Contemporary American Politics and Society

Issues and Controversies

Robert Singh

SAGE Publications
London • Thousand Oaks • New Delhi

For Hannah, with love

© Robert Singh 2003

First published 2003

SAGE Publications Ltd
6 Bonhill Street
London EC2A 4PU

SAGE Publications Inc
2455 Teller Road
Thousand Oaks, California 91320

SAGE Publications India Pvt Ltd
B-42, Panchsheel Enclave
Post Box 4109
New Delhi - 100 017

British Library Cataloguing in Publication data

A catalogue record for this book is available from the British Library.

ISBN 0 7619 4095 2
ISBN 0 7619 4096 0 (pbk)

Library of Congress catalog card number 2002109396

Typeset by Photoprint, Torquay, Devon
Printed in Great Britain by The Alden Press, Oxford

Contemporary American Politics and Society

ENDORSEMENTS FOR *CONTEMPORARY AMERICAN POLITICS AND SOCIETY*

In this volume the political scientist Robert Singh has selected and analyzed closely a set of topical issues and controversies in American politics – including gun control, capital punishment and cultural wars – as a way better to understand the United States. The result is an excellent text which conveys both the diversity of contemporary America and the complexity of issues often treated superficially in media accounts. I recommend the book highly.

Desmond King, Mellon Professor of American Government, Nuffield College, University of Oxford

Rob Singh is a master of style, and his book is the perfect companion for those who are interested in America's 'culture wars' but hitherto have been put off by the execrable jargon they have spawned.

Rhodri Jeffreys-Jones, Professor of American History, University of Edinburgh

For those who still believe that politics is normally, naturally, about economics, Rob Singh has gathered the evidence and dialed the wake-up call: seven major instances of an ongoing culture war meet a common analytic framework here in a lively and informative fashion.

Byron E Shafer, University of Wisconsin

For the student this is the perfect complement to a textbook. American politics is not just about institutions and processes, but also about current political issues and debates. Robert Singh's interesting book illuminates a range of social and cultural issues that divide Americans in the 21st century. All undergraduate courses on American politics should include it on reading lists for seminars, tutorials and classes.

Alan Ware, Worcester College, University of Oxford

Contents

List of Exhibits and Tables

Preface

As its title implies, *Contemporary American Politics and Society: Issues and Controversies* is a book about contemporary social divisions in America. It provides an analysis of the 'culture war' that has engulfed America since the later 1960s by focusing on seven highly divisive political issues at the heart of that conflict: abortion, gun control, capital punishment, pornography, gay rights, religion in public life and drugs. All of these issues fall within the rubric of 'cultural value conflict': conflicts of morals, ethics and matters of fundamental 'right and wrong'. Each issue is distinctive and important in the United States and each has received extensive analysis. Taken together, they form a powerful set of concerns that underpin, shape and sharpen the profound divisions that currently inform American politics at federal, state and local level.

Although the issues considered in this book are ones that generate deep and intense passions among Americans, their treatment here has been – as far as possible – dispassionate and balanced. The book does not take sides in the several controversies nor does it endorse a particular political viewpoint or analytical approach. My own views will, perhaps, appear more clearly in some chapters than others to curious readers. If so, the discussion of the issue should nevertheless remain balanced rather than one-sided. The aim of the book is to avoid prescription and provide students with a clear and rounded interpretation of each issue, and the several cultural conflicts taken together.

The various presentational devices – from summaries to 'exhibits' to discussion questions and web links – are intended to assist students in two ways. First, by presenting a common format that progresses from introduction, historical context and public opinion to an analysis of the politics of the governing institutions (president, Congress and courts, in particular) and intermediary organizations (concentrating on political parties and interest groups), readers should be able to follow each chapter clearly and, if they wish, to dip into each to compare and contrast particular features of distinct issues. Secondly, with the exhibits and tables focusing on particular dimensions of these complex issues, along with web sites dedicated to particular viewpoints or factual information, readers can follow whatever aspects interest or concern them in more detail as and when they (or their instructors) so wish. To the extent that a textbook can be 'user-friendly', hopefully this one meets that goal.

American politics is invariably fascinating and the study of it ought also, it seems to me, to be enjoyable. Some academics object to the analysis of issues such as gun control or gay rights as 'frivolous' compared to the serious stuff of congressional subcommittees or oversight of the executive bureaucracy. Equally, some scholars regard references to popular culture as 'dumbing down' or pandering to student prejudices. Perhaps because I came, like many students, to the study of American politics through a fascination with the land, people and popular culture (from music and novels to film) of the United States, my approach here regularly employs references to matters other academics reject. But there exists sufficient room today for different approaches to the study of America, ones that combine serious analysis with humour and an embrace of the types of concerns that make the United States simultaneously riveting and bemusing to non-Americans. Hopefully, readers of this book will find it informative, comprehensive and enjoyable.

Acknowledgements

I owe substantial debts of gratitude to many individuals who generously offered advice and suggestions – some directly, others indirectly – that had a tremendously positive effect on this book. Needless to say, the following bear no responsibility for any errors of fact or interpretation that remain.

The idea for, and initial work on, this book and its companion volume, *American Government and Politics*, occurred at the University of Edinburgh during 1996–99 but was completed at Birkbeck College, University of London during 2000–02. Most of the chapters were 'road-tested' in one form or another on my graduate and undergraduate students at both institutions and I should like to thank those students for proving to be such positive and pleasant critics. Revising and adapting courses and teaching styles helped greatly in identifying the problems associated with studying and writing about American politics. My students – whether consciously or otherwise – proved invaluable contributors to my continuing education, not only in terms of what I learnt from them, but also in clarifying the kinds of concerns that help to stimulate their interest and enthusiasm.

At Edinburgh, my colleague, friend and distinguished authority on modern Italy in the Department of Politics, Martin Clark (now retired), kindly read the chapters on pornography and gay rights and lent his exceptional knowledge to finessing their finer points. I should also thank my 'Americanist' colleagues in the Department of History for their consistent interest, assistance and support and the greater appreciation of the historical context to contemporary American politics that they helped to engender: Alan Day, Frank Cogliano, Rhodri Jeffreys-Jones and Owen Dudley Edwards. Robert Mason deserves special thanks for reading the chapters on abortion and capital punishment and providing very constructive suggestions on both. Of my politics students at Edinburgh, I should thank in particular Tim Nuthall, Eleanor Prescott, Juliette Cottrill and Ruth Walker who all read draft chapters. My warmest thanks go to them for their time and generosity.

At Birkbeck, I have benefited immeasurably from a set of highly supportive and imaginative colleagues in the School of Politics and Sociology. I should thank in particular Bill Tompson, for regular conversations on all matters American, and Samantha Ashenden, for illuminating discussions on all manner of cultural conflicts, reading two draft chapters of the book and offering very helpful observations on each. Many Birkbeck students also assisted – in classes, bars and public houses in the Bloomsbury area – to refine, revisit and revise the views and ideas contained herein. Of the many mature undergraduate and graduate students who have suffered my American politics courses with good humour, I should especially thank Kate Dixon and Darren Stevens for reading the chapters on abortion and pornography and offering valuable suggestions for revisions on both. Another former Birkbeck graduate, Andy Coath, offered many suggestions, rich and varied, that made their own distinctive contribution to the outcome and helped me to cope with the ups and downs of modern academic (and London) life.

Finally, I should thank Lucy Robinson and the staff at Sage for all their work on this book and its companion volume.

1 The Culture War and Contemporary American Politics

. . . This election is about much more than who gets what. It is about who we are. It is about what we believe, it is about what we stand for as Americans. There is a religious war going on in our country for the soul of America. It is a culture war, as critical to the kind of nation that we will one day be as was the Civil War itself.

Patrick J. Buchanan, Republican Party National Convention, 1992

. . . What is ultimately at stake in our current environment is literally the future of American civilization as it has existed for the last several hundred years . . . it is impossible to maintain civilization with twelve-year-olds having babies, fifteen-year-olds killing each other, with seventeen-year-olds dying of AIDS, and with eighteen-year-olds ending up with diplomas they can't even read. What is at issue is literally not Republican or Democrat or liberal or conservative, but the question of whether or not our civilization will survive . . .

Newt Gingrich, Washington Research Group Symposium, November 11, 1994

- American Politics and Culture in the Twenty-first Century
- What is the Culture War?
- The Significance of Cultural Value Conflict

- Traditionalists and Progressives
- Conservatives and Liberals by Another Name?
- Morals v. Lifestyles
- 'Exceptional' American Dilemmas?
- Choosing the Issues

Chapter Summary

America is currently convulsed not only by a war against terrorism but also by what many Americans regard as tantamount to a second civil war: a 'culture war'. Central to this conflict is a political battle among traditionalists and progressives whose ideas, values and beliefs differ substantially regarding the nature of American identity, the role of government and the balance between individual freedom and the state. The key issues dominating the conflict are abortion, gun control, capital punishment, pornography, gay rights, religion in public life, and drugs. On each issue, profound disagreements exist among Americans on the appropriate balance between federal, state and local power, the role of the federal government, the balance between individual rights and community control, and the Constitution's meaning in today's America. Neither progressives nor traditionalists have secured clear and consistent victories across the spectrum of these cultural conflicts, but traditionalists have proven remarkably resilient and increasingly effective since 1981. The culture war has nevertheless continued to divide and polarize America under President George W. Bush and the prospects of its reaching a decisive settlement or cease-fire remain distant and slim.

After the terrorist attacks of September 11, 2001, two events highlighted the centrality to contemporary American life of conflicts over cultural values. First, two days after the attacks, the Reverend Jerry Falwell, a leading evangelical Christian, placed part of the blame for the attacks on gays, feminists and civil libertarians, claiming that their activism during recent decades had led God to allow the barbarities to occur. Falwell was immediately condemned by many of his compatriots, suggesting that rationality, tolerance and non-judgementalism had achieved a much broader reach among most Americas.

But as the war in Afghanistan against the Taliban and Al Qaeda progressed to its rapid conclusion, a second and more poignant vignette occurred. John Walker Lindh, a young American who fought with the Taliban and Al Qaeda, had been captured by US forces. He was interrogated by Mike 'Johnny' Spann, a CIA operative. Shortly afterwards, in an insurrection by captive prisoners, Spann was killed. Walker was subsequently transported back to America to face trial. Many American commentators not only disagreed about his appropriate punishment but questioned how two Americans could end up in such diametrically opposed situations.

Spann had grown up in the heart of God-fearing Alabama, in a small town with no alcohol or cinema. He was a regular attendee at the local Church of Christ, a fundamentalist Christian church. Spann married a woman who had grown up just ten miles from his home town and, after graduating from university and joining the Marine Corps, joined the CIA. Lindh grew up in Marin County, California, one of the most notable locations for West Coast 'alternative' lifestyles. Named after John Lennon, he dabbled as a youth in Buddhism, popular black culture and (partly influenced by *The Autobiography of Malcolm X*) eventually turned to a militant version of Islam, travelling to Afghanistan to be trained by Al Qaeda and fight for the Taliban. The confrontation of two Americans so markedly different in their views of the United States eloquently and tragically summed up the fault-lines in a divided America.

Spann and Lindh arguably represented polar opposites, but to millions of Americans the types of cultural difference that they exhibited were notably familiar. To many Americans, cultural battles have been fought out since the end of the 1960s on many fronts scattered across the nation: from Washington, DC to Washington State, in the president's administration, Congress, and the federal and state courts; in state legislatures, governors' mansions, city councils and school boards; on network, cable and satellite television; in newspapers, magazines, radio shows and Internet chat-rooms; and in universities, colleges and high schools. These battles involve stakes that are supremely high, for they are focused on America's culture and national identity – what they once were, remain, and will be in years to come.

Just how far, and in what ways, America remains divided, even after September 11, is a matter to which this book will return in its conclusion. Strong arguments exist that America now possesses two quite distinct cultural traditions of traditionalism and progressivism, making the republic 'one nation, two cultures'. Equally, a powerful case can be advanced that, for all the many differences among its uniquely diverse people, America remains 'one nation, after all'. Once we have surveyed the central conflicts in the 'culture war', we will be in a better position to judge the merits of these competing views.

AMERICAN POLITICS AND CULTURE IN THE TWENTY-FIRST CENTURY

The 1990s saw some odd moments in American public life. In 1992, Vice President Dan Quayle criticized the Candice Bergen sit-com *Murphy Brown* for its positive portrayal of single mothers and negative take on fathers, the institution of marriage and the nuclear family. In the same year, President George H.W. Bush declared that American families ought to be more like *The Waltons* than *The Simpsons*. In 1994, Charlton Heston – shortly to become president of the National Rifle Association (NRA) – condemned the Time-Warner corporation for distributing 'Cop Killer', a controversial release by the rapper, Ice-T. Conservatives and liberals contested the values that the movie *Forrest Gump* promoted, while Republican presidential candidate Bob Dole attacked Hollywood in 1996 for producing 'violent' movies like *Natural-Born Killers*. In 1999 Reverend Falwell issued a 'parent alert' that identified the Teletubbies' Tinky-Winky as a degenerate gay icon, while Pat Buchanan launched his Reform Party general election campaign at Bob Jones University in September 2000 by declaring that the mass media and courts 'are abolishing America, they are deconstructing our country . . . they have dethroned our God'.

Such declarations by prominent public figures suggested that politics and popular culture had become enmeshed in a peculiarly intimate embrace. But they also spoke to the far more serious and deep-seated conflict within America over the nature and future of its cultural values, national identity and public policies.

Recent years have seen intense political conflicts develop over issues such as abortion, gun control, capital punishment, pornography, gay rights, religion in public life and drugs. To say that a 'culture war' exists is no exaggeration. Anti-abortionists have been arrested while attempting to block access to abortion clinics; some clinics have been fire-bombed; and some doctors have been murdered. Fierce arguments in state legislatures and the courts have occurred in many states over whether gay and lesbian couples should be allowed to marry and adopt children. Although most Americans want to keep heroin, cocaine and other drugs illegal, a significant number want to legalize (or at least decriminalize) drug use. The Supreme Court has ruled that children cannot pray in public schools, but this has not prevented many parents and school authorities from attempting to reinstate school prayer or 'prayer-like' moments of silence. Not just 'Monicagate', but the entire Clinton presidency offered a rolling and highly charged commentary on the values of the 1960s.

Unsurprisingly, these cultural conflicts have attracted some pungent antagonists, especially on the right. Perhaps the most well known and acerbic is Robert Bork. Nominated by President Reagan to the Supreme Court in 1987, the Senate rejected Judge Bork as an 'out of the mainstream' conservative by the largest margin in its history (58–42). Since then, Bork has railed against the 'unrelenting' assault now assailing traditional American civilization:

> We hear one day of the latest rap song calling for killing policemen or the sexual mutilation of women; the next, of coercive left-wing political indoctrination at a prestigious university; then of the latest homicide figures for New York City, Los Angeles, or the District of Columbia; of the collapse of the criminal justice system, which displays an inability to punish adequately and, often enough, an inability even to convict the clearly guilty; of the rising rate of illegitimate births; the uninhibited display of sexuality and the popularization of violence in our entertainment; worsening racial tensions; the angry activists of feminism, homosexuality, environmentalism, animal rights – the list could be extended almost indefinitely. (Bork, 1996: 2–3)

Partly because of concern for the nation's future, a strong focus of those occupied by issues of cultural decay has been on what is taught in schools. Thus, Burton Pines, author of *Back to Basics* (1982), claimed that American school textbooks were suffering from 'an anti-God, anti-religion, anti-patriotism, anti-capitalism, and anti-homemaker' bias. Conservative Republican activist Phyllis Schlafly echoed his views in her soberly entitled book, *Child Abuse in the Classroom* (1984). Noting that American children were being force-fed 'humanistic-inspired' ideas about participatory democracy, equal rights, sex education and global awareness, she called on parents to insist that schools instead 'use textbooks that teach the truth about the family, monogamous marriage, motherhood, American history and Constitution, and the private enterprise system' (Hellinger and Judd, 1994: 34).

Another conservative, whose views have won somewhat wider popular appeal, is William Bennett, who served as Education Secretary under President George H.W. Bush. Bennett also stresses the importance of rebuilding a sense of shared purpose in the political system, one founded not on material wealth but on appropriate values:

> Our problem is not economic. Our problems are moral, spiritual, philosophical, behavior . . . crime, murder, divorce, drug use, births to unwed mothers, child abuse, casual cruelty, casual sex and just plain trashy behavior. (quoted in Peele, 1998: 142)

Themes of societal regeneration were not confined to self-proclaimed conservatives. As part of a new 'Third Way' public philosophy, President Clinton consistently argued for an emphasis by government on individual responsibilities as well as rights in areas like education, welfare and penal policy during his two terms in the White House, while Hillary Clinton's book, *It Takes a Village* (1996), stressed heavily the importance of moral values in raising and educating children.

Such exhortations to restore a previously untarnished America conveniently overlook the presence of many of these problems from the republic's earliest years. It was a fundamental moral issue dating from before the republic's founding – slavery – that informed the Civil War. Value conflicts strongly underpinned the Progressive reforms of the early 1900s that sought to abolish child labour, regulate health and safety standards at work, and eliminate corruption from political life. Conflict over Prohibition – prohibiting alcohol production and consumption – was the quintessential cultural value conflict of the 1920s and 1930s (and began in the 1890s). The 'Scopes Trial' of the 1920s focused directly on the place of Darwinian evolution theory in schools and the challenge to fundamentalist religious beliefs that this posed. And moralism was the foundation of the movement for black civil and political equality in the 1950s and 1960s.

Political battles about the character and consequences of American culture are therefore not new. What is novel about the contemporary era is the scale, scope and intensity of these political exchanges. The isolated, important and prolonged cultural battles of the first half of the twentieth century were relatively few and far between and often limited to particular regions (especially the Midwest and the South). More importantly, they were much less significant politically than questions of 'guns and butter': issues of national security and domestic economic well-being.

Although George Washington famously warned America against 'foreign entanglements' when he left office, the nation did not heed his call. A succession of wars, from the First and Second World Wars to the Cold War against the Soviet Union and its communist allies, to various 'hot' engagements (Korea, Vietnam, the Gulf) and covert actions (in Cuba, Cambodia, Chile, Africa and the Middle East), provided the troubling international backdrop to domestic American politics. The nation moved from isolationism after the First World War to international engagement after the Second World War. Domestic scares over communism prompted riots in 1919 and the imprisonment of hundreds of Americans under the anti-

communist 'witch-hunts' of McCarthyism in the 1950s, while fears of domestic subversion led to the incarceration of Japanese Americans in prison camps during the Second World War (German and Italian Americans, being far larger populations, more dispersed voting blocs and with greater representation in federal and state government escaped this fate).

The increasingly interdependent nature of national economies also affected America in direct and disturbing ways. The Wall Street Crash-induced Depression of the 1930s unleashed terrible poverty and resulted in an unprecedented level of public support for the federal government intervening to offset the economic downturn. For the first time in its history, Americans turned their back on the notion that 'the government that governs best is the government that governs least'. Instead, shrewdly led by President Franklin D. Roosevelt, and bolstered by the successful war effort of 1941–45, Americans endorsed a 'New Deal liberalism' that sanctioned unheard-of levels of intervention by the federal government in economic and social life. Presidents Truman, Kennedy and Johnson all sought to extend this 'reform liberalism' tradition, with varying degrees of success, through the 1950s and 1960s.

But, increasingly shaken by urban riots, rising inflation and growing federal budget deficits from the disastrous war in Vietnam, oil price shocks then rocked the American economy in 1973 and 1978, leading to double-digit inflation and unemployment, a crisis of confidence in government, and the steady erosion of the New Deal era. The election of Ronald Reagan as president in 1980 at once expressed and assisted a slow but steady shift of Americans away from the public philosophy of reform liberalism, even though their embrace of conservatism is neither complete nor certain today.

Historically, then, cultural value issues took not just second place, but third, fourth and fifth place to these more immediate and pressing concerns about economic security at home and national security abroad. The recent emergence of cultural value conflict can be traced back at least to the end of the 1960s. What developed from that crucial and complex decade, the meaning of which still provokes heated disagreement, was not only economic downturn and foreign humiliation for America. In addition, a range of highly charged cultural conflicts erupted, encompassing millions across America. Crucially, the modern culture war was not confined to a particular region but became national in scope. Moreover, many Americans came to see these cultural battles not as isolated and unconnected exchanges, but as closely linked together.

So, although they do not form a completely seamless web, many of the same forces on one cultural issue often – though by no means always – occupy similar ground on others. For example, millions of those who favour legalized abortion also support liberal obscenity laws, while many who support the death penalty also oppose tougher gun control measures and 'abortion on demand'. This, then, is not a set of isolated exchanges waged by separate sets of small-scale guerrilla armies, but has become a full-blown culture war about the nature of America in the twenty-first century. The battalions on each side may wage individual battles over abortion or gun control, but they form part of two, much broader, armies in the ongoing cultural conflict.

WHAT IS THE CULTURE WAR?

While each particular battle in the culture war has distinctive characteristics, they share four features.

Clear popular views based on strong value systems

Many Americans hold strong, even instinctive, views on cultural value issues. Most tend not to go through a complicated analysis, examining competing arguments, balancing costs and benefits, considering the complexities that they raise. Instead, Americans mostly know, intuitively and immediately, where they stand. For many, these responses derive from a set of moral values based on profound religious conviction. For others, their values – no less deeply rooted – derive from conceptions about another secular form of faith: the 'political religion' of the American Creed – that amalgam of values and beliefs (liberty, egalitarianism, individualism, populism and laissez-faire economics) that have been argued to make up what it means to be an American citizen. According to the liberal historian Arthur Schlesinger, Jr., the Creed defines Americans in political, not cultural, terms:

> ... what has held the American people together in the absence of a common ethnic origin has been precisely a common adherence to ideals of democracy and human rights that, too often transgressed in practice, forever goad us to narrow the gap between practice and principle. (Schlesinger, 1992: 118)

As Schlesinger suggests, American history is replete with many disturbing and shameful instances where little goading to reconcile principle and practice in fact occurred – most notoriously in the South's embrace of slavery and, subsequently, state-sanctioned racial segregation, domestic repression of 'subversives', and exclusionary federal immigration policies based explicitly on race and ethnicity. But whatever the historic and current gaps between democracy's promise and its reality, most Americans tend to cling tenaciously to the Creed as the abiding essence of their national identity. And whatever their views on specific political issues, Americans hold values derived from the Creed, religious conviction and moral codes that powerfully inform their positions on matters of culture, values and identity.

Strong public salience

Many Americans feel sufficiently strongly about cultural issues to join organized interest lobbies, file briefs in courts, run as or work for candidates in elections, sponsor referendums, ballot propositions and recalls, donate money to political parties and individual candidates, take out advertisements in newspapers and on television, and demonstrate, boycott, and march for their causes. This is relatively unusual. Many commentators argue that Americans are depoliticized or pursue 'politics by other means'. They cite low turnout rates in elections, no tradition of mass membership of political parties, and the paucity of news, current affairs and political discussion programmes on American television in support. However, on the issues addressed in this book, many Americans have strong and clear views, sufficiently important to encourage active and direct participation in the political process.

Divisive social and political impact

Unlike many questions of economic or foreign policy that generate consensus, cultural issues tend to divide public opinion sharply. They often provoke a vociferous response among Americans that, occasionally, even finds violent expression. Cultural value issues tend to provoke deep divisions and intense disagreements. They polarize discussion and divide families and friends, classmates and professors, employers and workers.

This is partly because, for many Americans, cultural issues also form the litmus test between the maintenance of the traditional western values that have informed America's history since its founding, and the accusation by others that those dominant values are racist, sexist, homophobic and oppressive, requiring concerted and decisive challenge. So significant has this conflict become that cultural matters appear to some commentators to be the key to whether the historically United States is now 'disuniting' and, if so, whether, how and when that process can be halted.

Abiding federal–state tensions

Cultural battles involve two important spatial conflicts. One is between what can be termed the dictates of universalism and the demands of particularism. The growth of concern for universal individual rights lends force to those who seek nationally applicable policies to defend the rights of all citizens, wherever they reside. Against this, specific communities often wish to preserve their particular collective ways of life against outside intrusion.

A second conflict occurs between federal and state authorities. Since America is a federal system, certain specific powers are granted to the national government in the Constitution but the states and the people retain the remainder. This creates inevitable problems when competing claims of where power resides over particular issues occur.

These two conflicts are inextricably linked. Since the 50 states are so diverse economically, socially and politically, they are inexorably pulled against each other on a range of policy matters. Consequently, much cultural conflict now revolves around battles between one or more branches of the national government attempting to establish a nationwide public policy and individual states seeking to resist the imposition of policies that they oppose. The importance of this conflict is not confined to social issues – it occurs on issues from education to the environment and health care – but it is most vivid on matters of cultural conflict.

THE SIGNIFICANCE OF CULTURAL VALUE CONFLICT

Politics was once pithily defined as 'who gets what, when and how'. Cultural value politics is more 'who may do what, when and how'. Cultural conflict is not directly about the distribution of goods and services or the redistribution of tax dollars. Although these distributive questions form an important part of it (should the government use tax dollars publicly to fund abortion clinics or 'obscene' art shows, for example?), they are less central than questions about what an individual citizen is free – or unfree – to do. Can a woman in rural Alabama who has been the victim of a rape resulting in pregnancy legally procure the abortion she desperately desires? Can a young black American in downtown Los Angeles buy the cheap handgun he believes will protect his family from drug-dealing gangsters? Can a teacher who happens to be gay hold down a teaching job in Mississippi without being dismissed for his or her sexual orientation? These are the types of real-world situation that make the culture war so immediate, important and fraught for its many participants.

But some political scientists argue that cultural conflict matters little. Most analyses of presidential elections, for example, offer a straightforward account: in good economic times, the incumbent president wins; in bad, he loses. For example, George H.W. Bush had not altered his views on cultural issues from 1988 to 1992 (although his party's public image became more extreme), but in 1988, with a prosperous economy, he defeated his Democratic opponent, Michael Dukakis, by 54–46 per cent in the popular vote. In 1992, with the economy in a mild recession, he achieved just 38 per cent of the popular vote, and Bill Clinton won the election with 3 per cent less of the popular vote than Dukakis had lost by in 1988. Similarly, Clinton was not trusted as a person by millions of Americans in 1992 and 1996, but his impressive job approval ratings after 1994 survived all manner of personal crises, political disasters and 'character' questions.

On this view, then, cultural issues are marginal distractions from the 'pocket-book' concerns (taxation, income, jobs, health care and interest rates) that typically determine electoral outcomes. So prevalent has this view become that after 1984 (when the Democrats' presidential candidate, Walter Mondale, publicly admitted that he would raise taxes if elected and then suffered a landslide defeat against Ronald Reagan) politi-

cians in both America and Europe became loathe publicly to endorse tax increases, fearing that to do so would be to invite inevitable defeat.

Added to the 'primacy of economics' school is another important argument: 'single issues' do not determine election outcomes. That is, the proportion of voters who decide to cast their ballot on the basis of one issue that is of overriding importance to them (such as abortion) are so few as to be discounted. When deciding on how to vote, individual voters must think about all the issues that matter to them. They may well be pulled in different ways. They will probably have to prioritize some issues over others. Issues of taxation, jobs, education, crime and health care may rank as more important than abortion or gun control. Whatever their positions on cultural issues may be (pro-choice or pro-life on abortion, pro- or anti-gun control), they will cast their votes according to where they stand on the socio-economic ones. Hence, while cultural conflict is interesting, it provides an inaccurate picture of American politics.

Both of these points are important but neither should lead us to dismiss cultural issues. *How* much they matter compared to economics or foreign policy is not this book's primary concern. *That* they matter is sufficient reason to examine them. But let us be clear that they do.

First, cultural issues have an effect on presidential and congressional elections, as well as local and state-level contests: directly, in that some voters base their voting decisions on them, and others factor them into their decisions; and indirectly, in that presidential nominations and party nominations for Congress are heavily influenced by cultural issues and by activists who mobilize on them in party primaries and caucuses. Precisely because many party activists – especially convention delegates – often have fairly similar views on economic issues like taxation or social spending, we should expect the cultural cleavage to have a disproportionate effect in many primaries and caucuses. (Just how much will inevitably vary according to the particular year, the election context, and the field of candidates that are running.)

Secondly, focusing on the presidency neglects the rest of the federal government, while focusing on the federal level in turn neglects state and local politics. In all these cases, politicians have to be attentive to those portions of the constituency that do mobilize on the basis of cultural issues, even if these citizens are not a majority of the voting age population. As we will see in Chapter 4, for example, one of the explanations advanced for gun rights groups' powerful influence on firearms regulation is that losing the portion of gun-owners who vote in a constituency can be fatal for an elected politician – if not in a general election, then in a primary contest.

Thirdly, no 'single' issue may determine a politician's fate but what if several co-exist and either complement or cut across each other? What if, for example, voters face a candidate whose views on gun control, abortion, pornography and school prayer they all share, and an opponent with whom they differ across the board? In this case, voters may not simply have their positions on economic or foreign policy reinforced, but the social issues may even displace them in priority. Alternatively, the complexity of these issues may pose problems for a candidate working out the best strategy to win an election. Precisely because these issues are cross-cutting (one may be pro-choice but a gun enthusiast, pro-capital punishment but against censoring pornography), the dangers are that much greater. The nature of cultural value issues is that whatever stance a politician takes, he or she risks alienating some groups of voters.

So, cultural conflicts matter: to elections; to the fate of political parties; to who gets nominated as a candidate; to who occupies the White House and Congress; to who sits on the courts and in the federal bureaucracy. They matter, also, to the agenda of politics, which is crucial for what policy outcomes result from the interaction of the social base, intermediary organizations and government. Much political activity revolves around

agendas: getting discussion to be about what you want it to be about, preventing other topics from being considered. If a candidate knows, for example, that most voters share his or her distaste for gun control, but do not agree with his or her pro-choice position on abortion, it is important for that candidate that the election is focused on firearms, not abortion. This way, he or she has a much better prospect of winning, despite the fact that most voters do not share his or her abortion stance. Even if abortion does become an election issue, however, the candidate can still influence the outcome by shaping the terms of the debate. In this sense, cultural conflicts provide both opportunities and constraints. The former, in that posing the abortion debate in terms of 'choice' rather than 'life', for example, powerfully affects the terms of the discussion. The latter, in that cultural issues can intrude upon other areas – economic policy, trade, even foreign policy – and vastly complicate politicians' lives and desired public policies. For example, attaching an amendment about abortion to a bill on farm subsidies or support for the International Monetary Fund in Congress can force some legislators, who would otherwise support the original bill, to vote against it, with the result that the entire bill is defeated. Nominating a Supreme Court justice on the basis of his or her support for capital punishment has knock-on effects when he or she rules on litigation over trade or environmental matters. So, cultural issues can have wide-ranging and sometimes unanticipated effects.

But, in a sense, all of the above are rather extraneous and 'academic' reasons for the study of America's cultural conflicts. They neglect where cultural value conflict matters most: to the practical, real-world lives of hundreds of millions of citizens. The tensions generated by the culture war affect Americans' views on how well the government works, on how much influence ordinary citizens have over government, and on how much freedom should be granted to erstwhile political opponents. Above all, the culture war is not merely about what kinds of policy federal, state and local governments should adopt, but also about what kind of country Americans want to live in.

TRADITIONALISTS AND PROGRESSIVES

If the basis of the conflict is clear, how can the competing cultural forces best be characterized? Many popular metaphors exist to describe the mass of Americans who make up the 'mainstream' of the United States. 'Main Street' and 'Wall Street' were popular terms for several decades, contrasting, respectively, supposedly ordinary folks with a wealthy Northeast-coast elite. In 1969, President Nixon famously referred in a nationally televised address to a 'silent majority' of patriotic and hard-working Americans who rejected radical ideas and protest politics. 'Middle America' remains another commonly used term among journalists. But these can be improved upon for our purposes.

Writing about gun control in 1975, two historians identified that particular conflict as part of a more general cultural battle between 'cosmopolitan America' and 'bedrock America'. To illustrate the differences, they recounted a story about Gunnar Myrdal, the Swedish sociologist and author of the landmark 1944 study of race relations, *An American Dilemma*: shortly after Senator Robert Kennedy was assassinated in June 1968 (five years after his brother, John Kennedy, had been slain and just two months after Martin Luther King, Jr. had been murdered), Myrdal reportedly said that if the Constitution allowed such indiscriminate gun ownership, 'then to hell with the Constitution'. The historians noted: 'Cosmopolitan America would have found this food for sober reflection; bedrock America, without reflection, would have said: "To hell with Gunnar Myrdal" ' (Kennet and Anderson, 1975: 255).

Much of this division in world-view reflects concerns over status and 'high-brow'

versus 'low-brow' culture, but the cultural aspects of this division have expressly political, as well as social, features. Put crudely, cosmopolitan America has always been concerned about the nation's international image and global role; bedrock America has always been nativist, for whom the Middle East is Kansas and the Far East is Maine. Cosmopolitan America holds a barely concealed contempt for 'Joe Six-pack', while bedrock America revels in the anti-establishment attacks of populist politicians like Ralph Nader, Jesse Ventura and Pat Buchanan, radio talk-show hosts such as Rush Limbaugh, and Internet investigators like Matt Drudge. Cosmopolitan America cherishes visits to the New York Met to take in a Verdi opera, while bedrock America faithfully follows the Dixie Chicks. Cosmopolitan America celebrates Homer as the author of the *Iliad*, while bedrock America knows him to be Bart's happily dysfunctional father.

To adopt a more formal definition of our combatants, we can view the political conflict over culture as one between those who believe in 'traditionalist' or 'orthodox' values, on the one hand, and those who support 'progressive' cultural values, on the other. While this distinction is neither scientific nor perfect, it captures the key aspects of the contemporary political divisions (see Table 1.1).

Traditionalists tend to adhere to a conception of America as a uniquely blessed country with certain supremely admirable virtues. These have persisted throughout the nation's history and made it the best country in the world, a 'shining city on a hill'. Among these special traits are: a rugged individualism, antipathy towards government (especially the federal government), a strong religious (especially Judaeo-Christian) faith, belief in the sanctity of monogamous, heterosexual marriage and the nuclear family, robust patriotism, suspicion of foreigners and foreign ways, love of cars, and a relaxed attitude towards owning and using guns.

When it comes to values, traditionalists tend to believe that morality is as important as, or more important than, individual self-

---

TABLE 1.1   Traditionalist and progressive issue positions

The issue	Typical traditionalist position	Typical progressive position
Abortion	Pro-life	Pro-choice
Gun control	Against	In favour
Death penalty	In favour	Against
Pornography	Favours censorship	Opposes censorship
Gay rights	Against	In favour
Drug use	For prohibition	For decriminalization of 'soft' drugs

---

expression and that moral rules derive from the commands of God or the laws of nature – commands and laws that are relatively clear, timeless and independent of individual preferences. They tend to cherish the America whose essence they regard as deriving from European civilization, especially (white) Anglo-Saxon, Protestant immigration. Traditionalists also have a highly sceptical attitude to social and political changes that appear to threaten ways of life that have existed for many years, especially if these reforms are authored by federal government bureaucrats or judges. For many, movie stars like John Wayne and Clint Eastwood personify a ruggedly individualistic and strong America.

In contrast, progressives are typically more sympathetic to social change. By 'progressive', we do not mean that those who adhere to certain values are necessarily right, more intelligent or morally virtuous, progress, by definition, being 'a good thing.' Rather, we mean that progressives tend to base their views more on rational reflection than religious or moral codes. Progressives tend to think that personal freedom is at least as important as traditional moral rules, and that those rules must be (re)assessed in the light of the evolving circumstances of modern life – conditions that are neither divinely ordained nor timeless but complex, changeable and dependent on individual preferences.

Progressives do not always enthusiastically embrace social change, but they are generally more ready to recognize imperfections in the American way of life and more congenial to

attempts to remedy these. For example, progressives tend to be concerned by social problems such as racism, sexism, poverty, economic inequality and environmental decay, and are anxious to remove such blights on the American mosaic. They are hence generally content for government to address social problems by devising new programmes, agencies and laws. Progressives tend to see overt celebrations of America – from Reagan's 'Morning in America' campaign commercials to the Bicentennial of the Constitution in 1987 – as being complacent and occasionally even vulgar. Although mostly religious adherents, progressives are also more willing to accept alternative cultural traditions, lifestyles or attitudes as being as worth while as the historically dominant American one – as different, but not deficient.

Where traditionalists see America as having already arrived at a special destination that needs vigorous defending, progressives yearn to make America a better place, the journey to an ideal country having hardly begun after more than 200 years. While patriotic, progressives are less willing to equate America's being 'exceptional' with being unequivocally 'better'. Progressives are less willing automatically to support their country no matter what the circumstances, less likely to own and use guns, less likely to see divorce, abortion or sex before – and bearing children out of – marriage as actions to be censured as immoral, sinful or wrong. Where traditionalists regard sex education in schools as encouraging immorality and undermining marriage and the nuclear family, progressives view it as necessary to educating adolescents responsibly about the dangers as well as the pleasures of sex. Similarly, where traditionalists favour their children being taught Shakespeare rather than Puff Daddy (even if they may prefer John Grisham novels to both), progressives often see the study of 'dead white European males' as elitist, inappropriate, and socially exclusionary for America's diverse society.

The conflict between these traditionalist and progressive forces has become especially marked because the profound social changes originating in the 1960s have not only persisted but have also resisted attempts to secure their reversal. Traditionalists who opposed many of these changes found that, even when the candidates and parties that they favoured won elections, the progressive direction of social change went unaltered. Government proved unable to stop Americans following lifestyles, asserting rights, and engaging in acts of which many of their compatriots disapproved. Those of whom many traditionalists disapproved typically included 'liberated' women, gays, lesbians and bisexuals, single mothers, 'pornographers', 'anti-gun' advocates, welfare beneficiaries, drug users, immigrants (all illegal, and some legal, ones), and ethnic and racial minorities.

What makes those who oppose these progressive enemies an important and substantial force is primarily the role that religion continues to play. By comparison with other advanced industrial societies, America has unusually high levels of religious belief and observance. Moreover, Americans tend to adhere to a vast array of private sects, not to hierarchical churches with links to the state. Issues that are therefore at the fringes of politics elsewhere, simply because they are of secondary concern to most secular (i.e. non-religious) people, become centre-stage in many American states. The cultural confrontation between traditionalists, who would impose a return to an old moral and social

order (an idealized vision of 1950s America), and the progressives, who reject that vision as reactionary and exclusionary, has been waged in the political arena.

Critics who dislike traditionalist views often dismiss them as fanatical expressions of 'the religious right'. It is certainly the case that most conspicuous among the traditionalists are fundamentalist Protestants and 'born-again' Christians (who hold that they have personally met Jesus Christ and that the Bible is literal truth). It is also true that, as one British observer remarked:

> The moral and political issues which so divide American society – abortion, homosexual 'marriage', gay rights – cannot be solved or ameliorated by normal political methods when confronted with a significant section of the population which appears to believe that feminists fly around on broomsticks or that homosexuality has a satanic, Nazi connotation. (Esler, 1997: 158)

But many traditionalists are neither fanatical nor deeply religious, nor even especially right wing; they simply have strong views about issues like drugs, sexual morality and pornography.

Similarly, progressives include members of liberal Protestant denominations (Episcopalians and Unitarians, for example) and those without strong religious beliefs. Their critics often denounce and demonize them as immoral, anti-Christian radicals who have embraced an ideology of 'secular humanism', the belief that moral standards are entirely relative rather than absolute and that such standards do not require religious justification. Yet most progressives are neither immoral nor anti-Christian, nor do they regard secular humanism or relativism as their defining ideology.

Moreover, the culture war occurs not only between different religious denominations but also within them. Catholic, Protestant and Jewish leaders with traditionalist views tend to assign great importance to two-parent families, condemn pornography, denounce homosexuality, oppose ratification of the

Equal Rights Amendment to the US Constitution, and hold America to be a force for good in the world. Leaders of the same faiths who have progressive views are more likely to believe that legitimate alternatives to the two-parent family exist, that pornography and homosexuality are private matters protected by individual rights, and that America has been a neutral and sometimes negative force in world affairs.

CONSERVATIVES AND LIBERALS BY ANOTHER NAME?

Cultural traditionalists tend to support what is now (but was not always) the more conservative political party in America, the Republicans, while cultural progressives tend to side with the more liberal party, the Democrats. This being the case, why not follow the conventional path and simplify matters by describing the two sides as 'conservative' and 'liberal'? Three factors make this problematic.

Issue dimensions

Politics is not a simple matter of placing an individual's positions along a single-issue dimension, from left to right, and then coming up with an appropriate ideological identity-badge for him or her. Not only can we talk about different 'issue dimensions' that have little, if anything, to do with one another – economic policy, defence policy, social policy – but we can also hold several positions on each dimension that do not 'fit' together in any straightforward sense. One can, for instance, be in favour of strong environmental measures by government to protect the ecology (a 'liberal' position) but also be in favour of a large military budget (a 'hawkish' or 'conservative' position). That combination simply cannot be accommodated intelligibly on a linear spectrum of beliefs.

Again, the fact that on economic issues voters may endorse the government cutting taxes says nothing – as a matter of logic – about their views on whether government should ban the legal availability of abortion. To use the popular parlance, it is perfectly possible to be, simultaneously, an 'economic conservative' and a 'social liberal': to want government off our backs, out of our boardrooms and out of our bedrooms, to leave us as free as possible to do what we wish with both our private property and our private parts. But there is nothing inconsistent about being an economic and a social conservative: wanting government off our backs and boardrooms and in our bedrooms; or even being an economic and a social liberal: wanting government on our backs and in our boardrooms, but out of our bedrooms. Relatively few of us have truly 'consistent' ideological positions across the entire range of issue dimensions.

Ideology

Precisely because the American Creed has been so powerful and pervasive an influence, ideology remains a highly problematic concept when applied to America. Richard Hofstadter famously commented that, 'It has been our fate as a nation not to have ideologies, but to be one' (quoted in Lipset and Marks, 2000: 29). The ideological traditions familiar to Europe – socialism, communism, social democracy, Christian democracy and fascism – have had only the most marginal impact in America. Americans often throw political obscenities at each other that suggest strong ideological divisions, liberals sometimes being accused by their more zealous detractors of being 'pinko-commies', while conservatives are decried by their more emotive opponents as 'fascists', but these are comic and grossly inaccurate caricatures. (Historically, as Tom Wolfe sardonically observed (1993: 303), the political astronomy of the American left during the twentieth century tended to see the 'dark night of fascism' descending in America but somehow it always conspired to land in Europe.)

To the extent that their national identity is defined essentially in political terms, not cultural ones, Americans conventionally find that they can disagree on politics without having to appeal to 'foreign' ideas, most of whose key foundations (liberty, equality, democracy, the rule of law) are already subsumed under the all-encompassing 'American Creed.' The Creed that unites Americans as citizens is also what allows them to be divided on specific issues, by being selective about which of its competing values they appeal to. So, while Americans believe it is possible to act in an 'un-American' way, they frequently disagree about what kind of behaviour or attitudes qualify as being 'un-American'. One therefore has to be particularly careful in speaking of ideology in this context.

Party politics

The two main political parties have historically been broad and amorphous coalitions of distinct interests. There are cultural traditionalists in the Democratic Party and cultural progressives present in (and sometimes perplexed and perturbed by) the Republican Party. True, these are a relatively small and – most political scientists argue – declining proportion of each party, but they remain significant, especially when, as in 2001–02, neither party commands a clear majority in Congress. This breadth of party interests, in turn, reflects the social, economic and demographic diversity of the 50 states. So, for example, in a mostly traditionalist state like Alabama, most politicians, whether Democrat or Republican, will reflect traditionalist views. Conversely, in a more progressive state like Massachusetts, politicians from both parties will tend to assume progressive stances. (The choice of party for an aspiring politician typically depends on the state's history, the pattern of partisan identification among its citizens, and which party usually has a majority in the state legislature.) When one takes the national parties, a Democrat from Alabama may therefore be a very different creature from one from Massachusetts, but both choose – entirely rationally – to co-exist in the same party.

In the light of these complicating factors, it is best to stick to our traditionalist–progressive distinction. But if these two armies are fighting a war of cultural values, what exactly do we mean by 'culture'? And why has culture become the focus of such animated American passions?

MORALS V. LIFESTYLES

The term 'culture' is notoriously difficult to specify. Depending on the particular academic discipline (politics, sociology, history, cultural studies) and the individual author, many alternative definitions of culture are offered. Bork defines culture broadly, to refer to 'all human behavior and institutions, including popular entertainment, art, religion, education, scholarship, economic activity, science, technology, law, and morality' (Bork, 1996: 2). A more standard dictionary definition of culture describes it as 'the customs, civilization, and achievements of a particular time or people' (*Oxford English Dictionary*, 1992: 282). There are still some problems with this term, being rather sweeping and begging the question of what constitutes 'civilization', but it captures the essence of the issues now being contested across America. This definition is also one that our protagonists – traditionalist and progressive – can probably agree on.

But a second definitional difficulty arises, in that participants in, and observers of, America's culture battles often use different terminology to describe the same conflict. George Orwell's famous observation of political language in Britain is equally applicable to America: 'Political language ... is designed to make lies sound truthful and murder respectable, and to give an appearance of solidity to pure wind' (Orwell, 1957: 157). For example, some Americans talk about 'moral' issues; others of 'social' issues; still others of 'lifestyle' issues. Partly because of these differences in approach, the combatants in the cultural exchanges often appear to be talking at, rather than to, each other. In a sense, this 'war of words' is understandable, since each term captures part of the meaning of cultural conflict but none provides a full account. Using any one term prejudices the discussion in a particular direction (which is precisely why the combatants choose their language so carefully; as often occurs in politics, 'where you stand depends on where you sit').

Take 'moral' issues, for example. For many Americans – especially, but not only, the Christian Right – questions of whether or not a woman's pregnancy can be legally terminated or of whether cinemas and the Internet can show sexually explicit movies are ones fundamentally (even exclusively) about morality. There are few, if any, shades of grey here. Some actions are morally right, others morally wrong. The Bible (or the Koran, or the Torah or the Pope), says so. But for other Americans, this is misplaced. Abortion is not so much a question about the morality of terminating unborn life as it is primarily a matter about individual freedom: the autonomy of a woman to choose what to do with her own body, free from both government interference and the preferences and prejudices of others (not least, men, who can never labour under the burden of pregnancy). Similarly, many Americans disapprove of graphic images of sexuality, but do so on the practical grounds of its demeaning the status of women and leading to violence against them, not on grounds of morality; while many others see no problem at all in consenting adults choosing to watch other adults engage in sexual acts on their television screens in the privacy of their own home. To term these 'moral' issues is to enter the analysis already partially on the side of one set of combatants – normally the more traditionalist side.

But equally vexing problems arise when we use the term 'lifestyle' politics. This has become increasingly popular in America and, for many Americans, this is entirely what issues such as gay rights or pornography revolve around: what type of life does an individual citizen wish to lead? Can the fact that others, who happen to be in the majority at a particular time, prevent them from leading such a life merely because they disapprove of that particular lifestyle?

Again, issues of government power and individual freedom are inextricable from such considerations. The basic premise of liberal political theory since John Stuart Mill is that an individual should be at liberty to do whatsoever he or she wishes, providing his or her actions do not cause direct harm to another. If people wish to watch sexually explicit movies in the privacy of their homes or to engage in a consensual sexual act with an adult member of the same sex, they should not be prevented by public majorities who happen not to share their taste for an 'alternative' lifestyle. The point here is not just that others disapprove. They also act in the political arena, through government, to prohibit people's actions by force of law, to make them illegal and punishable by the state; and can do so because they are more numerous in the population and possess greater voting clout.

But, for other Americans, some actions are not only clearly right and some wrong as matters of morality, some forms of behaviour also have profoundly negative consequences, both for those involved and society as a whole. Hence, some lifestyles should be positively encouraged, others discouraged. It is the task of the government to intervene to promote the former and discourage, or even prevent, the latter from occurring: to 'enforce morality'. Describing these choices as ones of lifestyle reduces questions of fundamental moral principle to ones akin to forms of mass consumption. 'Choosing' to be gay or bisexual rather than heterosexual is no more weighty a decisional burden than selecting a healthy seafood salad over a diet-disastrous burger and fries. To many, this is grossly offensive, damaging to the social fabric and plain wrong. Again, if we use the term 'lifestyle' to describe these conflicts, we have already conceded important ground to the progressive side before beginning to dissect the issues.

To compound matters further, even secular, progressive groups sometimes slide into their erstwhile opponents' tactics, using the language of morality to defend their positions. Some feminist activists, for instance, frequently claim that to deny a woman the right to end her pregnancy is not only infringing her individual autonomy but is also 'morally' unjust. Similarly, for government not to recognize same-sex marriages as equal before the law to heterosexual ones is 'morally' wrong, many gay activists claim. (As discussed in Chapter 7, many argue that being gay is not a choice at all since sexual orientation is a 'given'.) So, just as many traditionalists oppose abortion or gay rights in moral terms, so many progressives resort to describing their preferences as urgent issues of morality and fairness.

This dispute is far more than a mere linguistic argument. It is one that animates intense divisions within America. It is also important because the otherwise neat and useful distinction in the cultural conflicts that Ware (1998) draws between 'moralists' and 'civicists' does not encompass the full range of issues that forms part of the contemporary culture war. Battles on gun control, drugs, welfare, multiculturalism and affirmative action, for example, are not so easily described as ones that pit moral campaigners against civic-minded foes. (Some Americans treat their firearms with an almost religious reverence, it is true, but it would be quixotic and incorrect to describe their opposition to gun control laws as deriving from moral convictions as such.) Still, these battles are as much a part of the rich mosaic of contemporary cultural conflict in America as abortion or gay rights. They simultaneously reflect and reinforce convictions about the values that Americans hold, the cultural traditions they see as requiring defence or challenge, and their conceptions of American identity.

It is preferable, therefore, to adopt a more neutral term in this book than moral or lifestyle issues: cultural value conflicts. What this definition involves is the notion that, whatever side they're on, and from whatever basis they hold their views (religion, morality, ethics, the American Creed), the participants in the battles profess a profound belief in certain values about American culture to support their positions on the political issues at hand. This strongly distinguishes them from the normal pattern of American politics.

So, for example, while one might argue that government subsidies for tobacco farmers is a 'good' or 'bad' thing, the policy would not be described as 'right' or 'wrong'. This makes such distributive policies especially well suited to the bargaining processes and compromises that are such essential features of American politics. By contrast, with abortion, for instance, many Americans would not describe government allowing women a legal abortion as a good or a bad policy; they would instead term it right or wrong. With the issues in this book, notions of right and wrong are almost always present, even in issues that do not seem obviously about morality (such as gun control). As a result, these cultural issues are much less amenable to definitive resolution in the incessantly compromise-demanding American political system. And therefore, in turn, cultural issues tend to be perennial political problems that surface with alarming regularity in national, state and local politics.

'EXCEPTIONAL' AMERICAN DILEMMAS?

The fascination with cultural issues is all the more acute to many outside America because European politics often seems less exotic, even less meaningful, by comparison. Europeans have been subject to developments that parallel those of America: industrial transformation, the retreat of the state, 'globalization', technological and communications revolutions, immigration and racial/ethnic tensions, changing sexual mores, feminism and environmentalism. In addition, several European states have witnessed intense political battles over abortion, divorce and gay rights, particularly those with a strong Catholic presence (France, Ireland, Italy and Spain). But European politics has not seen such widespread, prolonged and highly charged politico-cultural conflicts as America. The scope and persistence of cultural conflict generally has been less, even if the intensity has been comparable in particular cases. America still seems very 'different' from Europe, if no longer exceptional.

As the chapters in this book affirm, there are several reasons why this is so. The most significant, however, is religiosity. This is not only a matter of the extent of religious belief, but also of the intensity of sectarian, non-church-based religious practice. Where Western Europe has experienced secularizing trends since at least the Second World War, America has remained a nation whose citizens profess and practise religious beliefs on a far greater scale. Americans may not turn out to vote, but they do turn out to church, in remarkably large numbers. It is not America that is unusual here, but Europe. Across the world, religion is central to a majority of states, and some – theocracies such as Iran – are even built upon religious doctrines incorporated into law. However, it is largely because so many Americans profess strong religious beliefs that so many cultural battles have developed. Issues that provoke no, or relatively little, conflict in Europe are central, divisive and enduring in America.

Partly as a result of the religious resistance to postmodernity's progressive tendencies, another distinctive feature of American politics arises: the compromise that is central to the way America's governing institutions work is difficult to achieve on these issues. On questions of economic policy and international relations, finding a consensus is a necessary, familiar and habitual exercise for American politicians. Achieving a consensus on issues of cultural conflict is far harder. Yet the model of government established by the Constitution makes that search an unavoidable task, and the character of America's intermediary institutions – reflecting the constitutional design – again provides a distinctive contribution. Enthusiastic in articulating positions, political parties find it difficult to aggregate them, to bundle them together in a coherent whole. Parties cajole and encourage, but cannot compel, their members to support 'party positions'. They cannot deny their members renomination, much less re-election. Equally, interest groups confront no need to aggregate, but face every incentive to articulate their positions vociferously. Such factors help to prolong cultural conflict in America in ways unlike Europe. Without either a sudden mass religious conversion or a loss of faith of miraculous proportions, the American culture war is here to stay – as good a reason as any to treat it to a serious examination.

CHOOSING THE ISSUES

The selection of specific cultural issues for analysis in this book has primarily relied on three considerations.

Longevity

Some cultural conflicts, such as flag-burning, arose and disappeared fairly rapidly as discrete political issues. Many Americans disapproved of the Supreme Court's decisions in *Texas v. Johnson* (1989) and *US v. Eichman* (1990), that struck down as unconstitutional, respectively, state and federal laws criminalizing the desecration of the Stars and Stripes. But although the issue has seen political elites pursue it, the mass public has not been mobilized. Other issues that divide Americans do not (currently, at least) see much in the way of political action, not least because the division is one between the public and the 'political class' and the latter fear antagonizing the former by pressing for social change. (One example here is the issue of decriminalizing prostitution.)

By contrast, the issues selected for examination in this book have been more or less constant elements of the cultural war since the late 1960s. They have provoked significant political action among the mass American public and political elites. Some, such as abortion, pornography and gun control, have been the focus of controversy for at least three decades. Others, such as gay rights and drugs, emerged as national political controversies only since the 1980s. None are likely to disappear rapidly from America's political landscape, such is the extent of social division on these issues.

Availability of source material

One of the problems for students (and teachers) of American politics outside the US is discovering useful and authoritative materials, which are often contained in American political science journals or books that may not be held by their libraries. University budget constraints have meant that American politics texts are now one of the less successful exports that the US can boast.

The problem of source material also reflects the recent rise of the culture war. Because the presidency, Congress and other government institutions have been the staple for teaching American politics, cultural issues have suffered relative neglect. Poor cousins to the 'serious' stuff of budgetary politics or international relations, finding material on gun control or gay rights is rarely straightforward. Each chapter in this book therefore attempts to thread otherwise disparate sources together in a comprehensive account.

Coherence and comparability

An exhaustive survey of all the cultural value conflicts that exist in America would demand an extended treatment far beyond the scope of this modest volume. Rather, the chapters that follow seek to offer interpretations of the 'compare and contrast' mode. Because the particular issues selected share many features in common, but still differ in important respects, they offer an attractive set for analysis.

Taken together, the issues selected allow an evaluation of the significance of cultural value conflict and continuity and change therein. But before addressing them individually, the next chapter explains more fully why the culture war has become such an insistent part of American politics today.

2 The Rise of the Culture War

I find my blood pressure rising when Clinton's cultural shock troops participate in homosexual-rights fundraisers but boycott gun-rights fundraisers – and then claim it's time to place homosexual men in tents with boy scouts and suggest that sperm donor babies born into lesbian relationships are somehow better served.

> Charlton Heston, President, National Rifle Association, speech to the Free Congress Foundation, December 1997

I really believe that the pagans and the abortionists and the feminists and the gays and the lesbians, who are actively trying to make that an alternative lifestyle, and the ACLU, People for the American Way, all of them who have tried to secularize America – I point the finger in their face and say, 'You helped this happen'.

> Rev. Jerry Falwell, September 13, 2001

- The Origins of the Culture War
- The Social Base
- Governing Institutions
- Intermediary Organizations
- Conclusion

Chapter Summary

Although conflicts over cultural values and identity existed from the republic's founding, the contemporary culture war is particularly broad, intense and long-lasting. Once sporadic and peripheral, cultural battles have acquired a central role in American politics. Part of the explanation lies in the profound social changes that have occurred since the 1960s, especially in regard to post-industrialism, feminism, immigration and multiculturalism, and a powerful reaction to these by a resurgent conservative movement. But the intervention of the federal government was also critical, particularly the decisions of the Supreme Court that brought home to millions the extensive reach of the federal government in new, direct and disturbing ways. The reactions to these judicial decisions by America's governing institutions, organized interest lobbies and individual citizens – both supportive of and opposed to the sweeping changes they heralded – helped to transform the place of cultural issues in politics. Cultural value conflict thereby moved from the margins to the centre of political debate, a transition assisted strongly by the end of the Cold War and the renewed – albeit short-lived – focus on domestic affairs that this occasioned.

Three forces account for the prominence, pervasiveness and persistence of cultural conflict in American politics since the 1960s: a changing social base; the intervention of the federal government – in particular, the Supreme Court – on cultural value issues; and the responses of intermediary organizations. In this chapter, we review each, emphasizing how the three distinct forces interacted to transform the place of cultural issues into enduring subjects of profound political disagreement.

THE ORIGINS OF THE CULTURE WAR

As military historians invariably observe, wars do not develop in political vacuums. Their origins lie not in the spontaneous actions of a few national leaders but in complex patterns of political, social and economic relationships that evolve over time: historical events, social and technological developments, industrial and economic transformations, inward and outward migration patterns, crises, and the tactical and strategic calculations of greater or lesser national, sub-national and supranational powers. The culture war is no exception to this rule, requiring us to examine a particular constellation of distinct but overlapping forces that caused its outbreak and conditioned its subsequent character.

Although expressions of cultural conflict arose previously, it has only been since the later 1960s that such a broad cultural battlefield has emerged in America. It is conventional to examine the profound changes that have occurred in society since 1945, and especially since the 1960s, to explain the growth of cultural conflict. Most prominent among these are: the rise of – and reactions to – feminism, the growing presence of women in the workforce, the end of legally sanctioned racial segregation and new civil rights measures, rising levels of education, a shift from manufacturing to service industries, and new waves of external migration to, and migration within, America. These are certainly important factors in the growth of the culture war and its assuming the particular character it now displays. But the reasons for the new landscape derive from three sources – analytically distinct but interrelated in practice – that make up the basic architecture of American politics:

1 The social base.
2 The institutions of government.
3 The intermediary organizations that mediate how (1) and (2) interact.

So it is worth (re)examining these 'structural fundamentals' to consider how and why the cultural battles now occurring first arose. Only if we examine all three sources can we achieve a full explanation for the onset of these protracted political hostilities.

With regard to these three sources of change, Byron Shafer and Bill Claggett argue that in the post-WWII era:

> social, technological, and regulatory change, and, crucially, relevant interventions from the US Supreme Court, all created powerful

added emphases on the dimension of cultural values. When the active parties then diverged sharply on these matters, the latter were destined to assume a much larger role in national politics. (Shafer and Claggett, 1995: 179–80)

What they mean is concisely captured in Table 2.1. Although the table necessarily oversimplifies the complex and nuanced differences between pre- and post-1968 politics, it conveys the essence of the transformed political and social context. What we see occurring are profound changes in society, government and the organizations that link the two together. When considered as a whole, the result is an unprecedented expansion of the role and importance of the culture war in national, state and local politics and a

sharp polarization of the two main parties on this newly consequential dimension of political conflict.

THE SOCIAL BASE

The social base refers to the types of group that exist in society and the divisions among them. America's remarkable diversity in terms of these 'social facts' is well known. In terms of income, religion, race, ethnicity, region, gender, urban/rural/suburban locations and sexual orientation, America is extremely heterogeneous, but since the end of the Second World War, five important changes have occurred here: the transition from a Cold War to a post-Cold War (and

TABLE 2.1   The rise of the culture war: dynamics of change

	New Deal era (1932–68)	Divided government era (1968–)
Social base	Second World War/Cold War	Post-Cold War (1991–)
	Industrial economy	Post-industrial economy
	Class cleavage dominant	Competing cleavages of class, region, race, ethnicity, religion, gender, sexual orientation, urban/suburban/rural
	European immigration	Asian/Latino immigration
	Patriarchal gender relations	'Post-patriarchal' relations
	Apolitical Christianity	Politicized Christianity
Governing institutions	Liberal judicial activism	'Rootless'/conservative judicial activism
	New Deal coalition	'No majority' realignment
	Undivided control	Divided party control
	Modern presidency	'Post-modern' presidency
	Credit-claiming	Blame avoidance
	Collegiate/corporate congressional norms	Adversarial/entrepreneurial legislative behaviour
Intermediary organizations	Bipartisanship	Partisan polarization
	Intra-party divisions	Inter-party divisions
	Party convention	Primaries and caucuses
	Party-centred politics	Candidate-centred politics
	Fat-cat donors	Individual donors/PACs
	Interest group concentration	Interest group fragmentation
	Pluralism	Hyper-pluralism
	Broadcasting	Narrow-casting

now a post-September 11) context; the shift from an industrial to a post-industrial society; new sources of immigration; the sexual revolution and the onset of a 'post-patriarchal' society; and the counter-mobilization of the right. Consequently, the social base – unusually diverse since the latter half of the nineteenth century – has undergone further fragmentation that has intensified political conflict on cultural value questions on a national scale.

The end of the Cold War

Although the end of the Cold War is not strictly a feature of the social base in the sense that race, ethnicity or religion obviously are, the Cold War powerfully shaped American attitudes and beliefs for 44 years (1947–91). Not only did this affect American foreign policy, but it also pervaded domestic politics. Until the Vietnam War, both parties adopted the principle of containment of communism as the guiding principle of foreign policy and looked to presidential leadership to achieve the defeat of communism. Whether Democrat or Republican, strong anti-communism was a prerequisite for most elected officials and, both before and after McCarthyism, support for or association with communism represented a treacherous badge of 'anti-Americanism'. For almost 50 years, Americans were offered by their leaders an easily identifiable, powerful and dangerous enemy in the Soviet Union and its satellite powers.

With the revolutions in Eastern Europe in 1989 and the Soviet Union's collapse in 1991, American attentions shifted away from an enemy abroad to focus on domestic affairs. This facilitated some Americans (such as the militia movement) searching for enemies at home. While the culture war predated the collapse of the Eastern European and Soviet communist regimes, the transition to a post-Cold War environment encouraged some politicians and activists to describe domestic opponents in terms of being enemies out to destroy the American way of life: not least

'pro-abortionists', homosexuals, advocates of gun control and even bureaucrats in the federal government. The Cold War's end also helped to revive calls from forces on both the left and right of the political spectrum for America to focus directly on its domestic problems and to place domestic priorities before international commitments – until September 11.

Post-industrialism

America underwent an economic transformation from an industrial to a post-industrial society after the Second World War. Previously dominant manufacturing industry and agricultural sectors were increasingly supplanted by high-tech, service and tertiary-sector industries. Dependent upon advanced technology in economic production and communications, a vast expansion of education – especially higher education – became necessary to meet demands for a skilled and mobile workforce. This expansion created a set of 'knowledge-workers', who took up increasingly progressive views on social (but not economic) issues.

During the 1960s and 1970s, conflicts over poverty, racism and the Vietnam War convinced the new expanded cohort of college students that America needed radical change. Participants in an 'adversary culture' that prided above all else the right to individual fulfilment and self-expression in the realms of morality, sex and personal relations, traditionalist constraints – from wives and husbands to children, parents and the state – became impediments to the exercise of this individualistic right. The individual became viewed as at least as important as the community, personal freedom as important as traditional moral codes, and freedom of choice as crucial as conformity to conventional social norms.

But this legacy in turn confronted another important social development: newly affluent working-class Americans, who had benefited from the sustained economic growth of the 1950s and 1960s, experienced unprecedented levels of material affluence and social mobility, and were far less enamoured of unrestrained celebrations of unfettered individualism. Patriotic, skilled or semi-skilled, and suburbanites married with children, such Americans watched with a mixture of disbelief and horror at campus and black radicals, urban unrest and anti-Vietnam protests. They saw an 'American Dream' that had conferred on them unanticipated material riches demonized and derided by advocates of social change. While the 1970s therefore saw economic malaise at home and defeat abroad, they also featured a cultural crisis that threatened traditionalist morals and 'family values'. What rapidly emerged was a growing and deepening antagonism between the forces of progressive social change and of traditionalist resistance.

Immigration and multiculturalism

America self-consciously celebrates its status as a nation created and sustained by immigration. But, despite the Statue of Liberty's inclusive invitation to 'Give me your tired, your poor, Your huddled masses, yearning to breathe free', the republic was founded exclusively for white, Anglo-Saxon, European Protestant settlers; slaves and Native Americans were not members of the polity. From the 1840s to the 1920s, mass immigration by non-Protestant Europeans provoked vehement protests from nativists who feared that new immigrants were undermining basic cultural values. From the 1920s to 1965, a rigid immigration quota system was imposed that sought to exclude non-white Anglos from entry. Throughout America's history, many Americans tried either to prevent the admission of certain immigrants, deny them civil and political rights, or force them to abandon aspects of their traditions, beliefs and lifestyles.

Despite these efforts, however, America has continued to accept new immigrants. In 1998, the proportion of the population that was foreign-born was higher than at any time since the 1930s. Moreover, demographers

expect America's population to grow massively, from an estimated 261 million in 1995 to 392 million by the year 2050. Changes in the character of American immigration, however, together with changes in the indigenous population, raise important questions about America's evolving cultural identity.

Historically, America's social base has been so unusual that several metaphors competed to describe it. Most influential for several decades was Israel Zangwill's image of the 'melting-pot'. This term captured the idea that immigrants (from northern, and latterly southern, Europe) acquired a new political, cultural and national identity as Americans. It assumed that immigrants would sooner or later learn English and be assimilated into a society dominated by Anglo-Saxon, Protestant culture, thereby 'becoming' Americans in a quasi-religious, ideological experience. 'Melting-pot' envisaged the eventual elimination of distinct cultural identities and structured the way most Americans addressed identity issues throughout the twentieth century.

But once South America and Asia became the main sources of immigration over the final two decades of the twentieth century, this notion was strongly criticized as inappropriate and socially exclusive. Other terms, such as 'marble cake' and 'salad bowl', arose. These implied that Americans continued to share a political and national identity but also retained distinctive cultural traditions and beliefs. Latino and Asian immigration, and responses to it, contributed to 'disuniting' trends in the social fabric.

- *Discrimination*. America finally began to tackle racial segregation with the passage of the Civil Rights Act (1964) and Voting Rights Act (1965). The policies and strategies adopted to expand civil rights for blacks had implications for other minority groups defined by race, religion and language, and for women and gays. Respect for different identities and subcultures promoted the adoption of a range of policies and strategies ranging from affirmative action to mother-tongue education and ethnic heritage preservation programmes. It also encouraged a new and controversial emphasis within the education system on the roles of minorities and women in American history and culture, and efforts to reduce the attention devoted to the 'western canon' (the classics of western civilization were now criticized for representing only the views of 'dead white European men').

- *Multiculturalism.* Minority groups became more aggressive in defence of their distinct cultural identities. 'Multiculturalism' became the preferred goal for these groups, rejecting the allegedly dominant monoculturalism in favour of a 'co-equality of respect' for different traditions. This entailed profound consequences for public policy when, for example, it involved claims that a group's native language should be given parity with English, not merely employed instrumentally to prepare for participation in a culture dominated by the English language and an intellectual heritage drawn primarily from western Europe. Among African Americans, it also saw new emphases placed by elites upon Afro-centrism, black nationalism and racial separatism.

- *Population change.* By the twentieth century's close, America confronted an unprecedented demographic future in which Americans of Anglo-Saxon origin were predicted to become a minority by 2050. Latinos, especially, were expected to grow as a proportion of the national population, with substantial blocs already present in states such as California, Texas, Florida and New Mexico. (Although the greatest expansion of immigrants during the 1980s and 1990s came with Asian Americans, their educational and employment achievements – and their embracing English – caused less disquiet among whites.)

The conjunction of these three developments occasioned a strong reaction among traditionalists, who were concerned at the apparent threat they collectively posed to the historically dominant understanding of American identity as essentially that of white, English-speaking, Anglo-Saxon Europeans. National and state efforts occurred from the mid-1980s to bring forward constitutional amendments formally to entrench the status of English as America's official language. Individual states, such as California, held referendums in drives to eliminate mother-tongue instruction. Movements for monolingualism, as well as vocal rejections of multiculturalism, found powerful support among conservatives, in the Republican Party, and from some academics fearful of the erosion of constitutional nationalism as the basis of American identity. Crucially, though, these battles were not only about language but became a multifaceted struggle between different elements in America for control over the nation's cultural character. Disputes over bilingualism, welfare, immigration and multiculturalism all suggested an intense struggle about the nature of identity, culture and the kind of country that would exist in the twenty-first century.

The sexual revolution, feminism and 'post-patriarchy'

The post-Second World War years, and especially the 1960s and 1970s, unleashed many new social and political developments in America. One of the most enduring and important was the 'sexual revolution'. More a rolling set of incremental reforms than a revolution, the changes it heralded included the development of the contraceptive pill, the liberalization of laws on the age of consent, gay sex and obscenity, the teaching of sex education in schools, the striking-down of state laws prohibiting racial intermarriage, increasing public recognition of female sexuality, and the growing prevalence of sexual themes in popular culture from movies to music and advertising. While the extent to which male and female attitudes altered can be exaggerated, these developments affected the behaviour of millions of Americans, severing the act of sex from its traditional links to procreation, marriage and established moral codes. The extent to which the prime beneficiaries of these changes were men or women remains unclear, but the sexual revolution assisted the spread of a new individualism.

Related to this was the rising influence of feminism or, to be precise, 'second-wave' feminism. 'First-wave' feminists had campaigned through the nineteenth century to secure formal civil and political equality with men. Ratification of the Nineteenth Amendment in 1920 secured American women's right to vote. Although social and economic progress lagged far behind, the emergence of the pill and expanded education opportunities transformed the socio-economic environment for women. A range of feminist authors celebrated and popularized the growing challenge to male dominance or 'patriarchy' and women's organizations such as the National Organization for Women (NOW, formed in 1966) gave this new female assertiveness institutional expression.

While women have not yet achieved socio-economic parity with men, post-1960s America saw a 'post-patriarchal' society emerge that complemented (and relied on) the 'post-industrial' transformation of the economy. This is not to deny that sexist attitudes, prejudice and discrimination against women continued to exist, but where women were previously deemed by a dominant male America to be exclusively homemakers, wives and mothers, America now afforded remarkable new opportunities in education and employment. The legacies of the sexual revolution and 'feminization of the workplace' make the concept of a patriarchal society more problematic today.

Women's groups became active on many cultural value issues, but two proved especially important: abortion and pornography. Abortion became a vital issue for feminists. The ability of a woman to be able to decide to terminate her pregnancy symbolized the struggle for female equality and autonomy. Pornography, to many feminists, also represented a touchstone of whether America would accord women equal respect. By the 1990s, however, these issues had become more complex and the divisions over them more subtle as many women took up positions against abortion rights and others endorsed positions in favour of sexually explicit materials. Moreover, socio-economic issues related to work (sexual harassment, childcare, equal pay) and home (domestic violence and child-rearing) emerged as central concerns of many women. For both men and women in America, the social and economic uncertainties of their lives reinforced the widespread sense of a culture in flux.

Reaction on the right

The fifth and final legacy of the 1960s was one of reaction. Millions of Americans experienced an unfamiliar sense of 'culture shock': disorientation at being subjected to disconcerting political and social developments, being in the midst of an ongoing transition with no clear destination. The political reactions this engendered were the emergence of a 'New Politics' on the left and – ultimately of greater consequence – a powerful counter-mobilization by a revived right.

On the left, the most visible proponent of this new progressive politics was Senator George McGovern of South Dakota, who captured the Democratic Party's presidential nomination in 1972. Denounced by his opponents as the candidate of 'acid, amnesty, and abortion', McGovern was trounced by Nixon in the 1972 presidential election as being an 'out of the mainstream' liberal. Allegations that Democrats were 'soft' on communism abroad and crime at home would subsequently dog presidential candidates from 1972 to 1988, and helped to derail all but Jimmy Carter.

The most vocal spokespersons on the right were Ronald Reagan, governor of California from 1966 to 1972, and George Wallace, governor of Alabama. Denied the Republican presidential nomination in 1968 and again (more narrowly, against incumbent President Gerald Ford) in 1976, Reagan consistently espoused a simple mantra of conservative beliefs: reduce taxes and social spending programmes, build up national defence, and return power from the federal government to the states. A key component, also, was a traditionalist social agenda: opposition to abortion rights, affirmative action, drugs, welfare and pornography, strong support for school prayer, capital punishment, gun ownership and the nuclear family. Reagan did not alter his views from 1964 to 1980, but the Republican Party did change, with an infusion of conservative activists motivated more by issues (not least cultural ones) than particular candidates, spurred on more by 'purity' in the pursuit of desired policy goals than pragmatism in pursuit of electoral victories. By 1980, the Republican Party was in a position to nominate Reagan as its candidate for president.

Reagan's path to the presidency was partially paved by Wallace, whose great political achievement was to transcend a narrowly sectarian focus on race by broadening his attack to the federal government and 'pointy-headed intellectuals'. His 1968 campaign slogan summed up much traditionalist sentiment: 'Our lives are being taken over by bureaucrats, and most of them have beards!' Wallace exploited the fears and resentments of lower-income whites over taxes, law and order, intrusive bureaucracy and pacifist sentiments. His central contribution was to place cultural value issues at the forefront of public debate. As a Democrat, especially, he appealed to other traditional Democratic identifiers sympathetic to his populist and reactionary message.

But the force that reacted with most vigour was the 'New Christian Right' (NCR). No group of Americans was so deeply antagonized by the social changes of the post-Second World War years as evangelical Christians. Especially on abortion, school prayer, pornography and gay rights, the Supreme Court seemed to be directly imposing on their God-fearing communities policies that they overwhelmingly opposed – policies that neither the White House nor Congress managed subsequently to reverse. For some, these decisions suggested nothing less than a full-scale assault by an unrepresentative and unelected elite on the nation's traditionalist values. The preacher Pat Robertson observed in a typically dispassionate fundraising letter in 1992, for example, that: 'The feminist agenda is not about equal rights for women. It is about a socialist, anti-family political movement that encourages women to leave their husbands, kill their children, practice witchcraft and become lesbians.'

In order to safeguard their traditional beliefs and ways of life against feminism and a rampant 'secular humanism' (a culturally relativist public philosophy that viewed any and all lifestyles and moral codes as equally 'valid') participation in politics was a necessary, if insufficient, condition of reversing pernicious policies that were anathema to their most cherished values and beliefs. The unprecedented mobilization of impassioned Christians powerfully sustained the centrality of battles over culture into the twenty-first century.

GOVERNING INSTITUTIONS

While changes in the social base facilitated the rise of the culture war, the role of governing institutions was equally critical. A crucial factor in the timing of the rise of cultural value conflict concerned changing public attitudes about the role and scope of federal government intervention in social and economic life. America went from an era of mostly sustained economic growth during the 1950s and 1960s to one of inflation and unemployment in the 1970s, and growing budget and trade deficits in the 1980s and early 1990s. Significantly, this occurred while the military disaster of Vietnam, revelations of government secrecy at home and abroad under the presidencies of Lyndon Johnson and Richard

Nixon, and Nixon's eventual resignation over Watergate successively shocked, infuriated and dismayed Americans.

This in turn had two important effects. One was that the traditional scepticism about the role of government (especially the federal government) was revived. A second affected the politicians inhabiting the institutions of government at federal, state and local level. The changed economic environment meant that these politicians were no longer so able to 'claim credit' for dispensing government benefits (jobs, projects, loans). Instead, they were obliged to 'avoid blame' for allocating economic pain, advertise their activities more assiduously, and position-take more adroitly to satisfy an array of concerned constituents. Governing institutions thus rapidly acquired a crucial role in cultural conflicts, recognizing, encouraging and, eventually, becoming sites for political efforts to reverse, modify and entrench ongoing social changes.

Most important was the intervention of the Supreme Court. Under Chief Justice Earl Warren, the Court from 1953 to 1969 addressed a wide range of important issues: racial segregation, criminal defendants' rights, the reapportionment of congressional districts, birth control, public school prayer, and obscenity. The decisions handed down were controversial: striking down segregation; expanding the rights of criminal defendants (the 'you have the right to remain silent' caution, beloved of American cop movies, originated in a court decision, *Miranda v. Arizona* [1966]); requiring congressional districts to be redrawn on a one person–one vote basis; disallowing prayer in public schools; and liberalizing laws over pornography. As Martin Shapiro observed, 'Few American politicians would care to run on a platform of desegregation, pornography, abortion, and the "coddling" of criminals' (1990: 48). Fortunately for the justices, they did not face the 'problem' of electoral accountability.

To the disappointment of President Nixon (who appointed him), Warren Burger, Warren's replacement as Chief Justice, proved little better for traditionalists. Just at the moment when the post-1968 cultural conflict was at its sharpest, the Burger Court (1969–86) notched up several victories for social liberalism that seemed to validate exactly what Reagan and Wallace were claiming about an unrelenting progressive advance: in 1971, the Court struck down a legal distinction based on gender because it violated women's constitutional equality, and it authorized bussing schoolchildren to achieve racially mixed schools; in 1972, it ruled that capital punishment was unconstitutional; and in 1973 it declared a woman's constitutional right to an abortion.

These decisions were profoundly controversial, partly in their substance, partly because of the constitutional interpretations used to justify them, and partly because it was an unelected and unaccountable branch that was imposing these changes on American states. But an additionally important aspect of the decisions was to nationalize and politicize conflict on these divisive questions.

One of the virtues of a federal system of government is that it accommodates a socially heterogeneous populace. Defenders of the arrangement argue strongly that it provides a good balance between the wishes of majorities being implemented and the rights of minorities being defended. Individual rights guaranteed by the Constitution can 'trump' legislative majorities, if judges so decide. This is a vital element of the constitutional order that makes government 'limited'. Culturally conservative communities in Mississippi, for whom the conventions and norms of progressive Massachusetts were anathema, were thereby insulated from them, and vice versa. But because the Supreme Court gave the definitive ruling on what the Constitution allowed or disallowed, its decisions over abortion or capital punishment had a nationwide effect. Consequently, Court rulings brought home the universalizing reach of the federal government to many communities in profoundly unappealing ways. Parents whose children had recited the Lord's Prayer in school now found this declared unconstitutional. Communities who viewed abortion as murder found state laws forbidding pregnancy terminations that had existed since the nineteenth century suddenly struck down. Unsurprisingly, outraged traditionalists condemned these changes while progressives celebrated them – with large numbers of uncertain, persuadable Americans in between.

The effects of these decisions were far-reaching not only for society but also for other branches of government. At the federal level, members of Congress now became subject to public pressures to reinforce, revise or reverse the Court rulings. Pressure for constitutional amendments became a constant in American politics: to provide equal rights for women; overturn the Court's abortion rulings; stop 'forced bussing'; guarantee a balanced budget; mandate term limits for elected officials; ban flag desecration; make English the official language; and allow prayer in public school.

Presidents also became enmeshed in two ways. First, in using the veto, the appointment power and the signing of executive orders, presidents wielded formidable political influence. As if his leadership task were not tough enough, the occupant of the Oval Office now faced demands not only to deploy these formal powers for economic prosperity at home and a strong America abroad, but also for guiding the republic in the correct moral direction. Secondly, this new responsibility caused media commentators to examine not only presidential candidates' positions on cultural value issues, but also their own personal histories. This ultimately contributed to a blurring of the divide between private and public life. The unprecedented media coverage accorded President Clinton's adulterous affair with intern Monica Lewinsky in 1998 would have been unthinkable in John Kennedy's day; even if the 'inappropriate behaviour' most certainly was not.

One final point here is important. Thanks to the separation of powers, distinct tiers and branches of government and a staggered system of elections, America faces a constant election cycle. If the European Union suffers a 'democratic deficit', America arguably faces a 'democratic surplus'. Partly as a result, American politicians are unusually 'vulnerable' and tend to 'run scared'. Fearful of defeat in primaries as well as general elections, obliged to raise their own funds, construct their own campaign organizations and hire professional consultants to run their campaigns, elected officials confront their contests alone. Lacking party cover, they are politically naked. Therefore, they frequently pursue cultural issues for electoral advantage, to buttress their own support and discredit opponents. This is another important, but often neglected, institutional reason why conflict over cultural matters appears such a persistent feature of American politics.

INTERMEDIARY ORGANIZATIONS

As we saw above, cultural issues became important items on the national political agenda by the end of the 1960s. Voters who previously were motivated by 'bread-and-butter' questions alone now factored cultural issues into their decisions on how to cast a ballot. Abetting their new importance was the shift by the main political parties to assume opposing positions on cultural values. Where they believed it to be advantageous, party candidates would deliberately highlight their own, and their opponents', positions to attract votes. The overall effect was that where once voters had generally not thought about cultural value issues in elections and where, even if they had, there was nothing much to choose between the two parties, things were now more fluid. Not only were these issues sufficiently important to become voting considerations, but election candidates also had contrasting rather than complementary positions on them. A choice, not an echo, was offered.

One result of this change was that cultural conflicts came increasingly to define the main parties and encourage their ideological polarization. For Republicans, concern with issues such as abortion, pornography, school prayer and capital punishment extended the party's tradition of Protestant-derived moralism. But the Democrats, too, increasingly acquired a more morally coherent cast than had previously been the case. Democrats increasingly embraced moral liberalism, drawing sharp distinctions between private and public life and favouring the notion that individuals, not society, should decide whether and when to terminate a pregnancy, recite prayer in school, or watch 'adult' movies. More tolerant of different 'lifestyles', Democratic candidates – especially for the presidency – faced increasing problems in assuring voters that they shared their commitments to a strong defence, law and order, and traditional morality.

This polarization ran against the grain of party politics. The traditional picture of parties saw two broad and loose coalitions, as much divided within themselves as between each other, that came together only once every four years to select a presidential candidate, finance and run his campaign. These events were national landmarks, and the parties brokered deals in 'smoke-filled rooms' to choose the candidate with the widest voter appeal. Moderation was the order of the day. The key targets were centrist, swing voters. The result was that both parties selected nominees who could appeal across the nation: FDR, Truman, Eisenhower and Kennedy. This also assisted financial donations to the parties for their presidential campaigns from 'fat cats': business and labour unions. The overall image was of 'Tweedledum and Tweedledee' parties: unideological, unprogrammatic, disdainful of political extremism.

All this changed dramatically after the disastrous Democratic National Convention of 1968, to which both parties responded by democratizing their selection procedures. Ironically, however, the result was the selection of candidates who were *less* representative even of their parties' identifiers in the electorate, let alone the average voter, than previously. Frequently criticized for offering

voters mirror images, the parties now assumed clearer identities. Cultural value conflict 'cut across' the traditional class base of the Democrats' New Deal coalition. Voters who might otherwise have supported the Democratic candidate if the main issue was economic policy became cross-pressured by his stance on social issues and foreign policy, which were also now salient issues. Federal campaign finance legislation in the 1970s altered the political landscape, eliminating 'fat cats' in favour of political action committees (PACs) and individual contributors, limited in the total amounts they could donate to parties and candidates. For many traditional Democrats, the feeling was one of disillusionment. Though reluctantly casting votes for Republican presidential candidates such as Nixon, Reagan and the Bushes, who were closer to their views than their respective Democratic nominees McGovern, Mondale, Dukakis and Gore, the feeling of traditionalist Democrats was: 'I haven't left my party, my party has left me.'

At no point was this polarized party politics more clear than in the 1988 presidential election. Trailing Governor Michael Dukakis by ten points in May 1988, focus groups of voters showed the Bush campaign the way to victory. It was to exploit two cultural 'hot-button' issues: Dukakis's veto of a state law that would have made reciting the Pledge of Allegiance a daily requirement in Massachusetts schools; and the release on weekend parole – under a state programme initiated by a previous Republican governor but approved by Dukakis – of a convicted black murderer, Willie Horton, who raped a white woman and battered her husband on release (ironically, it was Al Gore who had initially used Horton to attack Dukakis in the 1988 Democratic primary campaign). In October, Bush personally took up the latter issue in a reference to a traditionalist icon: 'Clint Eastwood's answer to crime is, "Go ahead, make my day." My opponent's answer is slightly different. His answer is "Go ahead, have a nice weekend" ' (Hershey, 1989: 95). Bush did not win the election by cultural politics alone, but they proved an important part of his victory and showed how potent the culture war had become.

That this polarization occurred was, in one sense, predictable. Cultural issues are difficult to resolve by traditional political methods. The fragmented nature of government that the Constitution established makes compromise and incrementalism the essence of policymaking. But compromise and conciliation are more amenable to distributive politics than to cultural issues. Material goods can be divided on an acceptable basis but cultural values involve stark issues of right and wrong. Compromise means sell-out. Negotiation and concession are tantamount to defeat. Driven more by ideas than interests, demands for purity, whether from traditionalists or progressives, are invariably impossible to meet.

Assisting this sea-change in the parties' approach was the activism of organized interest lobbies. For the Democrats, civil rights groups, labour unions, environmentalist groups, feminists and gay rights activists encouraged their supporters to register to vote in primary elections. Delegates to post-1968 Democratic conventions were overwhelmingly highly educated, wealthy and progressive. For the Republicans, a new set of groups, led by fundamentalist Christians and social issue activists of the 'New Right', now began registering in their primaries and caucuses in substantial numbers. Forming PACs and using direct mail to mobilize sympathizers and tap their money, organized lobbies eagerly pursued policy goals, sometimes to the exclusion of considerations of electoral success. The result was that both parties' ideological profiles narrowed. To win the party nomination, candidates had to appeal to these new, issue-motivated and 'purist' groups – to narrow their views. This was more acute in the Grand Old Party (GOP), but the Democrats suffered too. The separation between the electoral and governing coalitions in America – always partial, because of federalism and the separation of powers – now became a gulf.

All of this was further assisted, albeit inadvertently, by the changing mass media. Two aspects were important: the development of an adversarial media and the emergence of television as the central platform, focus and disseminator of politics. The key events were Vietnam and Watergate. The Vietnam War was a prolonged national trauma, the first televised war and the first that America 'lost'. This, along with the uncovering of Watergate, led many journalists (many of whom had experienced the postwar expansion of education and 1960s radicalism) to see both themselves and public officials in a new light. They became charged with a duty to scrutinize government and politicians in the closest detail. Whether Republican or Democrat, whether president, Congress, or courts, all politicians and governing institutions were *prima facie* suspect. Aggressive, fearless investigation was henceforth a necessary part of the journalist's trade. The media had a responsibility – in the public interest – to assume an adversarial stance.

Because television had by now also become the main source of political news for most Americans, its importance to politicians increased. Prior to 1952, most American households did not own a television. Thereafter, with television the main medium by which Americans received their information about politics, cultural conflicts became increasingly in vogue. Television did not cause the rise of the culture war, but the prominence of cultural issues owes much to their being more amenable to succinct (and graphic) televised news coverage in the space of four minutes than the complex minutiae of the latest budget deal or free trade agreement. Television notoriously loves image over detail, simplicity over complexity, the concrete over the abstract, and the dramatic over the dull. The message it implicitly sends is that, to learn about globalization or environmental protection, read the *Wall Street Journal* or *Washington Post*. Politics on television (and radio) is more styled to light entertainment and drama than detailed discussion and complex information, and cultural conflicts are full of drama.

For candidates, getting time on television was crucial to getting their names well known and their views heard. Journalists became crucial intermediaries between politicians and the people. Ultimately, they were not just reporting news, but making it. They acted as 'gatekeepers'. Those whom they mentioned as 'serious' contenders for party nominations affected which politicians could raise money for prospective campaigns; what features of the campaign were covered – personality, issues or the 'horse race' of who is ahead, who is behind – affected voter perceptions of candidates and electoral outcomes; and how electoral results were evaluated in turn affected the decisions of candidates, campaign workers and prospective donors.

Another aspect of television (along with new technologies such as direct-mail communications and the Internet) was that it made it easier for the interest groups and activists on both sides to wage a cultural war on a large scale. Previously, preachers, writers and lecturers could reach at most a few hundred people at a time. Now, television evangelists, radio talk-show hosts, and the authors of direct-mail messages can wage a furious war of words reaching tens of millions of people and recruiting hundreds of thousands of followers. Images of protestors blocking abortion clinics or massing outside prisons to demand that a death penalty be implemented are simple, powerful and vividly direct in ways that diagrams about budget deficits are not. Partly as a result, a cultural war that once enlisted only a few activists could now mobilize mass armies on both sides of the divide.

CONCLUSION

The rise of cultural value conflict relies on several distinct but related features of American politics. Some derive from the changing social base and socio-economic infrastructure: post-Cold War politics, post-industrialism, immigration, feminism and a reaction on the right. Others stem from the actions of government, especially the Supreme Court. Still others emerged from the consequences of party reform, organized interest mobilization, and a newly aggressive, adversarial and far-reaching media dominated by television. These three dimensions affected each other, reinforcing and magnifying the dimensions of cultural conflict into one that was national in scope and spoke to basic questions of moral values and national identity. The cumulative effect was to enlarge the role of cultural issues in politics in an unprecedented, dramatic and far-reaching fashion, and to divide Americans as never before – sharply and persistently – on this newly important dimension of political conflict.

3 Abortion

This right of privacy, whether it be founded in the Fourteenth Amendment's concept of personal liberty and restrictions upon state action, as we feel it is, or, as the District Court determined, in the Ninth Amendment's reservation of rights to the people, is broad enough to encompass a woman's decision whether or not to terminate her pregnancy.

Harry Blackmun, for the Court, *Roe v. Wade* 410 U.S. 113 (1973), at 152

Today, Roe v. Wade *and the fundamental right of women to decide whether to terminate a pregnancy survive but are not secure. . . . I fear for the future. I fear for the liberty and equality of the millions of women who have lived and come of age in the sixteen years since Roe was decided. I fear for the integrity of, and public esteem for, this Court.*

Harry Blackmun, concurring in part and dissenting in part, *Webster v. Reproductive Health Services*, 492 U.S. 490 (1989), at 537–538

- **The Historical Context**
- **Public Opinion: Abortions as 'Safe, Legal and Rare'**
- **Explaining the Politics of Abortion**
- **The US Constitution**
- **Governing Institutions**
- **The Traditionalist Counter-revolution: Has *Roe* Been Eroded?**
- **Abortion and American Politics: The Wider Significance**
- **Conclusion**

Chapter Summary

Abortion has proven the most divisive and controversial cultural value conflict of the last 30 years. The key catalyst was the ruling of the US Supreme Court in *Roe v. Wade* (1973) that struck down the severely restrictive abortion laws of most American states. The decision was widely condemned by traditionalists, not only for its effect in decriminalizing abortion, but also because of its contentious constitutional basis. *Roe* galvanized both a 'pro-life' movement that sought to reverse the decision and a 'reproductive rights' lobby that viewed abortion as a proxy for broader issues of women's equality. Together, the abortion issue was nationalized and politicized. Although the Supreme Court has not overturned *Roe*, it has – in combination with Republican administrations, Congress and direct action by pro-life groups – effectively limited women's access to abortion. While most Americans concur with the current politico-legal settlement, in which a woman's right to terminate her pregnancy is recognized but so too are the rights of individual states to regulate conditions surrounding the exercise of abortion rights, the divisive nature of the issue has not seen an abatement of political conflict. The fundamental conflict of individual female autonomy versus community values has been especially controversial because of the involvement of a third party whose scientific, legal and constitutional status remains a matter of intense dispute: the foetus.

Norma McCorvey (aka 'Jane Roe') occupies an unusual position in American politics. She has been celebrated for her courage, moral strength, and for personifying what the modern-day struggle over the issue of abortion has been about – by *both* the 'pro-choice' and 'pro-life' movements. That exceptional niche has been the result of McCorvey being the woman responsible for bringing to federal courts one of the most important and controversial cases of the twentieth century, *Roe v. Wade* (1973), that established for the first time the constitutional right of a woman to terminate her pregnancy by abortion; and for then renouncing her behaviour 20 years later and joining the religious right. McCorvey's individual journey of 'redemption' provides an unusually clear mirror to the deeply emotive and complex subject of abortion – the most divisive and intractable cultural value conflict in modern American politics.

Some one and a half million American women currently avail themselves of the constitutional right to an abortion every year (approximately one-quarter of all pregnancies in America). This alone makes abortion a matter of profound and widespread political concern. Beyond this stark statistic, however, four additional factors make abortion a supremely highly charged and enduring political issue. First, abortion involves competing claims not only between the individual citizen and the state but also over a third party: the foetus. Secondly, an unelected, unaccountable federal judiciary, employing contentious methods of constitutional interpretation to overturn the established laws of most individual states, has powerfully shaped abortion policy. Thirdly, the abortion controversy pits groups who adhere closely to religious doctrine against an array of secular, progressive and feminist forces intent on protecting a woman's reproductive rights. Fourthly, the fragmentary nature of American government has stimulated intense competition within and between governing institutions over abortion and sustained the battle between political coalitions with markedly different social values, partisan leanings and views of the appropriate limits to individual freedom.

Before proceeding, however, it is important to note a point about political language. Journalistic shorthand often uses terms such as 'pro-abortion' and 'anti-abortion' to describe the combatants in the conflict, but this is misleading. No Americans favour abortions taking place as a positive state of affairs; all would readily embrace an America where no abortions had to occur. However much many Americans fear abortion becoming merely a routine form of contraception, the process of terminating a pregnancy is too painful – physically, emotionally and psychologically – for all concerned to deem the 'pro-abortion' tag remotely accurate.

Rather, the contending groups are best described in terms of being 'pro-choice' and 'pro-life'. Both groups use these terms, not least since it is conventionally deemed politically preferable to be for something than against anything in America. Even these classifications are not completely satisfactory (they imply, for example, that some Americans oppose freedom of choice for the individual while others are 'against' human life) but they nevertheless clarify the key concerns. In this dichotomy, those who side with the pro-choice forces differ in their views on the morality of terminating pregnancies but share the conviction that the decision should be primarily, or even exclusively, a matter for the individual woman alone (in consultation with a physician) to make. Government should have no role in intruding on her decision or setting up burdensome administrative or regulatory hurdles hampering her right to choose an abortion. Choice takes priority.

For the pro-life lobby, however, the sanctity of human life – including that of the 'unborn child' (a term conceptually distinct from the foetus) – is sacrosanct and hence abortion is morally wrong. While pro-lifers disagree about what kinds of government prohibition on abortion should exist and their extent (such as whether all abortions should be prevented, including those resulting from rape and incest), they share the core belief that substantial restrictions on terminations are appropriate, desirable and legitimate actions for governing authorities to undertake. The potential life of the unborn, not the autonomy of the living woman, is the priority consideration.

The disagreement on abortion is complex. It is not simply centred on the morality of abortion, but also on the competing claims of the foetus, pregnant woman and state. One can with perfect consistency maintain that termination of a pregnancy is immoral while simultaneously upholding the right of women to be free to choose to do so,

unhindered by government interference. Similarly, one can consistently believe that abortion is not, by definition, murder while supporting the right of individual states to regulate heavily the terms and conditions by which abortions are carried out, without establishing a uniform national regulatory regime. The absolutist pro-life position of prohibiting all abortions and the absolutist pro-choice position of prohibiting none are extremes that obscure many other more subtle and, in practice, commonly held stances on the issue.

The straightforward explanation most often advanced for the persistence of conflict over abortion – religiosity – is, then, inadequate. Although the social base of American politics remains dominated by Protestants and Catholics, many of whom view abortion as a sin against God, this situation has been the case since at least the nineteenth century. Admittedly, different degrees of religiosity exist in America and these particular groups tend to see abortion as a key issue. But to account for the politicization of abortion since 1973, it is necessary to examine the role of government, and especially the federal government. In particular, the Supreme Court's intervention in *Roe v. Wade* was crucial. Only since that landmark decision has abortion become a political issue of nationwide salience and controversy.

This is not to suggest that, prior to 1973, abortion generated no conflicts. But these pale by comparison with the bitter and protracted battles that have occurred since the Court's intervention. In a peculiar sense, both the pro-choice and the pro-life groups agree that abortion is a 'matter of conscience', one that should not be part of conventional political battles. But to take abortion 'out' of politics, both lobbies are convinced of the need to engage in concerted political action: either to entrench a woman's right to choose indefinitely (for pro-choicers) or to prohibit abortion more or less entirely (for pro-lifers). Ironically, from markedly dissimilar motives, the shared conviction that government should have nothing to do with abortion leads both sides to the widespread political activism that has compelled government authorities at state and federal levels continuously to intervene.

THE HISTORICAL CONTEXT

Abortions in America are as old as the republic. Reflecting their colonial origins, American states were originally guided on abortion policy by British common law, which permitted terminations until 'quickening' – the point about midway through a pregnancy when the woman first perceives foetal movement in the womb. Although abortion before quickening was socially acceptable and no grassroots pro-life movement existed in America before the twentieth century, a successful campaign to outlaw abortion in the nineteenth century was initiated – ironically, not primarily by religious leaders but by physicians, seeking to drive out of business the 'irregular' doctors most likely to perform abortions. With their professional power augmented by the formation of the American Medical Association (AMA) in 1847, and further strengthened by a political alliance with the anti-obscenity movement led by Anthony Comstock in the 1870s, abortion was outlawed by every state by 1900.

Crucially for the contemporary conflict, however, those prohibitive laws were authored by individual state legislatures, not Congress. Until fairly recently, the federal government had nothing to say on abortion, except in areas of federal jurisdiction (such as military bases). Judicial intervention by federal courts on constitutional grounds was also rare. The content of abortion laws therefore mirrored the dominant preferences of particular state populations – a uniform national regulatory framework was absent. America contained a patchwork of different rules and regulations, but, as Table 3.1 reveals, most laws were decidedly restrictive, prohibiting women from obtaining a termination in all cases except where the life of the mother was endangered or where pregnancy had resulted from rape or incest.

An inevitable result of this highly restrictive regulatory regime was that women seeking abortions frequently needed to travel outside their own state in order to obtain terminations. In 1972 (the year before *Roe* was decided), in 23 of the 50 states, *every* woman seeking an abortion had to leave her state of residence to obtain one; in only eight states did fewer than 10 per cent *not* have to do so (Craig and O'Brien, 1993: 76).

This powerfully restrictive pattern began to be challenged during the 1960s by two developments. The first was initiated largely by medical professionals in particular states. Concern over foetal abnormalities raised by the thalidomide drug scare and the rubella epidemic of the early 1960s, along with proposals by the American Law Institute, initiated a dialogue among lawyers and medical practitioners on the merits of abortion law reform. Growing professional and public concern over revelations about the number of illegal abortions also contributed to the changing context. Pressure to liberalize strict abortion laws began to mount on therapeutic (medical) grounds. In 1967, the state legislatures of California, Colorado and North Carolina passed laws widening access to abortion on health grounds. But these therapeutic grounds for abortion still left the ultimate decision on termination with the doctors, not the pregnant women.

The second development, which strengthened the forces for liberalization of abortion laws but politicized the issue dramatically, came with the activism of a new 'second' wave of feminist groups. For organizations such as the National Organization for Women (NOW), securing less restrictive abortion laws was not only a matter of women's health, but also an imperative part of the struggle to achieve 'reproductive autonomy' for women and equality with men. In some cases, this amounted to a campaign to achieve 'abortion on demand'. For example, after an acrimonious and bitter campaign, New York's state legislature passed a law

TABLE 3.1 State abortion laws before *Roe v. Wade*

	Reasons for allowed abortions			
Any reason (5 states)	To protect the woman's physical and mental health (13 states)	To preserve the woman's life and in cases of rape (1 state)	Only to preserve woman's life (29 states)	All abortions prohibited (3 states)
Alaska	Arkansas	Mississippi	Alabama	Louisiana
DC	California		Arizona	New Hampshire
Hawaii	Colorado		Connecticut	Pennsylvania
New York	Delaware		Idaho	
Washington	Florida		Illinois	
	Georgia		Indiana	
	Kansas		Iowa	
	Maryland		Kentucky	
	New Mexico		Maine	
	North Carolina		Massachusetts	
	Oregon		Michigan	
	South Carolina		Minnesota	
	Virginia		Missouri	
			Montana	
			Nebraska	
			Nevada	
			New Jersey	
			North Dakota	
			Ohio	
			Oklahoma	
			Rhode Island	
			South Dakota	
			Tennessee	
			Texas	
			Utah	
			Vermont	
			West Virginia	
			Wisconsin	
			Wyoming	

Source: Craig and O'Brien (1993: 75).

in 1970 effectively allowing abortion on demand during the first three months of pregnancy. Under pressure from pro-life lobbies, the state legislature then voted to repeal the measure in 1972 (but this was vetoed by Governor Nelson Rockefeller).

While conflict was emerging over abortion, its intensity remained relatively muted by occurring on a selective and state-by-state basis, federalism allowing for different state outcomes. Controversy over abortion was neither nationalized nor fully developed into a fundamental ideological or partisan battle, and the nascent pro-life and pro-choice lobbies could each claim selective legal and policy victories.

But this was transformed by the Supreme Court's intervention in 1973. The Court's involvement began with *Roe v. Wade* and its companion case *Doe v. Bolton*. In these landmark decisions, the Court found that the Constitution's 'right to privacy' encompassed a woman's decision whether or not to bear a child and the justices set out a 'trimester' scheme that legalized the abortion procedure prior to viability. *Roe* was a particularly sweeping decision by any historical or comparative measure: 49 state laws on abortion (all bar New York's) were rendered unconstitutional. As Byron Shafer observed, by 'legitimizing abortion nationwide, the decision not only increased sharply a previously proscribed activity. It also augmented the appearance of an increase even more, as previously private (and often illegal) abortions came into the legal public record' (Shafer, 1998: 121).

As evident in Table 3.2, the absolute number of legal abortions skyrocketed over 20 years, from 18,000 in 1968 to 1,590,000 in 1988. By the mid-1980s, the proportional change from the previous year had become less than 1 per cent, indicating that the annual number of abortions had stabilized. (The reasons for this reflected not simply legal availability but also social factors – births out of wedlock, contraceptive use and the effect of AIDS on sexual mores – and technological advances.) While the increase in abortions pre-dated the 1973 rulings, it would be wrong to infer that an equivalent increase would have occurred without the judicial intervention that constitutionalized and nationalized abortion rights. The Court's legalizing abortion contributed significantly to the substantial increase in recorded terminations.

One of *Roe*'s most immediate and dramatic political consequences was powerfully to antagonize evangelical Christians and Catholics throughout America. Admittedly, abortion was merely one part of a broader set of

TABLE 3.2   Legal abortions in the US, 1967–88

Year	Number	Change from previous year	Percentage change from previous year
1967	9,000	+1,000	+13
1968	18,000	+9,000	+100
1969	22,700	+4,700	+26
1970	193,500	+170,800	+752
1971	485,800	+292,300	+151
1972	586,800	+101,000	+21
1973	744,600	+157,800	+27
1974	898,600	+154,000	+21
1975	1,034,200	+135,600	+15
1976	1,179,300	+145,100	+14
1977	1,316,700	+137,400	+12
1978	1,409,600	+92,900	+7
1979	1,497,700	+88,100	+6
1980	1,553,900	+56,200	+4
1981	1,577,300	+23,400	+2
1982	1,573,900	−3,400	−0.2
1983	1,575,000	+1,100	+0.07
1984	1,577,200	+2,200	+0.1
1985	1,588,600	+11,400	+0.7
1986	1,574,000	−14,600	−0.92
1987	1,559,100	−14,900	−0.95
1988	1,590,800	+31,700	+2

TABLE 3.3   'Degenerative trends'

	Divorce		Illegitimacy		Crime	
Year	Raw number (1,000s)	Rate per 1,000	Raw number (1,000s)	Rate per 1,000	Raw number (1,000s)	Rate per 1,000
1990	1,175	4.7	1,225	43.8	12,430	66.5
1980	1,189	5.2	666	29.4	11,110	66.5
1970	708	3.5	339	26.4	5,208	34.9
1960	393	2.2	224	21.6	1,096	8.8
1950	385	2.6	142	14.1	737	7.6
1940	256	2.0	90	7.1	662	8.9

Note: Divorce rate is calculated per total population; illegitimate birthrate is calculated per total number of unmarried women; crime rate is per total population.
Source: Shafer (1998: 122).

developments connected with the perceived 'breakdown' of the family: a rising divorce rate; growing rates of births outside marriage; and increasing crime (see Table 3.3). These trends had been developing for several years and far outweighed the impact of judicial decisions on abortion in terms of social effects. Nevertheless, abortion became the most powerful touchstone for those activists mobilizing a mass constituency to protect 'family values'. Abortion rapidly emerged as the most critical symbolic social issue – a litmus test and proxy – for where Americans stood on the fate of the traditional family and

Exhibit 3.1   A progressive view: abortion as an equality issue?

Abortion is rarely debated in terms of equality of opportunity but for progressives and feminists it should be. Pregnancy automatically limits a woman's activities – to prohibit abortion is to deny her any escape. (After giving birth, her freedom is also limited in other ways although, in principle, she can put her child up for adoption.)

Both legal and moral judgements are involved. The legal conundrum is when a 'person' comes into existence. The Constitution's Fourteenth Amendment declares that no state is to deny any person the 'equal protection' of the laws. To speak of an 'unborn child' suggests that a human being exists, waiting to be born, which is plausible in the later stages of gestation but implausible in the earlier stages, when most abortions occur. In *Roe v. Wade* the Supreme Court took the position that a *person* does not come into existence until a live birth occurs. The embryo and foetus have no claim to equal protection but the pregnant woman is a person with both rights and interests that she is entitled to protect.

But even if it is assumed, as traditionalists typically do, that a foetus is a person, it does not necessarily follow that abortion is wrong and should be illegal. The organism in the womb is, in effect, a parasite, sapping the woman's energy, sometimes risking her health and even her life. Morality and law inevitably require individuals to take risks and make sacrifices for others, but pregnancy involves more risk and sacrifice than are required in almost any other connection. This suggests to many progressives that acceptance of those burdens, which men by definition do not share, should be a matter of individual choice, not state determination.

other issues (gender roles, sexuality, the place of Judaeo-Christian values, child welfare) intimately associated with that institution. For traditionalists, this period – the 1960s and 1970s – saw a broad and far-reaching assault mounted by the federal government in general, and the courts in particular, against the foundations of American society.

Crucially, the battle over values was also inextricably linked to questions of resources and class. Most pro-life women always valued their traditional family roles highly and arranged their lives accordingly. They generally did not acquire high-level educational and occupational skills because they married, and they married because their values suggested that this would be the most satisfying life option open to them. Pro-choice women, by contrast, tended to postpone (or avoid) marriage and family roles in order to acquire the skills (educational and occupational) to compete in traditionally male spheres and achieve career success and status. Equality of opportunity is therefore a central part of the pro-choice position for many progressives (see Exhibit 3.1). Each side in the controversy defended not only a moral position but also an entire way of life. Fundamental economic and social interests, as well as values, informed abortion conflict.

PUBLIC OPINION: ABORTIONS AS 'SAFE, LEGAL AND RARE'

America's political system has rarely confronted an issue so seemingly unamenable to compromise as abortion. For advocates of choice, abortion represents a fundamental right of reproductive freedom for women. For the pro-life movement, abortion is murder. Between those two positions there exists little room for consensus and political dialogue between pro-choice and pro-life movements has effectively been non-existent.

But most Americans see the issue quite differently from the partisans. Only a minority supports either the purist pro-choice position

of 'abortion on demand' or the absolutist pro-life stance of a ban on abortion in all (or most) circumstances. What makes matters more problematic is that there exists no single popular majority on abortion but two overlapping ones. On the one hand, many Americans are profoundly uneasy about government interference in intimate personal decisions. When pollsters pose the abortion issue as a question of whether the choices of individual women or government should be binding, results indicate a clear pro-choice majority. However, when pollsters put the question differently, they get another majority: most Americans think too many abortions are performed, reject most of the reasons that women give for terminations, and favour restrictions on abortion rights (such as requiring teenagers to get prior parental permission). Some polls have shown that a majority of respondents support legal abortion even as a majority of the same group considers abortion to be the equivalent of murder.

Alongside this complexity is the fact that neither men nor women occupy one side of the conflict. Although the most vocal activists on both sides tend to be women, the division of women and men more generally reflects the distinct prisms by which abortion is viewed: for pro-choicers, as primarily a matter of reproductive rights; for pro-lifers, as primarily a matter of motherhood and the life of the unborn child. As Table 3.4 shows, most Americans consistently opposed the decriminalization of abortion when asked in general terms, but support for *Roe* appears relatively high (see Table 3.5), although only 20 per cent of Americans support abortions in the second trimester of pregnancy (months four to six).

Moreover, as Table 3.6 shows, when asked about support for abortion in particular cases, such as foetal abnormalities or danger to maternal health, greater popular support is forthcoming for therapeutic abortions. Non-therapeutic reasons, such as being unmarried, are regarded less favourably. As always with opinion data, however, the answers must be treated cautiously, since the

TABLE 3.4 Respondents believing abortion should be legal, 1975–92 (per cent)

Date	New York Times	Gallup
April 1975	–	21
December 1977	–	22
February 1979	–	22
July 1980	–	25
May 1981	–	23
May 1983	–	23
September 1988	–	24
September 1989	40	–
November 1989	41	–
January 1990	39	–
April 1990	–	31
August 1990	41	–
June 1991	37	–
August 1991	41	–
September 1991	42	33
January 1992	40	–
March 1992	44	–

Note: – indicates that the survey was not conducted in that year.
Questions: (*New York Times*) 'Which of these comes closest to your views? (1) Abortion should be generally available to all who want it, or (2) Abortion should be available but under stricter limits than it is now, or (3) Abortion should not be permitted'; (*Gallup*) 'Do you think abortion should be legal under any circumstances, legal only under some circumstances, or illegal under all circumstances?' The percentages represent those who selected ('1') in the *New York Times* poll and 'under any circumstances' in the *Gallup* poll.

responses received partly depend on the manner in which the question is formulated.

Compared to the United Kingdom, Americans are proportionately more opposed to abortion. But as Table 3.7 records, even in the UK, majorities disapprove of abortion in the cases of unmarried women with a physically handicapped child and when a married couple does not wish to have any more children.

Although abortion is often perceived as the burning moral question of the modern era, for most Americans it is far from being a critical issue. A Gallup poll in July 1995, for example, asked respondents to list the important problems facing the country and abortion ranked eighteenth out of 22 problems mentioned (Golay and Rollyson, 1996: 196). That does not mean that Americans lack opinions on the issue, nor that it divides them, but it suggests that its importance is limited in terms of political participation.

Most Americans agreed with Bill Clinton's position that abortion should be 'safe, legal and rare'. For example, a *Los Angeles Times* poll in June 2000 found that 65 per cent of those responding (including 72 per cent of women) said that after the first three months of pregnancy, abortion should either be banned or allowed only in cases of rape, incest or to save the woman's life. But a contemporaneous *Newsweek* poll found that

TABLE 3.5 Support for *Roe v. Wade* (per cent)

Date	Harris	Gallup
February 1974	52	–
November 1974	–	47
April 1975	54	–
March 1976	54	–
August 1976	59	–
October 1976	60	–
July 1977	53	–
July 1978	–	–
February 1979	60	–
February 1980	–	–
May 1981	56	45
May 1982	–	–
June 1983	–	50
June 1984	–	–
September 1985	50	–
January 1986	–	49
January 1987	–	–
December 1988	–	57
January 1989	56	–
July 1989	61	58
August 1989	59	–
October 1989	58	–
October 1990	–	–
June 1991	–	52
July 1991	–	56
September 1991	–	57

Note: – indicates that the survey was not conducted in that year.

Questions: (*Harris*) 'In 1973, the US Supreme Court decided that state laws which made it a crime to have an abortion up to three months of pregnancy were unconstitutional, and that the decision of whether or not to have an abortion should be left to the woman and her doctor to decide. In general, do you favour or oppose the US Supreme Court decision making abortion up to three months of pregnancy legal?' (*Gallup*) 'In 1973, the Supreme Court ruled that states cannot place restrictions on a woman's right to an abortion during the first three months of pregnancy. Would you like to see this ruling overturned or not?'

[The wording of the question is inaccurate. The decision in fact legalized abortion in the first six months of pregnancy. In 1975, *Harris* found only 20 per cent approval for legalized abortion between the third and sixth months of pregnancy.]

62 per cent of respondents wanted any new Supreme Court justices to uphold *Roe* and continue 'protecting a woman's right to choose' (Taylor, 2000: 2207). To this extent, the mobilization on abortion has been driven largely by groups that are unrepresentative of most Americans in terms of both their intense concern and preferred policy outcomes.

TABLE 3.6   Respondents supporting legal abortion under special circumstances (per cent)

Year	Chance of defect	Wants no more children	Health endangered	Cannot afford	Rape	Not married	Any reason
1965	54.0	–	77.0	18.0	–	–	–
1972	74.3	37.6	83.0	45.6	74.1	40.5	–
1973	82.2	46.1	90.6	51.7	80.6	47.3	–
1974	82.6	44.6	90.4	52.3	82.7	47.9	–
1975	80.3	43.8	88.2	50.5	79.9	45.8	–
1976	81.6	44.6	88.7	50.8	80.4	48.2	–
1977	83.1	44.4	88.0	51.6	80.5	47.5	36.5
1978	80.1	39.0	88.3	45.4	80.4	39.6	32.2
1979	–	–	–	–	–	–	–
1980	80.3	45.2	87.7	49.6	80.2	46.3	39.4
1981	–	–	–	–	–	–	–
1982	78.4	43.4	87.5	46.7	79.8	43.2	36.5
1983	74.7	37.0	85.3	41.2	77.9	36.8	34.3
1984	77.4	41.1	87.0	44.4	76.7	42.6	37.2
1985	76.1	39.1	86.8	42.4	78.0	39.9	35.7
1986	–	–	–	–	–	–	–
1987	74.8	39.3	84.4	42.8	75.6	38.5	37.3
1988	76.2	38.8	85.6	40.4	76.7	37.6	34.6
1989	78.3	42.7	87.5	45.8	79.9	43.3	38.6
1990	78.0	43.2	88.8	45.3	80.7	43.1	41.5
1991	79.4	42.7	88.0	46.1	82.3	42.9	40.8

Note: – indicates that the survey was not conducted in that year.

Questions: 'Please tell me whether or not you think it should be possible for a pregnant woman to obtain a legal abortion if (A) there is a strong chance of serious defect in the baby, (B) she is married and does not want any more children, (C) the woman's own health is seriously endangered by the pregnancy, (D) the family has a very low income and cannot afford any more chldren, (E) she became pregnant as the result of rape, (F) she is not married and does not want to marry the man, or (G) the woman wants it for any reason?'

Source: Epstein et al. (1994: 599)

TABLE 3.7   Support for abortion in the United Kingdom, 2000

Circumstances	Approve	Disapprove	Don't know
• Where the woman's health is at risk by pregnancy	92	6	6
• Where it is likely that the child would be born physically handicapped	65	24	11
• Where the woman is not married	34	52	15
• Where a married couple do not want to have any more children	39	53	9
• Where the woman has chosen not to have the child	43	47	10

Note: The question posed was, 'Do you approve or disapprove of abortion under the following circumstances?'

Source: *The Sunday Telegraph*, May 28, 2000, p. 3.

EXPLAINING THE POLITICS OF ABORTION

That many Americans are disturbed by the current state of abortion law is hardly surprising. The combination of widespread and profound religious conviction, the influence of medical authority and technological change, the existence of broadly held demands for individual autonomy, and the presence of conflicting levels and contents of statute and common (judge-made) law makes for a potent and divisive struggle. That the issue has proven so bitterly contentious for so long, however, is less obvious. Abortion typifies cultural value conflict in that explanations for the persistence of the battle requires us to examine not only the social base of politics, but also the roles of governing institutions and intermediary organizations that are pressured by competing demands.

In some respects, abortion politics resembles the struggle over Prohibition that occurred during the early twentieth century. In 1919, the Anti-Saloon League and many religious and ethnic groups promoting 'moralist' causes won the initial battle with the ratification in 1919 of the Eighteenth Amendment to the Constitution, outlawing the manufacture, sale and transportation of liquor. Anti-Prohibition groups then had only one way to go: to win passage of another constitutional amendment to overturn Prohibition. After 14 years of social turmoil, they achieved precisely that with the ratification of the Twenty-First Amendment in 1933. Similarly, in the evolving abortion battle, 16 years after constitutionalizing abortion rights in *Roe v. Wade*, the Supreme Court upheld in 1989 a number of restrictions on abortion and appeared about to overturn *Roe*.

But the abortion struggle has been unlike Prohibition in important respects. First, the secular interest won the first triumph in abortion (securing a constitutional right to an abortion), and the religious–traditionalist position was forced to take up a counteroffensive. Secondly, the abortion struggle has also been over a Supreme Court decision, not a formal constitutional amendment. Thirdly, the institutional, partisan and interest group conflicts over abortion have occurred on markedly different – and shifting – political battlegrounds.

THE US CONSTITUTION

Much of the explanation for the continuing abortion controversy concerns the constitutional basis to *Roe*. It was not simply the fact of judicial intervention on abortion that strongly antagonized millions of Americans. Nor was the sweeping scope of its effect and the liberalizing content of the decision so troubling, though these were important and alarming to Americans who opposed abortion rights. It was also the contentious way in which the ruling was arrived at that fuelled outspoken criticism of the Court from many quarters for engaging in a blatantly unacceptable exercise of 'raw judicial power'. For prolife forces, a document that is holy writ was used to justify a deeply immoral policy. It is ironic yet typical of American politics that a contemporary national controversy should be stoked by a document composed in 1787.

Unlike gun control (where the Second Amendment contains a specific reference to arms) or capital punishment (where the Eighth Amendment contains a ban on 'cruel and unusual punishment'), no clause or amendment exists in the Constitution that expressly or directly refers to abortion. This is one of many issues where the Constitution seems to be 'silent'. No obvious or explicit guidance – whether to prohibit, allow or require abortions – is available from the document's text, but the Supreme Court controversially found that the Constitution had a strongly permissive voice when it came to abortion.

Roe v. Wade originated in a legal challenge to a Texas state law, litigation that eventually worked its way through the federal system for adjudication by the Supreme Court.

Norma McCorvey was a 21-year-old high school dropout, divorced with a five-year-old daughter and little money when she became pregnant in the summer of 1969. She unsuccessfully sought an abortion, which Texas prohibited unless it was necessary to save the woman's life. McCorvey recalled that, 'No legitimate doctor in Texas would touch me. . . . I found one doctor who offered to abort me for $500. Only he didn't have a license, and I was scared to turn my body over to him. So there I was – pregnant, unmarried, unemployed, alone and stuck' (Craig and O'Brien, 1993: 5). After carrying her pregnancy to term and giving up the child for adoption, McCorvey was persuaded to challenge the law's constitutionality as a class action suit (although the papers for the case were filed on March 3, 1970, the Supreme Court did not rule until January 22, 1973).

The core of the *Roe* decision was the 'right to privacy', the justices holding that this was broad enough to cover whether a woman could terminate her pregnancy. But a search through the words of the Constitution will nowhere reveal the words 'right to privacy', much less abortion. It will not even find the term 'privacy'. How then had the justices conjured this abortion right from a document that apparently said nothing about privacy, let alone terminations?

The justices had, in legal parlance, 'read this right into' the federal Constitution. The key decision had occurred eight years earlier, in *Griswold v. Connecticut* (1965), a ruling that aroused some academic attention but nothing in the way of the popular outcry that later accompanied *Roe*. *Griswold* concerned a 1937 law passed by the state of Connecticut (successor to a similar statute enacted in 1879) that prohibited the use of contraceptives, even by married couples. The law criminalized any person using 'any drug, medicinal article or instrument for the purpose of preventing conception'. Although unenforced – a difficult undertaking even if the authorities had wished to do so – it remained the legal requirement of the state. The executive director of the Planned Parenthood League of

Connecticut and the medical director of a New Haven birth control clinic brought a test case and the litigation eventually reached the Supreme Court. The majority ruled the state law unconstitutional as applied to married persons.

The majority in *Griswold* held that although the term 'privacy' appeared nowhere in the document, several amendments to the Constitution together suggested a 'zone of privacy' upon which the state could not intrude. The Third Amendment, for example, prohibited the quartering of soldiers in a private home during peacetime. The Fourth prohibited unwarranted searches and seizures of private property by government. Justice Douglas wrote for the majority that these clauses contained 'penumbras' (shadows) and 'emanations' that, when taken together, went to create another self-standing 'right of marital privacy' that is implicit in the document as a whole. The right, in effect, amounted to a declaration of individual sexual and reproductive autonomy that would be fleshed out over the next decade. In 1972, the justices extended the right to contraception to unmarried couples in *Eisenstadt v. Baird*. In 1973, they decided that the right was 'sufficiently broad' that it encompassed a woman's decision to have an abortion.

As Exhibit 3.2 reveals, *Roe* was heavily based on medical factors rather than constitutional law. The key constitutional provision concerned the Fourteenth Amendment's guarantee of protecting personal 'liberty' from state intrusion. Much attention focused on the first trimester (three months) but the decision effectively stated that women were free in consultation with their doctor to terminate a pregnancy for any reason up to six months and thereafter for serious health reasons.

Unsurprisingly, moral traditionalists and conservatives were outraged by this judicial move. To most, the step from quartering soldiers and searching property to allowing abortion was a rather odd, circuitous and tenuous one. Robert Bork, for whom abortion subsequently proved a decisive political

Exhibit 3.2   The trimester ruling of *Roe v. Wade* (1973)

By a 7 to 2 majority, the Court ruled that the Constitution's unenumerated 'right to privacy' protected a woman's right to terminate a pregnancy by abortion. This right was relative, not absolute: individual states had legitimate interests in abortion decisions, in particular preserving maternal health and protecting potential life. The Court therefore balanced the competing interests of the woman's right to a termination against the states' interests within a 'trimester' framework:

First trimester (one to three months)
In consultation with her physician, a woman may have an abortion. The state cannot interfere with her decision. Since abortion is medically safer than continuing pregnancy during this period, the state has no reason to prevent abortion to protect maternal health. Also, since the foetus is incapable of life outside the womb at this stage, the state has no reason to prevent the abortion to preserve potential life.

Second trimester (four to six months)
A woman remains free to terminate a pregnancy in consultation with her physician, but because abortion now poses a greater medical risk to her than continuing the pregnancy, the state's interest in preserving maternal health becomes a relevant consideration. The state can therefore regulate the conditions under which terminations occur, such as the kinds of hospital and clinic that may perform them. Since the foetus remains incapable of life outside the womb, the state cannot prevent abortion on grounds of its interest in preserving potential life.

Third trimester (seven to nine months)
Towards the end of sixth months the foetus becomes capable of life outside the womb, with or without artificial means of support. The state's interest in protecting potential life now becomes relevant. As well as regulating the conditions under which abortions occur, the state can prohibit them, subject to one important exception: if the woman's doctor(s) agrees that continuing the pregnancy poses a threat to her life or health, the mother may choose to have a termination.

albatross in his unsuccessful bid to win a Supreme Court seat in 1987, described the decision as a 'miracle of transubstantiation': 'Unfortunately, in the entire opinion, there is not one line of explanation, not one sentence that qualifies as legal argument' (Bork, 1990: 112).

Even *Roe*'s defenders reluctantly conceded that it was a shaky ruling. True, the Ninth Amendment was a get-out clause for pro-choice advocates: 'The enumeration in the Constitution, of certain rights, shall not be construed to deny or disparage others retained by the people.' This means that because the Constitution lists some specific rights, the fact that others do not appear explicitly in the document does not mean that

they do not exist. This is a matter for judges to 'discover' over time.

If, by composing the Ninth Amendment, the Constitution's authors themselves recognized that society would inevitably change over time, and hence they could not possibly cover every eventuality, surely the justices acted reasonably in *Roe*? The task of the courts is, after all, to interpret the document and apply it to new and unforeseen developments, thereby adapting it to a changing America without altering its fundamental meaning.

The difficulty here, however, is two-fold. First, the Ninth Amendment has been used extremely rarely by American courts, including the Supreme Court. Secondly, that judicial reluctance has traditionally reflected a key point about *Roe*: that if one took the logic of judicial 'discovery' of rights to underpin the beginning of judicial intervention, there exists no clear or obvious end to judicial legislating. (It is difficult to imagine the anti-government authors of the Bill of Rights having intended to grant such limitless discretion to judges.) The search for rights could realize some odd, hidden ones on this line of reasoning. Also, as the more perceptive liberals noted, given time and a suitably conservative president and Senate, respectively, to nominate and approve their appointments, the majority of federal judges could become conservative. A conservative court, reshaped by such appointments, could threaten the gains cherished by liberals through exactly the same mechanisms of 'creative' interpretation, albeit now to secure conservative policy results.

Moreover, if progressive advocates of the 'living Constitution' concept had their way, and judges interpreted constitutional provisions in the light of what most Americans deemed to be 'reasonable' or in line with 'civilized' values, then the Bill of Rights, which was designed to protect minorities from majority views, would effectively become a majoritarian instrument. Far from curtailing and limiting majority sentiment, the meaning of its provisions would come to rest on what majorities of the public preferred. For all these reasons, then, the Constitution proved to be central to abortion politics.

But the difficulty for conservatives was that to demand *Roe*'s overturning suggested, if successful, real-world results that most Americans would now deem repugnant. Reversing *Roe* would not amount to a ban on abortion – it would return America to the era where states could legislate as they saw fit. But the age in which most state abortion laws were passed was one in which women were viewed as chattel, tied to marriage, the family, bearing and raising children, and deferring to the patriarch of the house – husband or father – on pain of dire consequences. The

central explanation for the intensity with which pro-choice activists matched their pro-life opponents owes much to the conception of abortion as part of the broader struggle for female emancipation. It is also strongly informed by the majority of women obtaining abortions being young and unmarried. For feminists, being allowed to decide whether or not to terminate a pregnancy was hardly sufficient to achieve autonomy, but it did constitute a necessary part of female equality. To deny that right was to retard the day when women might realize their equality as human beings instead of being secondary citizens to men. Abortion rights therefore became enmeshed in broader cultural battles over the status and nature of the family, sexuality and gender roles.

Moreover, for courts to overturn *Roe*, as some conservatives recommended, would be to ignore precedent, a dangerous course of action for institutions dedicated to upholding the rule of law. As one respected jurist put it, however problematic their origins, to cast doubt on the Court's privacy decisions in *Griswold* and *Roe* is not necessarily to argue that they were wrong as '. . . a matter of constitutional law; it is to say that the Court was unable to come up with a satisfactory demonstration of their rightness' (Posner, 1992: 338).

GOVERNING INSTITUTIONS

Because of the controversial nature of abortion, most politicians prefer not to address the issue. But because of the intensity that many Americans bring to the struggle, politicians have simultaneously been unable to escape the electoral and financial pressures to take a public position on the issue.

Since 1973, both pro-choice and pro-life forces have claimed that their activism has led to the victory or defeat of particular candidates for elections to Congress and state offices. It is difficult to identify specific examples where a politician's stance on the issue caused his or her victory or defeat.

Nevertheless, it is clear that risk-averse elected officials, keen to capture the middle ground among voters, must tread with care on abortion. Even if the issue is insufficient alone to cause electoral triumph or catastrophe, it can contribute significantly to a victory or loss, whether in primary or general elections. In Republican and Democratic primaries, abortion is frequently a litmus test of political acceptability to party activists. Many voters feel sufficiently strongly on this issue to vote on it as the main – or a key – issue and to donate funds to campaigns on the basis of a candidate's abortion stance.

The disparity of lobbying resources among the competing coalitions is not nearly so great in the abortion case as over gun control. A coalition of ardently pro-life groups exists that is well financed, has a mass membership base that cares passionately about its cause, and has no qualms about mass mailing elected officials and the public to press its case. But a vocal and vigorous pro-choice coalition also exists, one no less vigilant in monitoring legislative action on abortion rights and mobilizing its popular base. As a result, abortion hovers on the political horizon like a storm cloud: 'No politician ventures into the field without formidable gear: polls, media consultants, and carefully worded position statements on when life begins and whether abortion should be legal' (Rubin, 1987: 253–4).

Campaigning on abortion is heavily dependent on emotive rather than rational appeals, portrays opponents as enemies and suggests an apocalyptic future about to descend unless immediate and decisive actions are undertaken. Mass direct mailshots are stridently worded, seeking to make voters angry. Pro-life shots often feature graphic photographs of terminated foetuses and testimony from women who had abortions and subsequently regretted the decision not to give birth to the baby that they were carrying. A fairly typical pro-life mailing, for example, called on voters to 'stop the baby killers':

These anti-life baby killers are already organizing, working and raising money to re-elect pro-abortionists like George McGovern. . . . Abortion means killing a living baby, a tiny human being with a beating heart and little fingers . . . killing a baby boy or girl with burning deadly chemicals or a powerful machine that sucks and tears the little infant from its mother's womb. (Chafe, 1991: 463)

Other pro-life appeals refer to abortion in terms of the Holocaust and cast supporters of abortion rights as being possessed by the Devil, since only satanic forces could permit thousands of abortions to occur annually in America (see *www.christiangallery.com/atrocity/*).

Pro-choice literature, by contrast, often features photographs of bombed abortion clinics, murdered abortion physicians, and pro-life groups blocking the entrances to clinics where terminations are performed. The objective of both lobbies is to galvanize action: the signing of a cheque, the decision to join an organization, or the journey to a polling station to vote for or against a particular candidate. Few occupants of America's governing institutions can easily ignore such provocative campaigns.

Ironically, however, precisely because the issue generates such controversy, candidate television campaign advertisements mostly avoided abortion until 1992. Most candidates feared the divisiveness that abortion appeals would cause among voters. In 1992 some challengers used spots on abortion (Indiana Republican challenger Michael Bailey used graphic anti-abortion footage during his race to unseat pro-choice incumbent Democrat Lee Hamilton), but of the 13 congressional candidates who did, only two won their primaries and none won in the general election (West, 1997: 49–50). In 1996, there was again fairly extensive use of television advertising on abortion. Johnny Isakson, for example, a candidate for the Republican nomination for the US Senate in Georgia, deployed an advertisement to distinguish himself from the other five Republicans in the party primary. Using a female announcer, and pictured with his wife and daughter, Isakson claimed his opponents would 'vote to ban abortions, making criminals out of women and their doctors', and stated that 'I don't believe our Government should fund, teach or promote abortion. But I will not vote to amend the Constitution to make criminals of women and their doctors. I trust my wife, my daughter and the women of Georgia to make the right choice' (Isakson lost).

Presidential politics

The presidency has been affected by, and in turn has shaped, the abortion conflict since 1968. Relatively little evidence exists to suggest that abortion directly influences presidential election outcomes. Although pro-choice and pro-life groups feel strongly on the issue, most Americans do not share their intensity and consider other issues to be equally or more important. Abortion's direct electoral impact has therefore been limited.

The choice of nominee for each party, however, has been influenced by abortion. Support for pro-choice positions on abortion has become an article of faith for Democrats, so much so that it has effectively become taken for granted that Democratic presidential nominees, such as Clinton and Gore, will be strongly pro-choice. In the Republican Party, greater conflict has occurred, with pro-lifers assuming a dominant position of influence since the end of the 1970s. Opposition to abortion was a crucial part of Ronald Reagan's campaigns to win the GOP nomination in 1976 and 1980, helping him to cement ties with the New Right and Christian fundamentalists as their preferred candidate. Unlike his Republican predecessors, Nixon and Ford (who wanted to return to the pre-*Roe* days of individual states determining policy), Reagan favoured bans on abortion. Both George H.W. Bush in 1988 and Bob Dole in 1996, who began as moderately pro-choice politicians, were forced to adopt strong pro-life positions to appease the religious right. George W. Bush was, like Reagan, adamantly

opposed to abortion but sensibly avoided making it an election issue in 2000.

In office, too, presidents have attempted to influence abortion policy in four ways:

- *Executive orders.* President Reagan used these to issue prohibitions on federal funds to organizations performing or promoting abortion overseas (see Exhibit 3.3) and to institute a 'gag rule' in 1988 that prevented doctors employed on federally funded health programmes from even discussing abortion with a patient. President Clinton reversed these bans in his first term of office and issued orders allowing women soldiers to receive abortions at military hospitals and to approve the use of the French abortion drug RU486.
- *Appointments.* Reagan, George H.W. Bush and George W. Bush appointed pro-life nominees to the federal bureaucracy and judiciary. In Reagan's case, prospective nominees were effectively screened by his Justice Department on abortion as a 'litmus test' of their suitability. His Supreme Court appointments of Sandra Day O'Connor (1981), Antonin Scalia (1986) and Anthony Kennedy (1987), and his appointment of William Rehnquist as Chief Justice in 1986, were intended to hasten the overturning of *Roe*. While the salience of the abortion issue receded somewhat with Clinton's election, it played a significant role in his decision to appoint Ruth Bader Ginsberg and Stephen Breyer to the Court. Both were judged to be moderately but clearly pro-choice. George W. Bush appointed a staunch abortion rights foe, former Senator John Ashcroft, as his Attorney General in January 2001.
- *Litigation.* Presidents Reagan and George H.W. Bush instructed their solicitors-general and Departments of Justice to intervene in abortion cases before the Supreme Court to urge the justices to reverse *Roe*. George W. Bush's choice for Solicitor-General, Ted Olson, was expected to argue

Exhibit 3.3   Abortion and foreign aid: the history of 'Mexico City'

1984. At the second UN International Conference on Population in Mexico City, the Reagan administration announced a new policy of denying assistance to any foreign, non-governmental organization that 'performs or actively promotes abortion as a method of family planning', even if that is done with the group's private funds. The directive became known as the 'Mexico City' policy.

1991. The House passes a foreign aid authorization bill that would remove the Mexico City restrictions but the measure ultimately fails, partly through President George H.W. Bush threatening to veto the bill over the provision.

1993. President Clinton rescinds the Mexico City restrictions in a memorandum to the director of the Agency for International Development, writing that 'These excessively broad anti-abortion conditions are unwarranted. Moreover, they have undermined efforts to promote safe and efficacious family planning programs in foreign nations.'

1995. Anti-abortion forces in the House – blocked in attempts to reinstate Mexico City through legislation – cut appropriations for international family planning programmes by 35 per cent and blocked payments until July 1996.

1996. Anti-abortion forces successfully delay payment of fiscal 1997 family planning funds until July 1, unless Congress votes separately to release them in March. Congress subsequently approves the early release.

1997. Negotiations on the fiscal 1998 foreign aid spending bill reach a deadlock over a House provision that would effectively reinstate the Mexico City restrictions. GOP leaders remove the provision but limit spending to the fiscal 1997 level, released at 8 per cent per month.

1998. House leaders keep anti-abortion restrictions off the fiscal 1999 foreign operations spending bill but the Mexico City policy is added to a State Department authorization bill, which fails.

1999. Clinton eventually agrees to a one-year deal on the fiscal 2000 foreign aid bill that prohibits aid to family planning groups that perform abortions – except in cases of rape, incest or to save the life of the woman – or that lobby to change abortion laws or government policies in other countries. Clinton can and does waive the restriction, but under the law this triggers a shift of $12.5 million in family planning aid to an account for child survival and disease prevention programmes.

2000. Republicans agree to increase aid for family planning programmes but the fiscal 2001 foreign aid spending bill prevents spending the money until February 15, after a new president is inaugurated.

2001. President George W. Bush reinstates the Mexico City ban by directive, writing that, 'It is my conviction that taxpayer funds should not be used to pay for abortions or advocate or actively promote abortion, either here or abroad.'

Source: Adapted from Pomper (2001: 235–6).

strongly against pro-choice rulings before the Court during 2001–05.

- *Veto power.* Presidents have been able to use, and threaten to use, their veto to strike down laws passed by Congress on abortion. President Clinton twice vetoed a law that banned 'partial-birth abortions' – used in some late-term abortions – that

had been passed by the Republican 104th Congress in 1996 (the first time that Congress had passed a law outlawing a specific abortion procedure). The operation was undoubtedly horrific – doctors bring the intact foetus down the birth canal and then crush the skull so that the head can be pulled out – but all late-term abortions involve crushing the foetus's skull (so that the mother does not have to go into labour to expel the foetus). Clinton vetoed the law because it did not permit the procedure when the mother's life was in danger. The arrival of George W. Bush in the White House increased the prospects that a prohibition on the procedure would be enacted.

It should be noted that rhetorical power can also be a formidable weapon. Reagan, in particular, used the White House as a 'bully pulpit' from which to try to shape public attitudes against abortion rights (see Exhibit 3.4). Although this informal resource lacks the direct influence of the four powers listed above, it can be significant. Given the president's unique position as Head of State and Head of Government, the only elected official able to speak to and for a national constituency, the president's championing a particular cause or position can help to shape popular sentiments on an issue. President George W. Bush, while rejecting Reagan's overt approach, emphasized the importance of 'life' and symbolically restricted federal funding to international family planning groups that provide abortion services on his

first day in office – the day of the twenty-eighth anniversary of the *Roe v. Wade* decision – in January 2001.

Congress

For many federal lawmakers, abortion is the type of divisive social issue that they would prefer to avoid, for whatever votes, campaign contributions and positive publicity may be attracted by taking one position may be lost through alienating another group. Prior to *Roe*, federal legislators were able to avoid controversy by arguing that abortion policy was the states' responsibility. After *Roe* nationalized policy, however, they could no longer avoid taking positions on the issue. Three broad types of congressional response have been generated:

- Proposals for *constitutional amendments* to ban abortions.
- *Statutory measures* declaring the foetus to be a person in legal terms, thereby enjoying the same rights to life and liberty as citizens. In 2001, for example, the National Right to Life Committee lobbied Congress to pass the 'Unborn Victims of Violence Act'. Under the bill, if an unborn child is

Exhibit 3.4   President Reagan's remarks to the Annual Convention of National Religious Broadcasters, January 30, 1984

This nation cannot continue turning a blind eye and a deaf ear to the taking of some 4,000 unborn children's lives every day. That's one every twenty-one seconds. ... We cannot pretend that America is preserving her first and highest ideal, the belief that each life is sacred, when we've permitted the deaths of fifteen million helpless innocents since the *Roe v. Wade* decision – fifteen million children who will never laugh, never sing, never know the joy of human love, will never strive to heal the sick, feed the poor, or make peace among nations. ...

This nation fought a terrible war so that black Americans would be guaranteed their God-given rights. Abraham Lincoln recognized that we could not survive as a free land when some could decide whether others should be free or slaves. Well, today another question begs to be asked: How can we survive as a free nation when some decide that others are not fit to live and should be done away with?

I believe no challenge is more important to the character of America than restoring the right to life of all human beings. Without that right, no other rights have meaning. 'Suffer the little children to come unto me, and forbid them not, for of such is the kingdom of God'.

Source: Craig and O'Brien (1993: 171).

injured or killed during the commission of a federal crime of violence against a pregnant woman, the child would be recognized as a victim. Supporters noted that pregnant women, if attacked in a federal jurisdiction and losing their baby as a result, could prosecute their attacker only for assault. Opponents saw the measure as designed to pressure the federal government to recognize the unborn as equivalent to living humans with identical rights under law.

- Bills to remove the *appellate jurisdiction* of the Supreme Court to hear abortion cases.

None of these measures has yet succeeded, partly through the opposition of pro-choice legislators and partly because of their radical nature. Most of these steps represent, in effect, direct attacks on the Supreme Court's legitimacy and its authoritative reading of the Constitution – something that most legislators are wary of doing to an institution that, for all the fall-out over particular decisions, remains one of the most respected parts of the federal government.

One important measure that Congress did enact, however, was the Hyde Amendment, passed in 1976. Named after its sponsor, Representative Henry Hyde (Republican, Illinois), the law became a regular subject of congressional conflict. The measure introduced an amendment to the Health, Education and Welfare Appropriations bill that cut off Medicaid funds for virtually all abortions (Medicaid is the federally funded health care programme for the poor). The Hyde Amendment allowed funds to be used for all health care associated with pregnancy but not even therapeutic abortions (medically necessary ones) would be covered unless the mother's life was otherwise in danger. (In 1993, exceptions to this ban were allowed by the Democratic 103rd Congress, in cases where pregnancy had resulted from rape or incest.)

The law effectively prohibited poor women from obtaining abortions. In 1978, the first full year of its operation, the number of Medicaid-funded abortions fell from 295,000

in the previous year to just 2,000. In 1981, the Adolescent Family Life Act provided grants to organizations to promote chastity among teenagers but no organization offering contraception or abortion counselling services was deemed eligible for funds. In effect, Congress used its power of the purse to undermine *Roe* indirectly, the brunt of the assault falling on poor women whose ability to exercise the fundamental citizenship rights declared in *Roe* depended largely on government funds.

But not all of the abortion laws passed by Congress in recent years have favoured the pro-life coalition. For example, in response to the attempts of militant pro-life groups like Operation Rescue to blockade abortion clinics, Congress passed the Freedom of Access bill in 1994, which made this a federal offence. Crucial here, however, was the existence of undivided Democratic control of the White House and Congress. Once divided party control re-occurred with the Republican victories in the midterm congressional elections of 1994, the prospects for new measures on abortion were much diminished.

For much of the period from 1968 to 1992, despite controlling the House throughout this time and losing control of the Senate only from 1981 to 1987, Democratic efforts at liberalizing laws on abortion were effectively doomed by the threat of vetoes exercised by Republican presidents. Divisions within the congressional Democratic Party – where, in particular, Southern Democrats often supported pro-life positions – also weakened the impetus for pro-choice measures. Once Republicans captured both houses of Congress in 1994 (and retained them in 1996, 1998 and, briefly, in 2000), however, the situation was reversed, with President Clinton standing as a veto to conservative measures making abortion laws more restrictive. The result was a deadlock on policy by Congress, leaving the key – mostly restrictive – action on abortion to the states.

Intermediary organizations

Americans' views on abortion transcend party lines but abortion politics is strongly partisan in character. Although significant exceptions to the rule exist, the Democratic Party has emerged since 1972 as the home of pro-choice activists, the Republican Party the main location for pro-life forces. In each party, a minority holds the opposite view to the majority of active partisans, making intra-party divisions as regular a feature of party politics on abortion as inter-party ones.

The reasons for the increasing (albeit incomplete) partisan polarization are clear. Since the later 1960s, moral traditionalists have been increasingly disaffected by a Democratic Party whose activists are strongly supportive (or tolerant) of 'alternative' life-styles, feminism, gay rights and 'unconventional' sexual practices. They see the Republicans as offering the most robust support for the 'traditional' two-parent family, the institution of (heterosexual) marriage and conventional gender relations. Progressives, by contrast, have increasingly viewed the Republicans as the home of oppressive, narrow-minded and intolerant puritans seeking to impose their own morals on others who do not share them. (That some pro-life Republicans during the 1990s proudly displayed T-shirts and bumper stickers with the phrase 'Intolerance is a beautiful thing' did not damage the progressive case.) Such is the extent of polarization that, in both 1992 and 1996, Robert Casey, the pro-life Democratic governor of Pennsylvania, was denied a speaking role at the party's national conventions while pro-choice Republicans have rarely been given such roles at GOP conventions since 1980.

Partisan polarization has reflected and reinforced the activism of organized interest lobbies. *Roe* was crucial in altering the interest group universe on abortion. Prior to 1973, a variety of groups had sought to liberalize American abortion laws. Some, such as the National Organization of Women, were women's groups for whom abortion was part of the broader agenda of reproductive freedom and gender equality. Some were specifically focused on reproductive issues, such as the National Association for the Repeal of Abortion Laws (NARAL) and the Planned Parenthood Federation of America. Others had a broader (mostly progressive) political agenda, such as the American Civil Liberties Union (ACLU). In addition, professional organizations joined the campaign, such as the American Medical Association, the American Psychiatric Association and the American Public Health Association. Ethnic and religious groups supportive of abortion rights, such as the American Jewish Congress, added to the coalition's breadth.

Partly because most state laws were already restrictive, pro-life activism prior to *Roe* was largely confined to the Catholic Church. Since then, however, the pro-life movement has flourished far beyond Catholic organizations. Social conservatives who saw abortion as part of the broader assault on traditional family values mobilized, with groups like the National Right to Life Committee, Focus on the Family, the Family Research Center, the League for Infants, Fetuses and the Elderly, the Christian Coalition and militant pro-life groups like Operation Rescue that advocate a civil disobedience approach (blocking clinics and trying to dissuade those women seeking abortions from entering). These groups engaged in several tactics: encouraging politicians to sponsor bills and constitutional amendments; filing litigation cases and *amicus curiae* ('friends of the court') briefs in state and federal courts (see Exhibit 3.5); waging public campaigns, such as the annual March for Life outside the Supreme Court on *Roe*'s anniversary (22 January); and evaluating legislators according to their abortion stance.

But it would be misleading to see either coalition as homogeneous. For example, take the National Right to Life Committee (NRLC), the leading pro-life group. Although its professional staff grew to 50 paid employees in Washington by the mid-1990s, it remained a largely volunteer organization

Exhibit 3.5   Filers of *amicus curiae* briefs in support of appellants, William L. Webster, Attorney General of the State of Missouri, in the Supreme Court case *Webster v. Reproductive Services* (1989)

Six US senators and 50 US representatives

Nine US senators and 45 US representatives

127 members of the Missouri General Assembly

260 state legislators

Alabama Lawyers for Unborn Children

American Academy of Medical Ethics

American Association of Pro-Life Obstetricians and Gynecologists

American Association of Pro-Life Pediatricians

American Baptist Friends of Life

American Collegians for Life

American Family Association

American Life League

Association for Public Justice

Attorneys general of Arizona, Idaho, Louisiana, Pennsylvania and Wisconsin

Baptists for Life

Birthright

Catholic Health Association of the United States

Catholic Lawyers Guild of the Archdiocese of Boston

Catholic League for Religious and Civil Rights

Catholics United for Life

Center for Judicial Studies

Certain members of the General Assembly of the Commonwealth of Pennsylvania

Christian Action Council

Christian Advocates Serving Evangelism

Christian Life Commission of the Southern Baptist Convention

Covenant House and Good Counsel

Doctors for Life

Elliott Institute for Social Sciences Research

Family Research Council of America

Feminists for Life of America

Focus on the Family

Free Speech Advocates

Holy Orthodox Church

Human Life International

International Right to Life Federation

Knights of Columbus

Lawyers for Life

Let Me Live

Lutheran Church–Missouri Synod

Lutherans for Life

Missouri Catholic Conference

Missouri Citizens for Life

Missouri Doctors for Life

Missouri Nurses for Life

Moravians for Life

National Association of Evangelicals

National Association of Pro-Life Nurses

National Legal Foundation

National Organization of Episcopalians for Life

National Right to Life Committee

New England Christian Action Council

Presbyterians Pro-Life

Right to Life Advocates

Right to Life League of Southern California

Rutherford Institute and the Rutherford Institutes of Alabama, Arkansas, California, Colorado, Connecticut, Florida, Georgia, Kentucky, Michigan, Minnesota, Montana, Nebraska, Ohio, Pennsylvania, Tennessee, Texas, Virginia and West Virginia

Southern Baptists for Life

Southern Center for Law and Ethics

Southwest Life and Law Center

Task Force of United Methodists on Abortion and Sexuality

United Church of Christ Friends for Life

US Catholic Conference

US Government

Value of Life Committee

Austin Vaughn and Crusade for Life

Women Exploited by Abortion of Greater Kansas City

that combined the roles of political organizer, legislative agenda-setter, public educator and legal challenger. Moreover, it takes no stand on birth control or other reproductive health issues. Contrary to common belief, many people who oppose abortion support family planning and birth control. NRLC would lose significant support, especially from younger Americans, if it took a position condemning birth control. Conversely, if it supported birth control, it would lose a large number of Catholics and evangelical Protestants who believe that abstinence is the only acceptable form of birth control. Not only is the NRLC therefore reluctant to work with other pro-life groups (whose broader agendas may dilute the abortion message), but it also refuses to work with Operation Rescue (albeit for strategic political reasons rather than because it opposes 'rescues').

Assessing the balance between the two coalitions is not easy, partly because this has fluctuated so frequently over time, often in reaction to election results and Court decisions (three months before *Webster* was decided, for example, a pro-choice 'March for Women's Lives' drew over 300,000 to Washington, DC to attend a rally that included celebrities such as Meryl Streep, Glenn Close and Leonard Nimoy). In terms of its accomplishments, the pro-choice movement ranks among the most important social movements that originated in the 1960s. Legalization of abortion was a major policy change with far-reaching social implications. Although the activism of some groups – especially the more assertive, absolutist women's lobbies – politicized abortion, their mobilizing popular support helped to sustain the constitutionality of *Roe*. Moreover, as Susan Staggenborg argues, it remains 'unlikely that any future restrictions placed on access to legal abortion will be able to reverse all of the changes that have resulted' (Staggenborg, 1991: 155). The movement became a powerful political force that aroused strong opposition from traditionalists in its turn, effectively institutionalizing the presence of both coalitions in the contemporary interest group universe. In terms of policy outcomes, however, the pro-life lobby's success has probably been the more impressive.

THE TRADITIONALIST COUNTER-REVOLUTION: HAS *ROE* BEEN ERODED?

Almost 30 years after *Roe* was decided, abortion remains a controversial political issue and a regularly divisive feature of federal and state election campaigns. That persistence is attributable largely to a pro-life coalition that will be content only when *Roe* is finally reversed for good and a pro-choice coalition fearful that a woman's constitutional right to choose has already been undermined. That both sides still feel so intensely says much about the peculiar politics of abortion and the distinct lenses through which it is viewed.

In several respects, pro-choice fears are well founded. A combination of presidential, congressional and judicial action at the federal level, and changes by state governments, has meant that American women currently face many more hurdles to obtaining an abortion than existed in the years immediately following *Roe*. The Supreme Court's intervention prompted a range of responses by the states whose laws were struck down as unconstitutional. Some refused to comply with the decision or sought to undermine *Roe* by adopting regulations intended to make it difficult for women to obtain abortions. Pennsylvania and Missouri, for example, enacted laws that required a woman seeking an abortion to obtain her husband's prior consent. Rhode Island passed a law stating that life begins at conception, a foetus is a legal person, and doctors performing abortions not necessary to save the mother's life would be liable to criminal prosecution. Some states surrounded the abortion decision with regulations and administrative procedures designed to deprive a woman of real choice. Still others banned abortions from being performed in public hospitals, leaving women reliant on private clinics, meaning that for women in rural and small-town areas, long journeys (sometimes to other states) were necessary, much as they were before 1973.

Given the intense competition between the

Exhibit 3.6   Key Supreme Court rulings on abortion, 1973–2002

Doe v. Bolton (1973). 7–2. Extended *Roe* in holding that just as states may not criminalize abortions, they may not make abortions unreasonably difficult to obtain. Struck down state requirements that abortions be performed in licensed hospitals, that a hospital committee approve abortions beforehand, and that two physicians concur in the abortion decision.

Planned Parenthood v. Danforth (1976). 5–4. Ruled that informed-consent statutes requiring the doctor to obtain the written consent of the woman after informing her of the dangers of abortion and possible alternatives are permissible if the requirements are related to maternal health and are not overbearing.

Maher v. Roe (1977). 6–3. Majority upheld the constitutionality of a Connecticut law cutting off Medicaid funds for non-therapeutic abortions.

Harris v. McRae (1980). 5–4. Upheld the Hyde Amendment, passed by Congress, which cut off Medicaid funds for non-therapeutic and therapeutic abortions, except where necessary to save the mother's life.

Akron v. Akron Center for Reproductive Health (1983). 6–3. Held unconstitutional an Akron (Ohio) ordinance placing various conditions upon a woman's right to choose an abortion. These included an 'informed consent' provision, a 24-hour delay between signing the consent form and having the operation, and a requirement that the foetal remains be disposed of in 'a humane and sanitary manner'.

Thornburgh v. American College of Obstetricians (1986). 5–4. Struck down several restrictive provisions of a Pennsylvania statute, similar to those in *Akron*.

Webster v. Reproductive Health Services (1989). 5–4. Upheld state laws restricting abortion providing they do not impose an 'undue burden' on access. Upheld the provisions of a Missouri law that (i) decrees that life begins at conception and that 'unborn children have protectable interest in life, health, and well-being'; (ii) requires a physician, before performing an abortion on a woman believed to be 20 or more weeks pregnant, to test the foetus's 'gestational age, weight, and lung maturity'; (iii) prohibits public employees and facilities from being used to perform an abortion not necessary to save the woman's life; and (iv) makes it unlawful to use public funds, employees and facilities for the purpose of 'encouraging or counselling' a woman to have an abortion except when her life is endangered. Only Justice O'Connor in the majority is unwilling to reverse *Roe*, Chief Justice Rehnquist declaring *Roe* to be 'modified'.

Hodgson v. Minnesota (1990). 5–4. The Supreme Court upheld a Minnesota statute requiring parental notification before an abortion could be performed on a woman under the age of 18.

Rust v. Sullivan (1991). 5–3. The Court upheld regulations of the Department of Health and Human Services that prohibited the use of Title X family planning funds for abortion counselling, referral or activities advocating abortion as a method of family planning.

Planned Parenthood v. Casey (1992). 5–4. Upheld the several restrictive provisions of a Pennsylvania statute similar to those previously declared unconstitutional in *Akron* and *Thornburgh*. The trimester system of *Roe* is abolished. However, to the surprise and disappointment, respectively, of pro-choice and pro-life forces, five justices vote to sustain the basic constitutional right to choose an abortion.

Madsen v. Women's Health Center (1994). 6–3. The Court upheld the decision of a Florida judge to enjoin (issue an order prohibiting) peaceful picketing by protesters outside abortion clinics, ruling that such injunctions do not necessarily constitute 'prior restraint' in violation of the First Amendment.

Stenberg v. Cahart (2000). 5–4. The Court held that a Nebraska law banning what abortion rights opponents termed 'partial-birth' abortions was too broadly drawn and presented an undue burden on a woman seeking an abortion. The Court also stated that it was unconstitutional because it did not contain an exception to protect the health of the woman. (The ruling also limited 30 other states with similar statutes.)

pro-choice and pro-life coalitions, and the for-midable resources they commanded, many of these state laws were referred to the courts. The outcome has been mixed but, over time and with increasing Republican appoint-ments to federal courts, has tended to favour allowing states to impose restrictions. Much of the Court's direction on issues of feder-alism since 1986 has been to return powers to the states from the federal government and abortion is a prime (and early) example of this shift. The combination of congressional action, state reforms and the changing judi-cial approach has meant that the symbol of *Roe* remains potent but its substance is now largely emasculated.

Two cases decided by the Supreme Court were especially important: *Webster* (1989) and *Casey* (1992). These involved challenges to newly restrictive state laws regulating abor-tion access. For political and technological reasons, pro-choice advocates feared the out-comes. Politically, five new justices had been appointed by Presidents Reagan and Bush by the time *Casey* was to be decided. In terms of technology, 'viability' was an increasingly shaky foundation for constitutional rights. In *Roe*, for example, viability had been defined as the point at which the foetus is 'potentially able to live outside the mother's womb albeit with artificial aid'. In 1973 that point was roughly 28 weeks but subsequent techno-logical advances moved that point back in some cases to 24 weeks. Contrary to popular expectation, however, neither decision over-turned *Roe*.

Webster produced no clear decision, with Justice O'Connor crafting a position that the restrictive Missouri regulations were per-missible but accepting these as compatible with *Roe*. Blackmun's dissent cautioned that *Webster* was 'filled with winks, nods, and knowing glances to those who would do away with *Roe* explicitly'. In *Casey*, the test of constitutionality was explicitly altered by the justices from the trimester ruling of *Roe* to one of whether or not state regulations imposed an 'undue burden' on access to abortion. The Rehnquist Court upheld most

of the Pennsylvania law's restrictions: women were required to be informed by doc-tors about foetal development, give their for-mal consent to abortion or, if they were minors, obtain parental consent and wait 24 hours between the consent and the ter-mination. But the Court struck down as an 'undue burden' the requirement that women notify husbands of abortion plans on the grounds that this exposed them to spousal abuse and possible violence.

The refusal of a key group of Reagan–Bush justices – O'Connor, Souter and Kennedy – to overturn *Roe* was made explicit, on the basis of the need for stability for women and a society governed by the rule of law. Although they implied that they did not necessarily agree with the foundations of the original decision in *Roe*, they also contended that to retreat in the face of political pressure would diminish respect for both the law and the Court as the authoritative interpreter of the Constitution. For pro-lifers who had cele-brated their appointment, the result was a grievous disappointment.

Of at least equal concern to the judicial developments making access to abortion more difficult has been the decline in the absolute number of abortion providers. Most states have decided not to use their own funds to pay for indigent women to obtain abortions which, when combined with the Hyde Amendment's prohibition on federal funding and the clampdown on abortions in public hospitals post-*Webster* and *Casey*, means that the right to an abortion is effec-tively dependent on the ability to pay. More-over, fewer doctors and clinics now offer abortion services. In 1992, 18 per cent fewer clinics provided abortion services compared to ten years earlier. By 1996, 45 of the 50 states had seen a further decrease in the number of abortion providers. As Table 3.8 records, in 23 states, over 90 per cent of counties had no abortion provider. The extent to which this has been a response to the direct activism and violence of some pro-life organizations is unclear, but it would be astonishing if their efforts had not succeeded in intimidating

TABLE 3.8 Abortions and abortion providers, 1992–96

State	Abortions per 1,000 women	Number of abortion providers			Percentage of counties without abortion providers
		1992	1996	Change (%)	
Alabama	15.6	20	14	−30	93
Alaska	14.6	13	8	−38	76
Arizona	19.8	28	24	−14	80
Arkansas	11.4	8	6	−25	97
California	33.0	554	492	−11	36
Colorado	20.9	59	47	−20	79
Connecticut	22.5	43	40	−7	25
Delaware	24.1	8	7	−13	33
Florida	32.0	133	114	−14	73
Georgia	21.1	55	41	−25	90
Hawaii	27.3	52	44	−14	0
Idaho	6.1	9	7	−22	93
Illinois	26.1	47	38	−19	90
Indiana	11.2	19	16	−16	93
Iowa	9.4	11	8	−27	96
Kansas	18.9	15	10	−33	95
Kentucky	9.6	9	8	−11	98
Louisiana	14.7	17	15	−12	92
Maine	9.7	17	16	−6	56
Maryland	26.3	51	47	−8	54
Massachusetts	29.3	64	51	−20	14
Michigan	22.3	70	59	−16	81
Minnesota	13.9	14	13	−7	95
Mississippi	7.2	8	6	−25	96
Missouri	9.1	12	10	−17	96
Montana	15.6	12	11	−8	89
Nebraska	12.3	9	8	−11	97
Nevada	44.6	17	14	−18	82
New Hampshire	18.2	16	16	−	50
New Jersey	35.8	88	94	+7	10
New Mexico	14.4	20	13	−35	88
New York	41.1	289	266	−8	42
North Carolina	20.2	86	59	−31	74
North Dakota	9.4	1	1	−	98
Ohio	17.0	45	37	−18	91
Oklahoma	11.8	11	11	−	95
Oregon	21.6	40	35	−13	81
Pennsylvania	15.2	81	61	−25	75
Rhode Island	24.4	6	5	−17	60

TABLE 3.8 Abortions and abortion providers, 1992–96 *cont.*

| State | Abortions per 1,000 women | Number of abortion providers | | | Percentage of counties without abortion providers |
		1992	1996	Change (%)	
South Carolina	11.6	18	14	−22	80
South Dakota	6.5	1	1	–	98
Tennessee	14.8	33	20	−39	93
Texas	20.7	79	64	−19	93
Utah	7.8	6	7	+17	93
Vermont	17.1	16	13	−19	43
Virginia	18.9	64	57	−11	79
Washington	20.9	65	57	−12	69
West Virginia	6.6	5	4	−20	96
Wisconsin	12.3	16	11	−31	93
Wyoming	2.7	5	4	−20	87

Source: NARAL/Alan Guttmacher Institute, 2000.

some physicians and nurses against performing terminations.

Even without a formal reversal of *Roe* – either by the Supreme Court or constitutional amendment – the right it promises to protect is only poorly safeguarded. Abortion therefore offers some important support to the arguments of some scholars that the Supreme Court is merely a 'hollow hope' for progressive social change (Rosenberg, 1991). As a symbolic measure, *Roe* remains the law; in practice, access is extremely difficult for women in most states.

No state can currently pass a law preventing a woman from obtaining an abortion, but the restrictions that several states have imposed since 1981 are significant, even if many have not followed suit. Admittedly, these have tended to focus on minors, so the obstacles to terminating a pregnancy for adult women are not insurmountable and, compared to pre-1973 laws, the regulatory environment remains relatively permissive (and, as Table 3.9 indicates, most states oper-

ate a 'judicial bypass' that allows judges to sanction minors' abortion rights). Moreover, federal and state laws criminalizing pro-life violence against physicians and clinics now exist. For the moment, a *de facto* compromise has been struck between the demands of those seeking universally applicable rules guaranteeing abortion rights and the wishes of particular communities to prescribe their moral and ethical views on regulating abortion in law. But whether post-*Roe* changes have represented merely 'conservative weather in a liberal climate' remains dependent on future battles. As Richard Posner notes, the current focus of pro-life groups on discouraging late-term abortions could increase the abortion rate: 'The more that early-term abortions are discouraged by parental notification requirements, lack of subsidization, picketing of abortion clinics, and scarcity of abortion providers, the more late-term abortions there will be simply as a consequence of

TABLE 3.9   Parental Involvement Laws, 2001

State	One parent	Two parents	Notice	Consent	Enjoined	Judicial bypass
Alabama	X			X		X
Alaska	X			X	X	X
Arizona	X			X	X	X
Arkansas		X	X			X
California	X			X	X	X
Colorado		X	X		X	
Connecticut						
Delaware	X		X			X
DC						
Florida	X		X		X	X
Georgia	X		X			X
Hawaii						
Idaho	X			X		X
Illinois	X		X		X	X
Indiana	X			X		X
Iowa	X		X			X
Kansas	X		X			X
Kentucky	X			X		X
Louisiana	X			X		X
Maine	X			X		X
Maryland	X		X			
Massachusetts	X			X		X
Michigan	X			X		X
Minnesota		X		X		X
Mississippi		X		X		X
Missouri	X			X		X
Montana	X		X		X	X
Nebraska	X		X			X
Nevada	X		X		X	X
New Hampshire						
New Jersey	X		X		X	X
New Mexico	X			X	X	
New York						
North Carolina	X			X		X
North Dakota		X		X		X
Ohio	X		X			X
Oklahoma						
Oregon						
Pennsylvania	X			X		X
Rhode Island	X			X		X
South Carolina	X			X		X
South Dakota	X		X			X

TABLE 3.9   Parental Involvement Laws, 2001 *cont.*

State	One parent	Two parents	Notice	Consent	Enjoined	Judicial bypass
Tennessee	X			X		X
Texas	X		X			X
Utah		X	X			
Vermont						
Virginia	X		X			X
Washington						
West Virginia	X		X			X
Wisconsin	X			X		X
Wyoming	X			X		X

Source: NARAL

unavoidable delay in arranging for an abortion' (Posner, 2001: 289).

ABORTION AND AMERICAN POLITICS: THE WIDER SIGNIFICANCE

For some, compromise on abortion remains a lowest common denominator fudge rather than a genuine, lasting and legitimate solution. Robert Bork's indictment of contemporary American politics is centred on its 'seduction' of the law. He cites abortion marches in Washington, both pro-choice and pro-life, that commence at the White House, proceed up Pennsylvania Avenue, ignore Congress and congregate outside the Supreme Court. Bork's point is a telling one for any supporter of representative democracy, for here are groups who see little or no reason to seek to persuade their elected officials of their views, preferring instead to seek redress of their grievances from unelected judges.

On closer analysis, however, the 'government of judges' is nothing of the sort, and the choice of ignoring Congress is perfectly rational. The reasons are straightforward. Congress has satisfied neither the pro-choice nor pro-life lobbies, partly because those

lobbies do not reflect majority opinion and partly because the lobbies are well matched on the issue. For defenders of the American design of government, one of its strengths is that where the society is divided, government is neither able nor willing to intervene decisively on either side. Cooperation is needed to overcome the many points of conflict built into the system of government. As Morris Fiorina (1992) argues, this means that while Americans may have less opportunity to gain from government actions, they also face less opportunity to lose because of government actions.

The result is as unsatisfactory to abortion activists on both sides of the controversy as it is reflective of where most Americans stand. As Posner notes, most opponents of abortion do not place the highest absolute value on foetal life – if they did, they would oppose abortion even when the mother's life was endangered, which they do not (Posner, 1998: 346) – but most Americans share the concerns of pro-life groups about the (im)morality of extinguishing potential life. Most also share the disposition of pro-choice groups against legally preventing a woman from going through with a termination. The irony of the abortion struggle is that, for all the volumes of outrage expended on the Court's rulings and the abiding congressional reticence to act decisively either for pro-choice or pro-life ends, the ultimate outcome reflects where most Americans stand on this complex issue.

CONCLUSION

The abortion conflict pits a well-resourced and tenacious coalition of pro-life groups, traditionalists, religious and conservative organizations against a somewhat less well-resourced group of pro-choice groups, women's organizations and liberals. Neither lobby accurately reflects the fairly centrist opinions of most Americans, who would prefer a world in which abortions were not performed because they were unnecessary, but who also recognize that they do not live in such a world and that banning abortions will not get them there. The question for most Americans is not whether there will be abortions but whether the terminations that occur will be legal and safe or illegal and unsafe. By their persistent activism and high-profile campaigning, the pro-choice and pro-life sides maintain abortion's salience to politicians, governing authorities and millions of voters. Abortion in turn affects election outcomes, the composition of courts and, hence, the rulings of what is and is not constitutional regarding abortion law.

Abortion demonstrates how the interaction of social base, governing institutions and intermediary organizations can bring a previously depoliticized issue to the forefront of national politics, sustain its salience and ultimately see far-reaching public policy changes as a result of intense political competition between and within the two main political parties. *Roe* politicized the abortion issue but its goal of securing abortion rights has been subject to constant attack since 1973. Because the fragmented and veto-ridden American system of government effectively precludes outright victories for any group, concessions and compromises are insistent features of legislative and judicial battles on abortion rights. But precisely because the two lobbies represent polar opposites that maintain purist principles, neither can be entirely satisfied by the outputs that result from bargains struck in and by government. The resort by these groups to judicial routes for change, while rational and in accord with the traditional litigiousness of American society, has also proven an imperfect solution.

Therein lies the inherent tension between the dictates of universalism and the demands of particularism in a federal system. Judicial intervention to secure the rights of individual citizens occurred at the expense of the autonomy of individual states to determine their abortion laws. If, as defenders of the system argue, this reconciliation has occurred slowly and with delays, U-turns and the expenditure of enormous resources, it has at least done so with a broad-based and deeply rooted popular legitimacy. In the absence of a formal reversal of *Roe*, either by judicial decision or constitutional amendment, pro-life forces whose faiths tell them that abortion is murder will be unassuaged. At the same time, faced by continued attacks on the substance of a woman's reproductive rights, pro-choice lobbies will continue to press for reforms to entrench reproductive and privacy rights. As America celebrates and condemns *Roe*'s thirtieth anniversary, no let-up in the seemingly intractable conflict is yet in prospect.

FURTHER READING

Laurence Tribe, *Abortion: The Clash of Absolutes* (1992) is a strongly pro-choice analysis by one of America's leading liberal constitutional scholars.

David Garrow, *Liberty and Sexuality: The Right to Privacy and the Making of Roe v. Wade* (1994) is a comprehensive, detailed and dispassionate history of the *Roe v. Wade* case by one of America's leading historians.

Barbara Hinkson Craig and David O'Brien, *Abortion and American Politics* (1993) is a very useful, detailed and wide-ranging textbook analysis of America's abortion politics.

Suzanne Staggenborg, *The Pro-Choice Movement: Organization and Activism in the Abortion Conflict* (1991) is a detailed analysis of the structure and tactics of the pro-abortion rights movement.

Robert McKeever, *Raw Judicial Power? The Supreme Court and American Society* (1993, Chapter 4) is a detailed discussion of the key Supreme Court rulings on abortion.

Richard Posner, *Sex and Reason* (1992) is an impressively balanced and careful analysis of abortion by one of America's most influential federal judges.

WEB LINKS

Pro-life organizations

Christian Coalition
http://www.cc.org

Family Research Council
http://www.frc.org

Eagle Forum
http://www.eagleforum.org

Focus on the Family
http://www.fotf.org

Abortion 'from a Christian perspective'
http://www.worthynews.com/abortion-breastcancer.htm

Christian Gallery (graphic)
http://www.christiangallery.com

The Rutherford Institute
http://www.rutherford.org

Pro-reproductive rights organizations and resources

National Abortion Rights Action League
http://www.naral.org/index.html

Planned Parenthood Federation of America
http://www.plannedparenthood.org/

Alan Guttmacher Institute
http://www.agi-usa.org/

Million for Roe campaign
http://www.million4roe.com/

Feminist Majority Foundation
http://www.feminist.org/

The Abortion Access Project
http://www.abortionaccess.org/

National Coalition of Abortion Providers
http://www.ncap.com/

Abortion Clinics on-line
http://www.gynpages.com/

Legal representation for minors
http://www.janesdueprocess.org

Pro-Choice Resource Center
http://www.prochoiceresource.org/

The Abortion Resource Handbook
http://www.idsonline.com/tarh/

Georgia Abortion Rights Action League
http://www.garal.org/

National Organization for Women and Abortion Rights
http://www.now.org/issues/abortion/

National Women's Political Caucus
http://www.incacorp.com/nwpc

Rock for Choice
http://www.feminist.org/rock4c/1_rock4c.html

QUESTIONS

- Notwithstanding the moral arguments over abortion, was the Supreme Court's decision in *Roe v. Wade* defensible on either constitutional or political grounds?

- Should individual states be allowed the freedom to determine their own abortion laws or should the federal government establish national standards?

- Has *Roe v. Wade* become merely a symbolic decision?

- Why has abortion proven such a divisive issue in American politics?

- To what extent, and why, have pro-life groups waged a successful counter-revolution on abortion since 1973?

4 Gun Control

Families like mine all across this country know all too well what damage weapons can do, and you want to arm our people even more. You want to add more magazines to the assault weapons so they can spray and kill even more people. Shame on you . . . all I have to say to you is, play with devil, die with the devil.

Representative Patrick Kennedy (Democrat, Rhode Island)

My wife lives alone five days a week in a rural area in upstate New York [and] has a right to defend herself when I am not there, and don't you ever forget it.

Representative Gerald Solomon (Republican, New York)

- **The Historical Context**
- **A Public Policy Problem?**
- **Public Opinion**
- **Explaining America's Gun Politics**
- **Governing Institutions**
- **New Challenges to the Gun Lobby?**
- **Exceptional America?**
- **Conclusion**

Chapter Summary

America is unique among industrialized democracies in allowing its citizens widespread legal access to firearms. Approximately 80 million Americans own some 270 million guns. For traditionalists, firearms have acquired a strong symbolic association with liberty, property rights and American history, representing the key defence against not only criminals but also despotic government. Attempts to regulate the manufacture, sale and ownership of guns therefore raise the spectre of a tyrannical government disarming the citizenry. For progressives, the substantial public health and criminal costs of legal access to firearms are too heavy to permit near-unfettered regulation. In 1998, 30,708 Americans were killed with firearms – in homicides, suicides and accidents.

In comparison, 33,651 Americans were killed in the Korean War and 58,148 Americans were killed in the Vietnam War. Most Americans, including many gun owners, want stronger regulations on firearms, but although over 20,000 exist, most of these are at state and local level. Federal action is rare and modest. Three factors combine to explain this continued resistance to pressure for stronger controls: the existence of a 'gun culture'; the protection that the Second Amendment to the Constitution is widely perceived to offer gun ownership; and the influential political role of gun rights lobbies, especially the National Rifle Association (NRA). Although recent outbreaks of gun violence and litigation against the gun industry have brought more public attention to the costs as well as the benefits of legal access to guns, the prospects for strongly restrictive federal gun regulation remain slight. The fact that most gun control groups do not seek bans on guns is powerfully suggestive of the extent to which firearms remain a mainstay of American life.

In Pearl, Mississippi, on October 1, 1997, 16-year-old Luke Woodham used a firearm to kill his mother and shoot nine students at his school, killing two of them, including his former girlfriend. On December 1, 1997, a 14-year-old boy, Michael Carneal, opened fire on a student prayer circle in a school in West Paducah, Kentucky, killing three and wounding five students. In March 1998, Mitchell Johnson, aged 13, and Andrew Golden, aged 11, fired 27 shots at Westside Middle School in Jonesboro, Arkansas, killing four classmates and a teacher. In Springfield, Oregon, on May 20, 1998, 15-year-old Kip Kinkel shot dead his parents and, the following morning, killed two classmates and injured several others at his school. On April 20, 1999, Eric Harris and Dylan Klebold, both aged 18, killed 12 classmates and a teacher and injured 16 others at Columbine High School in Littleton, Colorado.

After the horror of the killings at Dunblane Primary School in Scotland by Thomas Hamilton on March 13, 1996, successive British governments tightened already-strict gun laws. The Labour government in November 1997 passed a total handgun ban. One editorial in *The Times* observed that 'inactivity would have been inconceivable after the violent deaths of so many children'. In terms of the fatalities that result from gun violence, America suffers the equivalent of 2,000 Dunblanes every year, but the federal government has enacted few restrictive gun control measures. In its first systematic study of school crime, the US Department of Education reported that 6,000 children had been expelled from schools in 1997–98 for bringing guns and bombs to class. To many outside and within the United States, Americans cling to their guns with a tenacity that defies all reason.

For many outsiders, when they think of America what immediately comes to mind is neither the genius of the Constitution, the dignity of the Supreme Court, nor the president's State of the Union address, but guns of every size, shape and lethality. Americans own millions of firearms: handguns, rifles, semi-automatic and automatic weapons capable of reeling off hundreds of bullets within seconds. Certain images of guns have become legendary in popular American culture: Clint Eastwood's *Dirty Harry* vigilante cop declaiming 'make my day' while pointing a Magnum in an unfortunate's face; Robert De Niro turning himself into a one-man arsenal of psychopathic terror in *Taxi Driver*. It is impossible to imagine some Hollywood stars without guns (Eastwood, Stallone, Schwarzenegger). Firearms are as American as motherhood and apple pie, albeit considerably more lethal.

That popular conception is not without

merit. As America entered the twenty-first century, it remained doubly unique among liberal democracies in being governed by a document designed for the eighteenth century and possessing the most heavily (and legally) armed civilian population in the world. The two facts are closely related. Informed by history and myth, the gun has acquired an iconic status. For many who oppose all firearms controls as unacceptable intrusions on liberty and property rights, history shows that gun control is not about firearms but individual freedom and protection against tyrannical government. Millions believe passionately that their liberty and safety are bound inextricably to the widest possible legal availability of firearms. As Charlton Heston, then-President of the National Rifle Association (NRA) put it in 1999, the legal right to own guns is 'freedom's insurance policy'.

That notion may seem archaic, absurd and alarming to non-Americans, many of whom are as fearful of guns as millions of Americans are fascinated by them, but the contemporary gun controversy has been particularly heated since it speaks to some of the most important, enduring and emotive themes in American politics: the Constitution, property rights, liberty, crime, public order, responsibility, federalism and the role of government. Like abortion, debate over gun control is contentious. Deliberation is polarized and emotionally heated. Where progressives view the existence of large numbers of guns as a serious public policy problem, traditionalists regard it as a virtue, accounting for gun violence and crime in terms of a crisis of values rather than weapons. Unlike abortion, however, the policy outcome on firearms does not reflect what most Americans want. In this chapter, we seek to explain why, despite only a minority of Americans owning guns and a majority that consistently wants stricter controls, America continues to lack tough regulations.

THE HISTORICAL CONTEXT

George Bernard Shaw once quipped that Britain and America were two nations 'separated by a common language'. Perhaps nowhere has this notion proven so accurate as in regard to the legal ownership of guns by private citizens. Britons invariably look with a mixture of bemusement and horrified fascination at America's passionate love affair with firearms. Americans, equally, find the British way of life a curiosity. Content to allow government a monopoly of coercive power and criminals to threaten their victims in the knowledge that they will not be able to shoot back, the British way of life is alien, anachronistic and astonishing. Even the film star Robin Williams, an advocate of gun control, once caricatured the British police's quaint position as being able only to shout to criminals: 'Stop! Or . . . I'll say "Stop!" again!'

Ironically, the common law right of citizens to possess weapons was included as a 'true, ancient and indubitable right' in the 1689 Bill of Rights (albeit only for Protestants) and bequeathed to Americans by the English. At the time, the right was viewed in England as a mainstay of civic humanism, crucial to the maintenance of limited government and individual liberty. Despite becoming an increasing anachronism over the eighteenth and nineteenth centuries, it was not until 1920 that Parliament required certification for private possession of guns. In America, guns became associated with the revolutionary war, the struggle for independence and the conquering of the western frontier. With the beginning of mass production in the 1830s and the Civil War, the gun achieved a mass market. As the post-Civil War saying went 'Abe Lincoln may have freed all men, but Sam Colt made them equal'.

Many outside America think of the nation as awash with guns but without gun laws. Nothing could be more misleading. Over 20,000 laws and regulations exist governing the production, importation, distribution, sale and ownership of firearms, but most of

Exhibit 4.1 Federal firearms legislation, 1934–2002

National Firearms Act (1934). The violent atmosphere of the Prohibition era and the attempted assassination of President-elect Franklin D. Roosevelt in 1933 inspired passage of this act. The legislation imposed a heavy federal tax on the manufacture and distribution of gangster weapons (machine-guns, sawn-off shotguns and silencers) and required the purchasers of those weapons to undergo FBI background checks and gain approval from local law enforcement officers.

Federal Firearms Act (1938). Prohibited shipment of firearms across state lines by manufacturers or dealers lacking a federal licence, restricted interstate shipment of guns and banned firearm sales to known criminals.

Gun Control Act (1968). The assassinations of Martin Luther King Jr. and Robert Kennedy, along with increasing crime and violence, prompted passage of this law. The measure prohibited traffic in firearms and ammunition between states and required serial numbers on all guns. It denied access to firearms to specifically defined groups (convicted felons, fugitives from justice, drug addicts, mentally ill, minors) and banned mail-order sales of firearms and ammunition. It banned the importing of surplus military firearms and of guns and ammunition not certified by the Secretary of the Treasury as legitimate souvenirs or for sporting purposes. It restricted interstate shipment of guns and ammunition to manufacturers, importers and collectors who were properly licensed by the US government. It set a minimum age for purchases at 21 for handguns and 18 for long guns.

Firearm Owners Protection ('McClure-Volkmer') Act (1986). Described as the 'zenith' of NRA influence on Capitol Hill, it overturned many provisions of the 1968 legislation, making interstate sales easier. It also allowed gun owners to transport their firearms across state lines if unloaded and not readily accessible, and banned future sales and possession of machine-guns by private citizens.

Gun Free School Zones Act (1990). Made it a federal offence to carry a firearm within 1,000 feet of a school. It was ruled unconstitutional by the Supreme Court in *US v. Lopez* (1995).

Brady Handgun Violence Prevention Act (1993). Named after James Brady, who was shot during the assassination attempt on President Reagan in 1981, the law established a five-day waiting period (for states that did not already have one) in which background checks could be made on gun buyers. The background check provision was ruled unconstitutional by the Supreme Court in *Printz v. US* (1997), and the waiting period provision lapsed in 1998.

The Violent Crime Control and Law Enforcement Act (1994). Prohibited the manufacture, sale and possession of 19 types of semi-automatic weapon and copycat models, as well as some other semi-automatic guns. It outlawed magazines holding more than ten rounds of ammunition, banned juvenile possession of a handgun or handgun ammunition, with limited exceptions, and made it a crime to sell or give a handgun to anyone aged 18 or younger. It also barred firearms possession by someone subject to a restraining order because of threats of domestic violence. The Republican-controlled House of Representatives voted to repeal the Act in 1995, but was not supported by the Senate.

The Domestic Violence Offender Gun Ban (1996). Prohibited anyone convicted of a misdemeanour domestic violence offence from buying or owning a gun.

these are state and local rather than federal laws. At national level, the federal government enacted just eight laws regulating firearms during the twentieth century (see Exhibit 4.1). The issue which analysts of America's gun regime seek to address is therefore not why America has few gun laws, but rather why it has so few national laws and why the content of the federal, state and local laws that it does have is so weak in comparative terms: only six states (California, Connecticut, Hawaii, Maryland, Massachusetts and New Jersey) had enacted a statewide ban on assault weapons by 2002; only four prohibited the purchase of more than one gun per month; and, as Table 4.1 notes, 20 states administered neither a waiting period nor an instant check on gun buyers to investigate whether or not they had a criminal record.

Some toughening of federal gun laws occurred during the 1990s. After several years of partisan disagreement, and with President Clinton staking significant political capital on them, the Democratic Congress passed two measures – the Brady bill and a partial assault weapons ban – in 1993–94. The former established a five-day waiting period (for states that lacked one) before gun purchases could be completed, allowing a background check to be made on the buyer. The latter banned 19 types of semi-automatic machine guns for ten years. The key background check provision of the Brady law, however, was ruled unconstitutional by the Supreme Court in *Printz v. United States* (1997), while the House of Representatives voted to repeal the assault weapons ban in 1995 (though the Senate failed to support the measure). The Supreme Court, in *United States v. Lopez* (1995), also struck down as unconstitutional another federal law – the Gun Free School Zones Act of 1990 – that had banned the

TABLE 4.1 Waiting for a gun

States with waiting periods (16)	States with instant checks (14)	States with no checks (20)
California	Colorado	Alabama
Connecticut	Delaware	Alaska
Hawaii	Florida	Arizona
Illinois	Georgia	Arkansas
Iowa	Idaho	Kansas
Maryland	Indiana	Louisiana
Massachusetts	Michigan	Maine
Minnesota	New Hampshire	Mississippi
Missouri	Oregon	Montana
Nebraska	Pennsylvania	Nevada
New Jersey	South Carolina	New Mexico
New York	Tennessee	North Dakota
North Carolina	Utah	Ohio
Rhode Island	Virginia	Oklahoma
Washington		South Dakota
Wisconsin		Texas
		Vermont
		West Virginia
		Wyoming

knowing possession of firearms within 1,000 feet of a school.

At state level, the Republican-led impetus during the 1990s was decisively for decontrol measures: laws permitting citizens to carry weapons concealed in public. As Exhibits 4.2 and 4.3 show, that campaign was stunningly successful: most states will now issue a

Exhibit 4.2   Is that a gun in your pocket? Concealed carry laws

While British lawmakers reacted to the horrors of Dunblane by imposing tighter regulations on who could own a gun, what types could be possessed, and when and where they could be used, American legislators took a different course. By 2002, 42 states had enacted 'concealed carry laws' (Vermont, in addition, had no law requiring a permit or licence to carry firearms concealed, while seven states prohibited concealed carry entirely). Concealed carry laws allow citizens to apply for a licence to carry a weapon concealed (either on the person and/or in a vehicle). In 2002, 28 states operated 'shall issue' laws, whereby every qualified applicant is automatically granted a licence; the responsibility is on the state to explain why an applicant does not merit a licence. Fourteen states enacted 'may issue' laws, in which the state need not automatically grant a licence and the responsibility is on the applicant to explain why a licence is necessary (local police officers have the discretion to issue or deny concealed carry permits to civilians in this case). States also enacted laws to recognize the concealed carry permits of other states' citizens when travelling through their territory.

The NRA was one of the leading proponents of such laws, arguing that they represent powerful deterrents to crime. (So successful was the NRA that when the governor of Virginia proposed to prevent proprietors from putting up signs banning the carrying of concealed weapons in bars during the mid-1990s, the 'saloon bar' amendment was only narrowly defeated by the state legislature.) To paraphrase the old Mae West question from *My Little Chickadee*, the chances are today that, whether or not he's pleased to see you, the average American male may well have a gun in his pocket, coat or pick-up truck. By contrast, in Europe and Australia, even the strongest opponent of gun control would be unlikely to accept that carrying guns concealed represents an excellent method of reducing the likelihood of gun violence.

Shall issue states (28)		May issue states (14 and DC)
Alaska	North Carolina	Alabama
Arizona	North Dakota	California
Arkansas	Oklahoma	Connecticut
Colorado	Oregon	Delaware
Florida	Pennsylvania	District of Columbia
Idaho	South Carolina	Georgia
Indiana	South Dakota	Hawaii
Kentucky	Tennessee	Iowa
Louisiana	Texas	Maryland
Maine	Utah	Massachusetts
Mississippi	Virginia	Michigan
Montana	Washington	Minnesota
Nevada	West Virginia	New Jersey
New Hampshire	Wyoming	New York
		Rhode Island

Exhibit 4.3   Praise the Lord and pass the ammunition: concealed carry in Texas

Recent surveys suggest that almost 60 per cent of households in Texas have firearms in them, compared to 34 per cent of homes across America. Even so, Texas had banned civilians from carrying concealed firearms for more than a century, until George W. Bush was elected governor in 1994. Bush signed a 'shall-issue' concealed carry law that took effect in 1995, and also approved an amendment in 1997 that removed 'established houses of worship' from the list of places where permit-holders were prohibited from taking their guns (gun-owning clergy who resided in their buildings had protested that their civil rights had been taken away). To obtain a permit after completing a gun class, an applicant must attest that he or she has no felony record or certain types of pending charges, has not been diagnosed with a disqualifying mental illness, is not a drug addict or alcoholic, is not subject to a restraining order, and has not defaulted on back taxes, child support payments or a student loan. By 2000, over 204,000 Texans were licensed to carry concealed handguns. Men made up 80 per cent of permit-holders, and over 92 per cent of holders were white. The Department of Public Safety that issues the permits revoked 1,005 permits after 1996, after notification of crime convictions or other disqualifications. But no evidence of an increase in gun violence appeared after the law took effect. As one aide to a Texas state senator observed: 'There's this whole idea that we're a bunch of gun-toting hicks, a bunch of Bubbas with gun racks going around shooting everything up, and that's wrong. People have firearms around them their whole lives. We have a healthy respect for them. I feel safer in Texas because I know Texans understand guns.'

Texas concealed carry permit-holders (January 2000)

White:	187,161	Male:	164,145
Black:	8,886	Female:	39,780
Other:	7,878		

Source: Adapted from Paul Duggan, 'Gun-Friendly Record Expected to Be Issue', *Washington Post*, March 16, 2000, p. A1.

concealed weapon permit to any citizen without a criminal record who requests one. The number of states with such 'right to carry' laws increased from eight in 1985 to 42 by 2002.

Although these laws have proven politically controversial, pro-gun forces have cited empirical studies attesting to their effectiveness (see Table 4.2). One advocate endorsed decontrol by noting that 'an armed society is a polite society' wherein gun owners 'treat others with respect, tolerance and consideration. . . . The handguns that they pack are for those who just don't get the message until they look down the bore and get a glimpse of those pearly gates' (Verhovak, 1995a).

A PUBLIC POLICY PROBLEM?

Before we examine gun control politics, it is necessary to establish why gun ownership is so controversial. This is important because many Americans do not concede that a public policy problem exists or deny that it is firearms. The traditionalist view is summarized in two slogans favoured by gun rights groups: 'guns don't kill people, people kill people' and 'if guns are outlawed, only outlaws will have guns'. Outside America, many see a choice existing between the demands of public safety on the one hand, and the legal availability of guns for recreational purposes

TABLE 4.2   Crime rates in states and the District of Columbia that do and do not allow the carrying of concealed handguns, 1992

	Crime rate per 100,000 population		
Type of crime	States with non-discretionary concealed handgun laws	All other states	Percentage of higher crime rate in states without non-discretionary laws
Violent crime	378.8	684.5	81
Murder	5.1	9.5	86
Rape	35.0	43.6	25
Aggravated assault	229.9	417.4	82
Robbery	108.8	222.6	105
Property crime	3,786.3	4,696.8	24
Auto theft	334.2	533.4	60
Burglary	840.3	1,074.7	28
Larceny	2,611.8	3,088.7	18

Source: John Lott (1998: 46).

such as hunting and sport on the other. But in America many do not recognize this distinction. Guns are about both safety and pleasure.

At the individual level, this outlook is perfectly rational. Guns have attributes that empower otherwise weak individuals: they do not require strength to use; they can be employed at a distance from the target, unlike knives or fists; they can be used repeatedly, to defend or attack several persons at once; and, if a criminal knows that someone owns a gun, he may hesitate before attacking that person or his or her property (see Exhibit 4.4).

What applies to criminals also applies to governments. European countries, such as England and France, had a long historic tradition of an armed citizenry. They deeply distrusted standing armies. Monarchs and dictators from Charles I in England to Adolf Hitler in Nazi Germany deliberately tried to disarm their citizens. Similarly, many American traditionalists argue that, for example, if the Chinese demonstrators in Tiananmen Square in 1989 had possessed guns, the

Exhibit 4.4   Five good reasons to own a gun

Efficiency. Guns are far more efficient means of destroying objects than weapons such as knives, baseball bats or fists.

Strength. Guns are light to carry and use, making them more attractive weapons for the less physically strong, not least women and the elderly.

Distance. Whether using knives or bats or fists, proximity is necessary to the assailant/victim. With a gun, one can attack or defend from a distance.

Concealment. Handguns take up less space than bats, clubs and many knives, so they can be more easily concealed.

Lethality. Guns are more reliably lethal than other weapons such as knives, being one of the most efficient means of destruction ever devised.

Beijing government would have thought twice before sending tanks in to crush their protest. Guns, on this view, safeguard liberty by providing a potent defence not only against criminals but also against the state. For traditionalists, the UK's tough gun control laws can neither prevent criminals from running riot nor stop the government trampling on individual freedoms. The fact that, in the two years following the complete handgun ban, the number of crimes in which a gun was reported to have been used in the UK increased by 40 per cent (from 2,648 to 3,685) provides at least some support for the traditionalist case.

This traditionalist view receives support from some surprising quarters. For example, many black Americans are strong opponents of gun control. This is partly a matter of fear of crime, especially in urban areas, where gun-toting drugs gangs can endanger entire communities with virtual impunity, but it also reflects a distrust of the police, for which many examples exist. From Fred Hampton, a leading member of the Black Panthers, who was shot to death in 1969 by armed police while sleeping in his bed, to Amadou Diallo in New York City in 1999 who was shot 41 times, blacks have been wary of police brutality. An armed individual may be able to deter or resist the kind of treatment that was meted out to Rodney King in Los Angeles in 1992 by the police, on this view. Possessing guns for 'self-defence' has been a mainstay of black nationalists from Malcolm X in the 1950s to the Black Panthers. (Just as some pro-life groups have appealed to African Americans on the basis that abortion is a form of racial genocide, so gun rights groups have appealed to them by arguing that gun control has racist roots in southern states disarming their black citizens after Reconstruction – the era following the Civil War – had briefly promised them equal political and civil rights.)

Against this, however, progressives cite some startling statistics. More Americans have died since 1933 as a result of gun-related incidents than were killed in all the wars – Revolutionary, Civil, First and Second World Wars, Korea and Vietnam – that America has fought combined. During the 1990s, approximately 38,000 citizens annually suffered gun-related deaths (evenly divided between suicides and homicides) according to government figures. In 1995, 35,957 Americans died by gunfire: 18,503 in firearm suicides, 15,835 in firearm homicides, 1,225 in unintentional shootings, and 394 in firearm deaths of unknown intent. The incidence was disproportionately concentrated among the young, men and blacks. In just two years in the 1990s, then, more Americans died from gun violence than were killed in Vietnam. Since 1960, approximately three-quarters of a million Americans have died through gun violence.

As the above figures note, most gun deaths are suicides. Evidence suggests that most gun murders also result from arguments among people who know each other, not because of encounters with strangers or criminals. The federal government's Uniform Crime Reports in 1991 recorded that almost half of all murders that year (two-thirds of which were committed with firearms) were committed by an acquaintance or relative of the victim. Boyfriends or husbands killed more than a quarter of all women murdered. Arguments precipitated 32 per cent of all murders; only 21 per cent resulted from the commission of felonies such as arson and robbery. A *Time* magazine compilation of all 464 gun deaths during the week of May 1–7, 1989 found that most murders 'typically involved people who loved, or hated, each other – spouses, relatives or close acquaintances'. Only 13 of the gun deaths were law enforcement related, 14 were self-defence, 22 were accidents and 216 were suicides. So, although criminals frequently use guns (obtained legally and illegally), the notion that gun violence is a product of 'bad guys' misusing weapons that 'good guys' handle properly is something of a myth.

Compared to other democracies, America seems to have a serious public policy problem, as Table 4.3 and Exhibit 4.6 suggest. But

Exhibit 4.5   Gun control and abortion: comparisons and contrasts

American culture. Where traditionalists see abortion as no part of American cultural traditions, they view gun ownership as one of the key historical foundations of the nation and its culture.

State regulation. Where traditionalists seek state action to prohibit abortions, on gun control they mostly reject state intervention as intruding on individual liberty and constitutionally protected rights.

Constitutionality. Where traditionalists dispute the basis for the constitutional right to an abortion, claiming that the 'right to privacy' either does not exist or does not cover abortion, they claim a clear foundation for gun ownership in the Second Amendment, with its explicit reference to the 'right to keep and bear arms'.

Congress. Traditionalists have tried to force Congress to act on abortion while generally seeking to prevent congressional action on firearms. Moreover, where congressional action on abortion had far-reaching consequences (such as the Hyde Amendment), the stricter gun laws passed by Congress have mostly been limited in reach.

Life and death. Where traditionalists see preserving life as overriding other considerations on abortion, they mostly see the right to own guns as either outweighing – or, more commonly, preserving – life and liberty.

Technology. Just as scientific developments have meant that life can be viable at earlier stages, making abortion even more unacceptable to traditionalists, so technology has meant that firearms have become progressively more lethal over time, able to extinguish life ever more 'efficiently'.

even if they accept that this is the case, traditionalists and progressives strongly differ on the appropriate solutions. For the former, the key to reducing the dismally fatal indicators of social dislocation listed above is a combination of education, training and tougher crime laws (such as mandatory sentences for particular types of crime). The rights of law-abiding gun owners should not be trampled over because a tiny minority of individuals abuse firearms.

When one compares the proportion of gun deaths to the number of Americans who own guns, it is miniscule: approximately 38,000 annually to over 270 million guns in circulation. More Americans die on the road each year than through gun violence. Traditionalists note that, while the deaths that occur are tragedies, the overwhelming majority of legal gun owners do not commit homicides, take their own lives, engage in crime or have accidents with their firearms. In 1990, for example, the murder and non-negligent manslaughter rate in America was 9.3 per 100,000

persons – firearms were used in approximately two-thirds of these killings. Even if all guns were eliminated and those killers who used guns substituted another weapon instead, America's murder rate would still remain 3.1 per 100,000 people – higher than Canada (2.1), Sweden (1.4) and Japan (0.5). It is also significant in this regard that other countries with high gun ownership rates, such as Israel and Switzerland, have notably low rates of gun crime.

A much greater proportion of American homes contain firearms than is the case in other industrialized nations. Clearly, the gun homicide and suicide rates are also a large part of the overall American homicide and suicide rates, and they each dwarf the gun homicide and suicide rates of other nations. As Table 4.3 shows, the ratio of non-gun homicides in America was three times higher than in England and Wales between 1985 and 1990, but 50 times higher in terms of gun homicides and 150 times higher in terms of handguns.

TABLE 4.3   Gun and non-gun homicides in England and Wales and the US, 1985–90

	Average annual rate per 1 million		
	England and Wales	**US**	**England and Wales/ US ratio**
All gun	1.02	51.92	1:51
Handgun	0.26	38.97	1:150
Other gun	0.77	12.95	1:17
Non-gun	10.28	33.56	1:3
Total	11.30	85.48	1:8

Source: Home Office, UK.

But traditionalist arguments find some support in Table 4.4. First, the overall suicide rate is higher in several countries with far stricter gun laws (such as France, Finland and Belgium) than it is in America. Secondly, if one removes the gun homicides from the overall American homicide rate, the remaining rate per one million people is 31.3 – a figure that is still higher than those of every other jurisdiction surveyed except Northern Ireland. For pro-gun groups, this suggests that something other than guns is at work in American homicide levels – be it a heritage of violence and/or individual irresponsibility. Even in the England and Wales comparison in Table 4.3, three times as many homicides occur in America without a gun being involved.

For progressives, these figures suggest that the only step towards a rational regulatory regime is stronger gun control. This is not a panacea that will completely eliminate gun deaths but nonetheless represents a sensible step to take. The proportion of Americans who die through gun violence may be comparatively few and steadily declining, but no sane individual can reasonably tolerate over 30,000 gun deaths every year. A few progressives, such as the Violence Policy Center, advocate a total prohibition on handguns. More commonly, regulations such as waiting periods, background checks and registration requirements are strongly favoured. And, as the next section shows, the progressive cause has the public on its side.

PUBLIC OPINION

Far from being 'gun crazy', public opinion has been remarkably consistent in its support of greater governmental regulation of firearms. Since the advent of modern opinion polling, when a 1938 Gallup poll found that 79 per cent of respondents favoured 'firearms control', it has been rare for less than two-thirds of Americans to support stronger measures. As Table 4.5 shows, the proportion favouring stricter gun control has varied since 1975 but has always been well over half of those questioned. On specific proposals, results fluctuate more significantly, but majorities have consistently favoured selective stronger controls (owner registration, requiring a police permit before buying a gun, and waiting periods) since the early 1960s.

Opinion polls have also shown increasing support for outright bans on the sale and possession of handguns (with exceptions for police and other authorized persons). In 1980, only 31 per cent of the public supported prohibition, but by 1993 Harris and Gallup polls found that 52 per cent and 60 per cent,

Exhibit 4.6　Selected firearms facts

Gun victims

- Of the victims of non-fatal gunshot wounds from crime, 87% are male, 13% are female, 59% are black, 19% are white, 14% are Latinos, and 9% are other or unknown. Half of the victims are between 15 and 24 years old.
- There are approximately three non-fatal firearm injuries for every death associated with a firearm.
- For 12% of the victims of non-fatal gunshot wounds from crime, the term 'drive-by' was used to describe the assault.
- In 1996 there were a total of 14,327 firearm-related homicides out of 34,040 gun-related deaths. Louisiana had the highest total number of firearm deaths that year: 1,052.

Gun availability

- In 1998 and 1999, federally licensed gun dealers reported 27,287 lost or stolen firearms.
- Estimates are that 75 million to 86 million gun owners possess a total of 200 to 240 million guns.
- 80% of available guns in the US are manufactured in the US. From 1973 to 1993, 6.6 million .357-calibre Magnum revolvers, 6.5 million .38-calibre Special revolvers, 5.4 million .22-calibre pistols, and 5.3 million .22-calibre revolvers were manufactured.
- From 1990 to 1999 the net import of rifles, shotguns and handguns averaged 1 million firearms per year.
- Firearms sales are worth $4.5 million annually.
- In 1997 there were 191 US small-arms manufacturers with a combined total product shipment of $1.2 billion.

Guns used in crimes

- More than 70% of homicides are committed with a firearm.
- Of guns recovered and traced by the government in 1994, 5% came from Brazil, 3% from Germany, 3% from China, 3% from Austria, 2% from Italy, and 2% from Spain.
- In 1996 handguns were used to murder two people in New Zealand, 15 in Japan, 30 in Great Britain, 106 in Canada, and 9,390 in the United States.

Source: *National Journal*, September 22, 2000, p. 2362–3.

respectively, backed a ban. This was the first time that a majority of Americans had endorsed such a position in opinion surveys since 1959.

Over the early 1990s, public opinion also hardened against the gun rights lobby. In particular, a large and increasing percentage of Americans held that the NRA possessed too much influence on policy. According to Gallup, the proportion of the public having a favourable opinion of the NRA declined from 56 per cent in March 1989 to 32 per cent by June 1995. Those having an unfavourable opinion grew from 32 per cent to 51 per cent. When asked whether the NRA had a mostly positive or negative influence on the crime bill passed by Congress in 1994, 56 per cent said negative, 32 per cent positive, while 12 per cent had no opinion. By the end of the 1990s, however, the NRA's membership was

TABLE 4.4   Rates of homicide, suicide and gun ownership in 18 countries

	Rate per million				Percentage of households with guns
	Homicide		Suicide		
	Overall	With gun	Overall	With gun	
USA	75.9	44.6	124.0	72.8	48.0
Norway	12.1	3.6	142.7	38.7	32.0
Canada	26.0	8.4	139.4	44.4	29.1
Switzerland	11.7	4.6	244.5	57.4	27.2
Finland	29.6	7.4	253.5	54.3	23.2
France	12.5	5.5	223.0	49.3	22.6
New Zealand	20.2	4.7	137.7	24.1	22.3
Australia	19.5	6.6	115.8	43.2	19.4
Belgium	18.5	8.7	231.5	24.5	16.6
Italy	17.4	13.1	78.1	10.9	16.0
Sweden	13.3	2.0	182.4	21.2	15.1
Spain	13.7	3.8	64.5	4.5	13.1
W. Germany	12.1	2.0	203.7	13.8	8.9
N. Ireland	43.3	21.3	82.7	11.8	8.4
CSSR	13.5	2.6	117.8	9.5	5.2
Scotland	16.3	1.1	105.1	6.9	4.7
England and Wales	6.7	0.8	86.1	3.8	4.7
Netherlands	11.8	2.7	117.2	2.8	1.9

Source: Home Office, UK government.

TABLE 4.5   Public support for stricter controls

In general, do you feel that the laws covering the sale of firearms should be made more strict, less strict, or kept as they are now?

Year	More strict	Less strict	Same	No opinion
1975	69	3	24	4
1980	59	6	29	6
1981	65	3	30	2
1983	59	4	31	6
1986	60	8	30	2
1990	78	2	17	3
1991	68	5	25	2
1993	70	4	24	2

Source: L. McAneny, 'Americans Tell Congress: Pass Brady Bill, Other Tough Gun Laws', *Gallup Poll Monthly*, 1993/2.

estimated to have passed four million for the first time in its history.

Mass public support for the progressive position is remarkable not only for its consistency over time but also because public opinion usually tends to support existing government policy. Only infrequently do analysts find strong and durable support for policy options that have not already been enacted. Given such clear statistics, then, why have governing authorities proven so resistant to enacting the gun control laws that most Americans favour?

EXPLAINING AMERICA'S GUN POLITICS

Historically, significant public pressure for stronger gun control has been generated either by large increases in violent crime rates (during the Prohibition era in the 1930s, in the mid-1960s and the early 1990s) or by assassinations – successful or attempted – of presidents (FDR in 1933, JFK in 1963, Reagan in 1981) and other politically prominent individuals (Martin Luther King and Bobby Kennedy in 1968). Only rarely, however, has such pressure resulted in policy changes at federal or state level. The weak content of gun laws is normally explained by three factors:

- The nature of America's 'gun culture'.
- The Second Amendment to the Constitution.
- The lobbying influence of gun rights groups – especially, but not exclusively, the NRA.

America's gun culture

The historian Richard Hofstadter characterized America as a 'gun culture', a term that remains resonant. After the 1998 Jonesboro killings, for example, popular commentary stressed that handling a gun was as much a rite of passage for boys in rural Arkansas as fishing or learning to drive. Conservative and populist politicians cited a pervasive 'culture of violence' to account for the boys' crimes, not the permissive state of gun regulation, despite the presence of violent themes in popular culture worldwide and the absence of anything like American levels of gun violence in other industrialized countries. Gun rights advocates portrayed the teenage culprits as unrepresentative of the mass of law-abiding gun owners. Isolated and mentally unstable, their actions were prompted not by the availability of firearms but by a combination of psychosis and a violent culture. In essence, Hollywood and the music industry encouraged the killings. Portrayals of violence from *Dirty Harry* to *South Park*, and the violent content of popular music from 'gangsta rap' to Eminem, were responsible for glamorizing anti-social forms of behaviour to vulnerable individuals.

For progressives, such views are as nonsensical as they are disingenuous. Few supporters of tougher gun regulations deny that America has historically exhibited an attachment to firearms and that guns were central to achieving independence (though the historian Michael Bellesiles has persuasively refuted the pervasiveness of guns prior to the 1860s), but the fact that an historic link once existed does not justify perpetuating a lethal practice in changed circumstances and times. Thus, although Justice Department figures reported over 40 per cent of households owning at least one gun in 1996, a marginal fall from the 45 per cent of 1990, there remained almost as many firearms in America as people – more than 250 million by some estimates, in a population of 270 million.

While overall crime rates declined during the 1990s, gun crime and murders remained more common than 30 years ago and more frequent than in any other western industrialized nation. A 1998 UK Home Office survey of homicide rates in 29 European and North American cities during 1995–97, for example, showed four American cities (Washington, Philadelphia, Dallas and Los Angeles) leading this macabre league table. At 69.3 per 100,000 of the population, the murder rate in

Washington was 33 times that of London, at 2.1. Whatever the violent content of American culture, the ease of legally obtaining firearms is, for progressives, the principal reason for the high rates of gun violence. Passion for guns simultaneously expresses and reinforces the centrality of property rights and individual liberty to American political culture, but the disastrous social consequences seem equally as obvious.

Despite this, the gun culture explanation of resistance to strong controls is not entirely satisfactory. First, there is a circularity to it, insofar as what it purports to describe is also advanced as an explanation. So, the descriptive observation is made that Americans own many guns. Yet this is also treated as an explanation for why Americans resist gun control. Americans own millions of cars and toys, too, but are content for such consumer products to be subject to far more rigorous health and safety regulations than are firearms.

Secondly, public majorities have regularly affirmed their support for selective gun controls. Even if millions own guns, there is nothing inconsistent about their supporting tougher regulations. One might imagine that, precisely because law-abiding citizens would mostly have little to fear from measures such as police permits, support would be logical.

Thirdly, the proportion of Americans owning guns is a clear minority of the total population, and declined over the 1990s. At the end of that decade, one in six owned a handgun. While this is a vast number of gun owners in absolute terms, it is clear that most Americans do not possess handguns (easily the most popular weapon in terms of gun crimes). Yet in terms of their firepower, the firearms that were in circulation increased in lethality over the same period. By the beginning of the twenty-first century, fewer and fewer Americans owned more – and more powerful – guns (Diaz, 1999). However much gun culture is a necessary part of the explanation, it is not a sufficient one.

The Second Amendment: a constitutional right to guns?

Gun culture explanations receive support from the Constitution. The federal Constitution is a source of intense disagreement between traditionalists and progressives on firearms. Unlike abortion, however, the basis for the disagreement is clearly identifiable in a specific provision, the Second Amendment: 'A well regulated militia, being necessary to the security of a free State, the right of the people to keep and bear Arms, shall not be infringed.'

Even for some conservatives, the Second Amendment is 'dangerously anachronistic' (Posner, 1998: 233). It has been the object of little judicial interpretation and is arguably one of the worst drafted in the document. At one level, the fact that the clause specifically allows for the militia to be regulated suggests strongly that Congress can exercise its national legislative authority over firearms. For many traditionalists, however, nothing could be clearer than a specific provision of the Constitution guaranteeing a right to own firearms that 'shall not be infringed'. On this reading, the constitutional case suggests that the Amendment confers an unfettered individual right to gun ownership as part of what it means to be a citizen.

Exactly what the Framers originally intended by the provision remains unclear. James Madison, the principal author of the Second Amendment, seemed to indicate that its specific purpose was the protection of the arms of the population at large. During the ratification debates about the new constitution, Madison argued in *Federalist Papers*, No. 46 that the newly empowered national government need not be feared because citizens had 'the advantage of being armed, which the Americans possess over the people of almost every other nation'. Personal communication among Madison's contemporaries also suggested that the Amendment was added because of concern over individual freedoms, not just out of a desire to protect the militia system then in place.

Even if this is the case, the question of whether and to what extent the Framers' preferences should constrain Americans today is less certain. It is difficult to imagine that Madison and Hamilton envisaged an America in which the majority of citizens owning firearms did not belong to militias; where thousands of teenagers and children would regularly take their guns to class with impunity; and where ordinary Americans would feel the need to stockpile weapons such as assault rifles against their government and fellow citizens alike.

Unlike almost all the other Amendments in the Bill of Rights, the Second has never been 'incorporated' through the Fourteenth Amendment's guarantees of 'equality before the law' and 'due process' to apply to state governments as well as the federal authority. That is, even if one holds that the federal government cannot constitutionally enact strong measures, the Constitution does not prevent states and localities from so doing. The Second Amendment has been unusual in this respect. Most of the Amendments originally applied only to the federal authority. Judicial interpretation then applied them to the states as well so that neither federal nor state governments could infringe fundamental rights and liberties. But this has not occurred with respect to the Second Amendment.

Moreover, the asserted 'right to bear arms' is linked to participation in a citizens' militia – a group of impermanent armed citizens – dedicated to defending the state. Whether one regards this as historically irrelevant with the demise of such militias by the end of the nineteenth century, or believes that the National Guard (troops trained in the states but under federal control) has become the reference since the turn of the twentieth century, the obstacle that the Second Amendment poses to regulation is strongly contested. As six former US attorneys general observed in a letter to the *Washington Post* in 1992: 'For more than 200 years, the federal courts have unanimously determined that the Second Amendment concerns only the arming of the people in service to an organized state militia; it does not guarantee immediate access to guns for private purposes.'

This view was bolstered, albeit indirectly, by litigation in the federal courts. In the challenge to the Brady law in *Printz*, and previously in *amicus curiae* briefs filed in *Lopez*, the plaintiffs chose not to rely upon the Second Amendment. These cases were the first opportunities that the Supreme Court had to rule on the constitutionality of important federal firearms legislation since 1939. The gun rights lobby evidently realized (reluctantly) that even the Rehnquist Court would not strike down federal gun laws as unconstitutional on the basis of the Second Amendment.

Nevertheless, the Amendment remains a formidable impediment to gun control in the eyes of many, and perhaps most, Americans. Perceptions matter in political life, fuelling what is held to be 'reality'. However incorrectly, the Second Amendment is widely seen as effectively prohibiting strong federal firearms regulation. In the spring of 2001, Attorney General John Ashcroft affirmed 'unequivocally' that it confers an individual right to own guns, but even gun control advocates unwittingly reinforce this perception. As a defence against the attacks of gun rights groups, progressives frequently qualify their pro-control stance by noting that new measures do not threaten the 'constitutional right' to own a firearm. Ironically, proponents as well as opponents of gun control help to reinforce the apparent sanctity that the Second Amendment affords gun owners.

But even if one accepts the arguments of gun rights groups that the Amendment confers an individual right to gun ownership (and this is contentious), a fundamental problem still remains. What, if any, federal or state gun controls can be considered to violate that right? Just as the First Amendment's guarantee of free speech is relative – some restrictions, such as libel and, as Chapter 6 shows, obscenity, do not infringe the guarantee – so the Second Amendment's right to keep and bear arms is not absolute. Imagine, for example, what an absolute Second Amendment would permit: stock-piling bazookas? purchasing more than 50 guns per month? For gun control advocates, even if one agrees with the individualist argument, that does not prevent the imposition of reasonable regulations – registrations, background checks, permits – that are permissible as not infringing any fundamental right to own firearms.

The relevance of the Second Amendment notwithstanding, the Constitution does offer obstacles to gun control in its federal provisions and the allocation of powers to distinct branches of government. Sheriffs in Montana and Arizona challenged the Brady law, for example, and district courts held that it was unconstitutional for the federal government to tell local officials to perform background checks on gun buyers. Brady was then held by the Supreme Court (in a 5–4 ruling) in *Printz* to violate the Tenth Amendment for the same reason: the federal government lacks the constitutional authority to order local officials to execute federal policies (i.e. to administer background checks on gun buyers). In *Lopez*, it was the fact that education was a state matter not subject to Congress's right to regulate under the Constitution's Commerce Clause – possession of a firearm within 1,000 feet of a school was held neither to constitute nor affect commerce – that convinced a majority to strike down the Gun Free School Zones Act (carrying a firearm within a school remains a crime under most state laws).

Constitutional prohibitions at federal level are also replicated in the states. Forty-four states have 'right-to-bear-arms' type provisions in their state constitutions, some which reference militias in a manner similar to the Second Amendment, others whose language more closely resembles the First Amendment. Even here, though, the crucial question remains how absolute that right to possession may be. While some Americans, such as members of the militia movement, hold that right to be absolute, developments at the end of the 1990s added particular force to the argument that the right to own a gun does not always trump the authority of government to regulate the terms and conditions of its manufacture, sale, possession and use.

The gun rights lobby

The most common reason advanced to explain America's weak gun laws focuses on the political power of gun rights groups. In particular, the NRA gives powerful organizational expression to traditionalist sentiments on firearms and provides an energizing, and at times evangelical, impetus to the gun lobby that is shared by few others. Although neither the only nor the most extreme gun rights group, the NRA remains the key player in gun politics. Its resources are impressive: approximately four million fee-paying members in 2002, providing an annual income of over $100 million. The organization maintains a full-time staff of over 300 employees, including over 60 devoted specifically to lobbying efforts. With a vested interest in maintaining and expanding the market for guns, its pragmatic and ideological links with gun manufacturers make it the political wing and unofficial trade association of the firearms industry. The NRA's Institute for Legislative Action monitors state and federal action on firearms and prompts its members by direct mail 'alerts' to contact legislators when new regulations are being considered. Its Political Action Committee, the 'NRA Political Victory Fund', spent $6 million in 1993–94, making it the fifth largest PAC in America. Faced by such intense beliefs, extensive resources and vociferous mobilization, federal, state and local politicians who confront the constant election cycle that the Constitution prescribes typically avoid antagonizing gun rights supporters.

This case has conventionally dominated explanations of America's weak gun laws and it retains powerful contemporary force. If one takes election campaign contributions, for example, the balance of donations to federal candidates still strongly favours the gun rights lobby. According to Federal Election

Commission figures, the three most prominent gun rights groups (NRA, Gun Owners of America, and Safari Club International) donated some $800,000 to federal candidates over 1997–98. This overwhelmingly favoured Republicans, who received 78 per cent. By comparison, the leading gun control lobby, Handgun Control, donated only $48,000 to candidates for federal office, 97 per cent of which went to Democrats.

The partisan pattern of donations is important. Gun rights groups increasingly viewed the Republicans as their natural allies after the 1960s but, like most effective lobbyists, consistently donated campaign funds on a bipartisan basis. Incumbency mattered as much as ideology to the gun industry. With the Democrats' apparent lock on the House of Representatives from 1954 to 1994 and near-control of the Senate during these years (losing it only during 1981–87), this was eminently sensible. But while this bipartisanship remains the case for the gun lobby (though not for gun control advocates), the pattern of campaign contributions now substantially favours Republicans, for three reasons:

- *Congress.* The Republicans dominated national politics after they won control of Congress in 1994. Not only did this confer voting majorities on the floor and in committees, but it also provided procedural controls over pending legislation (time-tabling and amendments), particularly in the House of Representatives. This was a powerful incentive for gun rights groups to establish special ties with Republicans who chaired the committees, subcommittees and *ad hoc* task forces concerned with firearms issues. Given the traditionally high re-election rates of House and, to a lesser extent, Senate incumbents, this was a sound investment.
- *Ideology.* Ideology reinforced the incumbency advantage. The development of the Republicans as a genuinely conservative party in the later 1980s and 1990s cemented the GOP/gun rights lobby

alliance. Though substantial intra-party divisions remained, the party now bears scant resemblance – in ideology, regional composition, activist base or policy goals – to that of the 1960s or 1970s. With the (once segregationist and solidly Democratic) South now the most solid Republican base in presidential and congressional politics, providing most of the Republican congressional leadership, the party is more ideologically homogeneous and more supportive of gun rights than at any time since the Second World War.

- *The states.* State-level advances consolidated the Republican Party's attractiveness to potential donors. After the 1996 elections, Republicans led the Democrats in state governorships by 32 to 17 (with one independent), one of their largest margins ever. Moreover, while Democrats still held more seats in state legislatures (3,883 to the Republicans' 3,470), the lead sharply declined over the 1990s. One result, noted earlier, has been the steady growth of states allowing their citizens to carry concealed weapons. With Republicans in majority control of Congress and state governorships, gun control proponents went on the defensive. Despite the well-publicized gun massacres and accompanying public attention from 1997 to 2002, the gun lobby has had little to fear from Republican-held governing institutions.

GOVERNING INSTITUTIONS

Gun control is significantly different from abortion and capital punishment insofar as federal courts have played a peripheral role in its politics. Instead, it has been left to the elected branches of government to draw up appropriate laws and regulations. But since the gun rights and gun control forces share so little in common (other than agreeing that guns are efficient means of destruction and a mainstay of American history), the issue has proven as resistant to lasting resolution as other cultural value battles.

Presidential politics

Four presidents have died through assassination (Abraham Lincoln in 1863, James Garfield in 1881, William McKinley in 1901, and John F. Kennedy in 1963), but several modern presidents (including JFK, Reagan, and the Bushes) have been NRA members. In the case of Reagan, George H.W. Bush, and George W. Bush, a pro-gun stance was embraced partly to appeal to traditionalist voters. The data in Table 4.6 suggest that gun ownership, like opposition to abortion rights, is strongly correlated with support for Republican presidential candidates. This is not causation, but it confirms the tendency of gun owners to favour the GOP – a partisan position increasingly adopted by formally neutral gun rights groups like the NRA.

Bill Clinton was the first president since LBJ to take a vocal public position in favour of stricter gun control. Despite coming from Arkansas, a predominantly rural state in which firearm ownership is common and hunting remains a popular pastime, Clinton lobbied strongly in favour of the Brady and assault weapons bills in his first term, and in support of stronger background checks on gun buyers at gun shows and pawn shops in his second. Gun control proved to be one of the relatively few measures where the president's position was unambiguous, consistent and in tune with the popular mood throughout his two terms.

But even in the aftermath of a series of gun massacres that placed gun issues high on the public's agenda, the 2000 presidential candidates disagreed on what to do. George W. Bush responded to a gun massacre at a church in Fort Worth, Texas, in September 1999 by blaming 'a wave of evil passing through America', rejecting major new legislation by arguing that 'I don't know of a law, a governmental law, that will put love in people's hearts.' Vice President Al Gore asked crowds

TABLE 4.6   1992–96 presidential vote by gun ownership

	1992				
	Clinton	**Bush**	**Perot**	**All**	**N**
Gun owner	35.0	42.0	23.0	43.1	317
Non-owner	52.0	34.9	13.1	56.9	419

	1992				
	Clinton	**Bush**	**Perot**	**All**	**N**
Gun owner	25.9	52.4	21.7	44.2	1,247
Non-owner	52.2	38.9	8.8	55.8	1,571

	1996			
	Clinton	**Dole**	**Perot**	**All**
Gun owner	38	51	10	37
Non-owner	54	37	7	63

Source: Bruce and Wilcox (1998: 234).

at campaign stops, 'How can we allow guns in churches?', a not-so-veiled reference to the concealed carry state legislation that Bush had signed in Texas in 1997 (Bush supporters pointed out, however, that the gunman did not have a concealed carry permit and had not applied for one).

Beyond campaigns and the 'bully pulpit', another aspect to the president's role concerns enforcing federal laws. The Bureau of Alcohol, Tobacco, and Firearms (ATF) is charged with administering federal firearms laws. The successor to the Bureau of Prohibition (Elliot Ness of *The Untouchables* fame was a member), the ATF is formally part of the Department of the Treasury. The Bureau's role in regulating alcohol and tobacco has declined over time, leaving firearms the most prominent of its responsibilities, but the agency has been consistently attacked by the NRA for its role and its agents criticized as arbitrary and abusive. Members of Congress have threatened to reduce its budget or even dismantle it completely. In 1981, John Dingell (Democrat, Michigan) described ATF agents as 'a jack-booted group of fascists who are . . . a shame and a disgrace to our country' (Bruce and Wilcox, 1998: 27). Gun control groups see the agency as limited by weak legislative support and powerful opponents preventing it from executing its responsibilities, such as certifying that gun dealers are entitled to their licences.

Congress

Lawmakers are typically torn between two pressures on guns: the knowledge that most Americans passively favour stricter controls and the fear that voting for these will antagonize the active members of gun rights groups to vote against them in future elections. In 1996, for example, the NRA spent $4.5 million to elect its friends in Congress. But some lawmakers report that the human clout the NRA can muster is more intimidating. Members who vote against the lobby can return home to find town meetings and telephone lines dominated by angry gun rights

advocates. Partly as a result, Congress has achieved a mixed record, at times toughening controls (1968), at other points emasculating them (1986), and mostly failing to act at all.

Congressional voting on gun control reveals three patterns of political cleavage.

- *Regional.* The regional cleavage is most notable between the South and West and the rest of the country, with southern representatives and senators of both main parties particularly inclined to oppose firearms regulation. Private gun ownership is especially prevalent in the South and West, with well over half of southerners reporting to pollsters that they have guns in their homes (compared to fewer than one-third of easterners). Although reported gun ownership is roughly at the same level among westerners and Midwesterners, those in the West (and South) are substantially more likely to own two or more handguns than people in the East or Midwest.

- *Urban–rural.* Irrespective of regional and party differences, representatives from urban areas are much more likely to favour strict gun controls than members from rural areas. Far more guns are owned for hunting and other recreational purposes in rural areas than among city dwellers. Since cities tend to have high rates of violent crime, lawmakers from cities tend to vote for gun controls to keep weapons out of the hands of criminals and thereby reduce violent crime. For example, almost all urban House Democrats voted for the Brady bill and the assault weapons ban in 1993–94, and urban Republicans were more inclined to support these measures than their rural counterparts.

- *Partisanship.* In the 1960s, party affiliation was not a reliable predictor of gun voting and bipartisanship existed. A significant number of southern and western Democrats opposed federal gun regulation and a significant number of northern suburban Republicans supported gun control.

But from the early 1970s voting became increasingly polarized by party. Changing patterns of party politics in the nation and a steady polarization over the federal government's role in regulating citizens' behaviour affected congressional coalition-building on gun control issues as on issues generally. Gun control became an issue dividing the parties against each other and, since the 1990s, congressional decision-making evokes a sharply partisan response.

Gun control tends more to push law makers apart than draw them together, a problem complicated further by the bicameralism that requires both houses to agree the identical bill before it can become law.

Intermediary organizations

Partisan polarization is at least as strong on gun control as abortion. Again, dissenting members of both parties exist but, broadly speaking, Republicans have expressed long-standing support for gun ownership with minimal government regulation (except in the case of gun use by criminals), while Democrats have shown a similar consistency in favour of gun regulations. The gun issue first surfaced in the parties' presidential election-year platforms in 1968, since when both parties have usually addressed the issue in their platforms under the category of criminal justice. Positions on gun control have become part of a broader political battle over which party is more 'tough' on law and order issues.

The Republican Party has maintained a strong opposition to gun control, becoming more clearly 'pro-gun' with successive elections. The 1968 party platform of presidential nominee Richard Nixon urged 'control [of] indiscriminate availability of firearms' but also demanded 'safeguarding the right of responsible citizens to collect, own and use firearms . . . retaining primary responsibility at the state level'. But the 1976 platform stated simply: 'We support the right of

citizens to keep and bear arms.' In 1980, the platform under Reagan repeated the 1976 stand but added a phrase urging the removal of 'those provisions of the Gun Control Act of 1968 that do not significantly impact on crime but serve rather to restrain the law-abiding citizen in his legitimate use of firearms'. The 1988 platform of George H.W. Bush supported the 'constitutional right to keep and bear arms' and called for 'stiff, mandatory penalties' for those who used guns in the commission of crimes. Despite the NRA refusing to endorse Bush in 1992, that year's platform kept the 1988 wording and criticized efforts at 'blaming firearm manufacturers for street crime'.

By contrast, the Democrats have been consistently more supportive of gun control, although with varying degrees of qualification. The 1968 platform urged 'the passage and enforcement of effective federal, state and local gun control legislation'. The 1972 platform called for 'laws to control the improper use of handguns', as did that of 1976 – though, reflecting Jimmy Carter's more conservative views, the 1976 and 1980 platform urged tougher sentences for crimes committed with guns and affirmed the 'right of sportsmen to possess guns for purely hunting and target-shooting purposes'. The 1984 platform again called for tough restraints on cheap handguns, but the 1988 platform omitted the strong language of previous years and called only for the enforcement of 1986 bans on 'cop-killer' bullets. Clinton's party in 1992 called for waiting periods and a ban on 'the most deadly assault weapons', though affirming that 'we do not support efforts to restrict weapons used for legitimate hunting and sporting purposes'.

These partisan differences have not produced significant changes on gun control at the federal level, for two reasons. First, divided party control has been the post-1968 norm, placing partisan as well as institutional obstacles in the path of federal gun control measures. From 1968 to 1988, no measure to strengthen gun controls reached the floor of either house of Congress for a vote.

Secondly, although single-issue appeals rarely prove decisive in presidential or congressional elections, the gun lobby's threat is not only national in scope but is especially serious in a candidate-centred environment. The threat that funds will be withheld or donated to opponents, or that television and newspaper advertisements will be purchased by well-financed gun rights groups, invariably caution risk-averse elected politicians against taking strongly pro-control stances. As a result, partisan polarization has been sustained on this issue as much as on abortion.

Like the parties, interest groups are also strongly divided. The gun rights lobby is well financed and possesses an active, articulate and passionate membership. While the lobby is not identical with the NRA, the NRA is the most influential and prominent organization against gun control. Its web site is sophisticated and comprehensive, featuring not only articles and information but press releases and an on-line store (featuring clothes, cooking recipes and more). Groups such as the Second Amendment Sisters (SAS) and Pink Pistols strongly urge women and gays and lesbians, respectively, to take up the right to firearms. SAS claims that at least 17 million women own firearms in America and that as many as 200,000 use a gun every year to defend themselves against sexual assault. Pink Pistols claimed by 2002 to have established over 20 chapters across America dedicated to the legal, safe and responsible use of firearms for self-defence of the sexual-minority community on the basis that it is not 'the right of those who hate and fear gay, lesbian, bi, trans, or polyamorous persons to use us as targets for their rage'.

Whatever differences exist among gun rights groups such as the NRA, Pink Pistols and Gun Owners of America (probably the most absolutist organization on guns) pale when compared to their collective differences with gun control advocates. The pro-control coalition is a heterogeneous one, comprising many religious, educational and social organizations such as Common Cause, the United Methodist Church, the American Jewish Committee, the AFL-CIO, the American Baptist Convention and the Women's Political Caucus. But the fact that these are multi-issue concerns, not single-cause groups, has limited their effectiveness.

The primary opponent of the NRA is Handgun Control, Inc. (HCI). Founded in 1974, the organization began in partnership with the National Coalition to Ban Handguns (NCBH), but the groups soon parted ways and NCBH was renamed the Coalition to Stop Gun Violence (CSGV) in 1990. CSGV has mostly pursued a tougher stand than HCI, but HCI has grown larger and more visible.

Until the 1980s HCI had few resources and limited effect, but John Lennon's murder helped generate interest and funds, and by 1981 membership had passed 100,000. Although the group's focus on the Brady bill – named after Reagan's press secretary, James Brady, who was seriously injured in the 1981 assassination attempt on the president (his wife headed HCI from 1989) – and state-level measures was important, the main impetus for change was public opinion. By the mid-1990s, membership had reached over 400,000 and HCI's annual budget was over $7 million. The organization included a PAC and grass-roots mailing network but its resources were still dwarfed by the NRA.

Somewhere between these two antagonists lies Americans for Gun Safety (AGS), a lobbying organization established by dot-com billionaire Andrew McKelvey. Although claiming to respect the right to bear arms while simultaneously seeking reasonable regulations, the NRA has condemned AGS ('anti-gun sophistry') for its support for 'rational' gun laws. In 2001, AGS spent $250,000 on 30-second cinema adverts in 44 states featuring John McCain (Republican, Arizona) supporting the AGS stance on gun rights and personal responsibility. Its web site also contains a wealth of data that is not only balanced but (partly in virtue of this) decidedly uncongenial to NRA supporters.

NEW CHALLENGES TO THE GUN LOBBY?

If strong elements of continuity existed in gun politics at the beginning of the twenty-first century, there were also important elements of change. The key catalyst was the spate of murders over 1998–2001, which combined important properties. The victims were children (as well as adults), reflecting a dramatic increase in juvenile gun deaths (from 1985 to 1995 the number of juveniles killed by firearms increased by 153 per cent, according to Department of Justice figures). But the fact that the perpetrators were also children, and that in some instances they killed parents, friends and teachers, was even more shocking. (Notable also was the fact that the killings occurred in several states across the nation rather than being concentrated in a particular state or region.)

All this suggested powerfully that something was deeply amiss and reinforced trends that had been growing for several years that were discomforting to gun rights enthusiasts. On May 14, 2000, the Million Mom March in Washington, DC drew a crowd of approximately 200,000 women in the largest-ever demonstration in favour of gun control in American history (and prompted a smaller gathering by the Second Amendment Sisters in opposition). George W. Bush's ardent opposition to gun control was widely seen to have cost him suburban votes in the 2000 presidential election, although it also helped to galvanize gun owners to vote (48 per cent of voters in 2000 were gun owners, an increase from 37 per cent in 1996) and may have assisted Gore's defeat in traditionally Democratic states such as West Virginia.

The courts

The most significant development for gun control advocates was the intrusion of traditional American litigiousness into the firearms debate. The litigation battle against tobacco companies offered a powerful and, for the NRA, highly disturbing precedent. For 40 years after the Second World War, cigarette companies maintained an unblemished record of victories in the courts, with 813 claims filed against them but no losses and no damages paid out to plaintiffs. With a marked shift in public opinion against smoking during the later 1980s and 1990s, and 47 states suing to recoup the medical costs of smoking-related illnesses, the industry became sufficiently fearful to offer millions of dollars in compensation to settle pending lawsuits.

Firearms litigation again focused on reclaiming damages. In Chicago, for example, the estates of three young people killed by gunfire sought damages from the gun industry, charging that firearms companies deliberately manufacture, market and sell products to appeal to gang members and other criminals. A Los Angeles police officer wounded in a bank robbery sued gun-makers for marketing automatic assault weapons and armour-piercing bullets that were used in the shoot-out. In New York, families of victims of gun violence sued gun-producers and distributors on the basis that they intentionally oversupply southern states with lax gun laws in the knowledge that the guns will be resold – and frequently fall into criminal possession – in states and cities with tougher regulations. Finally, mayors in cities such as Philadelphia, New Orleans and Chicago instigated lawsuits to recoup costs for the millions of dollars expended by their administrations on the consequences of gun violence, from police expenses and hospital bills to literally cleaning the city streets. Ironically, given the criticisms of gun laws from outside the United States, many of the companies sued were subsidiaries of non-American companies, such as Smith and Weston (England), Beretta (Italy), and Browning (Japan) (Diaz, 1999).

The litigation strategy accorded with the Clinton administration's 'third way' approach to public policy problems, stressing individual responsibilities in addition to rights. Clinton sought after 1994 to harness duties to rights in areas such as welfare reform, education and penal policy, with reasonable success. The strain of individualism that permeates American culture therefore posed opportunities as well as problems for advocates of gun control. For while gun ownership is viewed, however mistakenly, as an inalienable individual right of citizenship, American traditions also call for rights to be exercised responsibly. Freedom should not be irresponsibly abused.

Whether such litigation strategies promise genuine inroads into the rates or patterns of gun violence is nonetheless questionable. The federal courts remain heavily populated by Reagan–Bush appointees whose instinctive preference may well be against adjudicating claims in favour of the victims of gun violence on the basis of new and controversial legal theories. Issues of what is 'reasonable' complicate judgments here. Where compelling evidence of deliberate strategies to sell to criminals exists (marketing guns as offering 'excellent resistance to fingerprints' for example), this seems a reasonably straightforward matter on which judges might sensibly order damages to be paid by the firearms industry. But even here, regulating how one may advertise what remains a legal product is likely to encounter serious First Amendment objections.

In this light, issues of reclaiming city expenses (the Philadelphia case), or prohibiting licensed dealers selling firearms to citizens unregistered as gun-owners with their local authority (the Chicago case) are even more contentious. Questions of interstate commerce arise in the Chicago case, for example, while the fundamental notion of making the producers and distributors of legal products liable for their illegal usage raises a thorny legal question. It is, moreover, these cases that would prove the greater threat to the gun industry, and judges may well baulk at the consequences of holding firearms manufacturers to account for the actions of citizens who use their products in dangerous, fatal and illegal ways. Established law, basic fairness, questions of free speech

and interstate commerce are powerful considerations that will be invoked by opponents of the lawsuits.

Moreover, lobbied hard by the NRA and other gun rights groups, several states, especially in the South and West, began making rulings and passing laws that deliberately pre-empted attempts to make manufacturers liable for the results of gun violence. In the spring of 2001, a federal court of appeals in New York ruled unanimously that victims of gun crime could not sue gun manufacturers. In May 2001, Florida became the twenty-sixth state in only two years to enact laws precluding lawsuits by trial lawyers against gun manufacturers. The constitutionality of these laws itself will likely be tested in federal court but, whatever the outcome, their enactment demonstrates that neither the gun industry nor its political allies will easily accept further restrictive regulation by courts or legislatures.

The gun lobby: shooting itself in the foot?

The opposition of groups like the NRA to virtually all gun control measures, most of which are supported by majorities of the public, has proved unacceptable to many Americans. NRA opposition to bans on plastic guns incapable of detection by airport security machines, for instance, alienated previously sympathetic and influential allies, including police organizations and pragmatic conservatives. President George H.W. Bush resigned his membership in 1992 in protest at the NRA's hyperbolic language about 'jack-booted government thugs' taking away Americans' guns. Former Governor Cecil Andrus of Idaho, whose hobby is hunting, described the NRA as the 'gun nuts of the world' for opposing a ban on armour-piercing bullets, observing that he had never seen an animal sport a bullet-proof vest.

The 1990s also witnessed a series of high-profile events involving arms (the Ruby Ridge, Idaho and Waco, Texas sieges, the growth of private militias, the Unabomber, the bombing of the Alfred P. Murrah federal building in Oklahoma in 1995 and the Atlanta Olympics in 1996) that seemed to many Americans to caution against minimally regulated access to arms. In this context, the opportunities for pro-control forces to gain momentum by portraying their opponents as 'gun nuts' increased considerably. Fierce resistance to almost all forms of control has been a mainstay of militias, right-wing talk-radio disc jockeys and so-called 'patriots'. While gun control advocates such as HCI were unable to match the NRA's resources – not least its funding – they proved fairly successful at exploiting mass public concern about gun zealots.

Augmenting this shift was another development that has been gathering pace for some years: the battle over guns has increasingly become an indelible part of the broader 'culture war'. The NRA responded to the pressure of increasing public hostility by electing the actor Charlton Heston to its presidency in 1998, in the apparent hope that Moses might rehabilitate the organization's tarnished reputation among ordinary Americans. Heston's elevation, and previously Tanya Metaska's efforts as executive director, steered the organization into uncharted and controversial partisan territory. In 1992, the NRA maintained its traditional non-partisanship by refusing to endorse President Bush for re-election, despite his pro-gun record and his opposition to a ban on semi-automatic weapons. Since then, however, NRA leaders have sought to identify the organization and the Republican Party as allies, not just on firearms but also on a range of other divisive social issues. To paraphrase the old (and redundant) adage about the Church of England being the Conservative Party at prayer, the NRA became the Republican Party on the shooting range.

However, tacking an organized interest lobby so clearly to the fortunes of one major political party involves constraints as well as opportunities. One of the dangers here is the Republican Party's risk of being portrayed by its opponents as a bunch of far-right extremists, a charge enthusiastically employed by the Democrats in the 1996 elections (albeit with more success at the presidential than congressional level). On its own, gun control is a discrete political issue where both economic and social conservatives generally find common cause. Once gun control becomes enmeshed with a broader and more contentious agenda of social issues, the potential for disunity within the party and for alienation of moderate voters rapidly increases.

Perhaps even more telling of the important links between the cultural battles is the behaviour of Larry Pratt, a former Virginia state legislator. Not only was Pratt the executive director of Gun Owners of America, but he also headed the Committee to Protect the Family Foundation, an organization that raises funds for anti-abortion activist Randall Terry and his direct-action Operation Rescue group. Pratt also founded 'English First', a 250,000-member group that sponsors efforts to block bilingual education in America. Campaigning across several fronts was crucial, according to Pratt, since:

> the bottom line is that this is a spiritual battle. This is not a political issue. This is something that comes first and foremost from the Scripture. What I see in Scripture is not that we have a right to keep and bear arms, but that we have a responsibility to do so. For a man to refuse to provide adequately for his and his family's defense would be to defy God. (Dees, 1996: 55–6).

EXCEPTIONAL AMERICA?

Several countries experienced horrific examples of gun violence resulting in mass murders during the 1990s: the UK, France, Italy and Australia. Their response was invariably to enact stricter laws and regulations governing the ownership, manufacture and distribution of firearms. The American context remains different. One analyst claims that 'the window of opportunity for gun control proponents has typically been brief because of the limited duration of the public's focus on gun issues' (Spitzer, 1995: 126). Why, then, is America so enduringly different?

One problem is that the American debate suffers from its emotive character. Two examples from 1993 are typical. The NRA sent a summary of Congress's legislative activities for the year to its members, stating: 'If Congress sent one message to America's gun owners in 1993 it was ... "You are the enemy." Indeed, hearing Congress rant and rave about gun control in recent weeks was enough to make any freedom-loving American sick.' Deploying only marginally less heated rhetoric, HCI sent its members a leaflet depicting six semi-automatic weapons with the blunt message, 'We must get these killing machines off our streets!' As Spitzer observes, 'rational policymaking recedes from view when the political combatants spend most of their time screaming political obscenities at each other' (Spitzer, 1995: 97).

NRA public relations errors and tactical mistakes resulted in a significant loss of popular support over the 1990s but this occurred from a relatively high level. Moreover, it did not happen at an especially critical moment as far as pending legislation was concerned. While passage of the Brady bill and assault weapons bans benefited from the NRA's intransigence, neither measure was far-reaching. Not only did the Republican congressional victories make further restrictions improbable, but the NRA's lobbying efforts at state level also assisted the success of decontrol. As one member of Congress noted, the NRA is still 'a lobby that can put 15,000 letters in your district overnight and have people in your town hall meetings interrupting you'. Its revival by 2002 was complete, with September 11 prompting a sharp upturn in Americans purchasing guns for self-defence.

Even the child murders of 1998–2001 produced no uniform public response to gun violence. This is nothing new. Massacres at Stockton, California in January 1989 (where a man using an AK-47 assault rifle killed five children and wounded 29 others in a shooting spree in a school playground) and

Killeen, Texas in October 1991 (when George Hennard killed 22 people and himself, and wounded 23 others, in a cafeteria), did not make the need for stricter controls apparent. While Stockton led to public majorities supporting (unsuccessfully) an outright ban on assault weapons, the response of Texans to the Killeen massacre – the worst in American history – was to repeal the 125-year-old law that prohibited the carrying of concealed weapons in 1995.

Both pro- and anti-gun groups see firearms as matters of life and death but draw opposite conclusions about what this implies about their legal availability. In the UK, in the balance between public safety and the liberty of individuals to own a firearm for recreational or occupation purposes, public opinion strongly favoured the former. But in America, firearms are seen not only as recreational devices but also as necessary guarantors of individual and collective safety in rural and urban areas. This explains the vehemence with which gun-owners defend their 'right' to firearms. Far from unifying Americans, to the extent that the policy battleground on guns is viewed in terms of morality, it divides them.

One final consideration concerns the mass media. In America, media fragmentation not only precludes a concerted national debate on gun control (such as occurred in the UK over 1996–97), but also reinforces the divergent responses that exist. Pro-gun groups are rarely forced to seek legitimacy in the public arena but, when necessary, they have a more sympathetic media in terms of the volume of outlets and their political outlooks than exists in Britain. The fact that the liberal *Washington Post* and *New York Times* consistently support gun control matters little in Mississippi or Maine. Moreover, precisely because the market is much more fragmented, individual articles or documentaries about guns have comparatively less influence on public opinion. In this context, the pro- and anti-gun lobbies are generally more concerned with maintaining an active membership base to pressure politicians than securing television or print publicity for their views.

It therefore seems highly improbable that major changes are imminent. The current climate is one where measures which non-Americans view as minimal steps towards a rational regulatory regime are decisively rejected by Congress. Although gun politics is now in a state of flux, divided party control of the federal government militates strongly against the proposal, much less the enactment, of new restrictive regulations. The abiding cultural affinity for guns is too deeply rooted to entertain serious challenge at present, and the recent popularity of decontrolling measures at state level amply illustrates a primordial mindset about the costs and benefits of firearms that differs substantially from almost all other nations.

CONCLUSION

Traditionalists have proven remarkably resilient and effective on gun control. Partly, this is because they have powerful political resources at their disposal that far outweigh those of the pro-control coalition. Not only do millions of Americans own and use firearms (with no hint whatsoever of irresponsible usage, much less criminal activity), but gun rights groups also provide a vocal and persistent lobbying force against gun control. Moreover, judicial reluctance to enter this 'political thicket' – even at the height of liberal activism during the Warren Court era – contrasts sharply with the intimate involvement of federal and state courts on most other cultural value conflicts.

Traditionalists also have several arguments that are serious, powerful and rational. Practical considerations loom especially large. Gun ownership is so widespread that hope of eliminating most guns altogether is utopian, even if desirable. The evidence is unclear about the relationship between the legal availability of guns and levels of gun crime. Decontrol measures have become popular at

state level precisely because many Americans find their logic – and the evidence to support them – compelling. In addition, in the unlikely event that prohibitive measures were to be introduced by Congress or the courts, enforcement of a gun ban would be immensely difficult to achieve with so many firearms already in circulation. Even relatively mild measures, such as the 1994 partial assault weapons ban, were evaded by manufacturers simply altering the names or modifying the shape of the prohibited guns. The fact that measures can be evaded is not necessarily a good reason for abandoning attempts to enact them, but the very move towards confiscation of guns would, for some, so threaten America's relative social and political stability that it is risky, perhaps even foolhardy, to contemplate its execution.

Moreover, the story of gun violence is a complex one. Remove the suicides and murders associated with urban gang warfare (violence which would not cease were guns magically to vanish) and the threat to public order posed by guns seems somewhat less serious. Again, causal links are not obvious. In terms of suicides, for example, logic intuitively suggests that easy availability of firearms increases suicide rates given their lethality, but the line of causality may equally work in the other direction: those who have decided to kill themselves may well purchase guns specifically for that purpose. Gun homicides, per capita, were higher in the 1920s and 1930s than they are today, despite the far larger number of guns now in private possession. As Dizard, Muth and Andrews note: 'As terrible as our national rates of violence are, as tragic as the murders are, the facts make it hard to support the notion that we are in the midst of an epidemic of gun violence' (Dizard et al., 1999: 13).

What contributes to the widespread sense of an epidemic is not only Hollywood and sensationalist journalism, but also the culture war over guns. Pro-gun forces portray a nation on the verge of anarchy that requires law-abiding people to arm themselves in self-defence. Any government attempt to regulate is suspicious. In farms in the middle of the Nevada desert, where the police would not even arrive for hours were they called to assist, this is not a ludicrous position. Anti-gun groups portray a nation awash with guns, held hostage to the impulsive acts of unstable individuals. Any refusal to endorse regulation is irresponsible by definition. When children take guns to class this, too, is a reasonable position. Paradoxically, gun rights and control groups feed each other's fears, thereby not only hardening mutual opposition but also reinforcing the pervasive sense of danger that grips millions of Americans less involved in the gun debate.

The issue of an armed citizenry is also one that is not peculiar to America, even if the American response remains singular. For those of us who have never hunted or shot for sporting reasons, it is close to unimaginable what it must be like to view having a gun in the house or car as part of everyday life, unworthy of comment much less controversy. Equally, for Americans, the idea that the state can possess a monopoly of coercive power and be relied on to defend us is quaint and bizarre. The cultural roots of Americans' attachment to firearms are therefore as deep and resilient as many non-Americans' resistance.

But equally deep-rooted is the republican form of government. American democracy prides itself on its representative credentials.

Americans have supported stronger gun control measures, consistently and by decisive margins, but the efforts to achieve these have been consistently frustrated by a vocal, active minority whose institutional influence is disproportionate to its popular support. In this instance, we do not see public policies that reflect broad public opinion – quite unlike the situation regarding, for example, abortion, the death penalty, gay rights and drugs.

Non-Americans may well continue to voice bewilderment when news of the latest gun-related American massacres occurs, but, in some respects, the wonder is not that these episodes occur regularly but rather that they remain relatively rare in a nation awash with firearms of every description and power. It is important to recognize that guns are not some bizarre preoccupation that is peripheral or incidental to the wider political culture. Rather, guns are intimately wedded to issues of the Constitution, property rights, liberty, federal–state relations and the individualism that form America's foundation stones. Precisely for that reason, neither progressives nor traditionalists can easily abandon the issue; for both, the costs of doing so are prohibitively high. Perhaps the most acute irony, however, is that for all their vociferous conflict, gun rights and gun control groups possess far more in common with each other than with the views of most non-Americans.

FURTHER READING

Michael Bellesiles, *Arming America: The Origins of a National Gun Culture* (2000) is an important historical analysis arguing that the existence of a gun culture from the founding of the republic is a myth.

John M. Bruce and Clyde Wilcox (eds), *The Changing Politics of Gun Control* (1998) is an excellent collection on the federal and state-level politics of firearms.

Tom Diaz, *Making a Killing: The Business of Guns in America* (1999) is a detailed analysis of the business forces driving the politics of gun rights groups.

Jan E. Dizard, Robert Merrill Muth and Stephen P. Andrews, Jr. (eds), *Guns in America: A Reader* (1999) is a superb compendium of 43 essays on all aspects of the gun debate, both pro- and anti-gun control.

Stephen Halbrook, *That Every Man Be Armed* (1984) is a strong pro-gun argument by one of the NRA's favoured lawyers that draws on a wide variety of authors, from ancient Greece to modern times, who support the notion of an armed citizenry.

Dennis A. Henigen, E. Bruce Nicholson and David Hemenway, *Guns and the Constitution: The Myth of Second Amendment Protection for Firearms in America* (1995) comprises three thoughtful essays by gun control advocates.

Jim Leitzel, 'Evasion and Public Policy: British and US Firearm Regulation', *Policy Studies* 19 (2) (1998), pp. 141–57 (1998) is a comparison of the effects of regulation and the ease of avoiding them on both sides of the Atlantic.

John Lott, *More Guns, Less Crime* (1998) is a detailed, if controversial, case made for the effectiveness of concealed carry laws in reducing crime.

Joyce L. Malcolm, *To Keep and Bear Arms: The Origins of an Anglo-American Right* (1994) is a powerful historical analysis arguing that the Second Amendment was intended to confer an individual citizenship right of gun ownership.

D.J. Mulloy (ed.), *Homegrown Revolutionaries: An American Militia Reader* (1999) is a comprehensive set of interviews, essays and original documents that demonstrate how important the Second Amendment and gun ownership is to the American militia movement.

Robert Spitzer, *The Politics of Gun Control* (2nd edition) (1995) is a readable overview of the key aspects of the politics surrounding gun control in America, sympathetic overall to the pro-control arguments.

WEB LINKS

Pro-gun rights organizations and resources

National Rifle Association
http://www.nra.org

Concealed Carry
http://www.concealcarry.org

Gun World
http://www.guns-world.net

Second Amendment
http://www.secondfreedom.net

Keep and Bear Arms
http://www.keepandbeararms.com

Second Amendment Sisters
http://www.sas-aim.org

Gun Owners of America
http://www.gunowners.org/

Women Against Gun Control
http://www.wagc.com/

Sexual Minorities' Self-Defense
http://www.pinkpistols.org/index2.html

Gun Owners of California
http://www.gunownersca.com/

Grassroots North Carolina
http://www.grnc.org/

Kentucky Coalition to Carry Concealed
http://www.kc3.com/

Tennessee Firearms Association
http://www.tennesseefirearms.com/

Jews for the Preservation of Firearm Ownership
http://www.jpfo.org/

Concerned Citizens Opposed to Police States
http://www.ccops.org/

Gun control organizations and resources

Americans for Gun Safety
http://www.americansforgunsafety.com

Brady Center for the Study of Gun Violence
http://www.bradycampaign.org

Coalition to Stop Gun Violence
http://www.csgv.org

Million Mom March
http://www.millionmommarch.org

Transcripts of CNN, April 27, 1999 *Crossfire* debate on gun control
http://www.house.gov/lofgren/dc/990427-crossfire.html

QUESTIONS

- What best explains the weak regulation of firearms in America?

- Assess the arguments for and against repealing the Second Amendment to the US Constitution.

- Should stronger federal gun control measures be enacted? What effect, if any, are they likely to have on gun violence, gun deaths, and gun crimes?

- What makes the NRA such a powerful gun rights lobby and gun control groups so ineffective?

- Evaluate the arguments for and against an armed citizenry in today's America.

5 Capital Punishment

In my view, the choice for the judge who believes the death penalty to be immoral is resignation rather than simply ignoring duly enacted constitutional laws and sabotaging the death penalty.

> US Supreme Court Justice Antonin Scalia (Associated Press, February 4, 2002)

People who want to commit murder better not do it in Florida because we may have a problem with our electric chair.

> Bob Butterworth, Attorney General of Florida (commenting after Pedro Medina 'withstood' an electric shock of 2,000 volts with flames shooting from his head and only ceased living after several minutes), *Le Monde*, March 28, 1998

- An American Way of Death
- The Historical Context
- The Death Penalty Today
- Explaining the Politics of the Death Penalty
- The US Constitution
- Public Opinion
- The Supreme Court Strikes Down the Death Penalty: *Furman v. Georgia*
- The Supreme Court Changes Its Mind: *Gregg v. Georgia* and after
- Traditionalists v. Progressives
- Politicizing the Death Penalty: The Traditionalist Triumph
- Conclusion

Chapter Summary

Capital punishment distinguishes America from other liberal democracies. Most American states allow for, and many implement, the death penalty as a legal punishment for certain categories of crime. Currently legal in 38 American states and for the federal government, 66 death row inmates were executed in 2001. Most executions occur in southern states, with Texas setting an American record for an individual state of 40 executions in one calendar year in 2000. Although the Supreme Court ruled the penalty unconstitutional in 1972 on grounds of arbitrariness in sentencing, it upheld revised state capital punishment laws in 1976. While some methods of execution are unconstitutional, the principle of judicial execution has not been held to violate the Eighth Amendment's prohibition against 'cruel and unusual' punishments. Most Americans endorse capital punishment, but public support declines substantially when alternative options such as life imprisonment are offered. However, American politicians have exploited the penalty as a symbolic means of demonstrating their 'toughness' on issues of law and order. Despite powerful arguments against capital punishment and growing popular concern about wrongful executions, a combination of judicial conservatism and a punitive Congress suggests that the prospects for the abolition of capital punishment in America are slim and distant.

In the autumn of 1998 near a town called Jasper, Texas, three young white men were driving down a rural dirt road in the early hours of the morning. They picked up a black man walking down the track, James Byrd, ostensibly to give him a lift home. Along the way, they forced him out of the truck, beat him and chained him to the back of the vehicle. They then drove three miles down the road, dragging Byrd behind, until his body was mutilated and head decapitated. They then deposited the headless corpse outside a local black church. In February 1999, a predominantly white jury found one of Byrd's killers, a white supremacist named William King, guilty of murder and sentenced him to death, to be administered by lethal injection. It was the first time that a white man had been sentenced to death for the murder of a black man in Texas since capital punishment was reinstated by the US Supreme Court as constitutionally sanctioned state law in 1976.

For many Americans, the appalling brutality of the crime – the sheer inhumanity – justified the imposition of a capital sentence and a judicial killing. For others, no matter how brutal the crime, the state is rarely, if ever, justified in taking human life. Based on a true account by Sister Helen Prejean of her work with two condemned men in Louisiana, the film *Dead Man Walking* represented Hollywood's attempt to illuminate the human story of both the murdered and the murderer in death penalty cases. As the movie implicitly recognized, much of the opposition to the death penalty in America has been based less on the sheer volume of executions that take place than on its arbitrary imposition, selective enforcement, and the possibility of innocent life having been extinguished by the state.

Partly as a result of such growing concerns being documented, George Ryan, the Republican Governor of Illinois, announced a moratorium on further executions in his state in January 2000 and established a commission to investigate capital punishment. By the millennium, more death row prisoners had been exonerated (13) in Illinois than executed (12) since 1977. After 16 years behind bars, Anthony Porter – convicted (wrongly) in 1982 for two murders – was released only two days before he was due to be executed, after journalism students at Northwestern University had helped to prove his innocence and discovered the real killer. The *Chicago-Tribune* found that, of 245 death sentences in the state since 1977, 40 per cent were tainted in some form. Thirty-five black death row inmates had been convicted by all-white juries, while 33 inmates had been represented at trial by attorneys who were subsequently banned or suspended from practice. In declaring the moratorium, Ryan stated, 'Until I can be sure with moral certainty that no innocent man or woman is facing lethal injection, no one will meet that fate.' Simultaneously, however, he stated his support for the principle of capital punishment.

The ironies that surround death penalty politics are many. For a nation whose citizens consistently profess a broad scepticism towards government, capital punishment proves a remarkable exception. For Americans, one acceptable – even fundamental – role of the state is preserving law and order. Such is the enthusiasm for punitive punishment policies that some states during the 1990s approved allowing the families of murder victims not only to give evidence in the sentencing trials and attend the boards charged with deciding whether to commute the death sentences of convicted murderers, but also to attend the killers' executions. The state legislatures of Texas and California – with the nation's largest death rows – debated whether to televise executions to the public. (Supporters and opponents of capital punishment contemplated the likely public reactions with a view to bolstering their cause; supporters on the basis that justice would literally be seen to be being done, opponents that revulsion at the gruesome scenes might turn Americans away from capital punishment.)

Until recently, public support for capital punishment has been strong. With many Americans despairing at significant, albeit, during the late 1990s, declining, levels of violent crime, surveys consistently showed around 75 per cent support. Ninety-eight prisoners were executed in 1999, the most in a single year since 1951. Other than Japan, America remains the only industrialized democracy to use capital punishment and one of the few nations (alongside Iran, Iraq, Nigeria, Pakistan and Yemen) that executes juveniles. Neither Bill nor Hillary Clinton opposed the penalty; nor did any of the four main contenders for the presidential nominations of the Republican and Democratic parties in 2000. George W. Bush presided over more executions than any other governor (152 during his six years as governor). In 2000, Texas set a record for the number of executions in a single state in one calendar year (40) and in June 2001 Timothy McVeigh became the first prisoner executed by the federal government since 1963 (for the murder of 168 people in the 1995 bombing of the Alfred Murrah Federal Building in Oklahoma City).

Conflict over the death penalty features all of the political traits that epitomize cultural value antagonism: an influential but strongly divided judiciary; a marked divergence between elite and mass opinion; profound federal–state tensions; progressives concerned with individual rights and traditionalists occupied by the collective views of local communities; intense conflict between competing moral and ethical claims; partisan polarization; and an active, fragmented and diverse interest group universe. Moreover, as with abortion and gun control, moral traditionalists, despite judicial and legislative setbacks, have emerged as the dominant force in capital punishment politics. Thus far, traditionalist concern for the quality of justice has trumped progressive concern for the quality of mercy in most of America.

AN AMERICAN WAY OF DEATH

Capital punishment penalizes those individuals convicted by judges and juries of certain classes of crimes by state execution. Although many societies still practise capital punishment, most 'developed countries' abolished the death sentence during the twentieth century. While prohibited in 12 American states and the District of Columbia, capital punishment remains legal in 38 others and for the federal government. Sanctioned methods of execution include death by firing squad, electrocution, poison gas, hanging and lethal injections – the last is the most common method since it was first introduced in Oklahoma in 1977.

In a comparative context, America is often viewed as unusual in continuing to allow and implement capital punishment. In 1998, for example, none of the 40 members of the Council of Europe carried out capital punishment. Death sentences were pronounced in several and ten nations retained the penalty on their statute books, but even these ten respected moratoria they had established

---

TABLE 5.1 Countries that retain and use the death penalty for ordinary crimes, 1996

Afghanistan	Guinea	Qatar
Algeria	Guyana	Russia
Antigua and Barbuda	India	Saint Christopher and Nevis
Armenia	Indonesia	Saint Lucia
Azerbaydzhan	Iran	Saint Vincent and the Grenadines
Bahamas	Iraq	Saudi Arabia
Bahrain	Jamaica	Sierra Leone
Bangladesh	Japan	Singapore
Barbados	Jordan	Somalia
Belarus	Kazakhstan	Sudan
Belize	Kenya	Swaziland
Benin	Korea (North)	Syria
Bosnia-Herzegovina	Korea (South)	Tadzhikistan
Botswana	Kuwait	Taiwan
Bulgaria	Kyrgystan	Tanzania
Burkina Faso	Laos	Thailand
Cameroon	Latvia	Trinidad and Tobago
Chad	Lebanon	Tunisia
Chile	Lesotho	Turkmenistan
China	Liberia	Uganda
Cuba	Libya	Ukraine
Dominica	Lithuania	United Arab Emirates
Egypt	Malawi	*United States of America*
Equatorial Guinea	Malaysia	Uzbekistan
Eritrea	Mauritania	Vietnam
Estonia	Mongolia	Yemen
Ethiopia	Morocco	Yugoslavia
Gabon	Myanmar	Zaire
Georgia	Nigeria	Zambia
Ghana	Oman	Zimbabwe
Grenada	Pakistan	
Guatemala	Poland	

Source: Bedau (1997).

Exhibit 5.1   World leaders in executions

In 1999, China easily led all nations allowing capital punishment with 1,077 executions, followed distantly by Iran (165), Saudi Arabia (103), the Democratic Republic of Congo (100) and, in fifth place, the United States (98).

Source: *Newsweek*, June 12, 2000, p. 25.

(*de facto* or *de jure*). Moreover, it is now a condition of membership – for existing and prospective members – in the European Union that no nation allows capital punishment.

But this popular impression of America's exceptional status needs to be qualified. First, the death penalty debate needs to be placed in its appropriate historical context. The shared Anglo-American legal tradition is one that, historically, cannot be said to have ever been 'soft on crime'. The prohibition on 'cruel and unusual punishment' contained in the Eighth Amendment to the US Constitution ('Excessive bail shall not be required, nor excessive fines imposed, nor cruel and unusual punishment inflicted') first appeared in the English Bill of Rights of 1689. When adopted by the United States in 1791, federal law provided that larceny (theft of private property) be punished by 39 lashes. Branding, pillorying and ear-cropping were also common punishments in late eighteenth-century America and for some years after ratification of the Bill of Rights.

Secondly, America needs to be placed in an appropriate comparative context. Compared to Europe, the legality and implementation of capital punishment are more the exception than the rule. Once the international comparison is broadened, however, to take a truly global perspective, America's status as a death penalty oddity is less obvious. As Table 5.1 reveals, as of 1996, 94 countries allowed capital punishment to be sentenced and most had implemented death sentences between 1985 and 1996. What is most immediately striking about this group is that very few of these countries display a particularly democratic form of government. Respect for civil

liberties and individual rights are rare, free and fair elections are mostly not the rule, and many are brutally totalitarian or despotic pariah states. That America should keep company with such nations (several of which have been declared 'rogue regimes' by its federal government) provokes considerable unease among progressives, as well as strong criticism from abolitionist lobbies such as Amnesty International.

Such isolation among liberal democracies was graphically revealed when, in April 1999, the United Nations Human Rights Commission voted in favour of the 'Resolution Supporting Worldwide Moratorium on Executions', which called for countries that had not abolished capital punishment to restrict its use (including not imposing the penalty for juvenile offenders). America was one of only ten countries, including China, Pakistan, Rwanda and Sudan, that voted against the resolution.

THE HISTORICAL CONTEXT

Like gun control and abortion, capital punishment provokes intense and emotive reactions that can sometimes undermine dispassionate, rational and reflective debate. All three issues entail fundamental questions of life and death, of reconciling the universal protection of individual rights and liberties with the need for public order and the legitimate expression of particular wishes of local communities in law, of the constitutionality of specific practices and of the appropriate balance between federal and state regulation. All three issues lend themselves to being portrayed in simplistic ways using graphic images (guns, foetuses, electric chairs) and what can initially seem like abstract constitutional debates have acquired a relevance for mass American publics in the twenty-first century. The same fundamental issues of proportionality and barbarity that surrounded questions of outlawing hanging, drawing and quartering in the eighteenth and nineteenth centuries now surround the use of electric chairs and lethal injections. The same basic questions of whether the community's response to particularly heinous crimes should include capital punishment now inform debates over whether the penalty should be used as a weapon in combating the drugs trade, rape and terrorism (international and domestic).

Controversy over capital punishment has become especially significant since the latter debates have become intermeshed with growing public concern over crime. Punitive public policies, such as 'zero tolerance' and the 'three strikes and you're out' law championed by President Clinton, won notable popular support (the latter entails that a conviction for a third felony requires life imprisonment without parole). Successive years have seen the list of states placing capital punishment on their statute books increase. Between 1988 and 1998, for example, Kansas, New York and New Hampshire reintroduced the death penalty while no states abolished it. With the defeat of Democratic Governor Mario Cuomo in 1994, who had previously vetoed attempts to re-establish capital punishment, New York (in 1995) became the thirty-eighth state to reintroduce capital punishment since its partial prohibition by the Supreme Court in 1972. In 1994, Maryland and Pennsylvania conducted their first executions since the 1960s. Even the US military resumed capital punishment in the mid-1990s, 30 years after a solider was last hanged on the orders of a military court. (The President, as Commander-in-Chief of the armed forces, is charged with signing the orders.)

Public support for retribution over rehabilitation is hardly new. For the supposed land of the free, America places an extraordinary number of its citizens behind bars. After Russia, America currently has the second-highest rate of imprisonment in the world per capita. Although constituting fewer than 5 per cent of the world's population, America accounts for 25 per cent of the global prison population. One in every 163 Americans is currently in jail or prison, a rate over six times the average in Europe. The millennium saw America imprison its two-millionth inmate.

America's zeal for imprisonment is usually attributed to a recent shift towards harsh law enforcement policies, especially against drug dealers and users, dating back to the later 1960s. To some extent, this is true – the number of people locked up has tripled since 1980. But this recent surge is not an anomaly. Bondage of one sort or another has played a central role in American history from the beginning. Historically, not only black Americans, but also a large proportion of white immigrants, arrived in chains: as prisoners, indentured servants or bonded labourers (though the latter two categories involved – ostensibly – voluntary decisions). As America was settled, jails and prisons were among the first public facilities to be built in newly founded communities. When larger state prisons were established, reformers sought more enlightened regimes. Rehabilitation through penitence had a particular vogue – hence the American term for prison: 'penitentiary'.

American zeal for punishment therefore has a long lineage. Part of the explanation for this concerns the practical circumstances (nation-building, frontier conquest, crime) that Americans faced, but key, also, are the markedly individualistic and religious tenets to which most Americans adhere. Since such a heavy emphasis is placed on individual effort and achievement, and the rewards commensurate with this, so too must punishment be appropriate to those individuals who violate shared norms. For many, this basic Creedal value is underpinned by deeply held religious beliefs about the sanctity of life and the legitimacy of inflicting death as a retributive punishment, regardless of any other purposes that may be served (such as deterrence of crime). While many of these beliefs have remained intact, though, the practical mechanics of capital punishment have altered significantly over time.

The changing death penalty

Like the 'right to bear arms', the historical origins of America's death penalty lie in England. During the colonial era, all 13 states followed traditional English practice, implementing capital punishment for certain categories of crime. Subsequent developments, however, saw five important changes occur

that shaped capital punishment as we know it today:

1　With the invention of degrees of murder, a distinction became commonplace between different *categories of crime*. Today, every American jurisdiction that authorizes the death penalty for murder does so by limiting it to those convicted of 'murder in the first degree' ('capital murder') rather than crimes such as manslaughter.

2　*Public executions* were gradually ended, beginning in New York in 1835 (although a century was to pass before every state followed its lead, public hangings occurring as late as 1936 in Kentucky and 1937 in Missouri).

TABLE 5.2　Abolition, partial abolition and restoration of the death penalty

Jurisdiction	Year of partial abolition	Year of complete abolition	Year of restoration	Year of reabolition
Alaska		1957		
Arizona	1916		1918	
Colorado		1897	1901	
Delaware		1958	1961	
DC		1973		
Hawaii		1957		
Iowa		1872	1878	1965
Kansas		1907/1973	1935/1994	
Maine		1876	1883	1887
Massachusetts		1984		
Michigan	1847	1963		
Minnesota		1911		
Missouri		1917	1919	
New Mexico	1969			
New York	1969		1995	
North Dakota		1915		
Oregon		1914/1964	1920/1984	
Rhode Island	1852			
South Dakota		1915/1977	1939/1979	
Tennessee	1915		1919	
Vermont	1965			
Washington		1913	1919	
West Virginia		1965		
Wisconsin		1853		

Source: Bedau (1997).

3 American jurisdictions in the nineteenth century began authorizing *trial juries* to make binding recommendations in capital cases, offering more scope for discretion and leniency in sentencing (judges were previously mandated to impose death penalties in many cases).

4 *Abolitionist movements* organized and campaigned, with selective successes, to end the death penalty in particular states during the nineteenth century (but, as Table 5.2 shows, several states that abolished capital punishment restored it at a later date).

5 The *variety of crimes* eligible was gradually reduced so that, until the 1990s, the only crime punishable by death – the only crime for which anyone has been executed since 1977 – was some form of criminal homicide (certain drug offences now also qualify).

THE DEATH PENALTY TODAY

Strong American approval for the death penalty is conventionally linked to issues of crime and violence, especially murder. But, contrary to the common perception outside America of a country dominated by acts of appalling brutality, homicide ranks tenth in the list of the main causes of death. That is not to minimize the absolute extent of murder in America, but merely to place it in its appropriate context. As Table 5.3 shows, nine other causes of death are more widespread and generate much less emotive responses from American (and non-American) publics, the mass media and policymakers alike.

Nevertheless, American states not only execute a large number of convicted persons (Table 5.4) and allow the death sentence to be imposed for a wide variety of criminal offences, but also execute by a variety of methods. As Table 5.5 shows, firing squads and hangings are still used in some states to dispense capital punishment (Delaware carried out a hanging as recently as 1994).

Furthermore, many Americans have few apparent qualms about the age at which a convicted criminal can be killed by the state. As Table 5.6 shows, Americans as young as 16 years of age can be subject to judicial executions in some states. For many within and

---

TABLE 5.3   Ten leading causes of death in the US, 1992

Rank cause of death	Number	Death rate	Percentage of total deaths
All causes	2,177,000	853.3	100.0
1. Heart disease	720,480	282.5	33.1
2. Cancer	521,090	204.3	23.9
3. Stroke	143,640	56.3	6.6
4. Chronic obstructive lung disease	91,440	35.8	4.2
5. Accidents and adverse effects	86,310	33.8	4.0
Motor vehicles	41,710	16.4	1.9
Others	44,600	17.5	2.0
6. Pneumonia and influenza	76,120	29.8	3.5
7. Diabetes mellitus	50,180	19.7	2.3
8. HIV infection	33,590	13.2	1.5
9. Suicide	29,760	11.7	1.4
10. Homicide and legal intervention	26,570	10.4	1.2

Source: *Statistical Abstract of the United States* (1996).

TABLE 5.4 Prisoners executed under civil authority, 1930–94

Years	Executed for murder			Executed for rape			Executed for other offences		
	Total	W	B	Total	W	B	Total	W	B
1930–39	1,514	803	687	125	10	115	28	14	14
1940–49	1,064	458	595	200	19	179	20	13	7
1950–59	601	316	280	102	13	89	14	7	7
1960–67	155	87	68	28	6	22	8	5	3
1968–76	–	–	–	–	–	–	–	–	–
1977–82	11	5	6	–	–	–	–	–	–
1983–94	256	151	98	–	–	–	–	–	–
Total	3,601	1,820	1,734	455	48	405	70	39	31

Note: W = white, B = black. 'Total' includes races other than white and black. Excludes executions by military authorities. The Army (including the Air Force) carried out 160 executions (148 between 1942 and 1950; three each in 1954, 1955 and 1957; and one each in 1958, 1959 and 1961). Of the total, 106 were executed for murder (including 21 involving rape), 53 for rape and one for desertion. The Navy carried out no executions during the period.
Source: *Statistical Abstract of the United States* (1996: 222).

outside America, this is especially controversial, given the vulnerability and immaturity at which such individuals commit crimes and the impossibility, if a sentence is enforced, of repentance or reformation. Moreover, as of 2000, 25 of the 38 death penalty states, including Texas and Virginia, allowed the execution of mentally retarded prisoners (generally defining retardation as dating to adolescence or earlier and as an IQ of 70 or less). It was only in June 2002 that the Supreme Court held in *Atkins v. Virginia* that executing the mentally retarded was unconstitutional.

The contemporary context is one in which the death penalty's legality is settled – only 12 states and the District of Columbia lacked death penalty statutes in 2002 (see Table 5.7). What unites these states is unclear. Geographically, they tend to form a northern tier across America but this does not explain their abolitionist stance. Some have what can generally be described as a more 'liberal' political culture than others, such as Hawaii, Massachusetts and Minnesota. But even these states witnessed efforts during the 1990s to (re)introduce the death penalty that only narrowly failed.

Even with a majority of states allowing the death penalty, implementation is – relative to the volume of inmates – rare. As Table 5.8 shows, in excess of 3,000 prisoners were held on death rows in 1999. 'Only' 98 inmates were executed during 1999, although some states that had not executed any prisoners since 1976 commenced doing so at the century's turn (Ohio, for example, in 1999 and Tennessee in 2000).

Not only has implementation of capital punishment been rare but it has also been geographically concentrated. As Table 5.9 documents, most executions occur in just five states: Texas, Florida, Georgia, Virginia and Louisiana. Conforming to its reputation for everything being bigger in Texas, the Lone Star state is the undisputed leader: in October 1995, for example, Texas carried out its one hundredth execution since resuming them in 1982 and by July 1999 the figure since 1976 had reached 178 (though, per capita of state

TABLE 5.5   Methods of lawful execution, by jurisdiction, 1994

Lethal injection	Electrocution*	Lethal gas	Hanging	Firing squad
Arizona	Alabama	Arizona	Delaware	Utah
Arkansas	Arkansas	California	Montana	
California	Connecticut	Maryland	New Hampshire	
Colorado	Florida	Mississippi	Washington	
Delaware	Georgia	Missouri		
Idaho	Indiana	North Carolina		
Illinois	Kentucky	Wyoming		
Kansas	Nebraska			
Louisiana	Ohio			
Maryland	South Carolina			
Mississippi	Tennessee			
Missouri	Virginia			
Montana				
Nevada				
New Hampshire				
New Jersey				
New Mexico				
North Carolina				
Ohio				
Oklahoma				
Oregon				
Pennsylvania				
South Dakota				
Texas				
Utah				
Washington				
Wyoming				

* By 2000, only Alabama and Nebraska required electrocution as the sole means of implementing a capital sentence.

population, Oklahoma is the leading executing state).

It is no coincidence that all five of the leading executing states were southern states in which traditionalist positions on cultural value issues are among the strongest and most widely held in the nation. For progressives, one of the peculiar ironies of the strong southern resistance to abortion is the region's enthusiasm for the state extinguishing lives by the death penalty. But for many in the South (and elsewhere), the universal and unconditional right to life typically ends with the taking away of someone else's – death

row inmates are the functional equivalents of abortionists. In this respect, the Bible Belt also represents the Death Belt – the Deep South. In 2000, for example, 89 per cent of the 85 executions in America occurred in southern states, with only three non-southern states carrying out any executions. As Hugo Adam Bedau puts it, in the South 'the death penalty is as firmly entrenched as grits for breakfast' (1997: 21).

Explanations vary for the southern conviction in capital punishment and few have won clear or convincing empirical support. Conventional analyses point to the relatively

TABLE 5.6   Minimum legal age for capital punishment, by jurisdiction, 1994*

Age less than 18		Age 18	None specified
Alabama	(16)	California	Arizona
Arkansas	(14)	Colorado	Idaho
Delaware	(16)	Connecticut	Louisiana
Florida	(16)	Federal system	Montana
Georgia	(17)	Illinois	Pennsylvania
Indiana	(16)	Kansas	South Carolina
Kentucky	(16)	Maryland	South Dakota
Mississippi	(16)	Nebraska	Utah
Missouri	(16)	New Jersey	
Nevada	(16)	New Mexico	
New Hampshire	(17)	Ohio	
North Carolina	(17)	Oregon	
Oklahoma	(16)	Tennessee	
Texas	(17)	Washington	
Virginia	(15)		
Wyoming	(16)		

* The Supreme Court invalidated some of these state laws as unconstitutional by ruling in 1988 that the minimum age for capital punishment of juveniles was 16. Anyone younger than this at the time of the crime could not be sentenced to death.

rural, religious and (at one time) racist attitudes of many native white southerners in

TABLE 5.7   States prohibiting capital punishment*

Alaska	Minnesota
Hawaii	North Dakota
Iowa	Rhode Island
Maine	Vermont
Massachusetts	West Virginia
Michigan	Wisconsin

* Plus the District of Columbia. After a white aide to Senator Richard Shelby of Alabama was killed, Congress passed a Shelby-sponsored bill that required a referendum on capital punishment to be held in DC in 1992. The voters rejected reintroduction by a 2:1 margin, but the results were decisively closer in the affluent white suburbs than in the overwhelmingly black areas of the capital.

the Deep South, for whom capital punishment represents 'nothing but the survival in a socially acceptable form of the old Black Codes and the lynch law enforced by the Ku Klux Klan' (Bedau, 1997: 23). Simplistic as this may be, there can be little doubt that southern enthusiasm for capital punishment has a long historic lineage that is powerfully connected with the subjugation of blacks – particularly men – and fears of white women being subject to inter-racial rape (Mississippi, it may be recalled from Chapter 3, allowed abortion on grounds of rape prior to *Roe* largely for this reason). As Table 5.10 notes, officially reported lynchings of blacks (and some whites) almost doubled the total number of *de facto* executions in some decades of the early twentieth century.

Also, the disproportionate representation of blacks on death row and the disproportionate sentencing and execution rates for blacks who kill whites (compared to murdering other blacks) plausibly bears

TABLE 5.8   Total number of death row inmates, by state, 1999

California	551	Nevada	87	Delaware	18	Kansas	3
Texas	458	Missouri	85	Washington	17	New York	3
Florida	393	Louisiana	85	Maryland	17	Wyoming	2
Pennsylvania	223	South Carolina	69	New Jersey	17		
North Carolina	221	Mississippi	62	Utah	12		
Ohio	196	Indiana	44	Nebraska	9		
Alabama	182	Arkansas	41	US Military	8		
Illinois	161	Kentucky	39	Connecticut	7		
Oklahoma	152	Virginia	32	Montana	6		
Georgia	130	Oregon	26	New Mexico	4		
Arizona	119	Idaho	22	Colorado	4		
Tennessee	103	US Government	21	South Dakota	3	Total: 3,625*	

* When added, state totals are higher because some inmates have been sentenced to death in more than one state.

Source: NAACP Legal Defense Fund, *Death Row USA*, September 1, 1999.

some connection to the mostly white composition of a majority of southern judges, juries and prosecutors. Georgia's notoriously death penalty-friendly and predominantly white Chattahoochee Judicial District, which includes the city of Columbus and Fort Benning, has even been labelled the 'Buckle of the Death Belt' because of the way that death sentences for black defendants are routinely meted out.

Nevertheless, the volume of death row inmates, the numbers executed, the sanctioning of judicial killings of juveniles and, as we shall see later, strong concerns about the arbitrary and capricious enforcement of capital punishment have raised serious doubts as to the legitimacy of the punishment.

EXPLAINING THE POLITICS OF THE DEATH PENALTY

THE US CONSTITUTION

Whatever the competing moral, theological and practical arguments for and against the death penalty, its constitutionality remains the central issue in American politics. Were the Constitution deemed to prohibit its use, no extra-constitutional arguments would suffice to ensure its implementation. A practice may be deemed immoral in America but that does not equate with being unconstitutional; it is the latter that is key.

As one might suspect, given its prevailing legality and occasional (albeit increasing) implementation, most judges have held that the federal Constitution allows – but does not require – individual states to administer the death penalty for those found guilty of certain crimes. Some progressives view this as an inaccurate interpretation of the Constitution as it pertains to capital punishment. As with gun control, constitutional interpretation, far from being an arcane and esoteric question, is literally a matter of life and death.

Unlike assessments of the 'right to bear arms' clause of the Second Amendment, however, historical interpretations of the Constitution have left little doubt as to the constitutionality of capital punishment. Three Amendments are especially relevant: the Fifth, Eighth and Fourteenth. As Exhibit 5.2 reveals, the phrasing of these Amendments suggests that the Framers of the Constitution

TABLE 5.9 Prisoners executed by jurisdiction in rank order, 1930–95 and 1977–95

Jurisdiction	Number executed 1930–95	Jurisdiction	Number executed 1977–95
US total	4,172	US total	313
Texas	401	Texas	104
Georgia	386	Florida	36
New York	329	Virginia	29
California	294	Louisiana	22
North Carolina	271	Georgia	20
Florida	206	Missouri	17
Ohio	172	Alabama	12
South Carolina	167	Arkansas	11
Mississippi	158	North Carolina	8
Louisiana	155	West Virginia	7
Pennsylvania	154	Illinois	7
Alabama	147	Oklahoma	6
Arkansas	129	Nevada	5
Virginia	121	Delaware	5
Kentucky	103	South Carolina	5
Illinois	97	Mississippi	4
Tennessee	93	Utah	4
Missouri	78	Arizona	4
New Jersey	74	Indiana	3
Maryland	69	California	2
Oklahoma	66	Washington	2
Arizona	51	Pennsylvania	2
Washington	49	Nebraska	1
Colorado	47	Idaho	1
Indiana	46	Montana	1
West Virginia	40	Maryland	1
DC	40	Wyoming	1
Nevada	34		
US Federal	33		
Massachusetts	27		
Connecticut	21		
Oregon	19		
Iowa	18		
Utah	17		
Delaware	17		
Kansas	15		
New Mexico	8		
Wyoming	8		
Montana	7		
Nebraska	5		
Vermont	4		
Idaho	4		
South Dakota	1		
New Hampshire	1		

Source: Bedau (1997: 22–3).

TABLE 5.10 Number of official lynchings and legal executions in the US, 1890s–1960s

Decade	Number of lynchings	Number of legal executions
1890s	1,540	1,215
1900s	885	1,192
1910s	621	1,039
1920s	315	1,169
1930s	130	1,670
1940s	5	1,288
1950s	2	716
1960s	–	191

Source: Mark Grossman (1998: 164).

deliberately intended to acknowledge the death penalty's constitutionality – not to require it but to allow states to impose it should they so desire. The Fifth and Fourteenth Amendments permit the 'deprivation of life' provided this is done according to 'due process' of law. Admittedly, the Eighth Amendment, applied not only to the federal government but also to the states through the Fourteenth Amendment's guarantees of 'equality before the law' and 'due process', prohibits inflicting 'cruel and unusual punishments'. But this was intended to deal with barbaric punishments (such as crucifixion or burning at the stake) rather than capital punishment as such – the mechanics rather than the principle. Certainly, no Supreme Court majority has ever interpreted that phrase to

Exhibit 5.2   Does the US Constitution sanction the death penalty?

Arguments in Favour of the Constitutionality of Capital Punishment

- The Fifth Amendment states: 'No person shall . . . be deprived of life, liberty, or property, without due process of law . . .'
- The Eighth Amendment states: 'Excessive bail shall not be required, nor excessive fines imposed, nor cruel and unusual punishments inflicted.'
- The Fourteenth Amendment states: 'No State shall . . . deprive any person of life, liberty, or property, without due process of law . . .'

Taken together, these strongly suggest that the original authors of the constitutional amendments allowed for, but did not require, the possibility of the death penalty being imposed by individual states. The only condition that affected the constitutionality of capital punishment was that it could not infringe 'due process of law' – in essence, fair legal procedures, especially regarding impartial and fair trials. For abolitionists, though, the need for consistency of application that 'due process' requires has not been met (and perhaps cannot ever be met). That is sufficient ground to rule the penalty a violation of the Fifth and Fourteenth Amendments, either outweighing claims that it is not 'cruel and unusual' or making capital punishment cruel and unusual.

prohibit all forms of capital punishment in all circumstances.

Controversy again centres, however, upon the extent to which the 'originalist' reading of the Constitution is correct and, if it is, how far current generations of Americans should be bound in perpetuity by the particular preferences of their ancestors. At one level, it seems clear that the death penalty is a paradigmatic instance of the concept of the 'living Constitution' favoured by progressives. Changing societal notions of what kind of behaviour is acceptable and unacceptable have meant that, over time, practices once seen as entirely conventional are now viewed as uncivilized, inhumane and barbaric. This suggests that what counts as 'cruel and unusual' is inherently a matter for judges to ascertain in the light of changing public opinion. Indeed, the Framers themselves seemed to be well aware of the likelihood of changing public sentiment in this case, by once again providing a constitutional clause that is inherently ambiguous, open to subjective readings and adaptation over time. On this view, America is clearly out of sync with the vast majority of countries which most Americans would instinctively regard as their fellow 'civilized' states in sustaining capital punishment.

Unlike the explicitly anti-majoritarian thrust of the First, Second, Fourth, Fifth and Sixth Amendments, the Eighth appears to guarantee only what the majority already believes to be morally required on this interpretation. That is, if the content of 'cruel and unusual' takes its meaning from what most Americans believe, there seems little point in its being part of the Bill of Rights. If so, the 'cruel and unusual' provision would serve only a rhetorical purpose. As Justice Joseph Story once wrote, the Amendment 'would seem to be wholly unnecessary in a free government, since it is scarcely possible that any department of such a government should authorize or justify such atrocious conduct'. If the Eighth Amendment's interpretation is too closely tied to the moral judgement of

American society, the clause is unnecessary, since it then represents merely a restatement of the primacy of the majority's will, not an independent curb on that primacy.

On the other hand, if some independent content exists in the words 'cruel and unusual', meaning that it is independent of the current values and mores of society, then the clause could be considered to be among the most essential of the Bill of Rights. After all, no class of citizens is less valued, more vulnerable to arbitrary treatment, and least likely to have its interests represented in the political arena than that of convicted criminals. But this type of independent and creative construction places the Supreme Court on dangerous political ground, subject to criticism that it is an 'imperial' judiciary 'legislating' moral standards rather than 'adjudicating' them.

The importance of changing social contexts seemed to be acknowledged openly by the progressive Warren Court in a ruling in 1958, *Trop v. Dulles*, where the Chief Justice wrote for the majority that the Eighth Amendment's meaning was not fixed forever at the time of its adoption. Rather, the notion of cruel and unusual punishment 'must draw its meaning from the evolving standards of decency that mark the progress of a maturing society'. This offered apparent hope to capital punishment opponents. But Warren went on to argue that 'the death penalty has been employed throughout our history, and, in a day when it is still widely accepted, it cannot be said to violate the constitutional concept of cruelty'. For no less a liberal than Earl Warren to argue for capital punishment's constitutionality was particularly significant.

The interpretative difficulty for death penalty opponents is a substantial one. Unlike the First Amendment, the Eighth contains an express limitation on the scope of its protections. It does not prohibit all punishments – only those held to be cruel and unusual. Unlike the Fourth Amendment, moreover, the Eighth's limitation is defined in terms of a normative judgement about the moral quality of a proposed punishment: it does not specifically prohibit 'unreasonable' punishments or costly, useless or discriminatory punishments. Concerns such as the costs of possible alternative punishments or the importance of using a particular punishment to achieve a political or social goal therefore seem to be considerations that are effectively excluded by the Eighth's language.

PUBLIC OPINION

While public opinion has clearly shifted over time in terms of what methods can be considered constitutionally permissible for carrying out death sentences, the principle of the constitutionality has only rarely been opposed by majorities of the public. Most states, as well as the federal government, either retained or reintroduced a death penalty statute. In 1972 (when the Supreme

TABLE 5.11   Public opinion on the death penalty, 1936–91

Year	GSS	Harris	Gallup	*New York Times*
1936	–	–	61	–
1937	–	–	65	–
1953	–	–	68	–
1960	–	–	51	–
1965	–	38	45	–
1966	–	–	42	–
1969	–	48	51	–
1970	–	47	–	–
1971	–	–	49	–
1972	52.8	–	57	–
1973	59.7	59	–	–
1974	62.9	–	64	–
1975	59.8	–	–	–
1976	65.4	67	65	–
1977	66.8	–	–	–
1978	66.3	–	62	–
1980	66.9	–	–	–
1981	–	–	66	–
1982	67.9	–	–	–
1983	73.1	68	–	–
1984	69.9	–	–	–
1985	75.2	–	–	–
1986	71.2	–	–	–
1987	64.1	–	–	–
1988	70.6	–	–	77
1989	73.7	–	–	71
1990	74.2	–	–	72
1991	71.1	–	76	–

Note: – indicates that the survey was not conducted in that year.
Questions: 'Do you believe in capital punishment for persons convicted of murder or are you opposed to it?';
(*Harris*) 'Do you believe in capital punishment or are you opposed to it?'
Source: Epstein et al. (1994: 591).

Court declared capital punishment unconstitutional as then administered) 39 states and the District of Columbia allowed capital punishment. In 2002, 16 years after its reinstatement as a constitutionally permissible punishment, 38 states and the federal government did so.

Opinion surveys also indicate strong public support (see Table 5.11). Although opposition hardened in the early 1960s, such that in May 1966 (for the first and only time) a majority of Americans (47 per cent to 42 per cent) opposed the death penalty for murder, this was exceptional. A succession of inner-city riots across 125 American cities during the mid-1960s and a fearsome rise in violent crime from the later 1960s assisted the reversal of the abolitionist trend, which has not subsequently revived. The violence that has caused almost 500,000 murders in America since 1975 has also helped to reinforce support.

Whether despite or because of declining violent crime rates, support for the death penalty, according to several polls, also increased over the 1990s. According to a CNN/Gallup/*USA Today* poll in February 1999, 64 per cent of Americans felt that the penalty was not imposed enough (25 per cent felt 'too often', 4 per cent 'about right' and 7 per cent had no opinion). As a tactical matter, death penalty supporters can therefore concede that were it to be considered to constitute cruel and unusual punishment, capital punishment would violate the Eighth Amendment. But they can do so knowing full well that the public does not currently believe this and, for the judges so to rule, they would again be flying directly and dramatically in the face of public opinion.

America is not alone here. As Jonathan Freedland (1998) has observed, Americans and Britons share a belief in capital punishment, a 1996 MORI poll putting British support at 76 per cent. Freedland's conclusion was straightforward, but disturbing for some in the UK:

opponents of judicial killing have hardly won the argument among the British people. Instead our political system has simply failed to express the popular will . . . what is often a cause for self-congratulation – with progressive Britons imagining ours to be a more civilized society than the US – should perhaps be a trigger for self-doubt. American democracy ensures that the public get their way, even if the result is not always pleasant. The British system cannot say the same. (Freedland, 1998: 31–2)

However, American support for capital punishment is not as monolithic as such accounts suggest. An ABC poll in January 2000 put support for capital punishment at 64 per cent, down from 77 per cent in 1996. A Gallup poll in early 2000 also found that support had declined to its lowest level in 19 years, falling 14 percentage points since 1994 to 66 per cent. Moreover, several studies show clearly that public support for the penalty declines significantly when alternative measures such as life imprisonment without parole are mentioned. As Table 5.12 notes, support for capital punishment is much higher among Republicans and Independents than Democrats, with majorities of the former two groups still supporting the death penalty even when life imprisonment is offered as an alternative. Similarly, although support declines when life in prison is offered to men and to whites, majorities of both still support death. Majority support among Democrats and women declines substantially when life imprisonment is offered as an alternative. The only group consistently opposed to capital punishment is blacks.

These qualifying factors have yet to register in changes to the regulatory regime but opposition has been politically significant. Until the 1970s, opposition to executing a capital prisoner assumed one of two forms: (i) using the appellate courts to challenge the procedures whereby the defendant was tried and sentenced, and (ii) pleading for a commutation of the death sentence at a clemency hearing. Not until the mid-1960s was any serious attempt made to challenge the penalty's constitutionality, when the Legal

TABLE 5.12 The demographics of support and opposition to capital punishment, 2000*

	Favour	Oppose	Death penalty	Life in prison
Republicans	73	19	57	35
Independents	73	21	53	39
Democrats	52	38	37	53
Men	73	22	57	35
Women	56	32	39	50
Whites	69	22	51	39
Blacks	38	54	26	67

* Figures show responses to questions on support for capital punishment, and then for support if life imprisonment is offered as an alternative to the death penalty.

N = 1,006, 3-point error margin.

Source: ABCNews.com survey, January 12–16, 2000.

Defense Fund of the National Association for the Advancement of Colored People (NAACP) mounted a bold campaign that was temporarily effective in achieving a moratorium on executions from 1967 to 1977.

THE SUPREME COURT STRIKES DOWN THE DEATH PENALTY: *FURMAN V. GEORGIA*

The abolitionist campaign reached a climax in June 1972 with the Supreme Court's ruling in *Furman v. Georgia*. The Court's ruling held that the death penalty as then administered was unconstitutional, primarily because existing laws gave judges and juries excessive discretion. Sentencing authorities did not know what factors should or should not be considered in deciding between a death or life sentence, and the Court concluded that without such guidance arbitrary and/or discriminatory sentencing results were inevitable. This decision required state courts across the nation to re-sentence more than 600 prisoners then awaiting execution. America experienced for the first (and only) time the constitutional abolition of the death penalty as then administered.

Five of the justices in *Furman* concluded

that the death penalty, as it existed at the time, was 'cruel and unusual' punishment. Only two (Brennan and Marshall), however, ruled it so by definition, regardless of the crime for which it was imposed. Brennan identified four principles that marked a punishment as 'cruel and unusual':

- Unusual severity, to the point of degrading the dignity of human beings.
- Arbitrary imposition.
- Rejection by contemporary American society.
- Excessiveness, in the sense of inflicting unnecessary suffering.

Any punishment that 'seriously implicated' each of the principles would, under this 'cumulative' test, be unconstitutional, even if it did not violate any of the principles standing alone.

Marshall was more direct: first, the death penalty was an excessive punishment, since it served no legitimate penological purpose. Retribution did not suffice as a moral justification, and empirical studies had failed to prove the deterrent value compared to life imprisonment. Secondly, public support was based on ignorance of the arguments against capital punishment, its discriminatory application, execution of innocents and negative effects on the criminal justice system.

Three of the remaining seven justices voted against the death penalty, without addressing the argument that the punishment was, in the abstract, cruel and unusual. Instead, each concluded that there was something wrong in the way the penalty was administered. William Douglas contended that racial and class discrimination plagued the death penalty's administration. Potter Stewart saw arbitrariness, not discrimination, as the problem: 'These death sentences are cruel and unusual in the same way that being struck by lightning is cruel and unusual.' Byron White concluded that the penalty was being imposed so rarely by the states that it could not possibly serve a useful purpose: the problem was its infrequent use.

Reaction to the decision was deeply hostile. The legal scholar Raoul Berger aptly characterized it when he wrote that:

> Justice Brennan recently acknowledged that his 'is an interpretation to which a majority of my fellow Justices – not to mention, it would seem, a majority of my fellow countrymen – does not subscribe. On this issue, the death penalty, I hope to embody a community striving for human dignity for all, though perhaps not yet arrived.' Baldly stated, he stubbornly insists on cramming his morals down the throats of a people who do not share his views. (Hickok, 1991: 304)

In dissent, the four remaining justices argued that:

- Federal courts should be loath to strike down legislatively authorized punishments as 'cruel and unusual'; since elected state legislatures and not life-tenured federal courts are the barometers of public opinion.
- The punishment of death was common in 1791, hence the Framers must have believed capital punishment not to be cruel and unusual.
- The fact that a majority of state legislatures, along with the federal government, authorized the death penalty was a reliable indicator of society's moral judgement about capital punishment.

- Opinion polls showed broad support for capital punishment. The fact that juries rarely imposed the death penalty was evidence not of societal rejection of the punishment but of the care and caution that juries properly brought to capital punishment cases.
- The efficacy of the death penalty, its actual deterrent value, is irrelevant under the Eighth Amendment.
- Even if its efficacy was relevant and it proved an ineffective deterrent, the death penalty serves an appropriate retributive purpose.
- The actual evidence about deterrence was equivocal, suggesting that the Court should best defer to the legislative judgments.

Despite their dissent, such was the nature of the majority holding that one of the dissenters, Chief Justice Warren Burger, predicted that: 'There will never be another execution in this country.' But Burger was decidedly premature.

THE SUPREME COURT CHANGES ITS MIND: *GREGG V. GEORGIA* AND AFTER

The progressive campaign to abolish the death penalty nationally and permanently by federal constitutional interpretation and court decree ultimately failed to achieve its main goal. Much as happened in reaction to *Roe*, the legislative backlash to *Furman* by traditionalist forces was ferocious, widespread and effective. States whose laws had been invalidated passed new legislation to repair the flaws identified by the Court in *Furman*. Fifteen states introduced mandatory death sentences for specified crimes. Another 20 passed new statutes providing for various degrees of guidance for juries who retained discretion in imposing capital sentences.

Even California moved against abolitionism. Prior to *Furman*, the state's Supreme Court had ruled that the death penalty violated the California Constitution's ban on 'cruel or unusual punishments'. But the necessary signatures were collected to force a referendum on a constitutional amendment to reinstate the penalty and in November 1976, the California electorate overwhelmingly approved Proposition 17 and capital punishment was reinstated the following year. Such actions dramatically exposed the fallacy that American society considered the penalty to be cruel and unusual.

Faced by such strong public reactions that yielded 35 new state laws in only four years, the Court reversed its position. Four years after it had declared death penalty statutes unconstitutional, in *Gregg v. Georgia* and allied cases from Texas and Florida, the Court declared in 1976 that the penalty was not always unconstitutional. Still focused on the issue of arbitrariness, the Court approved new laws that separated capital trials into two parts: one in which guilt or innocence was determined, and a second in which the sentence was decided after consideration of mitigating and/or aggravating factors.

The *Gregg* decision effectively sustained the constitutionality of capital punishment. From 1976 to 1994, over 4,800 people were sentenced to death by judges and juries under the newly approved procedures, although only a tiny fraction of that total (245) was executed. As Exhibit 5.3 documents, subsequent cases saw a gradual court-ordered refinement of the capital punishment regime, as the Supreme Court declared unconstitutional mandatory death sentences (*Woodson v. North Carolina*, 1976) and the death penalty for rape (*Coker v. Georgia*, 1977), while deciding that a racially disproportionate death penalty system is not unconstitutional (*McCleskey v. Kemp*, 1987). Such has been the federal judicial acceptance of capital punishment that the Court has ruled that states can execute juveniles and the mentally handicapped, those abetting a crime and, in dramatically curtailing *habeas corpus*, that the Constitution did not guarantee a full hearing of new evidence that was unavailable at the original trial of a condemned inmate.

One prominent death penalty opponent remarked that the fact that 'the Supreme Court has so far failed to reverse its ruling in *Gregg*, or to hold the states on a short tether where the death penalty is concerned, tells us more about the ideology and politics of the majority of the Court since 1975 than it does about the constitutionality of the death penalty' (Bedau, 1997: 459). But much the same observation could be made of almost any other rulings by the federal courts on moral issues, regardless of whether the outcomes pleased traditionalists or progressives. To suggest that judicial interpretations are shaped by political considerations as well as legal ones is neither surprising nor novel, much less an indictment of their lack of 'objectivity'. Nevertheless, it is clear that the Court's dramatic tilt of the capital punishment regime against convicted criminals has reflected the punitive politics surrounding the death penalty as much as a search for the Founding Fathers' original intent.

TRADITIONALISTS V. PROGRESSIVES

As Exhibit 5.4 illustrates, the arguments for and against capital punishment are complex and involve many competing claims, but they also encapsulate the division between traditionalist and progressive thinking on cultural values. Traditionalists draw heavily on moral theorizing. On this view, some acts are so morally offensive, degrading to human dignity and heinous that the only appropriate punishment is death. Over the course of American history, the range of such acts has generally been limited to forms of murder, but it is not exclusively limited to these (at either state or federal level).

Such an approach is one that can easily resonate with many citizens who might otherwise be sceptical. For example, the Court's ruling in 1977 that death sentences for rapists were unconstitutional was a decision that remains, in principle, contestable, given the graphic horror of many rapes. For example, according to official government

Exhibit 5.3 Key Supreme Court rulings on capital punishment, 1972–2002

Furman v. Georgia (1972). 5–4. Struck down the death penalty under the 'cruel and unusual punishment' clause of the Eighth Amendment. Three justices found jury discretion produced a random pattern among those receiving the penalty and this randomness was cruel and unusual. Two justices found capital punishment a *per se* violation of the Constitution, degrading to human dignity, arbitrarily severe, unnecessary and offensive to contemporary values. The dissenters argued that courts should not challenge legislative judgements about the desirability and effectiveness of punishments. The decision halted all executions in the then 39 states that sanctioned capital punishment.

Gregg v. Georgia (1976). 7–2. Reaffirmed constitutionality of death penalty. Upheld statutes that guide judge and jury when imposing capital punishment. Rejected claims that the death penalty was unconstitutional by definition.

Woodson v. North Carolina (1976). 5–4. Outlawed mandatory death penalty as unconstitutional. Stated that evolving standards of decency required that death penalty statutes treat the convicted as individuals, not as part of a faceless and inhuman mass. Most states after *Furman* reinstated the death penalty without automatic sentences.

Roberts v. Louisiana (1976). 5–4. Struck down a mandatory death sentence law for murderers of police officers in the line of duty because it did not allow for individualized sentencing.

Coker v. Georgia (1977). 7–2. Held that the Eighth Amendment's 'cruel and unusual punishment' clause prohibited punishments that are disproportionate to the crime. Such penalties are a purposeless and needless imposition of pain and suffering. Death penalty provisions were emphasized as needing to be proportional only to the crime of first-degree murder. Imposing the death penalty for rape was hence unconstitutional.

Booth v. Maryland (1987). 5–4. Prohibited 'Victim Impact Statements' (where the emotional consequences of the crime on the victim's family are detailed) from being introduced in the penalty phase of capital murder trials.

McClesky v. Kemp (1987). 5–4. Upheld Georgia's death penalty law, despite a statistical study showing that Georgia defendants convicted of killing whites were 11 times as likely to be sentenced to death as were those who kill blacks. The discrepancy was even greater when the killer was black and the victim white. Writing for the majority, Justice Lewis Powell held that the study 'at most indicates a discrepancy that appears to correlate with race'. Held that to prevail under the Equal Protection Clause of the Fourteenth Amendment, McClesky needed to prove discriminatory purpose on the part of the Georgia legislature or the decision-makers in his case. Also held that disparities in the treatment of homicide cases did not offend 'evolving standards of decency' under the 'cruel and unusual punishment' clause of the Eighth Amendment.

Tison v. Arizona (1987). 5–4. Court ruled that the Constitution does not restrict the death penalty to 'trigger men' but permits the execution of accomplices who took a major role in the crime that led to a killing and displayed a reckless disregard for the lives of the victims.

Thompson v. Oklahoma (1988). 5–3. Executions of offenders aged 15 and younger at the time of their crimes was held as unconstitutional.

Penry v. Lynaugh (1989). 5–4. The Eighth Amendment does not preclude the execution of mentally retarded persons who have been convicted of murder.

Exhibit 5.3   Key Supreme Court rulings on capital punishment *continued*

Stanford v. Kennedy (1989). 5–4. The Eighth Amendment does not prohibit the execution of juvenile murderers as young as aged 16 (that is, that they were over 15 years of age at the time of their crimes).

McCleskey v. Zant (1991). 6–3. The Court redefined the 'abuse of writ' doctrine, thereby limiting the number of writs of *habeas corpus* appeals death row inmates can make.

Payne v. Tennessee (1991). 6–3. Overturned *Booth v. Maryland* to allow the use of Victim Impact Statements as evidence in sentencing trials.

Herrera v. Collins (1993). 6–3. The Constitution did not guarantee the right to a full hearing of new evidence of a condemned inmate's innocence that had not been available at the time of the original trial.

Harris v. Alabama (1995). 8–1. The Court held that where a state allows for a jury's sentencing recommendation in a capital case, such a decision was not binding on the judge in his final disposition as to sentence.

Felker v. Turpin (1996). 9–0. The Supreme Court unanimously upheld provisions of the Anti-Terrorism and Effective Death Penalty Act of 1996, which imposed tight time limits on appeals and restrictions on federal courts' review of death sentences among other things.

Atkins v. Virginia (2002). 6–3. The Court ruled that the execution of the mentally retarded is unconstitutional, violating the ban on 'cruel and unusual' punishment.

Ring v. Arizona (2002). 7–2. Ended the practice of allowing a judge, rather than a jury, to decide whether 'aggravating' factors in crimes (such as extreme brutality) call for capital punishment.

Exhibit 5.4   Capital punishment: philosophical and religious views

- *Retributive arguments.* Employing the basic notion of 'an eye for an eye', on this view the murderer must be given the punishment he or she deserves. This has a value independent of any contribution to reducing the crime rate or expressing some sense of community denunciation or outrage against the criminal act.
- *Deterrent arguments.* Statistical and intuitive ('best-bet') arguments. Most empirical studies suggest that capital punishment does not deter the crimes that it is intended to punish. If statistics cannot prove a decisive effect or a genuine causation between capital punishment and reductions in crime, it may be that a gamble has to be taken.
- *Utilitarian arguments.* A 'cost–benefit' calculation is necessary to weigh the pros and cons of the death penalty. It may be that the psychological gratification and security of enforcing capital punishment outweigh the limited deterrent effects, the moral dilemma of state murder, and the concerns over miscarriages of justice.

figures, in 1994, 102,100 forcible rapes occurred and 12,907 were attempted, a rate of 92 per 100,000 females over 12 years old (*Statistical Abstract of the United States*, 1996: 205). Substantial sections of the American public clearly believe that rape is such a repugnant crime that the death penalty should be available to juries and judges to impose on convicted rapists, even if no murder is involved. Indeed, Justices Burger and Rehnquist, in their dissenting opinion in *Coker v. Georgia* (1977), observed that three states had recently re-enacted the death penalty for rape, turning the anti-death penalty 'evolving standards of decency' argument around by asking: '[I]f the Court is to rely on some "public opinion" process, does this not suggest the beginning of a "trend"?' (Progressive opponents of mandatory sentences claimed that they could encourage rapists to murder if conviction for rape alone would lead to a capital sentence – an interesting reversal of the deterrent thesis but one that seemingly concedes that laws on capital punishment can or do have an effect on criminal behaviour.)

Imposing the death penalty is, for many Americans, a measure that is justified by reference exclusively to retributive justice, as an expression of understandable community outrage, even if its deterrent effects are minimal and alternative methods of punishment exist that more or less guarantee that the offender will not threaten the community once more. As William Bradford Reynolds, a leading official in the Reagan administration, remarked: 'Some crimes deserve death, and nothing else will quench our righteous anger, or vindicate our humanity, or inspire sufficiently profound respect or reverential fear of the law and the underlying moral order. Serving justice at times demands imposing the ultimate sanction' (Hickok, 1991: 330).

Progressives tend, by contrast, to advance a case more on the basis of empirical data. Again, like the prohibitionist position on gun control, absolutist positions regarding capital punishment are a relatively recent, post-1960s development. Until that time, the only politically viable question for reformers was the constitutionality of particular mechanisms by which the penalty was implemented. The principle of the state taking life was not widely questioned. Since then, however, both the principle and the methods of its implementation have been doubted. In a dramatic admission in June 1994, the outgoing

Supreme Court justice Harry Blackmun, who had dissented against the abolitionist *Furman* ruling, stated that the courts had failed to develop adequate protections to ensure that the death penalty was applied fairly and accurately: 'I feel morally and intellectually obligated simply to concede that the death penalty experiment has failed.'

Eighth Amendment objections, given that the notion of the death penalty as such being unconstitutional as cruel and unusual is effectively defunct, focus on three areas:

- *Particular methods of punishment.* The Court upheld the constitutionality of death by shooting in 1879 and by electrocution in 1890. In 1985, the Court declined to review a challenge to the constitutionality of electrocution (thereby confirming its acceptability), but eventually took up a review of the method in the 1999–2000 term in relation to Florida's 'Old Sparky' (see Exhibit 5.5).
- *Guaranteeing proportional punishments.* Authorizing the death penalty for an overtime parking violation, for example, would seem disproportionate to the offence.
- *Guaranteeing procedural rights.* On this view, the cruel and unusual punishment clause is, in effect, a 'super due process' clause. If consistency in application is not achieved, the punishment constitutes a cruel and unusual penalty.

Much of the progressive opposition to the penalty is concerned less by the sheer volume of executions than a number of disturbing inconsistencies in the enforcement of the sentence. Underlying opposition to capital punishment currently are seven arguments.

- *The deterrent effect is minimal.* Only a small proportion of those convicted of homicide receive the death sentence and, of those, only a small proportion is executed. More than 20,000 criminal homicides occurred per year in America from 1975 to 1985, but the annual rate of twenty to thirty executions per year represented less than

Exhibit 5.5   Electrocuting killers: cruel, unusual and constitutional?

The Supreme Court had resisted reviewing the constitutionality of electrocution since New York became the first state to approve its use, in 1890. Since reinstating the death penalty in 1976, 144 prisoners had died on electric chairs by the year 2000. Electrocution had initially been introduced as a more humane method of execution than hanging, but by 2000 only four states required electrocution as the sole means of implementing a capital sentence and the method had proven unreliable. In 1983, for example, Alabama's electric chair, 'Yellow Mama', took 14 minutes to electrocute a condemned inmate. In Florida, public concern grew over the chair when in 1990 and 1997 flames leapt from the headpiece worn by prisoners during electrocution. 'Old Sparky' was put out of commission in 1997/98, but the new replacement chair also saw blood flow from Allen Lee Davis's nose during his electrocution in March 1999. (Witnesses also raised the possibility that a strap was suffocating him.) In September 1999, the Florida State Supreme Court held in a 4–3 vote that the use of the chair was legal and neither cruel nor unusual under the Eighth Amendment to the US Constitution. The case was appealed to the US Supreme Court. Florida's Republican Governor, Jeb Bush, sensitively expressed the hope in a news conference that 'the Supreme Court will see this exactly like the trial court and the Florida Supreme Court saw it: an argument over the nose bleed of a criminal who savagely murdered a pregnant women and her two daughters in 1983.' In early 2000, Florida and Georgia altered their laws to allow lethal injection as an alternative punishment, thereby rendering the litigation on the chair moot, and Alabama and Nebraska as the only states employing electrocution as the sole method of death.

0.2 per cent of the homicide rate. Moreover, states without the penalty experience no higher crime rates than those retaining it. (Traditionalists reply that, like gun control, we simply do not know how many individuals have been deterred from committing crimes since they are hardly likely to report this.)

- *Alternative punishments are available that guarantee protection for society from criminals.* The most obvious alternative punishment to the death penalty is life imprisonment. Providing that this is enforced, the prevention of criminals re-offending is maintained for society but the possible problems associated with the death penalty are avoided. (Supporters of capital punishment note, however, that in many states a future governor can commute a life sentence of a prisoner.)

- *The death penalty is arbitrarily handed out and enforced.* The death penalty is 'the privilege of the poor'. At least 90 per cent of death row inmates cannot afford their own attorney. Fewer than half have completed high school. The American Bar Association estimates that any death penalty case requires around 1,000 hours of legal preparation, with most lawyers demanding a minimum $50,000 fee upfront. Those able to afford this are unlikely to face an executioner. As Justice William Douglas remarked in his concurring opinion in *Furman*, 'One searches our chronicles in vain for the execution of any murder of the affluent strata of our society. The Leopolds and Loebs are given prison terms, not sentenced to death.' On this view, the death penalty is inflicted not on those who have committed the worst crimes but on those with the worst lawyers. Only those without capital receive capital punishment.

Many examples exist that support this case. In Georgia, for example, a death row convict with an IQ of less than 80 was sent through the appeals process with no lawyer at all in 1996, while in Texas a man was executed even though his lawyer's entire closing argument at sentencing was: 'You are an extremely intelligent jury. You've got that man's life in your hands. You can take it or not. That's all I have to say.' In one case, unconstitutionally composed juries in Georgia sentenced two co-defendants, a man and a woman, to death. Her lawyers challenged the jury composition; his were unaware they could do so. She got a retrial and a life sentence; he was executed in 1976.

Another case was that of Calvin Burdine, who was an openly gay man sentenced to death in Texas after being represented at trial by a lawyer called Joe Cannon. Cannon, who at an earlier court hearing had referred to gays as 'queers' and 'fairies' did not object to a statement by the prosecutor that 'sending a homosexual to the penitentiary certainly isn't a very bad punishment for a homosexual'. He also failed to exercise his right to remove three prospective jurors during jury selection who openly admitted to being prejudiced against homosexuals. Cannon did not interview a single witness in preparing Burdine's defence and fell asleep repeatedly during the trial. On appeal, the Texas Court of Criminal Appeals ruled that this had not been proven to have prejudiced the outcome.

- *The measure is racially discriminatory in effect, if not intent.* Approximately 42 per cent of death row inmates are black, although blacks make up only 12 per cent of the total population. Of the 98 inmates executed in 1999, although 61 were white, 33 were black, two were native Americans and two were Asians. In Virginia, between 1908 and 1962, all those executed for rape were black, although only 55 per cent of those imprisoned for rape were black. The race of the murder victim appears to play a large role in who is sentenced to death. Blacks and whites are victims of murder in almost equal numbers, yet 82 per cent of prisoners executed since 1977 were convicted of the murder of a white person. In

Kentucky, for example, every death sentence to March 1996 was for the murder of a white victim, despite over 1,000 homicide victims in the state being black. A recent study in Philadelphia also found that the likelihood of receiving a death sentence is nearly four times higher if the defendant is black, after taking account of aggravating factors. In early 1998, of the 26 people under federal sentence of death (military and civilian), only five were white. The US General Accounting Office found that the chances of a black defendant being executed rose further when a white victim was involved.

Despite this, the Court has not concurred in the death penalty's unconstitutionality. The majority opinion in *McClesky* stated that the unique nature of the capital punishment process, in which juries must consider a wide range of factors about both the crime and the defendant, made statistical evidence less compelling than in other cases where it had been accepted as proof of intent to discriminate. The minority, however, disagreed, holding that the study 'reveals that the risk that race influenced McClesky's sentence is intolerable by any imaginable standard'. At the very least, as Table 5.13 shows, the study used in the case proves demonstrably the higher chances of being sentenced to death for murdering whites.

The race of victim numbers show a continuing trend since the death penalty was reinstated of a predominance of white victim cases. Despite the fact that nationally whites and blacks are victims of murder in approximately equal numbers, 83 per cent of the victims in cases resulting in executions overall, and 76 per cent in 2000, have been white (see Table 5.14). Since this disparity is confirmed in studies that control for similar crimes by defendants with similar backgrounds, it implies that white victims are considered more valuable in the criminal justice system. The problems of race were reinforced in a

TABLE 5.13 Killer–victim racial combinations and death sentences in Georgia, 1973–79

Race of killer/victim	Number with death sentence	Percentage
Black/white	50 of 233	22
White/white	58 of 748	8
Black/black	18 of 1,443	1
White/black	2 of 60	3

Source: Haines (1996: 77).

study by the Department of Justice. Released in September 2000, the study found that 80 per cent of cases submitted for federal death penalty prosecution involved minority defendants and that 80 per cent of the resultant federal death row was also made up of minority defendants. In addition, the study highlighted the fact that a few regions of the country were responsible for a disproportionately high number of federal cases, while other major areas produced none.

For most critics, the main reason for this disparity is easily accounted for: the overwhelming majority of district attorneys and other officials who make decisions as to whether to seek the death penalty are white. In 1998, of the 1,838 such officials in states with the death penalty, only 22 were black and 22 were Latino. In Georgia, six of the 12 black prisoners executed between 1983 and 1999 were convicted and sentenced by all-white juries after black nominees had been removed.

Although a 1986 Supreme Court ruling held that jurors could only be removed for 'race neutral' reasons (*Batson v. Kentucky*), bias has not been eliminated. Both prosecutors and defending attorneys go to extraordinary lengths – even visiting the neighbourhoods of the pool of potential jurors – to make calculated judgements as to whom to try to retain and eliminate from juries at jury selection.

- *Wrongful execution.* The issue of taking innocent life goes to the heart of a liberal government's legitimacy. It is impossible to know how many, if any, innocent lives have been taken since each case must be examined on a case-by-case basis. A 1987 research paper by Bedau and Radelet, examining the testimony and trial evidence, identified what they claimed were 23 wrongful executions that had occurred since 1905. However, two officials in the Reagan administration's Justice Department, after examining a dozen of the same cases, concluded that each defendant was

TABLE 5.14 Racial breakdown of the 85 executions in 2000

Defendants			Victims in the underlying murders		
White	43	(51%)	White	87	(76%)
Black	34	(40%)	Black	21	(18%)
Latino	6	(7%)	Latino	2	(2%)
Native American	2	(2%)	Other	4	(3%)

in fact guilty. The House of Representatives Subcommittee on Civil and Constitutional Rights confirmed that 45 inmates had been released between 1976 and 1993, after their convictions had been found to be mistaken. According to the anti-capital punishment Death Penalty Information Center in Washington, DC, over the past 25 years, some 75 people have been released from death row and cleared of capital charges, out of some 6,000 who have been sentenced to die – about 1 per cent of capital convictions turned out to be wrong. Supporters of the death penalty argue that this merely proves that the process works, with mistakes corrected in time. Notwithstanding the psychological ordeal of being condemned to death and enduring years on death row, however, others are less sanguine about mistakes that were never caught.

- *Delays.* Even for those relatively few death row inmates who eventually suffer judicial killings, the amount of time between sentencing and execution is, many would argue, intolerably lengthy. In 1933, Giuseppe Zangara shot at President Franklin D. Roosevelt as he rode down a Miami street in an open car; a bullet hit Roosevelt's motoring companion, Chicago mayor Anton Cermak, and wounded him fatally. Twenty-two days after the shooting, Zangara confessed; 11 days after the confession, Florida's executioners put him to death in the electric chair. The contemporary process is no longer as speedy or streamlined. It is not unusual for a prisoner to have to wait six years or more between the sentence being handed down and its implementation.

The average wait between condemnation and execution is currently seven years and ten months. Retrials, writs of *habeas corpus*, appeals, stays and other lengthy and involved legal processes can sometimes delay a convict's execution for a dozen years and more. Although, as noted above, California reinstated its death penalty statute in 1977, the state only carried out its first execution in 1992 under the new law. In 1999, over 550 men and a few women were on California's death row.

- *Cost.* One by-product of extended legal processes is expense. A 1993 Duke University study of North Carolina murder cases found that it cost approximately twice as much to try, convict, sentence to death, and execute a killer as it did to secure a first-degree murder conviction with a sentence of 20 years to life in prison. Philip Cook and Donna Slawson determined that it cost the state $329,000 more for each case to secure the death penalty. Even after subtracting projected prison costs, they found, the net additional charge exceeded $160,000. The actual cost for each North Carolina execution amounted to $2.1 million. As they remarked:

> Common sense says that it's cheaper to supply a few jolts of electricity than to shell out the equivalent of tuition at Harvard for incarceration for the next twenty years. But when all the costs are weighed, just the opposite is true. The death penalty is more expensive because of the constitutional protections embodied in the judicial determination that death as a punishment is different. Lawyers are more expensive than prison guards (quoted in Verhovek, 1995b).

In a nation whose citizens are supposedly sensitive to paying taxes, opposed to wasteful government programmes, and keen on value for money, this might be an additional factor in evaluating the desirability of capital punishment. But for traditionalists and progressives, the death penalty is primarily a moral issue. It is either wrong for the 'killing state' to put people to death or right for those convicted of a first-degree crime to pay for it with their own lives.

These arguments amount to a powerful and internationally embarrassing indictment of America's capital punishment system for progressives. In July 1996, the Geneva-based International Commission of Jurists released a report, authored by four judges and lawyers from India, Sweden, Nigeria and Australia, that concluded that the death penalty in America was 'arbitrary, and racially discriminatory, and prospects of a fair hearing for capital offenders cannot . . . be assured'. But, as McKeever remarked: 'Rational or not, the evidence could not be clearer that at the present time, the arbitrary and discriminatory imposition of the death penalty has done nothing to convince Americans that it violates standards of decency' (McKeever, 1993: 72). The way that politicians have exploited the death penalty is one major reason for this.

POLITICIZING THE DEATH PENALTY: THE TRADITIONALIST TRIUMPH

Given the widespread popularity of the death penalty among Americans, it might be objected that this issue does not actually form part of the contemporary culture war. But this would be to miss the remarkable extent to which the penalty has become politicized since 1972.

Curiously, the interest group universe displays a remarkably lopsided weighting towards the anti-death penalty position. Partly, this is a function of the strong public support for existing death penalty laws. In contrast to gun control, traditionalists tend no longer to fear the government emasculating death penalty laws since *Furman* was reversed. The incentive to organize is greater for those progressives seeking to overturn established public policy rather than to sustain it. Supporters of the death penalty experienced the most severe threat to their position in 1972. The overwhelmingly negative public response to the court's intervention was such that few could envisage capital punishment coming under renewed threat from the unelected judiciary. Any abolitionist assault on capital punishment would now

have once again to occur, as opponents of judicial activism argued it should, in the legislative arena.

But the death penalty has acquired a profound symbolic political significance for elected officials, making it highly unlikely that elected branches of government would attempt to curtail capital punishment. Indeed, it is difficult to identify another cultural issue on which presidents, members of Congress, governors, attorneys general, mayors and state legislative officials almost all take up such clear and unequivocal traditionalist positions. Much as abortion, pornography and gay rights became associated with notions of a 'permissive culture' having taken hold in the later 1960s, so the death penalty formed a crucial symbolic role in public policy debates on crime and 'law and order'. Support signalled an unequivocally 'tough' stance on crime, siding with the police and law enforcement agencies against criminals; opposition signified being 'soft' on crime and criminals. When one considers the complexity of the issue of how to combat criminal activity, it is perhaps surprising that the death penalty should assume such significance. Yet evidence suggests powerfully that a politician's stance on this issue shapes the broader public perception of his or her general approach to issues concerning crime.

Many politicians therefore take the competition over who is toughest on criminals to extraordinary lengths. For example, in 1990, Mark White, candidate for governor in Texas, aired a deliberately unsubtle television advertisement featuring him walking past portraits of inmates he had sent to death while serving a previous term as the state's governor. Al Checchi, a prospective Democratic candidate for governor in California, launched his campaign in late 1997 with a promise that, if elected, he would extend the use of the death penalty to include repeat child molesters and serial rapists who, he said, 'kill the spirit of a woman or a child'. Pete Wilson, the incumbent governor and a Republican, had previously advocated the execution of children as young as 14. Both misled the public, since neither proposal was constitutionally permissible: the Supreme Court had already ruled such measures unconstitutional.

Partly as a result of this 'tough' environment, once elected to office, American governors are also increasingly reluctant to commute sentences. Capital clemency, once quite common, is effectively a political death sentence for governors. According to the Death Penalty Information Center, clemency in the 1990s was only granted in about one case a year.

In addition, politicians are often publicly critical of the time taken to complete the capital appeals process. In 1997, for example, three months before the 'off-year' elections, the relatively moderate Republican Christine Todd Whitman, then governor of New Jersey, publicly demanded to know why none of the state's 14 death row inmates had been executed. Her political opponent criticized her for waiting over three years before taking action, claiming that he 'would take action on the death penalty from the first year' in office.

Not only governors suffer the focus on capital punishment. At the local level, the district attorney of the county where the crime occurs decides whether or not a particular murder should be prosecuted as a capital offence. This discretionary power may frequently be influenced by political pressures or personal preference and can cause arbitrary administration. For example, more than half of Pennsylvania's death sentences have been handed down in Philadelphia County, an area that contains only 14 per cent of the state's total population. Just one of the 79 counties in Texas accounts for almost one-third of the state's death row prisoners: 132 of the state's 437 condemned prisoners were sentenced in Harris County (a sprawling region of more than 100 square miles that takes in the city of Houston), as of January 1998, whose execution rate ranked ahead of entire American states such as Florida and Mississippi.

In most states whose laws provide for the death penalty, district attorneys as well as some judges are elected officials, some on party political lines. Hence, both those who prosecute and adjudicate in capital trials may be vulnerable to political or electoral pressures. In late 1994, for example, the District Attorney of Oklahoma City campaigned for re-election on his record of having 'sent 44 murderers to Death Row'. The 'Texas Terminator', the Chief Prosecutor for Harris County, John Holmes, Jr., was elected four times as the Republican candidate for prosecutor and went unopposed in 1996. His view of the death penalty was clear: 'There's nothing worse than having a law and not enforcing it. That promotes disrespect for the law' (Langton, 1999: 29).

Presidential politics

Presidents Nixon, Reagan, George H.W. Bush, Clinton and George W. Bush all used the death penalty symbolically to demonstrate their hard-line credentials on law and order. For the Republicans, capital punishment provided a convenient issue on which to label Democrats as 'soft' on criminal justice since 1968. Woodward and Armstrong described capital punishment as a 'hot' political issue in the 1972 presidential campaign, occurring in the aftermath of the *Furman* decision: 'Nixon had made the death penalty a foot soldier in his war on crime (Woodward and Armstrong, 1979: 207). Its actual effect on the election was unclear, but Reagan certainly employed the death penalty in 1980 to help embellish the image of Carter as a president who had reneged on his 1976 election image as a cultural conservative. Most notable of all, George H.W. Bush relentlessly exploited Michael Dukakis's opposition to capital punishment in the 1988 election (see Exhibit 5.6). The first question put to Dukakis during one of the televised presidential debates asked him how he would feel about the death penalty if his wife Kitty were brutally raped and murdered. Dukakis's coolly dispassionate answer made him sound overly detached and intellectual on the issue, which Bush

Exhibit 5.6   Willie Horton and the death penalty

In 1988, a commercial sponsored by *Americans for Bush*, a group nominally independent of the official Republican campaign, ran nationwide. In 30 seconds, voters saw and heard the following:

Side-by-side photographs of Bush and Dukakis appear on the screen. An unseen announcer says, 'Bush and Dukakis on crime'.

Switch to a picture of Bush. 'Bush supports the death penalty for first-degree murders.'

Switch to a photo of Dukakis. 'Dukakis not only opposes the death penalty, he allowed first-degree murderers to have weekend passes from prison.'

Switch to a menacing mug shot of an African American man, Willie Horton. 'One was Willie Horton, who murdered a boy in a robbery, stabbing him 19 times.'

Switch to another photo of Horton, with a wild Afro and raggedy beard, dressed in army fatigues, and towering over a white police officer, who is evidently placing him under arrest. 'Despite a life sentence, Horton received 10 weekend passes from prison. Horton fled, kidnapped a young couple, stabbing the man and repeatedly raping his girlfriend.' The words 'kidnapping', 'stabbing', and 'raping' flash on the screen.

Finally is a photo of Dukakis. 'Weekend prison passes. Dukakis on crime.'

proceeded to exploit for the remainder of the campaign (on leaving the debate, Dukakis, recognizing his error of judgement, confessed to aides 'I blew it').

For some critics, 1988 suggested once more that the voice of reason was well represented in the Democratic Party while that of reaction surfaced vividly among Republicans. But successive Republican onslaughts taught Bill Clinton an unmistakable lesson about death penalty politics. Clinton notoriously travelled back to his home state of Arkansas in April 1992, interrupting his primary campaign, in order publicly to refuse to exercise his prerogative as governor and commute the sentence of Ricky Ray Rector, a mentally retarded black death row inmate. Rector's comprehension of his imminent execution was so limited that, on the night of his execution, he put the dessert of his final meal on one side to 'save it for later'. One of the general election campaign advertisements for the Democratic presidential ticket declared that Clinton and Gore were 'a new generation of Democrats' who 'sent a strong signal to criminals, by supporting the death penalty', actions calculated deliberately to demonstrate being 'tough' on crime. Clinton's enthusiasm, along with the conversion of

previous opponents of the death penalty (such as Atlanta's former black mayor Andrew Young, when he ran for governor of Georgia in 1990), suggest powerfully that the populist clamour for retention of capital punishment strongly pressures members of both main political parties. It was not coincidental, in this regard, that an act of presidential clemency, when Clinton granted a six-month reprieve to convicted murderer Juan Raul Garza, who was due to become the first federal inmate executed in 37 years, only arrived on December 7, in the penultimate month of his two-term presidency.

Congress

Although much of the pro- and anti-capital punishment attention focused on the individual states after 1972, the 1990s witnessed a new willingness of the federal government to broaden the scope of the death penalty. Such actions accorded with the perceived sense of a popular fear of crime (especially violent crime) and the need to tighten up 'Fortress America'. Congress has rarely been unwilling to intervene strongly on death penalty issues.

Members of both the pro- and anti-death penalty lobbies have sought to change existing laws.

During the first Clinton administration, for example, a coalition of members of the Congressional Black Caucus (CBC) and other white liberal Democrats sought to include a 'racial justice' provision in the 1994 omnibus crime bill. This would have allowed defendants to challenge their death sentence by producing statistical evidence of racial discrimination in the judicial process. But this measure proved exceedingly controversial and was ultimately dropped from the final bill in 1994. (Kentucky became the first American state to pass this type of legislation in 1998.)

Pro-capital punishment forces enjoyed significant successes during Clinton's time in office, exploiting the president's much-touted toughness on crime. With the Republican take-over of Congress in 1994, and a fearful reaction to the Oklahoma bombing of 1995, the punitive context increased still further. Three measures were especially important:

- *New capital offences.* The 1994 crime bill created 60 additional federal crimes subject to the death penalty, including certain drug offences. Although the courts had previously ruled that capital punishment is unconstitutionally harsh for crimes in which a life is not taken, Congress took little heed. Signed into law by President Clinton on September 13, 1994, the Federal Death Penalty Act (FDPA) mandated the death penalty for 60 crimes not previously covered in federal statutes. The law supplemented the Anti-Drug Abuse Act of 1988, which allowed for the federal execution of so-called drug kingpins. Cited as Title VI of the Crime Control Act, the FDPA mandated death for:

    any offence for which a sentence of death is provided, if the defendant, as determined beyond a reasonable doubt at the hearing under 3593 – (A) intentionally killed the victim; (B) intentionally inflicted serious bodily injury that

resulted in the death of the victim; (C) intentionally participated in an act, contemplating that the life of a person would be taken or intending that lethal force would be used . . . and the victim died as a direct result of the act; or (D) intentionally and specifically engaged in an act of violence, knowing that the act created a grave risk of death to a person . . . such that participation in the act constituted a reckless disregard for human life and the victim died as a direct result of the act.

The act also required death for specified crimes, such as the murder by an inmate serving a life sentence in a federal penitentiary; the murder of a federal law enforcement official; a drive-by shooting committed in the course of certain drug offences; car-jacking resulting in death; the foreign murder of American nationals; and murder by escaped federal inmates.

- *Reducing sentence/execution delays.* Reacting to concerns over delays in implementing death sentences, Congress also sharply restricted death row appeals. The 1996 Anti-Terrorism and Effective Death Penalty Act, affecting both federal and state prisoners, extended recent Court decisions limiting death penalty appeals, imposing several new restrictions on death row inmates' access to federal courts. Inmates are now allowed only one appeal in a federal court within six months of sentencing (although the Supreme Court ruled in 1997 that the crime bill did not apply to inmates with pending petitions). The average time between sentencing and execution is now expected to decline from the nine years of the 1980s to three or four in the first decade of the twenty-first century.

- *Terminating funding for appeals.* One of the first acts of the Republican Congress in 1995 also ended federal funding to help pay for death row inmates' legal appeals. Congress terminated its financing of resource centres charged with helping indigent death row inmates find a lawyer (the American Bar Association, distressed by such due process problems, called for a moratorium on executions in 1997). In 1995, House Speaker Newt Gingrich demanded death for drug smugglers, suggesting that mass executions ('twenty-seven or thirty or thirty-five people at one time') could provide an excellent deterrent.

Neither caution nor clemency figured high in these legislative priorities, but together they meant that Congress had effectively nationalized the death penalty in America and extended it for crimes other than murder. The measures permit the federal prosecutor in a state to pre-empt jurisdiction from the state prosecutor; and if the federal prosecutor secures a conviction under the federal statutes, it does not matter whether or not the state law provides a death penalty for the crime in question. It remains to be seen whether there will be any or many federal prosecutions for crimes in states where the crime in question is not capitally punishable under state law.

Intermediary organizations

Opponents of capital punishment have made most of the running on the death penalty. Initially, these proved relatively successful, and their activism was rewarded by the *Furman* decision. Subsequently, however, with the politicization of the death penalty, the vocal opposition of public majorities to abolition, and the exploitation of this by populist politicians of both parties, the progressive coalition has proven far less effective.

The Legal Defense and Educational Fund (LDF) of the NAACP took the lead role in the abolitionist campaign. The American Civil Liberties Union (ACLU) assumed a secondary role, partly because of uncertainty about rank-and-file support. (The ACLU only assumed a formal position of opposition to the death penalty in 1965, a mark of the political weakness of abolitionism even among liberal political forces.) The LDF's campaign attempted first to achieve a *de facto* moratorium on executions by appealing every single death sentence. The hope was to jam up death row to such a level that resuming executions on a large scale would be too repugnant for public authorities to contemplate. Ultimately, the LDF succeeded by resorting to class action suits, which yielded some important successes: no death row prisoner was executed in the United States between 1968 and 1976 (inclusive).

The success was all the more notable for the relative absence of substantial allies. While intellectuals, influential newspapers (such as the *New York Times*, *Washington Post*) and select individuals took clear positions against the death penalty, relatively few organized lobbies followed suit. Even the American Bar Association, for example, failed to come out against the death penalty (in 1978, its House of Delegates heavily defeated a motion calling for states to abolish capital punishment, by 168 votes to 69).

The strength of the pro-death penalty position has militated against the need for organized action. In the 1970s, the National Association of Evangelicals (NAE), representing more than 10 million conservative Christians and 47 different denominations, and the Moral Majority were among the Christian groups supporting the death penalty. NAE's successor, the Christian Coalition, also strongly supports the death penalty. Fundamentalist and Pentecostal churches as well as the Church of Jesus Christ of Latter-day Saints (Mormons) typically support the death penalty on biblical grounds, specifically citing the Old Testament. Although traditionally a supporter of the capital punishment, the Roman Catholic Church, following the lead of Pope John Paul II, now opposes the death penalty, as do most Protestant denominations (Baptists, Episcopalians, Lutherans, Methodists, Presbyterians and the United Church of Christ).

But supporters can face troublesome cases, especially in instances of women prisoners. Of 5,680 offenders sentenced to death between 1976 and 1995, 116 (1.9 per cent of the total) were women (Grossman, 1998: 269). Most of these were not carried out, but one notable case concerned the execution of Karla Faye Tucker in Texas, in February 1998, sentenced for two vicious axe murders that she had committed. While on death row, Tucker educated herself and became deeply religious. She never denied her involvement in the murders for which she had been sentenced to death, but claimed to have become a born-again Christian and spoke of her desire to help others learn from her experience. The case saw a plea from the Pope for clemency, along with religious conservatives. Despite her acknowledged reform, however, the then governor of Texas, George W. Bush, refused to grant clemency and, on February 3, 1998, Tucker became the first woman to be executed in Texas (by lethal injection) since the Civil War and one of only three women to be executed in America since 1977 (43 others remained on death row as of June 1998; women have constituted only 3 per cent of total US executions).

CONCLUSION

There can be little doubt that in framing the Constitution the Founding Fathers envisaged the death penalty as a punishment that individual states, along with the federal government, could constitutionally approve and administer. Less clear, however, is the extent to which the death penalty now violates those key constitutional provisions that promise to protect due process of law and the equal protection of the laws, and that prohibit cruel and unusual punishment. Appeals to biblical injunctions provide conflicting views on the morality of state-sanctioned murder,

while the empirical data that exists overwhelmingly refutes the case that capital punishment has a significant deterrent effect. Given this, along with the relative infrequency with which those sentenced to death are executed, it may be that the death penalty should be viewed primarily as a moral issue. But the Supreme Court's attempt to give a moral lead during the 1970s revealed that 'mounting the tiger's back was far easier than descending unscathed' (McKeever, 1993: 51). Such is the judicial acceptance of capital punishment's constitutionality that it may better be regarded as a political issue for the states.

Were the Framers to return to the America of the twenty-first century, would they still approve of legal homicides as methods for dealing with those who perpetrate illegal ones? At least in principle, it is possible to imagine a time when public majorities decide that the death penalty constitutes a violation of the Eighth Amendment. Arguments against the measure are many and strong and its erstwhile supporters have offered few convincing refutations of the empirical case against the penalty: arbitrariness, racial imbalance and class biases. But those pro capital punishment argue that these problems are about the implementation of the penalty, not the principle. These are correctable, at least in theory; whether the class, racial and regional biases can be eliminated in practice is another matter. Moreover, such is the public support for capital punishment that its defenders have hardly felt it necessary even to try to muster empirical support for their case. Indeed, some now argue that death row inmates often prefer capital punishment to life imprisonment since the latter is more 'cruel and unusual'.

The new concern generated by revelations of innocent deaths and erroneous sentences has occasioned significant movement in the conflict over capital punishment but, ultimately, it is difficult to envisage any major change in American public sentiment occurring with any great rapidity. Much of the debate over capital punishment in the 1990s concerned not its prohibition (partial or absolute), but extending it to a new series of offences at state and federal level and making its execution more efficient. The notorious Benetton campaign 'Sentenced to Death' in 2000, featuring death row prisoners clothed in Benetton, resulted not in a changed public sentiment but the closure of the company outlets with mainstreet supplier Sears under public pressure. By 2000, American manufacturer McFarlane Toys was successfully producing 'Death Row Marv', a figurine whose eyes glowed red and declaimed 'Is that the best you can do, pansies?' as his electric chair switch was flipped.

As long as questions of homicide, property crime and terrorism continue to occupy American concern, the death penalty will remain a powerful resource – in the public mind, at least. Moreover, abolitionists can sometimes fall into the trap of romanticizing death row inmates, most of whom have, without doubt, committed brutal and barbaric crimes. While European states press the United Nations to condemn capital punishment, even in supposedly 'civilized' nations such as Britain public majorities have long professed support for restoring the death penalty, a position consistently denied them by their elected representatives. In America, where religiosity is much more widespread and politically influential, fear of violence is understandably pervasive and the public appetite for retribution against those who act with criminal irresponsibility remains powerful, constitutional interpretation seems settled and the prospects for abolition appear decidedly weak.

It is ironic that in traditionally 'strong state' Europe, opposition to the death penalty reflected deep-seated concerns over the state taking human life, while in traditionally anti-statist America a majority of states view government as entirely justified in executing American citizens found guilty of certain categories of crimes. Opponents of the death penalty face a double difficulty, however.

Some tend to base their rejection on empirical studies. Ironically, though, those such as Brennan who have held that by not being routine it is inevitably unusual and hence cruel, have fuelled their opponents to make sure that more crimes are subject to the death penalty, more sentences are carried out, and executions occur more rapidly. However, avoiding practical considerations leaves death penalty opponents reliant on a strong moral position that the state is never justified in taking life in peacetime – one that is simply unaccepted by most Americans.

Perhaps the difficulty here is where a precise line can reasonably be drawn. We can no doubt all agree that individuals who perpetrate acts of mass genocide deserve to die, but what of those who murder, say, 20 people? What of those who murder in particularly foul ways? What of those who murder children, or who take pleasure in brutally raping women? Few who witnessed the 1995 bombing of the federal building in Oklahoma, or who learnt of the brutal murder of James Byrd, can easily resist the argument that there are some crimes for which life imprisonment is an insufficient punishment, even if the likelihood of the criminal harming society again is minimal. These are moral and ethical judgements, of course, but they are also inherently political ones, for they involve competing conceptions of power and appropriate public policy. Whatever the constitutionality of the death penalty, it is unlikely in the foreseeable future that Americans, given the cost–benefit calculus that they currently assess, will easily countenance the abolition of what many outside the United States view as an obvious and blatantly 'cruel and unusual punishment'. Given the conflicting principles at stake, and the mosaic of state laws, political action on capital punishment resembles that over gun control and abortion: incremental changes to a predominantly traditionalist regime rather than frontal progressive assaults.

FURTHER READING

Hugo Adam Bedau (ed.), *The Death Penalty in America: Current Controversies* (1997) is a superb compendium of arguments and data about capital punishment, with contributions from both sides in the controversy.

Mark Grossman, *Encyclopedia of Capital Punishment* (1998) is a comprehensive A–Z of entries on capital punishment around the world.

Herbert H. Haines, *Against Capital Punishment: The Anti-Death Penalty Movement in America, 1972–1994* (1996) is a comprehensive analysis of the strategies and tactics of the various lobbies opposed to the death penalty.

Eugene Hickok (ed.), *The Bill of Rights in America: Original Meaning and Current Understanding* (1991, Chapters 20–22) offers arguments for and against the constitutionality of the death penalty.

Joseph L. Hoffman, 'The "Cruel and Unusual Punishment" Clause: A Limit on the Power to Punish or Constitutional Rhetoric?', in David J. Bodenhamer and James W. Ely, Jr. (eds), *The Bill of Rights in Modern America after 200 Years* (1993) is a discussion of the cases for and against the death penalty being 'cruel and unusual' punishment.

William McFeeley, *Proximity to Death* (2000) is an account by an abolitionist historian of his involvement with several death penalty cases.

Robert McKeever, *Raw Judicial Power? The Supreme Court and American Society* (2nd edition) (1995, Chapter 3) is a balanced discussion of the key Supreme Court capital punishment decisions.

Helen Prejean, *Dead Man Walking* (1993) is a detailed account of a Catholic nun's experiences in counselling inmates and campaigning against the penalty in Louisiana.

Austin Sarat (ed.), *The Killing State: Capital Punishment in Law, Politics and Culture* (1999) is a collection of essays on the law, politics and cultural representations of capital punishment.

WEB LINKS

Abolitionist and reform organizations

Amnesty International
http://www.rightsforall-usa.org

American Civil Liberties Union
http://www.aclu.org/executionwatch.html

Death Penalty Information Center
http://www.deathpenaltyinfo.org

National Coalition Against the Death Penalty
http://www.ncadp.org

The Justice Project
www.TheJusticeProject.org

National Committee to Prevent Wrongful Execution
www.constitutionproject.org

'Pro'-capital punishment organizations and resources

State of Texas
http://www.state.tx.us

Texas Board of Pardons and Paroles
http://link.tsl.state.tx.us/tx/BPP

Pro-death penalty resource centers:
http://www.dpinfo.com
http://www.prodeathpenalty.com

Victims' Rights
www.murdervictims.com

QUESTIONS

- Are the arguments for the right of individual states to impose the death penalty more persuasive than those against the death penalty?

- Is the principle of the death penalty itself unconstitutional or merely particular mechanisms by which the penalty is implemented?

- Under what conditions, if any, can capital punishment in America be considered 'cruel and unusual punishment'?

- How far have democratic values triumphed over those of liberalism in the case of the death penalty?

- What best explains American support for capital punishment?

6 Pornography

. . . no pornography, no male sexuality . . . the major distinction between intercourse (normal) and rape (abnormal) is that the normal happens so often that one cannot get anyone to see anything wrong with it.

> Catharine MacKinnon (1989: 139, 146)

If the First Amendment means anything, it means that a State has no business telling a man, sitting alone in his own house, what books he may read or what films he may watch.

> Justice Thurgood Marshall, for the Court, *Stanley v. Georgia*, 394 U.S. 557 (1969), at 565

- **The Historical Context**
- **Porn in the USA**
- **Public Opinion**
- **Traditionalists v. Progressives**
- **Explaining the Politics of Pornography**
- **The US Constitution**
- **Governing Institutions**
- **Conclusion**

Chapter Summary

The Supreme Court's intervention on pornography transformed the politics of the issue in America in the latter half of the twentieth century. The Court's attempts after the Second World War to define 'obscenity' in such a way as to include sexually explicit material (and hence deny it the free speech protections of the First Amendment) but exclude serious works of art with a sexual content proved lengthy, convoluted and at times comical. Since the 1960s, in reaction to the rapid growth of America's sex industry and what they perceived as the federal judiciary emasculating state and community norms, a combination of feminist groups and moral traditionalists has sought to reverse the liberalization of laws governing sexually explicit materials and conduct. Although the traditionalist–feminist forces won some important victories in the battles over free speech, the importance of the First Amendment and the lucrative financial rewards to be gained from the American sex industry have provided substantial political and legal support for diverse forms of 'sexpression' in America. Despite attempts to equate pornography with 'hate speech', the fundamental idea that no expressions can be prohibited on grounds of the content of their message – the essence of the First Amendment and subsequent jurisprudence – remains a cornerstone of America's liberal democracy.

The story of how pornography toppled the two Republican leaders of the US House of Representatives in 1998 is an odd and exotic one – even a very American one. In August of that year, Independent Counsel Kenneth Starr delivered the long-awaited report of his investigation on President Clinton to Congress, recommending impeachment of the president on charges of obstruction of justice, witness tampering and perjury. The Republican congressional leadership rapidly decided to allow maximum public access to the report by putting it on the Internet. The report contained detailed testimony from a former White House intern, Monica Lewinsky, about the number and nature of her sexual encounters with the president in and around the Oval Office. Among other things, it included extensive and detailed references to phone-sex, thong underwear, semen-stained dresses, masturbation, and the use of a cigar as a sexual aid. Some commentators made the point that, under legislation that the Republican 104th Congress had passed and Clinton had signed (but the Supreme Court had struck down as unconstitutional) two years earlier – the Communications Decency Act of 1996 – the material would probably have been impermissible to broadcast on the Net on indecency grounds.

In November 1998, after unexpected Democratic gains in the congressional mid-term elections to the House, Speaker Newt Gingrich accepted the blame for the Republicans' relatively poor showing and mistaken tactics, resigning as Speaker in the midst of the Clinton impeachment crisis. Bob Livingstone, a respected Republican lawmaker from Louisiana, was due to take his place, but Larry Flynt, the flamboyant multimillionaire owner of the American porn magazine *Hustler*, then aired revelations of Livingstone himself having committed adultery. The Republican then refused to accept the Speakership. (Flynt also offered substantial financial rewards to any Americans who could prove sexual misdeeds by prominent politicians, particularly those Republicans recommending impeachment. He was not short of suppliers, and issued his own *Flynt Report* in the spring of 1999, detailing the alleged ethical question marks surrounding several congressional Republicans seeking to impeach the president.) In the peculiar mix of moralism, media and money that characterizes contemporary America, the porn-king dethroned the Republicans' newly anointed saviour.

Much like the public reaction to *The Starr Report*, pornography evokes a mixture of reactions: prurience and Puritanism, embarrassment and enthusiasm, voyeurism and vituperation. Pornography has been a prominent battle in the culture war for three decades, a legacy of traditionalist and women's organizations reacting strongly (but not entirely successfully) against the growth of America's sex industry and federal court decisions liberalizing laws on obscenity. The ironies surrounding the issue – some might also suggest the contradictions and hypocrisies – abound. Pornography has seen seemingly incongruous alliances of radical feminists and the religious right, liberal

Democrats and conservative Republicans, civil rights groups and the sex industry. Allegations of porn consumption – linked, as feminist groups sought, to those of sexual harassment – almost derailed the nomination by President George H.W. Bush of Judge Clarence Thomas to the Supreme Court in 1991. Yet subsequent allegations of harassment, adultery and even rape against President Clinton were alternately suppressed and ignored by many of the same liberals and feminists who had narrowly failed to persuade the Senate to reject Thomas. In 2001, intelligence sources even suggested that Al Qaeda terrorists posted messages to each other on a porn site on the Internet.

Like abortion, gun control and capital punishment, technological developments also play a key role. Just as the invention of the camera, film and video did before them, so 'dial-a-porn' telephone services provided by carriers like AT&T, 'adult videos' offered by hotel chains like Sheraton and, most importantly of all, the Internet steadily transformed the dissemination of, and the debate on, pornography in America at the end of the twentieth century. But like gun control, the evidence on which contending arguments about the regulation or prohibition of pornography are based is strongly contested by opposing sides in the controversy. In particular, whether the consumption of pornography leads to a breakdown in traditional moral structures, encourages violence against women, and either causes or reinforces sexist attitudes are all hotly disputed questions. Where some Americans view pornography as at worst a harmlessly benign 'safety valve' and at best liberating, others see nothing in such material but exploitative coercion, degradation and ruthless victimization.

The essence of cultural value conflict is therefore exemplified by the pornography issue: religious and traditionalist values pitted against secular, 'modern' and libertarian norms; particular local and state preferences against universalizing federal requirements; individual liberty matched against demands for group equality and community autonomy; and federal and state courts intervening to very mixed and sometimes inconsistent effect. In this chapter we examine the extent of pornography consumption, attitudes towards it, and whether (and in what circumstances) the First Amendment protects an individual's 'right' to consume sexually explicit materials.

Historically, the commitment to individual freedom enshrined in the Bill of Rights has been tempered by occasional outbreaks of illiberal tendencies that seek to prohibit activities or ways of life – to enforce morality. McCarthyism was the most obvious case of this, such that the term has been used since the 1950s to attack those who sought to impeach Clinton as 'sexual McCarthyites' and to charge proponents of 'hate speech' codes as 'leftist McCarthyites'. Based on demands for group equality, feminist attempts to ban pornography and the growth of campus speech codes against offensive speech represent two of the more recent examples of classical American liberalism transformed into a creed for conformity. Thus far, however, the balance between democratic values and traditional liberal ones has remained mostly on the side of liberalism. Even speech that is considered widely offensive remains largely protected by the First Amendment.

THE HISTORICAL CONTEXT

Depictions of sex in art and literature date back to antiquity, as do the controversies surrounding them, but the modern battles over sexually explicit materials are especially intense and occasionally vituperative, for three reasons:

- *Technological developments.* The invention of film, video and the Internet has created a formidably large mass market for sexually explicit materials. While many depictions of sex existed in literary and artistic forms from the founding of the United States, it has only been since the end of the

Second World War that a genuine sex industry has developed, to cater for (and, in turn, shape) Americans' varied sexual practices, preferences and imaginations. Most estimates suggest that approximately half of all Internet traffic comprises sex-related sites, a substantial proportion of which are US-based.

- *The 'sexual revolution'.* However complex and contested the social and political legacies of the 1960s and 1970s remain, there is no doubt that they witnessed a marked liberalization of sexual regulations and practices that transformed the place of questions of sex and sexuality in American public life. Once tied exclusively to the institution of marriage and to child-bearing, developments such as the contraceptive pill, increased female employment and the 'second wave' of feminism together undermined the traditional concepts that sex was something to occur only between husbands and wives and primarily (even exclusively) for purposes of procreation. For many women and men, sex became a matter not just of biology but of personal autonomy, a component part of the very definition of individual freedom – not just sex outside marriage, but sex outside long-term relationships became legitimate to millions of Americans. Because sex and sexuality now comprised such vitally important parts of the individual identity of many citizens (for both women and men, heterosexuals and, as the next chapter documents, homosexuals), the availability of explicit sexual materials also emerged as a vexed and highly charged issue. While some saw this as part of a broader emancipatory process, others regarded such materials as repugnant to both morality and equality.

- *Gender equality.* Pornography speaks to broader questions of the relations between the sexes and the role of women in American society. Even the most ardent male chauvinist would be hard-pressed to deny that women have suffered all manner of prejudices, discrimination and violence at the hands of men through the ages, and that, however much this may have declined, it continues today in America and elsewhere. A central theme in late twentieth- and early twenty-first-century industrialized liberal democracies has been to further the long process of improving the socio-economic status of women and safeguarding their rights and liberties from male intrusion. For both those who see pornographic depictions of women as perpetuating a second-class status, and those who see prohibitions on pornography as maintaining a paternalist attitude to women, questions of equality loom as large as those of individual freedom. (The growth of gay activism and movements for equality from the late 1960s also contributed to the increased prominence of such egalitarian considerations in American debates about sex and sexuality.)

In one respect, conflict over pornography resembles that on gun control in that many basic facts are contested. In the gun control case, the relationship between the legal availability of firearms and the levels of gun violence provoked strong disagreement. In the case of pornography, three of the central claims made about sexually explicit material – first, that it leads to harm against women, secondly, that it causes or reinforces sexist and demeaning attitudes to women among men, and thirdly, that it contributes towards a breakdown in society's moral structure – are not accepted by many critics. But an important difference from gun control is that the subject of pornography itself is not easily defined or identified. We know what a gun looks like, sounds like and does. The issue for lawmakers then centres on what, if any, regulations on its legality, sale, distribution and use should exist. But, contrary to Justice Potter Stewart's famous 'definition' ('I know it when I see it'), we do not necessarily know – at least, reasonable persons may disagree – about what constitutes 'pornography'.

As with abortion, an important initial point therefore concerns language, which is again far from neutral and is powerfully influenced by particular political agendas. The terms 'pornography' and 'pornographic' are generally regarded as forms of abuse. So, too, is the notion that something is 'obscene' – the legal definition for material that is outside the free speech protections of the First Amendment to the Constitution. By contrast, 'erotica' is a term typically used to depict expressions of sex and sexuality of which the speaker or writer approves. As is sometimes said, 'one person's erotica is another's pornography' and pornography is simply 'erotica that offends'.

Crucially, then, subjective assessments of the erotic or pornographic status of works of film, literature and art abound. In fact, pornography originally meant 'writing about prostitutes' (from the Greek *grapho*: writing; and *porne*: prostitute). The standard dictionary definition is therefore, simply, writing or pictures 'intended to arouse sexual desire'. In itself, this immediately suggests the subjectivity inherent in the debate, since material intended to arouse may well not have that effect, while many of us may be aroused by images or objects that were never purposefully intended to stimulate such responses. Pornography has thus become a convenient but misleading short-hand term for all manner of works that some find offensive: depictions of sexual acts; images of violent or coercive sex; magazines with a sexual content, whether mild or strong; and even television programmes or rock, rap and comedy albums containing 'bad language'.

All that can generally be said with certainty is that some kind of explicit depiction or description of sex intended to arouse has to be present, whether in words or pictures, for something to be designated pornographic. But even this minimal definition is inherently subjective, since definitions of explicitness differ both between and within cultures and are also subject to change over time. Literature which western scholars now term 'classic' and view as sexually mild (D.H.

Lawrence's *Lady Chatterley's Lover*, for example, or Vladimir Nabokov's *Lolita*) was once deemed so racy as to be banned by government as socially inflammatory. As will be seen later, attempts by judges and anti-porn crusaders to define what constitutes either obscenity or pornography have proven disastrously ineffectual. All that traditionalists and progressives can agree on is that pornography is intended to arouse sexual feelings in the consumer. In this chapter, references to pornography therefore treat it as a neutral term that simply describes or depicts sexually explicit acts that may either arouse and/or offend; no value judgement is attached for or against the material in using the term.

Since the 1980s, conflict over explicit sexual materials has also become part of a broader political struggle to define and regulate what is conventionally termed 'hate speech'. This category of speech refers to expressions of animus towards groups, especially racial and ethnic minorities, but also women and gays. Drawing analogies with the struggle by African Americans to secure civil rights in the 1950s and 1960s, women's groups and gay lobbies have both sought to make expressions of hostility towards them questions of civil rights and discrimination. For many feminists, pornography represents hate speech against women in the same way that racist speech expresses hatred of particular racial and ethnic groups, denying them civil equality. The questions of whether government can seek to prohibit such expressions and, if so, to what extent and by what permissible means, are the central political and legal dilemmas in the cultural conflict.

PORN IN THE USA

Despite being the cradle of the 'sexual revolution' and the largest producer of sexually explicit materials worldwide, in many respects contemporary America remains an essentially puritan nation when it comes to matters concerning sex. Pornography is one example of this, but it is not alone.

Americans have battled over sex for many decades. One lasting legacy of this has been that American law on sexual issues is generally complex and varied, with some practices being legal in one state and illegal in an adjoining one. Practices and acts that have long been decriminalized in most of Europe are still illegal in many states (including adultery, oral sex, anal sex and voyeurism). Defining what might qualify as 'normal' or conventional behaviour in America is therefore notoriously difficult and arguably futile. Perhaps not surprisingly, the graphic revelations of President Clinton's 'inappropriate relations' with Lewinsky and his particular sexual predilections found millions of Americans simultaneously revolted and riveted.

Some observers might consider it rather anomalous that Americans are both dedicated followers of religion and avid consumers of pornography. How far the two aspects of American life are connected – how far pornography consumption is confined to the irreligious – is not at all clear. What is certain, however, is that pornography is big business. Critics of the sex industry have long attacked it for being 'un-American', yet in many respects there is something quintessentially American about the mix of sex and money, massive financial fortunes rapidly won and lost, new personal identities assumed and discarded, and regular rituals of public condemnations of private obsessions. As one critic observed: 'Largely fuelled by loneliness and frustration, the sex industry has been transformed from a minor subculture into a major component of American popular culture' (Schlosser, 1997: 43).

To describe pornography as part of mainstream popular culture might seem an extreme assertion but sceptics might consider the statistics. For example, according to *Adult Video News* (an American sex industry publication), the number of 'hard-core' pornographic video rentals in America rose from 75 million in 1985 to 490 million in 1992 and 665 million in 1996 (more than double the number of guns in circulation). Video rentals of 'hard-core' in America now far exceed those of *Disney*. In 1996 alone, Americans spent over $8 billion on sexual entertainment (videos, strip joints, computer porn and sex magazines), an amount larger than Hollywood's total domestic box office receipts for the year and much larger than all the revenues generated by American rock and country music recordings combined. In 1999, Forester Research estimated that successful US Internet sex sites received 50 million hits each month, collectively generating $1 billion of revenue annually and growing faster than any other part of the e-economy. Not only has the American sex industry successfully imitated mainstream film titles, in which, for example, *Saving Private Ryan* metamorphoses into *Shaving Ryan's Privates*, but it even boasts its annual Oscars equivalent for the industry's 'actors', producers and directors.

Moreover, most of the substantial profits generated by pornography are earned by businesses not traditionally associated with the sex industry: 'mom and pop' video stores renting out sex videos that major distributor chains like *Blockbuster* refused to stock; long-distance telecommunications carriers such as AT&T offering phone-sex channels; cable companies like Time-Warner and hotel chains like Marriott, Hyatt and Holiday Inn supplying sex programming to their customers. American pornography has also become one of the nation's prime cultural exports, dominating overseas markets despite stiff competition from Europe. Approximately 150 porn videos per week are now released in America and rentals of these movies account for between 15 per cent and 30 per cent of overall video rentals. And, notoriously, the most popular computer sites on the Internet are those with a clear or graphic sexual content, most of which originate with American providers.

It probably comes as no surprise that men are the largest consumers of pornography in America, but a substantial proportion of American women also consume hard-core material. A survey during the late 1980s by

Redbook magazine (a woman's magazine famous for its cooking recipes and household tips), for example, found that almost half of its readers regularly watched pornographic movies in the privacy of their homes. Marjorie Heins, a feminist defender of pornography, claims that women – either alone or in couples – annually comprise over 40 per cent of those Americans renting adult movies (Heins, 1993: 144). A survey in the mid-1990s by the *Advocate*, a leading American gay magazine, also found that 54 per cent of its lesbian readers had watched an 'X-rated' video in the previous 12 months. Justice Thurgood Marshall may have referred only to men in the *Stanley* ruling of 1969, but state intervention on pornography also has a clear impact on a substantial number of female consumers.

Unusually for such a success story, however, the public profile of pornography hardly boasts of a commercial giant, rich in its variety and an international market-leader for the USA. Americans have not taken pornography to their heads even if they have taken it to their hearts (and elsewhere). Instead, the religious and traditionalist dimensions of America's social base powerfully reinforce the combination of prurience and Puritanism that alternately consumes and condemns pornography. Pornography forms part of the broader dangers posed by sex to orthodox notions of appropriate behaviour and values. In particular, the institutions of marriage and the family are viewed by traditionalists as 'threatened' by the type of sexual licence that is the mainstay of pornography, be it sex before or outside marriage, homosexuality or 'unconventional' sexual practices (gay, lesbian or bisexual sex, group sex, wife-swapping, masturbation, voyeurism, and so on). Untying sex from procreation and marriage was, for many Americans, a deeply retrograde product of the 1960s, with profoundly troubling consequences in terms of illegitimate births, increasing divorce rates and family disintegration. Adultery and fornication remain publicly frowned upon in today's America.

Indeed, the 1960s sexual legacy remains potent in many political and social respects. Such was the growing popular concern about sexual permissiveness that, during the 1990s, an organization termed 'Promise Keepers' gained hundreds of thousands of members nationwide, consisting of husbands who promised to (re)honour their marriage vows. Campaigns for sexual abstinence among the young – most notably True Love Waits – sprang up across the nation and won endorsement from then 'First Lady' Hillary Clinton, who, countering conservative critics' characterization of her as a degenerate child of the '1960s' counter-culture', advocated that sex should not be engaged in before long-term, adult (post-20s) relationships and (ideally) marriage. The sexual taboo about miscegenation that historically informed state laws against inter-racial marriage remained powerful (although the Supreme Court had struck those laws down as unconstitutional in *Loving v. Virginia* [1967]). (Only in 1998, for example, did voters in South Carolina approve a ballot proposition to remove the ban on inter-racial marriage that had been part of the state's constitution; Alabama did likewise in 2000 but 40 per cent of those voting cast ballots against the repeal). In 1998, as Exhibit 6.1 explains, Alabama became the seventh state to ban the sale and distribution of vibrators as harmful consumer products (the sale and distribution of firearms, by contrast, remained legal). And despite the powerful arguments in its favour, the decriminalization of prostitution is still not a subject of public debate in America, much less legislative action (except in parts of Nevada).

While there exists a shared traditionalist heritage, the diversity of the individual states' social bases, combined with the federal nature of the political system, yields a rich variety of laws on sex in general, and pornography in particular. Although widely considered the quintessential private activity in America, sex is 'blanketed by laws' such that crossing a state boundary can involve 'stepping into a different moral universe' (Posner and Silbaugh, 1998: 1–2). Oral sex, for example, was illegal in 15 of the 50 states in 1999. Adultery remained a crime in 24 of them. Thirty-three states had no statutes relating to fornication but in 17 it was considered a misdemeanour or felony. Incest was a felony in 48 states but only a misdemeanour in Virginia and did not even merit a statute in Rhode Island. Prostitution was only a misdemeanour in most states (see Exhibit 6.2), while the strongest condemnatory language in American sex law ('unnatural', 'lascivious', and 'a crime against nature') was reserved for 'sodomy' – although a total of 23 states had no statutes at all pertaining to the practice.

Exhibit 6.1   Bad vibrations: a fundamental right to an orgasm?

Shortly before the midterm elections of 1998, the state legislature of Alabama passed a new bill. As state Assistant Attorney General Courtney Travers put it, 'This is really a case about the power of the legislature to prohibit the sale and manufacture of products it deems harmful.' The products in question were not handguns or assault rifles but vibrators and dildos. The Alabama law forbade the selling or distributing of 'any obscene material or any device designed or marketed as useful primarily for the stimulation of the human genital organs'. Although the Founding Fathers had famously declared everyone's right to the 'pursuit of happiness' in 1776, the state of Alabama in 1998 declared that its women had no 'fundamental, constitutional right to an orgasm', which, when the Constitution is considered, is true enough. In their defence, the Alabama prohibitionists pointed out that the state's women could travel to neighbouring Tennessee (not conventionally noted for being a lax bastion of moral depravity) to buy and bring back the 'contraband' – sex toys – if they so wished. Alabama thereby joined Colorado, Georgia, Kansas, Louisiana, Mississippi and Virginia, all of which had outlawed the sale of any device designed to stimulate the genitals of their wholesome, God-fearing citizens.

Source: Younge (1999).

Exhibit 6.2   Prostitution in America

There is considerable argument as to what percentage street prostitution represents of the total 'sex trade' in America. However, the consensus figure suggests that some two million women and men are engaged in prostitution in the United States (in context, this is equivalent to two-thirds of the entire population of the Republic of Ireland). Of these, it is believed that probably a maximum of 20 per cent is represented by street prostitution, the remainder being taken up by escort services, massage parlors and 'nightclubs'.

Officially, it is only in Nevada that prostitution is lawful (though, curiously, it is illegal in Las Vegas). Since 1971, it has been the position in the state that cities with less than 250,000 people are allowed to operate brothels quite lawfully. A 'Nevada Brothel Association' ensures that prostitutes are tested at regular intervals.

Although the remaining states criminalize prostitution with varying degrees of severity, the enforcement of state laws is not uniform. Some states are tougher than others (for example, a 1989 law passed in Portland, Oregon permits city police to confiscate the motor vehicles of street crawlers or of the clients of prostitutes). One survey reported that America's major cities 'spent an average of $12,000,000 each on controlling prostitution'.

Source: Richard Goodall (1995).

Theoretically, to take the Alabama example again, the state sanctions sex with donkeys and corpses (no state law exists against either bestiality or necrophilia) but punishes oral sex between husbands and wives (there exists a law against oral sex that does not discriminate between married and unmarried persons or heterosexuals and homosexuals).

Naturally, many of these state laws are unenforced. It would require a highly intrusive – indeed, totalitarian – state to do so. Nevertheless, the diversity in regulation illustrates two important points about American attitudes towards sex and sexuality. First, strong differences continue to exist on the enforcement of morality and regulation of sexual matters. Secondly, those critics who discerned in public reactions to 'Monicagate' during 1998–99 a decline or even disappearance in the Puritanism often attributed to America ('Americans have become French', as some jocularly put it) were somewhat premature. Pornography is one particular case illustrating both of these points.

PUBLIC OPINION

Millions of American men and women consume sexually explicit material on a regular basis and in a variety of forms (albeit discreetly). In line with the world's foremost consumer society, the types of pornography that are available in America are as varied as the human sexual impulse itself. But as Table 6.1 shows, consistent and clear – though not overwhelming – majorities of Americans increasingly professed a belief over the 1980s that the availability of pornographic materials causes a breakdown in public morality. (Of course, the causal chain may also plausibly work in the other direction: a weakening of religious or moral conviction may prompt individuals to seek out sexual materials.)

Significantly, between 40 and 49 per cent of Americans do not see pornography as causing a moral breakdown. Such figures suggest strongly that there is a substantial mass

TABLE 6.1 Americans believing that pornography leads to a breakdown in morals, 1973–91 (per cent)

Year	Percentage of respondents
1973	52.8
1975	51.3
1976	54.6
1978	56.8
1980	60.0
1983	58.3
1984	61.3
1986	61.9
1987	59.0
1988	61.8
1989	62.1
1990	60.8
1991	59.6

Note: Question: 'Do sexual materials lead to a breakdown in morals (yes/no?)'
Source: Epstein et al. (1994: 601).

market for sexually explicit materials, but we should be cautious before inferring that it is this group in particular that accounts for the consumption of pornography. The figures are so large that at least some consumers of pornography are probably to be found among those traditionalists who (publicly claim to) see it as a degenerative social force. (Though there is nothing inconsistent as such here, in as much as we can regard something as bad for us but nonetheless continue to consume it.)

TRADITIONALISTS V. PROGRESSIVES

The battle between traditionalists and progressives in the culture war is somewhat more complicated in the case of sexual materials than abortion and gay rights. In particular, two questions dominate the debate over pornography. Although distinct, they are closely related – effectively inseparable –

in terms of deciding whether and when the state may regulate, and even prohibit, the sale and distribution of pornographic material:

- *Is the material 'speech'?* If the material in question (a film, book, painting or photograph) is not considered speech, then no question of it being protected by the First Amendment even arises. In this case, the government is free to regulate or ban the work without any constitutional issue of free speech being raised. To qualify as speech, however, the key question is whether it has any 'cognitive' content. That is, does the work convey or communicate ideas in any way?
- *Can the state regulate or prohibit explicit sexual works?* If the work qualifies as speech, the issue of whether it can be regulated or banned by government becomes more complex. Competing arguments can be invoked, not least over the free speech rights of the individual, the preferences of local communities, and other claims about the broader social consequences of pornography that may either recommend or require the state's intervention. Normally, however, the First Amendment's protection of free speech would 'trump' any legislative attempts to prohibit the sale or distribution of the work.

The obvious contrast with pornography in these respects is with an act like flag-burning (see Exhibit 6.3). Justice William Brennan declared for the 5–4 Supreme Court majority in *Texas v. Johnson* (1989) that 'If there is a bedrock principle underlying the First Amendment, it is that the Government may not prohibit the expression of an idea simply because society finds the idea itself offensive or disagreeable'. But many Americans object that, unlike burning a flag, which is generally seen as conveying an important political message of protest (however disagreeable), a depiction of an orgy is not necessarily expressing any 'ideas' at all. Hence, such sexual works do not merit comparable protection under the First Amendment as other forms of speech or expression.

Using the two questions above as our test, the conflict over pornography yields a fourfold typology of political outlooks, as outlined in Exhibit 6.4. These positions are:

(1) *Prohibitionist Feminists.* For many (but not all) feminists, the availability of porn is merely part of the broader structure of patriarchy that has long oppressed women as second-class citizens. The fact that such materials remain available after other struggles for childcare benefits, sexual harassment laws, abortion rights and prohibitions on violence against women have largely been won is a glaring indictment of a still-patriarchal social structure. Many feminists hold that sexual material is speech but that government can (and should) ban certain forms of this material. Pornography does convey ideas but these are fundamentally violent and degrading messages about women. Pornography remains the most powerful and pervasive indicator that women remain viewed by men primarily as objects available for sex, not human beings equal to men. On grounds of both violence and degradation, then, the state is correct and legitimate to override any First Amendment issues when anti-pornography statutes are under consideration.

A particularly influential strand of this argument is associated with the 'prohibitionist feminists', most notably the scholar/activists Catharine MacKinnon and Andrea Dworkin. MacKinnon and Dworkin argue that pornography not so much represents but actually constitutes violence against women, denying them equality. Pornography is a form of sex discrimination, whereby women are victimized by being forced to perform pornographic acts, by acts of violence stimulated by pornography, and by the sexual attitudes and roles resulting from such sex discrimination. As MacKinnon puts it: 'Pornography, in the feminist view, is a form of forced sex . . . an institution of gender inequality. . . . [P]ornography, with the rape and

Exhibit 6.3   Desecrating the Stars and Stripes

The American flag is a potent and revered symbol of the nation, protected under both federal and state law. Partly because of this, destruction of the flag, its misuse or desecration, is a powerful means of expressing protest against the policies of the nation (for those within and outside America). These two realities came into conflict when the Supreme Court decided *Texas v. Johnson* (1989). While the 1984 Republican National Convention was taking place in Dallas, Texas, some political demonstrators were engaged in a protest against the policies of the Reagan administration. During this, one protestor, Johnson, unfurled the American flag, doused it with kerosene and set it on fire. While the flag burned, the protesters chanted: 'America, the red, white and blue, we spit on you.' Johnson was charged with the crime of violating a Texas statute that prohibited desecration of a venerated object. Desecration included any physical mistreatment 'in a way that the actor knows will seriously offend one or more persons likely to observe or discover his action'.

Johnson's conviction was overturned, 5–4, by the Supreme Court on the ground that 'the statute as applied to him violates the First Amendment'. The Texas law was concerned with the communicative harm (public offence) that would flow from Johnson's expressive conduct, but the majority argued that such content-based provisions infringed the First Amendment's free speech guarantees. In dissent, Justice Rehnquist argued that the public burning of the flag 'was no essential part of any exposition of ideas, and at the same time it had a tendency to incite a breach of the peace.' Emphasizing the flag's status as a unique symbol that transcended political differences, he argued that flag-burning should be categorized as 'low value speech' not entitled to normal First Amendment protection.

The decision prompted enormous political controversy. President George H.W. Bush declared that the Court was wrong and that a constitutional amendment was needed to protect the flag. To forestall this, Congress enacted a new federal law, the Flag Protection Act of 1989, which prohibited the 'knowing mutilation, defacement, burning, maintaining on the floor or ground, or trampling upon' any flag of the United States. But in *United States v. Eichman* (1990), the same five justices of the Court again struck down the new federal anti-desecration law as unconstitutional. Once more, they argued that the government's asserted interest in the statute was clearly related to the suppression of free expression and concerned with the content of the message. Writing for the majority, Justice Brennan declared: 'Punishing desecration of the flag dilutes the very freedom that makes this emblem so revered.' Pressure to enact a constitutional amendment to protect the Stars and Stripes has grown steadily since that decision, with Republicans at the forefront of the campaign to criminalize attacks on the American flag. (Many progressives oppose such an amendment on grounds of free expression trumping offence, yet simultaneously seek to prohibit public displays of the Confederate flag on grounds of the offence it causes many African Americans.)

prostitution in which it participates, institutionalizes the sexuality of male supremacy.' As a discriminatory act rather than expression as such, pornography cannot be tolerated since it offends a civil right – the right to gender equality. The victimization of women as a class, which pornography simultaneously represents and fosters, justifies the enactment of anti-pornography laws, which

amount not to censorship but to the promotion of civil rights.

(2) *First Amendment Absolutists.* Civil libertarians also tend to agree with those feminists who claim that pornography is speech, but in contrast they hold that government cannot prohibit it. For some, this is simply because material cannot be censored on the basis of its viewpoint, no matter how offensive the

Exhibit 6.4   Four sexually explicit positions

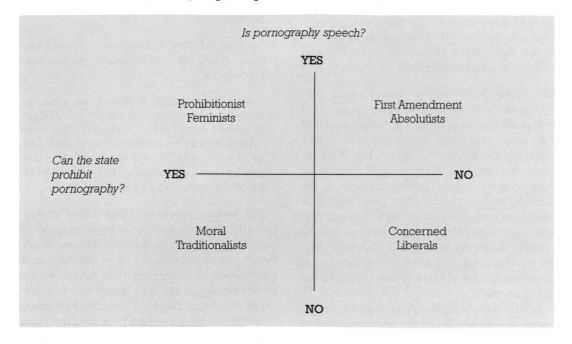

message conveyed nor how unimportant it may seem compared to other forms of speech, be these political acts (such as flag-burning) or literary works (such as *Tropic of Cancer* or *Ulysses*). Attempts to suppress the expression of ideas on the basis of their content are invariably suspect. A marketplace of ideas requires that all ideas – even pernicious or bad ones – circulate freely.

For other libertarians, such as Nadine Strossen and Marjorie Heins, pornography is not merely tolerable but constitutes a liberating device with a radical message to convey. While they concede that a small proportion of it is degrading and/or violent, most of it is not. Part of the criticism of the radical feminist position is precisely that censorship has frequently sought to reinforce prevailing male views of an appropriate female role. On this view, the alliance of feminists and conservatives is fundamentally misguided, its ultimate result being the notion that women should be protected from graphic images of sex and sexuality by paternalist male judges

and public officials. Some critics argue that it is precisely the availability of pornography that acts as a radical, 'anti-establishment' force in a fundamentally puritanical, sex-negative and racially charged American culture, allowing individuals access to words and images – from same-sex acts to inter-racial ones – that challenge 'orthodox' notions about sex and that legitimize their particular sexual preferences. Even if it could be proven that a relationship existed between the availability of such materials and sexist attitudes or violence against women, the prohibition of such materials would be too high a price to pay. As with firearms, the costs of outright bans exceed the benefits of legal availability.

(This is not to suggest that no regulations are ever acceptable to libertarians. Laws against pornography involving children, for example, are legitimate since they are directed at non-adults who are, by definition, unable to exercise informed consent. Participants, both adults and children, who are coerced into movies can also be targeted by criminal laws. But the suppression of material that does not fall into these categories is typically unjustified. Anti-pornography laws foster the very paternalistic attitudes and values they seek to combat.)

(3) *Moral Traditionalists.* Traditionalist conservatives tend to see pornography as either not qualifying as speech or as being speech of the most worthless character, and hence being legitimate for the state to ban if its citizens so desire. Unlike feminist censors of pornography whose central concern is the harm to women produced by porn, traditionalists emphasize morality. Such explicit sexual materials offer a view of sex that is without social context, untied from meaningful relationships or marriage, dislocated from procreation, and ultimately demeaning to the act of sex itself.

While many traditionalists would acknowledge the centrality of sex and sexuality to great works of art from antiquity to the present (from *Ovid*'s poems to the paintings of the Italian Renaissance and Shakespeare's plays), these works are of a qualitatively different nature from modern materials. Even mainstream movies such as *Basic Instinct*, much less 'hard-core' porn, are open to the above criticisms, as gratuitous exhibitions of sex without context. On this view, women should not necessarily be modest, chaste and dignified, but if they are not, there exists a time and place for such wanton behaviour (the marital bedroom). To portray women as sensual hedonists, celebrating their freedom through their sexuality and enjoying sex in the ways that many men do, is disturbing to the traditional social order and dangerous to the women.

For some, this is just a matter of revulsion against what they view as worthless filth and smut. Pat Buchanan, for example, bewails

> the damage that thirty years of judicial activism have done to this wonderful country. By breaking down all local barriers to filthy speech and dirty books, the Supreme Court permitted America's popular culture to be

converted into a public sewer, in which some of the world's worst pornographers now contentedly swim.

Betraying a hitherto unknown environmentalism, Buchanan vehemently denies that there exists a

> constitutional 'right' to befoul our airwaves any more than there is a constitutional right to pollute our rivers. . . . Polluted ideas have caused greater injury to mankind than polluted water, and the marketplace of ideas is in greater need of watching than the marketplace of goods. (Van Dyke, 1995: 195)

For others, however, there exists a profoundly negative worth to pornography, in that it undermines traditional notions of sex being something that is tied to marriage and procreation. It celebrates unorthodox forms of sex from gay sex and group sex to interracial sex (Larry Flynt was shot and confined to a wheelchair in Georgia by a man who was outraged not at *Hustler* magazine's explicitness, as such, but rather at a photo-spread of a mixed-race couple that it contained). Ironically, these traditionalists share the view of some libertarian feminists, that pornography constitutes a powerful social force in America. The key difference is that they see its power as profoundly negative rather than positive. Writing in the conservative Heritage Foundation journal *Policy Review*, Holman Jenkins argued:

> Nobody has heard of self-help groups for people claiming to be 'addicted' to sexual innuendo in *Friends* or to violence in Arnold Schwarzenegger films. Yet in the past few years, not only have organizations popped into being to aid people who feel a compulsive 'addiction' to view pornography; the subject has also begun to arise with alarming frequency in divorce and custody proceedings. Internet porn, at least in the collective mind of the counseling industry, has emerged as a major threat to marriages. (Jenkins, 2001: 6)

Whether extinguishing pornography would, even if feasible, make marriages more stable, and whether stable marriages, however desirable, are preconditions of civilization and humanity, remains unclear, but the link between porn and moral breakdown is central to the traditionalist case.

(4) *Concerned Liberals.* Progressives occupy the more difficult and ambiguous ground compared to the relative clarity of the previous three positions. They tend instinctively to side with the individual against the state on matters of free speech. Many progressives also worry that the same logic that underpins allowing states to prohibit hard-core material could be used against explicit rock songs, films and other forms of art and literature dealing with sex. But this position becomes more complicated on pornography, partly due to the arguments of scholars such as MacKinnon about its (direct and indirect) effects on women, and partly due to notions that pornography, even if it is speech, is clearly in a lower category of speech than political speech, and hence is entitled to less stringent First Amendment protection. The ambiguity is inherent in American liberalism, which embraces freedom (including the freedom to indulge in sexual materials) but also condemns attitudes and practices that inflict harm on others and deny them equal treatment.

The conclusions that progressives reach are therefore mixed. Some maintain a predominantly libertarian position on principle. Others are more pragmatic in deferring to the wishes of local communities and states. Still others, such as Justice Brennan, advocated libertarian positions on pragmatic grounds of the impossibility of developing satisfactory definitions that cover all cases involving depictions of sex. Yet others support government action against pornography on the egalitarian ground that it robs women of their dignity and self-respect, demeaning and degrading them arbitrarily as a group and placing them under a burden that men do not share.

Whether the effect of such materials is to induce violent feelings and behaviour (or simply boredom) remains in dispute among social scientists. Much of the basis for the claim that it does cause violence against women rests on the testimony of rapists and killers, and on 'laboratory experiments' that expose men to porn films and monitor their emotional and psychological responses (curiously, women's responses have thus far not elicited comparable empirical study). But libertarians argue that pornography consumption may in some cases be an expression of pathological behaviour, but is not its cause. Also, critics claim that laboratory experiments are, by their very nature, neither conclusive nor accurately reflective of 'real-world' conditions.

Some critics of MacKinnon and Dworkin also argue that their objection is not to materials that graphically depict heterosexual sex as such, but more to the act of heterosexual sex itself. Richard Posner, for example, argues that:

> The audience for pornography is interested in sexual stimulation, not in sexual politics. Pornography does present women as sexual objects, but in moments of sexual excitement even egalitarian men conceive of women in this way. It might make a difference how steady a diet of pornography a given man consumed. It seems to me that only a man truly immersed in the stuff would find his ideas about the proper status of women altered; and we must consider whether a man prone to such immersion is, as it were, redeemable for feminism by being denied the bath he seeks. (Posner, 1992: 371)

Moreover, the kind of sexist attitudes condemned by feminists such as Dworkin generally permeate those cultures – such as Islamic cultures – that are the most zealous in banning 'adult' magazines such as *Playboy*. Although it does not confirm the existence of a causal relationship, the correlation of those societies where women face a profoundly unequal social status with the strongest suppression of sexual materials is a strong one, as is that between greater social and economic egalitarianism and permissive laws on pornography (such as Scandinavian nations).

Equally, whether it is pornography or more 'conventional' sexual images – in advertising, movies and television – that is the main cause or reinforcer of sexist attitudes in western societies is unclear.

The empirical connection between the status and security of women and the availability of pornography is therefore far from being clear or settled, but this failure to reach agreement has not made the struggle over pornography any less vehement or bitter in modern American politics. If anything, the absence of compelling evidence one way or the other has fuelled rather than muted the controversy.

EXPLAINING THE POLITICS OF PORNOGRAPHY

THE US CONSTITUTION

Like gun control, the federal Constitution appears to contain a specific provision that speaks clearly and directly to pornography: the First Amendment. This provides a constitutional guarantee for free expression: 'Congress shall make no law respecting an establishment of religion, or prohibiting the free exercise thereof; or abridging the freedom of speech, or of the press; or the right of the people peaceably to assemble, and to petition the Government for a redress of grievances.' At least in theory, Americans can communicate whatever messages they wish and Congress cannot pass a law to prevent or punish them on grounds of the content of those messages. Being the very first amendment to the federal Constitution, its symbolic political importance was, and remains, especially pronounced. Most Americans can instinctively invoke it because they know what its core value is about, even if they cannot recite it accurately line for line or quote how the courts have implemented its guarantee in practice.

But the apparent simplicity of this constitutional guarantee is severely complicated by its application to real-world contexts. As was the case with the 'right to bear arms' clause of the Second Amendment, the application of the free speech right in specific cases is highly complex and contentious. Most importantly, the constitutional guarantee is a relative, not an absolute, one. Not all speech in all instances is protected, with some types, such as libel and slander, subject to criminal penalties. It is the function of the courts to decide when, where and why laws regulating expressive speech violate the constitutional protection normally afforded by the First Amendment. In principle, at least, there exists no reason why *Debbie Does Dallas* should not merit the same level of free speech protection accorded *The Federalist Papers* or *The Gettysburg Address*.

Like abortion policy, federal and state courts did not begin to address this important question until the twentieth century. The First Amendment applied originally only to the federal government, not the states. Only with its 'incorporation' since 1925 (beginning with *Gitlow v. New York*) have states also been subjected by the Supreme Court to its guarantees of free expression. A second factor was that until the twentieth century, American legal doctrine about speech drew heavily on British experience, especially regarding obscenity, which was based on the nineteenth-century English ruling of *Regina v. Hicklin* (1868). That ruling allowed prosecutions of those publishing obscene works based on the tendency of selected excerpts of the work to 'deprave and corrupt' the most susceptible part of an audience.

Not surprisingly, the changing regulation of such material was connected to broader changes in American society over the postwar period. The new jurisprudence was both celebrated by progressives and condemned by traditionalists as simultaneously reflecting and reinforcing the social trends of 'permissiveness' that many Americans perceived to be sweeping their nation during the 1960s. The key Supreme Court decisions were handed down in *Roth v. United States* (1957) and *Miller v. California* (1973).

In *Roth*, the justices of the Warren Supreme Court worked out a distinction between 'obscenity' and pornography. Justice Brennan, for the majority, began from a highly speech-protective premise: 'All ideas having even the slightest redeeming social importance – unorthodox ideas, controversial ideas, even ideas hateful to the prevailing climate of opinion – have the full protection of the [First Amendment] guarantees, unless excludable because they encroach upon the limited area of more important interests.' But obscenity did not fall within that principle since, 'implicit in the history of the First Amendment is the rejection of obscenity as utterly without redeeming social importance'. The result was that 'obscenity' became defined as a legal term for a category of speech that is entirely without First Amendment protection. If something is deemed obscene, it lacks First Amendment protection and can be banned.

But the critical point in the conflict over explicit sexual materials is that pornography is not, by definition, obscene. Whether or not it is depends on how one defines obscenity, and then whether the pornographic work in question actually meets that definition. It is possible – and, in practice, reasonably common – for a sexually explicit work to be deemed by judicial authorities to be pornographic but not obscene, and hence to be protected by the Constitution's free speech provision. In *Roth*, the majority defined obscenity in terms of 'whether to the average person, applying contemporary community standards, the dominant theme of the material taken as a whole appeals to the prurient interest'. Prurience was seen as a 'shameful' or 'morbid' interest in sex. In this definition, only 'hard-core' pornography was likely to be considered obscene and hence unentitled to free speech protection.

The effect of *Roth* was not what had been intended, since it effectively exempted almost all materials dealing with sex from existing obscenity laws. The exclusion of obscenity from First Amendment protection made it essential that the courts identify a test of obscenity that was sufficiently clear and narrow so as not to sweep in otherwise protected speech. But following *Roth*, defining obscenity became increasingly akin to squaring the circle. In *A Book Named 'John Cleland's Memoirs of a Woman of Pleasure' v. Attorney-General* (1966), also known as the *Fanny Hill* case, Brennan, for a plurality of the Supreme Court, significantly revised the *Roth* test. Three elements now had to be satisfied to characterize a work dealing with sex as obscene:

(a) the dominant theme of the material taken as a whole appeals to a prurient interest in sex; (b) the material is patently offensive because it affronts contemporary community standards relating to the description or representation of sexual matters; and (c) the material is utterly without redeeming social value.

But this judicial test left open the question of which community (national, regional, local?) had to be offended and whether the inclusion of, say, a quote from Plato or Einstein among a collection of pornographic pictures could 'redeem' a book and accord it First Amendment protection. The result of this ambiguity was a legal quagmire of epic and sometimes richly comical proportions, in which the Court had to review obscenity convictions on a case-by-case basis. The solemn dignity of the nine black-robed justices promising 'equal justice under law' thereby met the squeals, thrusts and grunts of decidedly disrobed porn stars and starlets in the Supreme Court's basement cinema. Even here, the inherent subjectivity of obscenity definitions was manifest. Justice White, for example, would tolerate 'no erect penises, no intercourse, no oral or anal sodomy', while Brennan did not object to penetration provided no erect penis was shown (dubbed by his clerks as the 'limp dick' test). Justice Potter Stewart's 'definition' ('I know it when I see it') was routinely declaimed by law clerks at appropriately 'climactic' moments as the films rolled (McKeever, 1995: 229). But some

Exhibit 6.5   Chief Justice Earl Warren: the Puritan confronts the obscene

The Warren Court was widely blamed by traditionalists for a series of liberal decisions, not least allowing pornography to 'pollute' American society. During the 1960s, some tradition-alists even displayed bumper stickers and posted billboards calling on Congress to 'Impeach Earl Warren'. Yet ironically, although supporting most of the liberalizing decisions from *Roth* on, Warren never shed his conventional middle-American attitudes or his deep-rooted Puritanism. He reportedly told his law clerks in reference to *Roth* that 'If anyone showed that [dirty] book to my daughters, I'd have strangled him with my own hands'. The otherwise humanistic chief's defensiveness about sexual expression made rational decision-making and opinion-writing in this area difficult. To him, 'smut peddlers' instinc-tively had no First Amendment rights at all. Their concern was neither art nor literature nor even communication, and their conduct was not only a personal affront but also a peril to American's longer-term moral fibre. But Warren's deep respect for free expression weighed heavily on the Chief Justice in First Amendment cases. As his closest colleague on the Court, Justice Brennan, noted: 'Warren was a terrible prude. Like my father was. If Warren was revolted by something, it was obscene. He would not read any of the books. Or watch the movies. I'd read the book or see the movie and he'd go along with my views.'

Source: Adapted from De Grazia (1993: 274).

justices simply refused to watch the 'filth' (see Exhibit 6.5).

The majesty of American law arguably suffered at least as much indignity as some of those participating in the movies the justices watched. But beginning with *Redrup v. New York* (1967), the Court began a liberalizing process, reversing lower court obscenity convictions, and overturning 31 such convictions between 1967 and 1973.

The Court finally tired of this subjectivity and confusion by 1973 when, with four new Nixon appointees and under Chief Justice Warren Burger, a majority of the justices forged a new definition of obscenity in *Miller v. California*:

(a) whether 'the average person, applying contemporary community standards' would find that the work, taken as a whole, appeals to the prurient interest; (b) whether the work depicts or describes, in a patently offensive way, sexual conduct specifically defined by the applicable state law; and (c) whether the work, taken as a whole, lacks serious literary, artistic, political, or scientific value.

Miller was an attempt by a court that had a

new set of four Nixon appointees to allow local communities to place restrictions on sexual materials, on the basis that the people of Mississippi or Maine need not accept material found acceptable in New York. *Miller* also attempted to require that even if a work had social value, it could be labelled unprotected obscenity. But the criterion of 'serious' value remained an inherently sub-jective assessment. Ultimately, the universal-ist spirit that underpins the First Amendment was substantially more influential than the particular objections of certain localities to being exposed to sexual materials. The Court succeeded in *Miller* in disengaging itself from reviewing the finding of obscenity on a case-by-case basis, but in leaving the definition of the obscene to lower courts it signally failed to stem the production and distribution of most pornographic material.

The basic intent of the justices had been relatively clear and sensible: to establish a regulatory regime where genuine works of art that contained sexual depictions could not be suppressed, while simultaneously allow-ing (though not requiring) states and local communities to prohibit the more explicit forms of hard-core pornography. In practice, however, drawing an effective body of case law to achieve these dual ends proved impossible. The effort was perhaps doomed from the start, but it certainly reached that state by the time *Miller* was handed down.

For some justices in both federal and state courts, the danger in limiting First Amendment protection – to allow authorities to curb legitimate publications – was far greater than the need to prevent the consumption of porn. This was especially so since, as part of the culture war, school boards were under intense pressure on curricula and library holdings from the 1970s. According to the American Library Association, for example, 52 books were banned from school libraries across America in 1986 alone (Hellinger and Judd, 1994: 35). These included *The Diary of Anne Frank* ('sexually offensive passages'), *Cujo* by Stephen King ('profanity and strong sexual content'), *The Color Purple* by Alice Walker ('troubling ideas about race relations') and *To Kill a Mockingbird* by Harper Lee ('undermining of race relations').

Similarly, the suppression of non-pornographic works under a guise of attacking 'smut' concerned many progressives and women's groups. Feminist women are especially keen to the harms of censorship since, historically, information about sex, sexual orientation, reproduction and birth control has been banned under the guise of 'protecting' women. Such restrictions have not only failed to reduce violence against women, but also led to the jailing of birth control advocates such as Margaret Sanger and the suppression of feminist works from *Our Bodies, Ourselves* to the plays of Karen Finley and Holly Hughes. Since women are as varied as any citizens of a democracy, the prospect of agreement among them as to what images are distasteful or even sexist is minimal, with or without the intervention of the state.

As Exhibit 6.6 shows, under pressure from traditionalists after 1969, the Burger and Rehnquist Courts enhanced the power of community controls on pornography and sexual expression generally, but without expanding the domain of the prohibitable. Obscenity law generally maintained a balance between democratic and liberal values that favoured classical liberalism – the freedom of the individual from state control. The current application of the law could be made easier if the Supreme Court adopted a fully liberal standard that reconciled sexual expression with most other expression as equally worthy, but such a reconciliation would be difficult to achieve politically, being tantamount to the abandonment of democratic control in such a highly charged and politicized issue.

It was not only traditionalists who mobilized against pornography in response to Court decisions. While the Burger and Rehnquist Courts sought to respond to community concerns, some women's organizations attempted to make pornography an issue of gender equality and civil rights. Most prominent were MacKinnon and Dworkin, who popularized the argument that porn is 'an institution of gender inequality' and 'a practice of sex discrimination, a violation of women's civil rights'; the very act of watching pornography is an act of male domination. In order to counter this, they developed their own detailed definition of what constitutes pornography and when it can and should be banned (laid out in Exhibit 6.7 below). They argued that they were not anti-sex, but that permissible erotica, as distinct from pornography, was sexually explicit material 'premised on equality'.

The MacKinnon/Dworkin ordinance was first introduced in Minneapolis, Minnesota, in 1983. Supported by a coalition of feminists and conservative anti-pornography activists, the ordinance was passed by the City Council only to be vetoed by the liberal Democrat mayor. The ordinance was finally passed into law in Indianapolis, Indiana, in 1984, backed by conservative Republicans. But the ordinance was ruled unconstitutional by the Indiana federal court, a decision confirmed by the federal court of appeals in *American*

Exhibit 6.6   Key Supreme Court rulings on pornography, 1957–2000

Roth v. US (1957). 6–3. The First Amendment does not cover obscene works, those that 'taken as a whole' appealed to the 'prurient interest' of 'the average person' and were 'utterly without redeeming social importance'. Effectively removed from threat of obscenity laws most works, even those dealing explicitly with sex, whose goal was to convey ideas rather than provide sexual stimulation.

Jacobellis v. Ohio (1964). The Court recognized that it had to make its own independent judgment of the nature of allegedly obscene material in each case.

Memoirs v. Massachusetts (1966). Material was obscene if its dominant theme is prurient, it is 'patently offensive because it affronts contemporary community standards', and it is 'utterly without redeeming social value'. Only the most explicit material could meet his test, which shifted *Roth*'s emphasis on prurience to patent offensiveness and the presence or absence of even minimal social value. The test effectively required the prosecution to prove a negative, a difficult task. Pornography producers resorted to their 'actors' quoting Aristotle or Einstein at the end of a sex scene to suggest some value that redeemed the product. Subsequently, the Court overturned virtually all obscenity prosecutions unless the material was sold to minors or advertised salaciously.

Stanley v. Georgia (1969). 9–0. Ruled that the constitutional right of privacy prohibited criminally punishing an individual for the private possession of obscene material in the home.

Miller v. California (1973). 5–4. Revised prior tests of obscenity, to identify material as obscene if its predominant theme is prurient according to the sensibilities of an average person of the community, it depicts sexual conduct in a patently offensive way, and if, taken as a whole, it 'lacks serious literary, artistic, political, or scientific value'. Attempted to restore power to communities to control sexual materials.

FCC v. Pacifica (1978). 5–4. Upheld the decision of the Federal Communications Commission to limit (but not ban) the availability of non-obscene 'indecent' expression in broadcasting.

City of Renton v. Playtime Theatres, Inc. (1986). 7–2. Allowed zoning control of non-obscene pornography.

Osborne v. Ohio (1990). 6–3. Narrowed scope of *Stanley* by upholding the conviction of an individual for the possession of child pornography, under an Ohio law that banned the possession or viewing of any materials depicting minors in a state of nudity. The majority argued that the interest of the state in suppressing child pornography far exceeds the interest of the state in proscribing the possession of obscene materials.

Barnes v. Glen Theatre, Inc. (1991). 5–4. In a case concerning nude dancing in public, the Court conceded that such dancing could be considered expressive conduct, and was hence protected speech. But it also ruled that it was only marginally so and that the regulation of such conduct by the states was constitutionally permissible. Indiana's public indecency law 'furthers a substantial governmental interest in order and morality'.

Reno v. American Civil Liberties Union (1997). 9–0. The Court unanimously strikes down the Communications Decency Act of 1996 as unconstitutional. The law had made it a crime to put 'indecent' or 'patently offensive' words or pictures online where children could find them.

United States v. Playboy Entertainment Group, Inc. (2000). 5–4. The majority said that restrictions on the broadcasting of adult material, enacted by Congress in the 1996 telecommunications law (PL 104–104), placed an undue burden on the exercise of free speech.

Exhibit 6.7   The MacKinnon/Dworkin definition of pornography

Pornography is the graphic sexually explicit subordination of women, whether in pictures or in words, that also includes one or more of the following: (i) women are presented dehumanized as sexual objects, things or commodities; or (ii) women are presented as sexual objects who enjoy pain or mutilation; or (iii) women are presented as sexual objects who experience sexual pleasure in being raped; or (iv) women are presented as sexual objects tied up or cut up or mutilated or bruised or physically hurt; or (v) women are presented in postures of sexual submission, servility or display; or (vi) women's body parts – including but not limited to vaginas, breasts and buttocks – are exhibited, such that women are reduced to those parts; or (vii) women are presented as whores by nature; or (viii) women are presented being penetrated by objects or animals; or (ix) women are presented in scenarios of degradation, injury, torture, shown as filthy or inferior, bleeding, bruised or hurt in a context that makes these conditions sexual.

Source: Quoted in De Grazia (1993: 595).

Booksellers v. Hudnut (1985) and affirmed without discussion by the Supreme Court.

The courts agreed that, unlike obscenity laws, the ordinance singled out material for condemnation based on disapproval of its viewpoint (presumed advocacy of the sexual subordination of women). Such viewpoint discrimination was at the heart of the protections afforded by traditional First Amendment jurisprudence. As Judge Easterbrook argued in striking the ordinance down: 'This is thought control. It establishes an approved view of women, of how they may react to sexual encounters, of how the sexes may relate to each other. Those who espouse the approved view may use sexual images; those who do not, may not.'

Many progressives and feminists disagreed with this view, arguing that pornography is, at best, low-value speech that enjoys only diminished protection under the First Amendment. Others argued that the collective costs of pornography (for women as a social group and for particular communities) outweigh any free speech rights of the individual to consume it. Yet for still others, defining pornography as a form of discrimination against women hardly narrowed the field, allowing the censor to address the more familiar examples of American cultural

sexism that appear every day in outlets as varied as romance novels, detergent commercials and (not least) the Bible. The fact that the courts largely erred on the side of individual liberty encouraged progressives but has not made the political battles any less settled. Renewed efforts by the feminist–fundamentalist coalition yielded new attempts at the suppression of 'sexpression'.

GOVERNING INSTITUTIONS

Presidential politics

The term 'State of the Union' might perhaps have been coined for the president to discuss pornographic couplings but, perhaps unsurprisingly, presidents have had little to say publicly on the subject. Presidents Johnson and Reagan both took the issue of pornography sufficiently seriously to establish presidential commissions to investigate the competing arguments about sexually explicit materials and recommend action (see Exhibit 6.8). This also had the happily convenient effect of exempting their administrations from taking immediate action. Nevertheless, the decisions to establish the bodies, and the two commissions' markedly different recommendations, reflected the temper of their respective times and had important political and social consequences. In particular, after the Meese Commission reported, the federal bureaucracy under Reagan and Bush acted fairly aggressively on porn distributors in a deliberate attempt to crack down on the mass market for sexual material.

As well as these commissions, porno-graphy has also formed an occasional part of presidential campaigns, especially for Republicans, where appeals to ban 'smut' are perceived to have a receptive audience in GOP primaries and caucuses. Pat Buchanan, for example, colourfully attacked George H.W. Bush in 1992's Georgia Republican Party primary for supporting the National

Exhibit 6.8 Three views on the links between pornography and anti-social behaviour: no, maybe and yes

The Lockhart Commission (1970). President Lyndon Johnson appointed a commission to study the operation of America's obscenity laws in 1967. It reported three years later (with Nixon as president) that it had found no evidence that pornography was harmful: 'In sum, empirical research designed to clarify the question has found no evidence to date that exposure to explicit sexual materials plays a significant role in the causation of delinquent or criminal behavior among youth or adults. The Commission cannot conclude that exposure to erotic materials is a factor in the causation of sex crimes or sex delinquency' (1970: 27). The real problem was rather 'the inability or reluctance of people in our society to be open and direct in dealing with sexual matters'. The Commission's central recommendation was for the repeal of existing obscenity laws. Even before it reported, President Nixon denounced its findings as 'morally bankrupt' while his Vice President, Spiro Agnew, declared: 'As long as Richard Nixon is President, Main Street is not going to become Smut Alley.'

The Williams Committee [United Kingdom] (1979). Set up by the British government and chaired by the philosopher Bernard Williams, the Committee reported that: 'It is not possible, in our view, to reach well-based conclusions about what in this country has been the influence of pornography on sexual crime' (UK Home Office, 1979: 80).

The Meese Commission (1986). In 1985, Edwin Meese III, President Reagan's Attorney General, convened another commission. Chaired by a zealous anti-pornography prosecutor, Henry Hudson, the barely hidden agenda was clearly to discredit the previous Commission's liberal conclusions. Although admitting that the scientific evidence was inconclusive, the Commission (over two dissents) announced that this evidence, along with their own common sense, nevertheless led them to believe that pornography caused sexual crimes: 'We have reached the conclusion, unanimously and confidently, that the available evidence strongly supports the hypothesis that substantial exposure to sexually violent materials as described here bears a causal relationship to antisocial acts of sexual violence, and for some subgroups possibly to unlawful acts of sexual violence' (1986: 326). The Commission refused to recommend new laws, but of its 94 recommendations, the most important was the creation of a National Obscenity Enforcement Unit (NOEU) within the US Department of Justice, empowered to bring prosecutions against distributors of sexual materials. The NOEU was charged with aggressively promoting the enforcement of existing federal and state laws. In alliance with local groups (often from the Christian Right), the NOEU enjoyed significant success in bringing prosecutions against distributors of sexual materials and in encouraging outlets not to stock material with a sexual content. Only with Bill Clinton's election in 1992 did the rate of such lawsuits diminish from 1993 to 2001.

Endowment for the Arts which, he claimed, subsidized allegedly pornographic and obscene artists.

During the 1990s, the pornography issue also became entangled in broader popular concerns over the violent and explicit content of much television and film entertainment in America. President Clinton signed legislation to require new televisions to contain a 'V-chip', allowing parents to prevent children from accessing certain channels. He also signed the Republican 'Communications Decency Act' in 1996 to tighten regulation of the Internet and prevent the transmission of 'indecent' programming. Such acts were designed to reinforce the president's traditionalist credentials among voters. Despite, or perhaps because of, the revelations surrounding his own 'inappropriate behaviour' in 1998, Clinton also commissioned federal investigations into the effects of explicit popular culture on youth in 1999. The president's unique position in the American constitutional order helped to ensure that demands for a restoration of 'moral leadership' fell with great regularity at the door of the White House.

Congress

In 1967, when moves began to impeach Supreme Court Justice Abe Fortas, part of the drive against him by some senators focused on the votes he had cast as a member of the Warren Court on movies he deemed were not obscene. Fortas had been a supporter of many liberal positions on the Court and President Johnson was keen to nominate him to succeed Warren as Chief Justice before the 1968 election. Conservatives who were dismayed at the liberalism of Warren and Fortas vowed not to let that happen, and pornography proved one issue on which they could exploit the justice's vulnerability. A 'Fortas Obscene Movie Show' on Capitol Hill formed a prominent part of the campaign to discredit the justice. Fortas was eventually forced to withdraw his nomination and Richard Nixon nominated Warren Burger in his place.

For most in Congress, pornography is a 'win–win' issue. Subject to the need to regularly win electoral majorities, lawmakers are rarely keen to take positions that suggest support for unconventional lifestyles or sexual practices (as part of the 1996 Welfare Reform Act, for example, Congress even included provisions for federal grants for sexual abstinence programmes – the only federal funding specifically allocated for any kind of sex education). Pornography provides an opportunity not only to take public positions that claim to defend the traditional family, but also to placate the otherwise unlikely electoral duo of feminists and religious groups (especially Christian evangelicals and Catholics). The electoral costs of such a stance are, at best, marginal. Those constituents who might care passionately about 'pornography rights' are unlikely to be so numerous as to prove decisive in re-election battles, much less to be vocal about their cause.

There are, of course, a few notable exceptions. For those members representing the handful of districts or states where the production and consumption of pornography is a lucrative market and an important source of employment (particularly in California's San Fernando Valley), too vocal an anti-porn stance is unwise. Equally, many politicians are able to avoid, as it were, full-frontal defences of pornography by using the broad cloak of free speech and the First Amendment. Ironically, of course, those progressives who resist the calls for bans on pornography tend to resort to the same type of 'slippery-slope' arguments that the National Rifle Association uses on gun control. That is, they argue that bans on porn will inevitably lead to prohibitions on other forms of communication dealing with sex and sexuality, from novels to paintings.

Partly for these reasons, then, pornography has not seen the type of partisan polarization that characterized abortion and gun control. But, like gay rights, pornography has been a useful issue by which Republicans have been able simultaneously to appease core elements of the party's coalition (especially Christian evangelicals and pro-family organizations) and attack Democrats as defenders of the 'permissive Sixties'. By introducing bills to restrict or prohibit forms of sexual speech, cut funding for (or eliminate) the National Endowment for the Arts (NEA), and censor the Internet, the GOP has placed Democrats in the unenviable position of having to oppose them, and thereby be portrayed by opponents as 'the pornographer's friend'.

By the mid-1980s, the Senate Commerce Committee held nationally televised hearings on 'obscene' lyrics in music by artists as varied as WASP, Cyndi Lauper and Prince. Controversy over the National Endowment for the Arts also featured heavily during the 1980s and 1990s. Having given federal grants to museums and galleries that featured the homo-erotic photographs of Robert Mapplethorpe and the irreligious work of Andres Serrano, the NEA was an obvious target for social conservatives. Led by Senator Jesse Helms (Republican, North Carolina), social conservatives sought to prohibit the NEA from donating to institutions that put 'obscene and indecent' art on display. As he put it: 'There's a big difference between "The Merchant of Venice" and a photograph of two males of different races on a marble tabletop. This Mapplethorpe fellow was an acknowledged homosexual ... the theme goes throughout his work' (De Grazia, 1993: 622).

Established in 1965 to fund non-profit arts projects, the agency has made more than 110,000 grants for undertakings ranging from the design of the Vietnam Veterans memorial in Washington to the first workshop production of the musical *A Chorus Line*. Fewer than 50 of those grants have proven controversial (see Exhibit 6.9). However, the NEA was especially politically exposed, since conservatives could attack its funding decisions not simply on the basis of the offensive content of certain works of art, but because of the taxpayer source of its funding. As such, criticism of the NEA provided a relatively rare opportunity to bring social and economic conservatives (traditionalists and libertarians) together. The conservative commentator

William Buckley observed: 'If a democratic society cannot find a way to protect a taxpaying Christian heterosexual from finding that he is engaged in subsidizing blasphemous acts of homo-eroticism, then democracy isn't working' (quoted in De Grazia, 1993: 627).

Responding to pressure from religious groups and traditionalists, in 1990 Congress passed legislation that: (a) officially relieved the NEA of the task given to it by 1989 legislation administratively to censor artists by rejecting arts projects considered by the NEA to come within the *Miller* definition of the obscene; (b) the NEA was given the explicit authority to defund (require the repayment of a grant already paid out to) any artists or art organization found by it (after a hearing) to have been found by a court of law to have created or disseminated with financial assistance from the NEA any work that was legally obscene; and (c) the NEA was for the first time required to refuse to fund arts projects that in its judgement – not a court's – might violate 'general standards of decency' or fail to show 'respect for the diverse beliefs and values of the American public'. By 2000, the NEA's funding had been cut from $175 million (in 1991) to $98 million.

Another important example of congressional responsiveness to anti-permissive forces occurred in the mid-1990s. When the Republicans took control of Congress after the 1994 election, one of the measures they introduced was the Communications Decency Act (CDA) – an attempt to keep sexually explicit materials off the Internet. President Bill Clinton signed the bill into law, as another prop in his traditionalist conservative social agenda that reinforced his 'New Democrat' image for the 1996 presidential election. The Act made it a federal crime to transmit 'indecent' or pornographic messages via e-mail or the Internet. The law made it a crime for a person to send indecent messages by way of an interactive computer network to anyone under the age of 18. It also banned Internet displays of pornography that would be accessible to someone under age 18. The law did not clearly or precisely define the

Exhibit 6.9   Art wars: the National Endowment for the Arts

- *1989*: Artist Andres Serrano, a grant recipient, creates 'Piss Christ', a photograph of a crucifix in a jar of urine. Photographer Robert Mapplethorpe, another grantee, creates an exhibit featuring graphic displays of unusual gay sex practices. Congress responds by passing the first ban on federal funding for works that could be considered obscene and that do not have 'serious literary, artistic, political or scientific value'.
- *1990*: During the conference on the fiscal 1991 Interior spending bill, the Senate agrees to adopt House language to lift the ban and add language directing the agency's chairman to take into account 'general standards of decency and respect for the diverse beliefs and values of the American public' in judging grant applications.
- *1991*: Senator Jesse Helms offers an amendment to the fiscal 1992 Interior appropriations bill to bar the NEA from funding materials that depict 'in a patently offensive way, sexual or excretory activities or organs'. During floor debate on the conference report, Helms brandishes a magazine called *Performance Journal*, which he said featured a 'blown-up' photo of a vagina. The amendment is tabled, 73–25.
- *1993*: Helms offers an amendment to the fiscal 1994 Interior appropriations bill that would eliminate all $170 million earmarked for the NEA. The amendment is defeated, 15–83.
- *1994*: A controversial show by an HIV-positive performance artist in Minneapolis draws new attention to NEA grants. The artist cut himself and another performer, then blotted up the blood on paper towels and hung them over the audience. The Walker Art Center, which received $104,500 from the endowment in fiscal 1994, says it spent less than $150 in federal funds to present the show. Helms offers an amendment, tabled 49–42, to the fiscal 1995 Interior appropriations bill that would have barred funding for content that depicts 'human mutilation, or invasive bodily procedures on human beings dead or alive; or the drawing or letting of blood'.
- *1995*: Senator James Jeffords (Republican, Vermont) attaches an amendment to the fiscal 1996 Interior appropriations bill that bars funding of projects that 'denigrate the objects or beliefs of the adherents of a particular religion' or 'depict or describe, in a patently offensive way, sexual or excretory activities or organs'. The amendment is adopted by voice vote.
- *1998*: The Supreme Court upholds the 1990 law requiring the NEA to consider decency standards when it decides who should receive grants.

Source: Julie Hirschfeld, 'NEA and the Art of Pleasing Congress', *CQ Weekly*, June 10, 2000, p. 1374.

material to be banned but referred to 'patently offensive' and 'indecent' portrayals of sexual or excretory activities. Convicted violators of the CDA could be fined $25,000, sentenced to two years in prison, or both.

CDA supporters held that the law served a compelling public interest – the common good of protecting the moral development of pre-adults. But opponents denounced the CDA as an unconstitutional limit on free expression. The American Civil Liberties Union (ACLU) and the American Library Association filed suit and, on appeal in *Reno v. American Civil Liberties Union* (1997), the Supreme Court unanimously struck down the law as an unconstitutional infringement of the First Amendment. Despite the appointment of conservative justices to the Court by Reagan and Bush (arguably their most important political legacy), free expression remained an area where a majority was exceedingly wary of upholding legislative restrictions on communication. Justice Stevens wrote for the Court that:

Not withstanding the legitimacy and importance of the congressional goal of protecting
children from harmful materials, we agree . . .
that the statute abridges the freedom of
speech protected by the First Amendment. . . .
The interest in encouraging freedom of
expression in a democratic society outweighs
any theoretical but unproven benefit of
censorship.

The case was especially significant in applying free speech precedents to the new
electronically driven media.

Intermediary organizations

Pornography has largely been peripheral to
the national parties. Partisan polarization has
been less evident on the issue than with
regard to abortion and gun control. Election
years have sometimes seen the parties' platforms make declaratory statements, generally
of a hostile or condemnatory type. As might
be expected, neither party has sought to take
an explicit stand in favour of pornographers,
but the Republicans have been more likely to
advocate restrictions on sexual materials and
to exploit Democratic defences of free speech
rights and the First Amendment. Even so, in
August 2000, Al Gore and other leading
Democrats condemned a proposed Democratic Party fundraiser to be held at Hugh
Hefner's *Playboy* mansion in Los Angeles
during the party's national convention (the
event was eventually moved).

Although the parties are less pressured by
well-resourced interest lobbies on this issue
than on abortion and gun control, the interest
group universe nevertheless contains a wide
variety of activists on pornography, both for
and against. The coalition that defends
pornography is itself unusually eclectic. Civil
liberties groups such as the American
Civil Liberties Union actively oppose the prohibitionist lobby. Groups such as Feminists
for Free Expression have sought to articulate
a defence of pornography within the
women's movement. The sex industry itself
has attempted, without undue fanfare but
with some success, to protect its wares and

livelihoods. It established a suitably dignified
title for its main interest group, the Free
Speech Coalition, dedicated to opposing, for
example, the California state legislature
imposing a 'sin-tax' on the producers
working in San Fernando Valley. And even
Hollywood film studios have stepped in –
occasionally, discreetly and indirectly – to
assist the cause of free expression and oppose
regulations on distribution and tax issues.

The opposing coalition is also heterogeneous. Feminist organizations have been
strongly active, especially on pressuring cities
and institutions to adopt the MacKinnon/
Dworkin ordinance. Opposition to pornography has also been a prominent element of
the 'purity' agendas of New Christian Right
organizations. 'Pro-decency' activists and
major fundamentalist organizations such as
Donald Wildmon's American Family Association and Citizens for Decency Through Law
(the anti-porn organization of disgraced Sav-
ings and Loan financier, Charles Keating)
were active during the 1980s and 1990s in
alleging that a causal link between pornography and criminal behaviour existed.
Other conservative and traditionalist groups
have made the fight against pornography
part of a broader attempt to defend the traditional American family and Judaeo-Christian
values, such as the Christian Coalition, the
Family Research Council and the Eagle
Forum. Their concerns have taken in not only
sexually explicit programming, but also television shows as diverse as *Ellen* and *South
Park*.

On balance, the centrality of freedom to
American culture has limited the success
of the anti-pornography coalition. Pro-
censorship groups have also suffered from
the more general diffusion of representations
of sex and sexuality into culture since the
1960s. As the historic battles between 'purity'
advocates and their opponents from the nineteenth century to today have demonstrated,
definitions of conventional and unconventional sexual practices are notoriously fluid.
By the turn of the twentieth century, Hollywood began to produce mainstream movies

Exhibit 6.10   *The People vs. Larry Flynt*

The unsuccessful impeachment of Bill Clinton helped to reinforce the image of Larry Flynt as a populist champion of free speech and opponent of hypocrisy about sex. Flynt's notoriety had begun some years earlier, when he won a libel action after his magazine had published (in 1983) a Campari ad parody in which the prominent Christian fundamentalist, Reverend Jerry Falwell, purportedly described his first sexual experience – with his mother in an outhouse. Falwell's $45 million lawsuit against Flynt was ultimately unsuccessful, with the US Supreme Court arguing that, since Falwell was a public figure, the parody was protected by the First Amendment. The film *The People vs. Larry Flynt* celebrated Flynt's eclectic story but remained, for influential feminists such as Gloria Steinem, a deeply misleading and dangerous account.

Gloria Steinem	*Milos Forman*
Let's be clear: A pornographer is not a hero, no more than a publisher of Ku Klux Klan books or a Nazi on the Internet, no matter what constitutional protection he secures. . . . In this film, produced by Oliver Stone and directed by Milos Forman, *Hustler* is depicted as tacky at worst, and maybe even honest for showing full nudity. What's left out are the magazine's images of women being beaten, tortured and raped, women subject to degradations from bestiality to sexual slavery.	One can't really argue with Gloria because she's accusing the film of something it is not. It does not glorify pornography. [This] is like saying Romeo and Juliet glorifies teenage suicide. The film is about free speech and the price we pay for it. When the Nazis and Communists first came in (to Czechoslovakia), they declared war on pornographers and perverts. Everyone applauded: who wants perverts running through the streets? But then suddenly, Jesus Christ was a pervert, Shakespeare was a pervert, Hemingway was a pervert. It always starts with pornographers to open the door a little but then the door is open for all kinds of persecution.

Source: Adapted from Gloria Steinem, 'Hollywood Cleans Up *Hustler*', *New York Times*, January 7, 1997, A13; and Bernard Weintraub, '*Flynt* Receives Thumps Up by New Reviewers: ACLU', *New York Times*, February 21, 1997, B3.

about the porn industry (such as *Boogie Nights*, *The People vs. Larry Flynt* and *The Fluffer*) that suggested a substantial mass market for popular artistic treatments even of the genre itself, while 'art-house' cinema also began to include 'hard-core' scenes in movies such as *Romance* and *Intimacy*. Even here, however, debate raged between proponents of free speech and advocates of group equality. As Exhibit 6.10 shows, pornography continues strongly and bitterly to divide many who would otherwise occupy the same ground in American political life.

CONCLUSION

In the midst of 'Monicagate' during 1998, when Clinton's future as president seemed in doubt, there existed one certainty: that the porn industry would produce its version of the president's 'inappropriate behaviour'. Sure enough, *Scenes from the Oral Office* subsequently provided a hard-core parody of the Starr Report's more clinical descriptions of the presidential liaisons (Tang, 1999: 12).

Justice Robert Jackson wrote in *West Virginia State Board of Education v. Barnette* (1943) that: 'If there is any fixed star in our constitutional constellation, it is that no official, high or petty, can prescribe what shall be orthodox in politics, nationalism, religion, or other matters of opinion or force citizens to confess by word or act their faith therein.' Pornography is a cultural conflict where a range of political actors have steadily sought to unfix that star, and it threatens to remain a prominent battle in the culture war. This is partly because the market for explicit sexual materials has continued to grow and to be supplied by numerous outlets, and partly because millions of Americans continue to disapprove of certain forms of conduct, even if it occurs in the privacy of someone else's home. Unlike abortion, however, the disapproval of certain acts is not confined to traditionalists, but finds support among groups who would normally count themselves as strongly progressive.

Justice John Harlan was undoubtedly correct when he wrote in *Cohen v. California* (1971) that 'one man's vulgarity is another's lyric'. Traditionalists who yearn for an idealized version of the 1950s in which square dances, *South Pacific* and Bing Crosby uplift rather than contaminate American youth seem doubly mistaken. First, American popular culture has always contained a subversive streak, from Mark Twain's novels and

H.L. Mencken's prose through Marx Brothers comedies to *The Simpsons* and *South Park*. Secondly, as Posner notes, 'The popular culture of the 1950s was not as raunchy as today's, but today's popular culture does not ridicule obese people, ethnic minorities, stammerers, retarded people, and effeminate men, as the popular culture of the 1950s did' (Posner, 2001: 304).

Guarantees of free expression are relative rather than absolute, and for many Americans it is for the people, expressing their will through elections, to decide what and where restrictions on free speech should legitimately be imposed. The powerful strain of moralism that remains in American culture also confronts the antipathy of most Americans towards government, especially on issues of sex and sexuality. Perhaps nowhere is the cultural battle between those who seek equality and those who value individual liberty so pronounced as on the issue of free speech, whether in regard to pornography or racist or homophobic expressions. It is a marked irony, though not necessarily an inconsistency, that the identities of the prohibitionists and libertarians on this very American issue contrasts starkly with those on gun control and drugs.

FURTHER READING

Robert Bork, *Slouching Toward Gomorroh: Modern Liberalism and American Decline* (1996) is a strongly traditionalist view of how American values and institutions have been subverted by secular humanists, relativists and radical feminists.

Edward De Grazia, *Girls Lean Back Everywhere: The Law of Obscenity and the Assault on Genius* (1993) is a lengthy compendium of cases involving free speech and sexuality through American history, sympathetic to libertarian approaches to the First Amendment.

Andrea Dworkin, *Pornography: Men Possessing Women* (1981) is arguably the classic radical feminist text that equates pornography with male dominance and draws strong – and highly contentious – analogies with the nature of heterosexual sex more broadly.

Susan Easton, *The Problem of Pornography: Regulation and the Right to Free Speech* (1994) is a detailed analysis of the issues surrounding the debate over pornography.

Marjorie Heins, *Sex, Sin and Blasphemy: A Guide to America's Censorship Wars* (1993) is a readable polemical analysis that takes a strongly libertarian line against restrictions on free speech.

Catherine MacKinnon, *Only Words* (1993) is a short polemical work in which MacKinnon forcefully argues the case that pornography is hate speech and a denial of women's civil rights.

Richard Posner, *Sex and Reason* (1992) is a detailed, careful and dispassionate analysis of a range of issues concerning sex and sexuality, including pornography.

Richard Posner and Katharine Silbaugh, *A Guide to America's Sex Laws* (1998) provides detailed coverage of how individual state laws differ on everything from voyeurism to bestiality.

Nadine Strossen, *Defending Pornography* (1995) is a leading ACLU advocate who contests the MacKinnnon–Dworkin view of sexually explicit materials as oppressive to women.

Isabel Tang, *Pornography: The Secret History of Civilisation* (1999) is an excellent account of the development of sexually explicit materials (and the controversies about them) from antiquity to the present.

WEB LINKS

Anti-censorship organizations and resources

American Civil Liberties Union
http://www.aclu.org

Anti-Puritan Action
http://www.burn.ucsd.edu/~mai/sex.html

Free Speech Coalition
http://www.freespeechcoalition.org/

National Coalition Against Censorship
http://www.ncac.org/

Electronic Privacy Information Center
http://www.epic.org/crypto/

COYOTE ('Call Off Your Old Tired Ethics')
http://www.bayswan.org/COYOTE.html

Feminists for Free Expression
http://www.well.com/user/freedom

First Amendment Cyber Tribune
http://www.trib.com/FACT/index.html

National Coalition Against Censorship
http://www.ncac.org

Traditionalist organizations

Morality in Media
http://www.moralityinmedia.org

Christian Coalition
www.cc.org

True Love Waits
http://www.lifeway.com/tlw/

QUESTIONS

- Does the First Amendment's protection of free speech include protecting erotic or pornographic expressions?

- 'The First Amendment affords more protection to some kinds of speech than others, therefore the argument that it protects pornography, which barely qualifies as "speech", is redundant.' Discuss.

- How far have traditionalists succeeded in mounting a sexual counter-revolution?

- If a link between sexually explicit materials and *either* violence against women *or* moral breakdown could be reliably proven, should First Amendment protection of pornography be ended?

- Under what, if any, conditions should government be allowed to regulate expressions of hatred towards particular social groups?

7 Gay Rights

. . . The Supreme Court has never had occasion to declare that young lovers have a fundamental constitutional right to embrace one another lustily as they dance the night away. But that right, too, is there waiting to be proclaimed against any state or locality so prudish as to insist that the young couple conduct themselves with greater decorum.

Laurence Tribe (1992: 99)

Many of the same people involved in Adolf Hitler [sic] were Satanists, many of them were homosexuals – the two things seem to go together.

Rev. Pat Robertson, founder of the Christian Coalition (Esler, 1997: 158)

- **The Historical Context**
- **Public Opinion**
- **Explaining the Politics of Gay Rights**
- **The US Constitution**
- **Governing Institutions**
- **Presidential Politics**
- **Conclusion**

Chapter Summary

Gay and lesbian Americans have made enormous progress since the 1960s. Openly gay women and men now serve in Congress, at the highest levels of corporate America and in the professions. Public laws and policies have accorded gay Americans legal protections against employment discrimination in many states, but despite increasing levels of tolerance existing in America, many Americans continue to view same-sex relations and homosexuality as immoral. Until the 1960s homosexuality was classified as an illness and it was not until the end of that decade that gays and lesbians began mobilizing forcefully in the political arena. Although social change has occurred steadily in advancing civil rights since the Stonewall protests of 1969, the process has been neither clear nor consistent in regard to sexual relations, discrimination or same-sex unions. In 1986, for example, the Supreme Court upheld as constitutional a Georgia state law criminalizing homosexual sexual relations. While, in 1996, the Court struck down a Colorado constitutional amendment that had sought to prevent cities and towns in that state from protecting homosexuals against discrimination, four years later it held that the Boy Scouts of America had a First Amendment right to bar homosexuals from becoming scout-masters. By 2002, most states had enacted laws defining marriage explicitly and exclusively as a heterosexual compact, but the issue of whether same-sex unions can be denied the same financial and legal benefits as heterosexual couples remains for the courts to adjudicate. For gay rights advocates, the issue of homosexual equality is about fundamental liberties and rights, directly analogous to prior struggles of African Americans and women. For traditionalists, however, the issues concern fundamental conceptions of the family, marriage and the rights of communities to express their particular moral and religious codes in law. Although many overtly and covertly anti-gay laws are not enforced by public authorities and increasing legal protections now exist, homosexuals remain comparatively unequal. Moreover, the achievement of increasing acceptance has sharpened divisions within the gay rights movement. With few but significant exceptions, traditionalists remain in the political ascendancy on gay equality despite increasing popular support for gay rights.

Note: I use the terms 'gay and lesbian' and 'homosexual' interchangeably. References to the gay rights movement include bisexuals, transgendered and transsexual Americans.

In August 1998, three advertisements appeared in newspapers across America. In the first, Anna Paulk, 'wife, mother and former lesbian', explained how God had helped her to 'overcome homosexuality'. Having been sexually abused by a teenage boy as a child, she had subsequently turned to a lesbian life. But she eventually 'discovered God' and was able to 'leave' homosexuality. A second advertisement featured several hundred people pictured together under the headline, 'We're standing for the truth that homosexuals can change'. The text beneath explained how Christian groups were motivated 'more by love than hate' and offered solutions to the 'problems for homosexuals that even condoms can't fix'. Finally, a third advertisement featured a black former pro-footballer turned evangelical minister, Reggie White, whose belief that homosexuality was sinful had earned him widespread abuse from gays and lesbians: 'I've been called homophobic. I've been called stupid. I've been called unintelligent, and I've been called a nigger by so-called gay activists' (Kettle, 1998: 2).

The advertisements represented a new stage in the evolution of the Christian Right's antipathy to the notion of equal rights for gays. Viewing same-sex acts, much less loving relationships or unions, as a sin against God, homosexuality had never occupied a place close to evangelical hearts. But the appropriate political response was now deemed to be that employed for most faith-related attempts at 'healing': conversion. The adverts' message was clear: the state of homosexuality may be sinful but the righteous individual can, through hard work, faith and Godliness, depart that unholy state, be forgiven and emerge redeemed. That gays are capable of racism also suggested that attempts to equate the homosexual struggle for equal rights with that of blacks was either mistaken or insulting. But for many homosexuals, the adverts represented merely a crudely veiled attempt to mask a vehement anti-gay bigotry under a façade of Christian compassion.

Gay rights is a supremely highly charged and multifaceted cultural conflict. It pits fundamental values of individual liberty and equal opportunity against the rights of states in a federal system to legislate their own moralities and strongly held religious beliefs about the immorality of certain forms of behaviour. It is also an issue where a traditionally tolerant people who generally try to adjust to social and cultural change while preserving traditional structures and established lifestyles, still frequently make an exception. As Alan Wolfe remarked, 'Homosexuality is the one area where people still use words like "sinful, abnormal, wrong and immoral." Middle Americans don't identify with gay people who talk about marriage or children or living in the suburbs' (Kettle, 1998: 3).

The response of many of those on the American right, whom gays and lesbians frequently condemn as hate-filled bigots, has been to reject calls for equal rights for homosexuals as pleas for 'special rights' and to adopt in their place the mode of offering 'help' to the 'suffering'. This is not confined to evangelical Christians. For example, on June 18, 1998, the Majority Leader of the Republicans in the Senate, the Mississippian Trent Lott, gave an interview to a local cable television station about his views on homosexuality. A well-rehearsed and politically targeted, but apparently spontaneous, set of thoughts emerged:

My father had a problem with alcoholism. Other people have sex addiction. Other people are kleptomaniacs. I mean, there are all kinds of problems and addictions and difficulties and experiences of this kind that are wrong. But you should try to work with that person to learn to conquer that problem.

Although Lott had been on record as saying that homosexuality was a sin, he now carefully avoided biblical denunciations or advocating any form of legal discrimination against gays. Rather, homosexuality was portrayed as a matter of individual choice (the wrong one) and human frailty, a problem – like excessive drinking or shoplifting – to be challenged and conquered.

But the homophobic tendencies in American public life are not confined to the right. For example, supposedly liberal California voted by 61 per cent to 39 per cent in March 2000 for Proposition 22, a ballot measure which limited legal marriage in the state to only 'a man and a woman'. Louis Farrakhan, leader of the black separatist organization, the Nation of Islam, also joined the call against homosexuality, seeing it as akin to a disease in need of a suitable cure. Comparing AIDS to the era when no cure for tuberculosis existed (and ignoring the incidence of the disease among heterosexuals), gays should be 'taken out' of society until they were cured and could be readmitted. Despite their shared history as victims of prejudice, discrimination and violence, the mass of African Americans, though not their political leaders, have consistently been opposed to gay rights.

As with the other cultural issues in this book, gay rights involves conflicts between two coalitions whose world-views are poles apart: on the one side, a group for whom their sexual orientation is a genetic given and that defines what is most essential about them as human beings; on the other, groups who see being gay as a conscious choice and who reject that orientation as threatening to family values and morality. Gay rights also encompasses a strong, and increasing, level of tension between the federal government and individual states over questions of same-sex marriage, child-bearing, child-rearing and adoption, and anti-discrimination laws. Majority opinion also appears strongly traditionalist and the parties have polarized steadily on the issue.

THE HISTORICAL CONTEXT

Although classical Greece had a relatively tolerant attitude towards gay men (albeit selectively so and tied to misogynist views towards women), the history of social policy towards homosexuals in western culture has predominantly been one of disapproval, ostracism, legal discrimination, and at times ferocious punishment. One important aspect of the west's 'sexual revolution' during the twentieth century was a slow but gradual improvement in the political, legal and social status of homosexuals. In most European nations, for example, homosexuals today generally labour under few legal, and relatively few social, disabilities and are mostly accorded the same formal civil and political rights, and even respect, as heterosexuals. But the position in America is more mixed.

Homosexuality and homophobia pre-dated the republic's founding. Condemnation of gay and lesbian love is not confined to religious traditionalists but disapproval of homosexuality has particularly strong roots in the Judaeo-Christian tradition (see Exhibit 7.1) that traditionalists view as a mainstay of American civilization. From the Old Testament (in particular Leviticus) through disciples in the Roman world such as St Paul and on to the days of the colonies of the New World, homosexuality has been publicly damned as a sin against God and could be punished by legal murder (the bundles of wood stacked around those burned alive were called 'faggots').

For many Americans, contemporary attitudes towards homosexuality come close to being as strident as attitudes about abortion. The cultural conservative Pat Buchanan, who once denounced Mayor David Dinkins of New York City for offending and insulting Irish Catholics 'by prancing with sodomites' in a St Patrick's Day parade, is among the most outspoken, arguing that: 'A visceral recoil from homosexuality is the natural reaction of a healthy society wishing to preserve itself. A prejudice against males who engage in sodomy with one another represents a normal and natural bias in favor of sound morality' (quoted in Van Dyke, 1995: 193). Similarly, in 1995, Robert Knight of the conservative Family Research Council claimed that 'lesbianism is the animating principle of feminism. Because feminism, at the core, is at war with motherhood, femininity, family, and God. And lesbians are at war with all these things' (Durham, 2000: 54).

But some conservatives dispute the notion that hatred or animosity informs their disapproval of homosexuality. Robert Bork, for example, writes that: 'Moral objection to

Exhibit 7.1   The biblical view: homosexuality as sin

Religious belief informs many Americans' views of homosexuality at least as much as the Constitution. Since 'born-again' Christians see the Bible as literal truth, its pronouncements on moral issues have profound importance to millions of Americans. On homosexuality, the biblical view is unequivocal. Leviticus 20:13 prohibits sexual relations between men, defines them as an 'abomination' and places them under the death penalty. Ethical considerations such as consent, coercion or power imbalances in adult–child relations are not legally relevant in these passages (nor in levitical laws on adultery, incest and bestiality). So, regardless of the sexual relationship of the participants (consenting men, an adult male rapist, a child victim), all are equally culpable, since all are equally defiled.

Paul in Corinthians 6:9–10 states that 'the ones who lie with men' will not 'inherit the kingdom of God', describes male–male sexual relations as 'impurity' and asserts that such men 'deserve to die' (Romans 1:24–32). He extends the prohibition to include sexual relations between women, as do other post-biblical Jewish writers. Like other writers in the Roman world, Paul sees same-sex relations as transgressions of hierarchical gender relations. The reference to 'unnatural' (Romans 1:26) refers to women's attempt to transcend their supposedly passive, subordinate role accorded them by nature, while the men have relinquished their superordinate role and 'descended' to the level of women.

homosexual practices is not the same thing as animus, unless all disapprovals based on morality are to be disallowed as mere animus. Modern liberalism tends to classify all moral distinctions it does not accept as hateful and invalid' (Bork, 1996: 113). Nevertheless, there exists a significant element of animus among much traditionalist opposition to homosexuality in America.

Partly as a result of the colonial Christian inheritance, individual states were not slow in drawing up laws that banned 'sodomy'. Such was the overwhelming social consensus against homosexuality that the US Senate issued a report in December 1950 entitled *Employment of Homosexuals and Other Sex Perverts in Government*, linking homosexuality to communism as a security threat. President Eisenhower issued Executive Order 10450 in 1953, allowing federal employees to be dismissed for 'sexual perversion'. As late as 1961 the laws of all states made sodomy a crime and the laws of 25 states did so as late as 1995. It was not until 1962 that the American Law Institute's model Penal Code recommended that consensual, adult homosexual sex be decriminalized and not until 1973 that the American Psychiatric Association removed homosexuality from its list of psychiatric disorders (followed two years

Exhibit 7.2   Traditionalists v. progressives: homosexuality as nurture or nature?

One of the most important issues about homosexuality is whether, and to what extent, homosexuality is a matter of individual choice or biology. Sexual love between members of the same sex, unlike that of heterosexuals, is widely regarded as unnatural. It involves oral or anal sex, which the Bible condemns as 'sodomy' and which many regard as immoral. But the case that homosexuality is perverse also involves another assumption: that it is a matter of preference. No one has discovered in either men or women a genetic characteristic that clearly determines sexual orientation, which makes it possible to hold that this important aspect of a person's life is a matter of choice. But homosexuals overwhelmingly claim that they were born that way and that their sexuality is a natural state beyond individual control. On this view, people range along a scale from being exclusively heterosexual through those who are bisexual to those who are exclusively homosexual (the majority being at the heterosexual end). Those near the bisexual portion may perhaps have a 'choice' but whether the others do is an unresolved question.

Americans who continue to see homosexuality as a choice argue that they are justified in seeking measures to penalize those making the 'wrong' choice. Those who, by contrast, see homosexuality as natural hold that discrimination is no more justified than that based on race or sex. Penalizing gays for a genetic condition makes no more sense than penalizing people who are left-handed.

Two considerations are also particularly relevant regarding state regulation of same-sex relations:

- Since some homosexuals lead celibate lives – just as some heterosexuals do – those who seek to penalize homosexuality face the question of whether sexual *orientation* is sufficient to bring on penalties or whether the focus must be exclusively on sexual *conduct* (this question has been especially pertinent to the issue of homosexuals in the military).
- 'Sodomy' (whether defined as oral or anal) is not a sexual practice exclusively confined to homosexuals. Why should what is conventionally considered a private matter between a man and woman come under the purview of the state if practised by gays and lesbians?

later by the American Public Health Association and the American Psychological Association).

Although 32 states had repealed or nullified laws banning homosexual sex by 2002, several had not, and even among those that did the age of consent for homosexual sex was often higher than that for heterosexual sex. The armed forces have an inflexible policy, albeit erratically enforced, of banning gays and lesbians. A few organizations, such as the Boy Scouts, hold that homosexual persons are unacceptable as leaders. In practical terms, known homosexuals are still routinely excluded from jobs involving national security, federal judgeships and teaching jobs in many elementary and secondary schools. In the case of teaching and the Scouts, suspicion of homosexuals is frequently linked, explicitly or implicitly, to a symbolic association of predatory males abusing vulnerable children.

A gradual challenge to homophobic views and discriminatory regulations was advanced at the end of the 1960s. Homosexual and lesbian organizations had existed previously (such as the Mattachine Society and the Daughters of Bilitis) but they were typically discrete, cautious and relatively depoliticized. Thereafter, a combination of the steady assault by the women's movement on traditional institutions and gender roles, the concomitant increased focus on sexuality as a component and expression of individuality, and the prominence of protest movements more generally (especially over civil rights and Vietnam) together encouraged gay groups to organize.

The police raid on the gay bar, the Stonewall Inn, on Christopher Street in Greenwich Village, New York City, on June 28, 1969 proved a landmark event. Refusing to submit to police harassment, the customers of the Inn resisted and barricaded the police inside the bar. This event was followed by three days of protest punctuated by the chant 'Gay Power'. Stonewall was a significant step in increasing the visibility of homosexuals and has become a rallying cry of parts of the gay rights movement to this day. It also proved a catalyst for the formation of the Gay Liberation Front and the annual Christopher Street parade.

Since that time, many more homosexuals have 'come out of the closet', thereby becoming visible to the broader public and organizing as an influential political force. While prejudice and violence against homosexuals are still common, the fact that many more homosexuals are openly so indicates that the 'costs' of being identified as a gay and lesbian are somewhat less than they once were. Living an openly homosexual lifestyle and forging a sense of identity built around it is a more viable choice than before for many gay and lesbian Americans.

Nevertheless, increasing visibility has met with strong opposition from religious groups and advocates of 'family values'. The AIDS epidemic, in particular, brought unprecedented attention to the homosexual community. As Table 7.1 records, the official number of reported AIDS cases grew dramatically after 1981. The number of male cases almost tripled from 1987 to 1995, while that of women increased six-fold. For many social conservatives, this allowed them to exploit anti-gay sentiment by portraying gays as not only forces of immorality but also spreaders of disease.

One commentator, who argues that AIDS was a 'very American disease' that unleashed a new Puritanism, notes that:

> Once AIDS was identified as 'a gay disease', the political response became largely a response to the gay movement, and the problems of AIDS were equated with the needs of 'the gay community'. That this meant a greater degree of visibility and strength for the gay community than ever before should not hide the reality that it was a potentially dangerous development (and one that ignored large numbers of other cases). Only when AIDS threatened to cross the boundaries that confined it to 'high-risk groups', most obviously in the case of blood transfusions or blood products, was there a widespread response to it as a problem of public health, and then, because of the homosexual label, it was very easy to promote the

TABLE 7.1   AIDS cases reported in the US, 1981–95

Year(s)	Total	Men	Women
1981–86	28,348	26,222	2,136
1987	21,478	19,643	1,835
1988	30,657	27,375	3,282
1989	33,559	29,921	3,638
1990	41,639	36,766	4,873
1991	43,653	37,997	5,656
1992	45,839	39,507	6,332
1993	102,605	86,173	16,432
1994	76,561	62,684	13,877
1995	71,547	58,007	13,540
Total	496,896	425,295	71,601

Source: *Statistical Abstract of the US* (1996: 142).

distinction between the 'innocent' (haemo-philiacs, babies, receivers of blood transfusions and heterosexual partners of AIDS 'carriers') and the presumed guilty (homo-sexuals, drug users, prostitutes and, though less clearly, Haitians). (Altman, 1986: 191–2)

Exhibit 7.3   AIDS, Americanism and the paranoid style in American politics

Some observers discerned in the reactions to AIDS what Richard Hofstadter termed the 'paranoid style' in American politics. The history of AIDS poignantly illustrates that uneasy balance between attraction to moral crusades and respect for civil liberties that underlies much of American life. The widespread tendency to see most matters in fundamental terms of good and evil was vividly illustrated in the rhetoric of both Moral Majoritarians, who saw AIDS as stemming from the wrath of God, and gay activists, who saw such language as the first step on the road to American concentration camps. Right-wing attacks on homo-sexuals as bearers of the new plague were matched by some in the gay movement who saw such responses as symptomatic of a larger homophobia. With no cure or vaccine in existence, some even engaged in conspiracy theories that accused government agencies such as the CIA as having deliberately invented the HIV virus.

But AIDS also saw a curious reversal in the positions of traditionalists and progressives over conventional 'nature versus nurture' debates. Many saw in AIDS a powerful metaphor for the clash between different sets of values concerning sexuality and 'lifestyle'. Because AIDS was perceived by many to be an illness intrinsic to homosexuals, some interpreted it as their just reward for flouting the laws of God and, by extension, when it afflicts others this can be explained by homosexual perfidy. Even more secular observers noted a symbol of the identity between contagion and desire. It has usually been progressives who have associated disease with environmental and lifestyle factors; conservatives have usually stressed a narrower medical model. In the case of AIDS, it is the rhetoric of conservatives that has tended to emphasize lifestyle, whereas most progressives have tried to explain the disease in terms of an infectious organism.

Despite these concerns, issues of homosexual rights rarely entered mainstream politics. National party campaigns did not begin to address gay rights seriously until the 1990s. In the early 1980s, gay issues were only beginning to be discussed, generally in those Democratic Party primaries and local congressional races where (especially in urban areas) the gay vote was of significant influence. During the 1980 Democratic presidential primaries, for example, candidates Ted Kennedy and Jerry Brown attended gay fundraising events in California, ensuring that prominent hopefuls for the party's nomination at least needed to pay lip-service to gay rights. In 1984, Jesse Jackson and Walter Mondale endorsed proposals for a federal gay rights bill and pledged to sign an executive order banning discrimination against gays in all federal employment (including the military). Jackson, in a nationally televised speech at the Democratic Convention in San Francisco, made the first national public reference in history by an aspirant presidential candidate to the existence of homosexuals as a political group. But while gay and lesbian activists were forming local, state and national organizations and mobilizing voters across America, their issues remained largely absent from the agenda of either national party.

By 1988, the 'gay vote' was beginning to enter public discussion and was considered largely up for grabs between the two major parties. Despite being unattached to either party, gay and lesbian political leaders were ambivalent about both parties' candidates because neither side offered more than subtle appeals. According to some Democrats, Michael Dukakis feared being linked to another 'special interest' group. His campaign director, Susan Estrich, commented that, 'The Republicans were painting us as liberal, so we stayed away from causes like gay rights that played into that' (Frymer, 1999: 187). George H.W. Bush, in turn, feared angering the Christian Right, for whom opposition to gay rights was a prerequisite for political support.

Gay and lesbian voters resemble black voters in that a number of significant strategic factors potentially work in their favour. They are predominantly located in crucial Electoral College states such as California, Florida, Illinois, New York and Texas. In California alone, gay and lesbian voters were estimated to comprise approximately 10 per cent of the state's total electorate in 1992. Party leaders in California, with 54 Electoral College votes and a history of close party competition between Democrats and Republicans, recognized that these unaffiliated voters could potentially provide the critical electoral margin. Nationally, gay and lesbian voters are estimated at approximately 4 per cent of the electorate, roughly equivalent in size to the Jewish vote and twice the number of Asian American voters.

Equally, if not more importantly, gay and lesbian groups consistently spend substantial sums of money in electoral campaigns. In 1992, for example, gay rights organizations donated an estimated $3.5 million to Bill Clinton's presidential campaign. According to the Human Rights Campaign, pro-gay organizations gave approximately $2.5 million in 2000 to federal political candidates – five times as much as pro-gun control groups and $400,000 more than environmental organizations.

In 1992, activists mobilized gay communities and politicized gay issues in an unprecedented attempt to influence a presidential campaign. Partly, this was due to the vocal and unapologetic homophobia of aspirant Republican presidential candidate Pat Buchanan. In February 1992, during the Georgia GOP primary, Buchanan's campaign aired a television advertisement, 'Freedom Abused' featuring clips from a Public Broadcasting Service documentary – subsidized by the National Endowment for the Arts – about gay black life, called 'Tongues Untied'. Superimposed over slow-motion images of partially dressed, young gay black men dancing on a stage were the words 'pornography', 'blasphemy' and (ironically) 'too shocking to show'. An announcer intoned that:

In the last three years, the Bush administration has invested our tax dollars in pornographic and blasphemous art too shocking to show. This so-called art has glorified homosexuality, exploited children, and perverted the image of Jesus Christ. Even after good people protested, Bush continued to fund this kind of art. Send Bush a message. We need a leader who will fight for what we believe in.

The message seemed to be that homosexuality, or inter-racial homosexuality, equalled blasphemy. Buchanan argued that the ad 'has nothing to do with anti-gay prejudice. It has to do with not spending people's tax dollars on values that insult them' (West, 1997: 79). Deriding the Democrats as a 'pro-gay' party, Buchanan's speeches during the Republican nomination battle politicized gay issues for the first time in a national election.

Equally important to mobilizing the gay and lesbian vote was that Clinton also placed their issues on the national agenda, announcing in a speech to gay political leaders relatively early in the 1992 campaign that 'I have a vision and you are a part of it'. By actively reaching out for their votes, Clinton represented the first major-party presidential candidate to speak openly about gay rights and publicly court gay votes. Among his pledges, Clinton promised to appoint gays and lesbians to prominent administration positions, increase the amount of federal funding targeted for AIDS research and awareness programmes, and lift the ban on gays serving in the armed services. Clinton spent considerably more time discussing gay issues than black issues in his co-authored book with Al Gore, *Putting People First* (1992).

With the Democratic Party's encouragement, gay groups and activists enthusiastically mobilized support for the Democratic candidate. Gay activists were prominent members of the campaign staff, and Clinton, though not centring his campaign on gay issues, at no point attempted to distance himself from them. While Republicans attacked the Democrats as the party of gays and lesbians, public opinion polls showed that key

groups of national voters rejected this. As Republican consultant Kevin Phillips commented: 'There was a thought that this would be the new Willie Horton. But the [Bush] Administration overdid it. The gay bashing turned people off. It's become a minus for the Republicans.'

After Clinton's U-turns on gays in the armed services in 1993, gay issues effectively disappeared from the national political agenda until the Republicans brought them up again during the 1996 election year. In response to a Hawaii Supreme Court ruling that same-sex marriages were constitutional, the Republican-controlled Congress passed – with extensive Democratic support – the 'Defense of Marriage Act' (DOMA). The DOMA precluded states and the federal government from having to recognize gay marriages – and the concomitant tax and other benefits – that were allowed in other states. While proclaiming ambivalence, Clinton announced immediately that he would sign the bill, prompting one gay activist to call it 'this year's Sister Soulja – a way to show he isn't beholden to gay people'.

But despite gay disgruntlement at their treatment by the Democratic Party, their significant numbers in key electoral states, their propensity to spend money in campaigns, and the absence of a long-standing historical tendency to vote solidly Democratic (in 1988, an estimated 40 per cent of the gay and lesbian vote went to George Bush), the Republican Party generally made no appeals for their votes. In 1995, Bob Dole accepted, then refused to accept, and finally accepted again a donation of $1,000 from the 'Log Cabin Republicans', a group made up of approximately 10,000 gay and lesbian Republicans.

Confronted by the continuing reluctance of Democratic party leaders, gay political groups have been faced with the frustration of being, like blacks, effectively 'captured': they have nowhere else to go. A former executive director of the National Gay and Lesbian Task Force observed:

The gay movement has established a beach-head in Washington by mobilizing some wealthy people and delivering some votes. But unlike the gun lobby (or the tobacco industry or the health insurance industry or any other major Washington force), we follow a pathway to political power that leads us to the locked, steel gate of anti-sexual cultural attitudes about homosexuality. The gay movement's use of politics of access cannot overcome the stigma of homosexual behaviour. (Frymer, 1999: 192)

An expected protest in San Francisco by gay activists shortly after the signing of the Defense of Marriage Act never materialized because gay leaders divided over the potential effects it would have for their preferred presidential candidate, Bill Clinton, against Bob Dole. By 2000, as discussed below, gay issues had receded to become one of the proverbial 'dogs that didn't bark', with 25 per cent of the gay vote going to George W. Bush.

PUBLIC OPINION

Without question the 1960s and 1970s heralded important changes in American sexual practices and attitudes that ultimately proved beneficial to gays and lesbians. But, as Table 7.2 reveals, the 'sexual revolution' of recent decades has not fully established the legitimacy or moral equality of homosexuality. A steady transformation has taken place in which most Americans tolerate gays and lesbians but many remain hostile to homosexuality.

Two aspects of the figures are especially significant: first, the scale of the majorities who hold homosexuality to be wrong is decisive, at over 70 per cent of respondents; and, secondly, it is consistently so. That this should be the case in the face of the profound changes that have occurred in society, increasing exposure to alternative viewpoints on morals, privacy and sexuality, and devastating epidemics such as AIDS, together suggests a deep-seated attitude towards

TABLE 7.2 Respondents believing homosexual behaviour is wrong, 1973–91

Year	Percentage
1973	76.3
1974	71.8
1976	72.5
1977	73.7
1980	75.5
1982	76.2
1984	75.1
1985	76.7
1987	79.2
1988	78.2
1989	74.2
1990	77.1
1991	74.2

Note: Question: 'Do you believe that sexual relations between two adults of the same sex is always wrong, almost always wrong, wrong only sometimes, or not wrong at all?'
(Figures in the table include 'always' and 'almost always' responses.)
Source: Epstein et al. (1994: 601).

homosexuality that is strongly, albeit not immutably, resistant to alteration.

The extent of popular disapproval of homosexuality is also revealed in Table 7.3. It is perhaps unsurprising that most Americans do not believe that communists should be allowed to engage in activities such as teaching. But only marginally fewer think that homosexuals should be allowed to teach in college. Given the pronounced antipathy to communists and atheists as 'un-American', the markedly hostile attitude towards gays that remains widespread is unmistakable. (According to historian Michael Beschloss (1997: 248, n1), Senator Joe McCarthy claimed during the 1950s that State Department leaks about foreign policy were the partial result of closet homosexuals in the department who were blackmailed to surrender classified information.)

The trouble that homosexuality causes some Americans extends more broadly. For

TABLE 7.3 Respondents allowing groups to perform specified activity (per cent)

Year	Community			Library			College		
	H	A	C	H	A	C	H	A	C
1973	60.7	65.3	59.7	53.5	60.8	58.2	47.3	40.6	38.9
1974	62.3	61.7	57.7	54.8	59.8	58.4	50.1	41.7	41.6
1976	61.8	64.0	54.5	55.4	59.5	55.9	52.0	41.3	41.4
1977	61.7	62.2	55.3	55.2	58.4	55.0	49.2	38.7	38.6
1980	65.9	66.1	55.1	58.1	61.9	57.2	54.6	45.3	40.5
1982	63.5	61.3	53.9	54.0	57.6	53.8	53.9	43.3	42.6
1984	67.9	68.0	59.1	59.3	63.6	59.3	58.7	45.7	45.6
1985	66.6	64.6	56.8	55.3	60.4	57.0	57.8	45.3	44.1
1987	67.1	67.9	58.6	56.5	64.1	59.3	56.1	45.6	46.0
1988	69.7	69.7	60.2	60.3	63.7	59.3	56.5	45.2	47.5
1989	76.1	71.6	64.1	63.8	67.1	61.3	63.3	51.0	50.2
1990	73.5	72.3	64.2	63.9	66.4	63.7	62.3	50.2	51.4
1991	75.7	71.8	67.1	68.3	69.1	67.2	63.2	51.9	53.6

Note: H = homosexual, A = atheist, C = communist.

Questions: (Community) 'Suppose someone who admits he is a homosexual wanted to make a speech in your community, should he be allowed to speak or not?' (Library) 'If some people in your community suggested that a book he wrote in favour of homosexuality should be taken out of the library, would you favour removing this book, or not?' (College) 'Should such a person be allowed to teach in a college or university, or not?'

Source: Epstein et al. (1994: 587–9).

example, according to a 1997 *USA Today/ CNN/Gallup* poll, 46 per cent of adults said that there are too many homosexual portrayals on television today, an increase of 9 per cent from 1995. A 1997 Gannett News Service poll also reported that 23 per cent of respondents said that television programmes should feature fewer 'gay' characters and another 33 per cent wanted no 'gay' characters at all on television.

Certain other aspects of Americanism complicate the picture. Beliefs in individualism, equality of opportunity, and the rule of law make governmental discrimination against gays – as opposed to moral disapproval of homosexuality and opposition to 'affirmative' measures to advantage gays and lesbians – much less supported than at first might be imagined. Beyond this, media attention to both vicious homophobia (such as the murder of Matthew Shepard, a gay college student, in Wyoming in 1998) and the heroism of gay Americans (Mark Bingham, for example, helped thwart the terrorist hijackers on the United Airlines flight that crashed in Pennsylvania on September 11, 2001) has assisted showing that gay people have the same types of lives, losses and concerns as heterosexuals.

Although opinion surveys are not completely consistent, a trend appears to have emerged rejecting overt or purposeful discrimination. A *Newsweek* poll on September 14, 1992 revealed conflicting signs: 78 per cent of respondents held that 'homosexuals should have equal rights in job opportunities' and 51 per cent opposed the statement that gay rights are 'a threat to the American family and its values'. A majority (53 per cent) nevertheless held that homosexuality was not an 'acceptable alternative lifestyle'. A Gallup poll in September 1994 reported that 58 per cent of respondents were opposed, and 39 per cent supported, extending civil rights protections for homosexuals

(Golay and Rollyson, 1996: 180). The Gallup opinion survey during the 1996 elections found that 67 per cent of Americans opposed the legalization of gay marriage, with 28 per cent in favour (Ladd, 1997: 11).

A National Election Survey in 1992 asked a series of questions on homosexuals. Three out of five people favoured laws to protect gays against job discrimination and a similar proportion felt gays should be allowed to serve in the armed forces, but only 28 per cent felt they should be allowed to adopt children. Similarly, a *Newsweek* poll in June 2000 found that 46 per cent of respondents did not want any new Supreme Court Justices to allow 'groups to exclude gays and lesbians if they feel homosexuality is morally wrong'. Yet 56 per cent of the same survey agreed with the 5–4 Supreme Court ruling that the Boy Scouts had a constitutional right to block gay men from becoming troop leaders (Taylor, 2000: 2208). In a sign of a possible shift in opinion, though, a Gallup poll in May 2001 found that 85 per cent of Americans held that homosexuals should have equal rights in terms of job opportunities, and 44 per cent said they favoured giving lesbian or gay couples the right to form civil unions.

In sum, although Americans still hold sexual relations between persons of the same sex to be wrong, tolerance of same-sex relations has increased and is increasing. Most Americans also support equal rights for gays and lesbians and oppose employment discrimination on the basis of sexual orientation.

EXPLAINING THE POLITICS OF GAY RIGHTS

Much as public opinion is characterized by conflicting tendencies towards tolerance and disapproval, so the politics of gay rights exhibits a combination of respect for individualism and political exploitation of an unpopular minority group. Most members of America's governing institutions have not been at the forefront of protecting equal rights for gays, and the federal courts, the traditional focus for such protection in the post-1953 era, have achieved a mixed record in this regard. Moreover, the main political parties have steadily polarized on the issue since 1972, offering both obstacles and opportunities for advocates of homosexual equality.

THE US CONSTITUTION

We saw previously how the Constitution remains central to political conflict but how strong disagreement about its contemporary meaning and the application of its provisions often prolongs that conflict. As with capital punishment, what society deems to be a reasonable or acceptable practice at a given time strongly influences judges in their interpretations of constitutional clauses. Societal attitudes towards homosexuality provide another important case of constitutional interpretation hinging partly on what the judges conclude about the broader social and political context. Unlike the Supreme Court's decisions in *Roe* and *Furman*, however, gay rights is an issue where the federal judiciary has rarely led public opinion or directly challenged prevailing social mores in favour of minority rights.

Gay rights currently offers one of the most controversial issues for courts to adjudicate. The Constitution said nothing explicitly or directly about homosexuality. Unlike some states today (such as South Africa), inserting into the Constitution a specific protection against discrimination based on sexual orientation would have struck the Founding Fathers as an absurd or abhorrent idea. The Framers did not explicitly protect either heterosexual marriage or a broader 'right to privacy' on social matters in either the 1787 document or the Bill of Rights. Much more so than with issues like gun control or capital punishment, the constitutional protection afforded individual citizens' sexual behaviour is unclear and unsettled.

Despite increasing litigation since the 1970s, efforts to secure more expanded constitutional protection for homosexuals have been only partially successful. Given the role of the judiciary in defending the liberties and rights of individuals against majoritarian abuse, one might have expected that courts would be pro-gay rights. As a minority social group facing prejudice, discrimination and overt hostility from others in society, gays and lesbians should be able, like blacks, women seeking terminations or criminal defendants, to seek judicial protection. But the courts have shown at least as much reluctance to protect gay rights as those of death row inmates. Instead of keeping the state out of private domains, they have allowed federal, state and local governments significant leeway to enter American bedrooms and workplaces. Three areas are especially important here:

- Gay sexual relations.
- Discrimination concerning gays.
- Same-sex marriages.

Gay sexual relations

Despite liberalizing decisions regarding the individual's right to reproductive autonomy since *Griswold v. Connecticut* (1965), homosexuals have not managed to secure the right to sexual autonomy from the federal courts. Most notably, in *Bowers v. Hardwick* (1986), the Supreme Court refused to interpret the 'right to privacy' as protecting consensual homosexual activity by adults in their homes. At the time of the ruling, 24 American states and the District of Columbia had laws prohibiting sodomy. The 5–4 majority on the Court held that such laws had a 'rational basis'. Writing for the majority, Justice Byron White, who had supported the 'right to privacy' in *Griswold*, maintained that the right did not confer a general right to sexual autonomy but was limited to questions of marriage, family and procreation, concluding that homosexual activity bore no connection to those: 'The Court is most vulnerable and comes nearest

to illegitimacy when it deals with judge-made constitutional law having little or no cognizable roots in the language or design of the Constitution.'

Yet this was precisely the criticism levelled at *Roe* by traditionalists. The resort to a 'right to privacy', heralded by progressives then as a necessary act of judicial creativity that protected civilized values, now appeared to secure exactly the opposite result. Quite why that right protected terminations of pregnancies, the use of contraceptives and watching child pornography in the home, while it did not protect adult homosexuals from engaging in consensual sex in their homes, seemed beyond many critics.

The criminal punishment of homosexual acts between consenting adults was surely as offensive to contemporary notions of the proper scope of government as Connecticut's ban on contraceptives. If the creation of homosexual rights was contrary to millennia of moral teachings, so was (at the time of *Griswold*) the creation of a right to use contraceptives; the moral teachers were the same and in both cases their social influence had declined substantially since the 1920s. Half the states, for example, had inserted privacy guarantees in their state constitutions. Half had also repealed their sodomy laws. In the half that retained them, the laws were no longer enforced unless there was clear evidence of coercion, public indecency, abuse of minors or other aggravating circumstances. Non-enforceability suggested strongly that these restrictive laws were more 'reports of public opinion' than vehicles of criminal law enforcement. Homosexuality was not approved of in these states but it was tolerated – the will to punish homosexuals as criminals had effectively died. Unsurprisingly, gay rights groups condemned *Bowers* as their equivalent of *Dred Scott* (see Exhibit 7.4).

Anti-discrimination statutes

The most immediate concern of many lesbians and gay men is not imprisonment for

Exhibit 7.4   The state in the bedroom: *Bowers v. Hardwick* (1986)

Bowers v. Hardwick was of profound symbolic importance. Until 1986, federal court decisions regarding gays were simply one-sentence affirmations of lower court rulings, made without legal argument or public discussion. *Bowers* promised a definitive resolution of the issue of equal rights for gays, yet it must stand as one of the strangest decisions to have been decided by the Court. The ruling eloquently revealed the mixture of conflicting beliefs about liberty, equality and religious values that surround gay rights.

The state of Georgia had a law on its books that prohibited heterosexual and homosexual sodomy (defined as oral and anal intercourse). On the night of August 2, 1982, in Atlanta, a police officer knocked on the front door of the house of a 29-year-old bartender, Michael Hardwick, to serve him with a warrant for public intoxication. A houseguest pointed the officer towards Hardwick's bedroom door, which he opened, and there saw Hardwick engaging in oral sex with another man. Hardwick was duly arrested and charged with sodomy. The charge was later dropped, but the American Civil Liberties Union persuaded Hardwick to take the state to court to test the constitutionality of its sodomy law.

Before the Court on March 31, 1986, Hardwick's lawyers argued that his right to privacy in consensual sexual matters in his bedroom was equivalent to that which the Court had recognized in *Griswold* and *Roe*. Georgia attorney general, Michael Hobbs, aggressively defended the state's right to ban homosexual activity. Warning that striking down sodomy laws would open 'a Pandora's box' and result in the repeal of laws banning polygamy, incest, prostitution, homosexual marriages and adultery, he cited the writings of Leviticus, Romans and Thomas Aquinas to support his assertion that homosexuality was immoral. He noted that homosexuals had been considered heretics in the Middle Ages and claimed that the law was needed to prevent the spread of AIDS and protect marriage, the family and the 'collective moral aspirations of the people'.

Justices White, Burger, O'Connor and Rehnquist were supportive of the sodomy laws, while Blackmun, Brennan, Stevens and Marshall were convinced of the right to privacy. Initially, Lewis Powell voted with the latter, but then changed his mind on the basis that Georgia had not enforced the law. (Others later suggested he had a less judicial concern: to avoid being known as the man who legalized homosexuality in America.) By a 5–4 majority, the Court held that the right to privacy did *not* extend to homosexual acts between consenting adults, even in their homes. The majority claimed that the Court lacked the judicial authority to expand further the types of behaviour classified as 'fundamental' and hence entitled to protection as 'constitutional' rights. The ruling made no reference to heterosexual sex, focusing exclusively on 'homosexual sodomy'.

Writing for the majority, Justice White ruled that the nation's sodomy laws had 'ancient roots' stemming from 'millennia of moral teaching'. In a concurring opinion, Chief Justice Burger argued that no relationship existed between the issues in *Bowers* and previous decisions on abortion and birth control because the latter related to 'family relationships, marriage, or procreation' and 'no connection between family, marriage or procreation on the one hand and homosexuality on the other has been demonstrated'. Exhaustive footnotes recorded when states had enacted their sodomy laws (Connecticut in 1791, Georgia in 1784) led White to conclude that it was 'facetious' to argue that gays' right to privacy was 'deeply rooted in our Nation's history and traditions'. Half the states banned homosexual acts and ruling these unconstitutional could lead to judicial logic that would also enfranchise acts of incest, providing they occurred in private.

In a scathing dissent, Justice Blackmun ridiculed the majority's 'obsessive focus on homosexuality', arguing that the case was 'about the most comprehensive of rights and the right most valued by civilized men, the right to be left alone'. He mocked the notion that sodomy could be a criminal offence because it had been for hundreds of years and argued

Exhibit 7.4 **The state in the bedroom:** *Bowers v. Hardwick* (1986) *continued*

that homosexual orientation was not a matter of choice but 'may well form part of the very fiber of an individual's personality. The fact that individuals define themselves in a significant way through their intimate relationships with others suggests, in a Nation as diverse as ours, that there may be many "right" ways of conducting those relationships, and that much of the richness of a relationship will come from the freedom the individual has to choose the form and nature of these intensely personal bonds.'

However much the decision was unenforceable, it stood as a profound symbolic statement. Libertarians compared the ruling to the *Dred Scott* decision in 1857 that upheld the Fugitive Slave Act with the logic that since blacks were not 'citizens' they were unentitled to constitutional guarantees of freedom. Gay rights advocates argued that those states that criminalize oral and anal sex not only deprive homosexuals of their privacy rights, but also discriminate against heterosexuals. *Bowers* effectively left gays with the status of unapprehended felons. A Gallup poll showed that 57 per cent of Americans did not believe that the state should have the power to forbid sexual relations between gay people, while 34 per cent approved of such laws. Laurence Tribe contended that the Court had missed the point, which was not what Hardwick was doing in his bedroom but what the state of Georgia was doing there.

Eventually, in November 1998, the Georgia state Supreme Court struck down the law as violating the right to privacy guaranteed by the state's constitution. Writing for the 6–1 majority, Chief Justice Robert Benham wrote: 'We cannot think of any other activity that reasonable persons would rank as more private and more deserving of protection from governmental interference than consensual, private, adult sexual activity.' Mere disapproval, even if based on morality, was insufficient to overcome the right to privacy. But other states with comparable sodomy laws remained – in the absence of a federal ruling striking them down – committed to retaining the status of unapprehended criminals for their active homosexual citizens.

sex (an unlikely occurrence, given the lack of enforcement of sodomy laws), but discrimination at the workplace, in securing housing, and in gaining custody of their children – in some cases adopted or the product of artificial insemination, in some cases one partner's children from a prior heterosexual relationship. While some federal and state courts have granted First Amendment protection for such activities as public acknowledgement of one's homosexuality, gay rights advocacy and forms of symbolic speech, the Supreme Court has been reluctant to extend broad First Amendment protection to homosexuals. Most notably, it has consistently denied *certiorari* (or 'standing') in cases concerning the dismissal of schoolteachers by local school boards because of their known homosexual status.

Partly as a result of this judicial reluctance, but also as a result of increasing gay rights activism, many cities passed local ordinances that prohibited discrimination against people because of their sexual orientation during the 1980s and 1990s. Colorado was one of the most prominent examples. But most of the state's voters did not approve of such action. In response, they voted in favour of a state constitutional amendment in 1992 that made it illegal to pass any law to protect persons based on their 'homosexual, lesbian, or bisexual orientation'. The amendment did not penalize gays and lesbians but stated that they could not become the object of specific legal protection of the sort traditionally accorded racial and ethnic minorities since 1964. In effect, the law repealed gay rights ordinances existing in Colorado cities and prohibited any future local or state law granting civil rights protections to homosexuals.

In *Romer v. Evans* (1996) the Supreme Court struck down the Colorado constitution's provision as a violation of the equal protection clause of the Fourteenth Amendment to the US Constitution by singling out as unworthy of protection a specific group of citizens. The Court held that the state's decision to withdraw protection accorded homosexuals was motivated only by animus and therefore could not stand under the rationale of the equal protection clause, noting that 'it is not within our constitutional tradition to enact laws of this sort'. In dissent, Justice Scalia described the Colorado provision as a

> rather modest attempt by seemingly tolerant Coloradoans to preserve traditional sexual mores against the efforts of a politically powerful minority to revise those mores through the use of the laws ... [the Court's decision] places the prestige of this institution behind the proposition that opposition to homosexuality is as reprehensible as racial or religious bias.

Scalia concluded that the Colorado provision

> was an entirely reasonable provision which does not even disfavor homosexuals in any substantive sense, but merely denies them preferential treatment. [It] is designed to prevent piecemeal deterioration of the sexual morality favored by a majority of Coloradoans, and is not only an appropriate means to that legitimate end, but a means that Americans have employed before. Striking it down is an act, not of judicial judgment, but of political will.

Whatever the merits of the contending views on the Colorado provision, the end result has been an unsatisfactory constitutional muddle on gay rights. A state can, for example, pass a law banning homosexual activities (federal courts have yet to overturn *Bowers*), but cannot pass a law preventing cities within the state from reversing that ban (the *Romer* decision made no reference to *Bowers*). Neither consistency nor coherence,

two of the more important attributes of the rule of law, are apparent here.

Nevertheless, significant movement has occurred at federal, state and local levels in spite of judicial equivocation. In 1998, for example, President Clinton issued an Executive Order that prohibited employment discrimination in federal government departments, agencies and commissions on grounds of sexual orientation. By 2002, 12 states (including California, Massachusetts and Nevada), the District of Columbia and many cities (including Los Angeles, New York and Washington, DC) had passed non-discrimination laws and ordinances banning discrimination based on sexual orientation in public employment (another five had similar laws through gubernatorial executive orders). Moreover, hundreds of corporations (including 154 of the *Fortune* 500 companies) provided domestic-partner benefits; another 297 of the 500 have non-discrimination policies.

Same-sex marriages

With the goals of developing intimate and loving ties between members of society and providing stable environments in which to raise children, the federal government has for several decades encouraged Americans to marry and respect the marital relationship. Federal policies typically promote marriage by according married couples reduced income, inheritance and gift taxation liabilities, providing social security benefits to a surviving spouse, giving preferences in immigration and citizenship to the spouse of an American citizen, and mandating unpaid leave from work to take care of a sick family member. Federal rules of evidence also accord marital partners special privileges (for example, allowing each partner to avoid testifying against the spouse).

Although the Constitution does not refer directly to the status of marriage, courts have over time regarded the institution as a fundamental part of the 'right to privacy'. The Supreme Court has affirmed the right of the states to prescribe most of the conditions of

Exhibit 7.5   Key Supreme Court rulings on gay rights, 1975–2002

Rose v. Locke (1975). The Court held that the non-specific statutory language of sodomy laws is not unconstitutionally vague when applied to the particular acts in question or when the law can reasonably be interpreted as covering the acts in question.

Doe v. Commonwealth Attorney (1976). Affirmed without explanation the lower court dismissal of a suit that had challenged the constitutionality of Virginia's anti-sodomy law.

Bowers v. Hardwick (1986). 5–4. Upheld the constitutionality of Georgia's anti-sodomy law, rejecting arguments that the right to privacy covered private, consensual, same-sex sodomy.

Hurley v. Irish-American Gay, Lesbian and Bisexual Group (1995). The justices unanimously ruled that the state of Massachusetts could not use a public accommodation law to force the sponsor of the Boston St Patrick's Day parade to admit a contingent that wanted to march behind a banner proclaiming its gay identity.

Romer v. Evans (1996). 6–3. Invoked the Equal Protection Clause of the Fourteenth Amendment to strike down an amendment to the Colorado state constitution that prohibited protections accorded to homosexuals.

Boy Scouts of America v. Dale (2000). 5–4. The majority found that a law requiring the Scouts to admit homosexuals as leaders violated the free association rights of a private, non-commercial association to select its own members and leaders without government oversight. The Scouts had argued that hiring openly gay leaders would interfere with their First Amendment rights to express the view that homosexuality is wrong and to associate – or not – with whomever they pleased. Dale countered that the issue was not the group's right to exclusivity but whether a group like the Scouts (which generally welcomes all boys) could claim being anti-gay as part of a core value.

marriage. Before the twentieth century, the Court generally held that states had to recognize the legitimacy of marriage entered into in other states. But with *Reynolds v. United States* (1879), in which the Court refused to recognize polygamy as protected by the First Amendment, it began to create a national standard of marital rights. In the 1960s, the Court limited state marital regulations significantly by protecting the rights of individuals to wed. For example, 30 American states had laws prohibiting racial inter-marriage prior to the Second World War. In *Loving v. Virginia* (1967), the Court struck down as unconstitutional Virginia's law – one of 16 southern states that still prohibited inter-racial marriage. (Significantly, its ruling declared the law to violate the Fourteenth Amendment's equal protection clause, avoiding the vexed 'right to privacy'). Writing for a unanimous Court, Chief Justice Warren declared that: 'Under our Constitution, the freedom to marry, or not to marry, a person of another race, resides with the individual, and cannot be infringed by the State.'

Until the passage of the DOMA in 1996, the federal government accepted state determinations of marriage for purposes of distribution of federal credits and benefits. It will no longer do so for same-sex couples. Congress refused to do so since, by accepting same-sex marriages, it would be encouraging and nurturing same-sex unions, as it did with mixed-sex unions through its policy involvement with the family. Simply by respecting a state's traditional regulatory powers over its domiciles, the federal government would be nationalizing the state policy on same-sex marriages and forcing all Americans to subsidize such marriages. But by refusing to

Exhibit 7.6 The US Constitution and marriage: for straights only?

Western marriage has traditionally been defined as the joining together of a man and woman by the state or a church. Same-sex couples have lobbied for the right to marry and obtain the same legal recognition and government benefits as heterosexual couples: family insurance, health benefits, joint tax returns and tax breaks, family visitation privileges in hospitals and automatic inheritance rights. Traditionalists oppose such recognition.

In 1993, the Supreme Court of the state of Hawaii ruled in *Baehr v. Miike* that the state's refusal to grant marriage licences to three gay couples violated the state constitution's explicit prohibition of sex-based discrimination. The court declared that unless the state could show compelling reasons for restricting marriage to heterosexuals, the discrimination would have to end. The Hawaii state legislature responded by passing a law in 1994 that stated that marriage licences must be restricted to 'man–woman' units capable of procreation. But the state Supreme Court ruled that this law, too, violated the state constitution.

Traditionalists feared that gay couples from other states would travel to Hawaii to marry in the expectation that their home states would have to recognize their marriages. Article IV of the US Constitution requires that 'full faith and Credit shall be given in each State to the Public Acts, Records, and judicial Proceedings of every other State'. Just as states must recognize the birth certificates and drivers' licences issued by other states, so, according to some, they must recognize marriage licences and divorce decrees issued by other states. (Some years ago, for example, Nevada had more liberal laws on divorce than other states and couples seeking a 'quickie divorce' went to Nevada, knowing that their home states would have to recognize the divorces because of this provision in the federal constitution.)

Traditionalists have sought to end what they view as this dangerous possibility by pressuring state legislators expressly to outlaw same-sex marriages. By 1997, eight states had laws banning them, and 30 had laws describing marriage specifically as a civil contract between a man and a woman. The Defense of Marriage Act, passed by the Republican 104th Congress and signed into law by President Clinton in 1996, intended to 'inoculate' states against having to recognize same-sex marriages occurring in other states and precluded the granting of federal monies such as Social Security and veterans' benefits to same-sex couples. Proponents of these laws argue that they should be effective – and, if challenged, be held constitutional – because the second part of the 'full faith and credit' clause states that 'Congress may by general Laws prescribe . . . the Effect' of this article on the states. At the same time, California established official registries to recognize domestic partners and Vermont, in 2000, adopted the first civil unions law (providing legal recognition of same-sex partners and most of the legal benefits and duties of marriage).

recognize such marriages, the federal government is establishing itself as the ultimate arbiter of who may and may not marry. This approach, too, injects it as a policymaker in matters traditionally reserved to the states.

The Court could, in principle, adopt the 'full faith and credit' approach of cross-recognition. But as Ken Kersh points out

The text of the clause is ambiguous; nothing

in the history of its application and, importantly, nothing in the larger history of the operating norms of the American federal system – with its values of comity concerning marriage – supports the arguments that the cross-state recognition of same-sex marriages should be compelled on Article IV grounds. (Kersh, 1997: 136)

Also, the Court has a distinctive role in the federal system of setting out vertical definitions of national rights. On this approach, the Court could, instead, plausibly follow the path it adopted regarding anti-miscegenation laws in *Loving*, by ruling under the equal protection (or due process) clause of the Fourteenth Amendment that same-sex couples have a fundamental right to marry that cannot be denied by state law.

The conflict is unlikely to cease until the Supreme Court has offered a clear decision – and perhaps not even then. In December 1999, Vermont's Supreme Court ruled that gay couples had the legal right to the same benefits and protections as heterosexual married couples. The court left it to the state legislature to determine whether equal benefits for gay couples should be instituted through formal marriage or through a system of domestic partnerships that would guarantee equivalent rights under law. The difficulty for the federal judiciary is granting recognition, thereby nationalizing a policy opposed by most states, or refusing to do so, thereby leaving same-sex couples denied the rights of heterosexuals.

Such is the dilemma that even committed progressives currently caution against too radical an intervention. As the constitutional law scholar Cass Sunstein, a supporter of homosexual rights who holds them to have a sound constitutional grounding, argues, were the Supreme Court to impose the requirement that all states authorize same-sex marriages:

> . . . we might well expect a constitutional crisis, a weakening of the legitimacy of the Court, an intensifying hatred of homosexuals, a constitutional amendment overturning the Court's decision, and much more. Any Court should hesitate in the face of such prospects. It would be far better for the Court to do nothing – or better still, to start cautiously and to proceed incrementally. (Sunstein, 1999: 161)

Such a view is unlikely to win support from the many Americans for whom questions of homosexual rights represent ones of equality before the law, citizenship, and freedom from discrimination no less immediate today than those for African Americans were in the 1950s and 1960s. But Sunstein's case, however much it is based on pragmatic considerations, merits scrutiny. Were the Court to strike down the DOMA as unconstitutional and a constitutional amendment defining marriage exclusively as a man–woman unit then to be enacted – a feasible occurrence, given most Americans' views on marriage – the dangers for homosexuals would be clear. Were it ratified, the prospects for overturning such a constitutional amendment – requiring two-thirds support in Congress and three-quarters of the 50 states – would not be great. In an effort to safeguard equality for gays and lesbians, the Court could unwittingly provoke a repudiation of that effort. The examples of abortion and capital punishment suggest that a self-consciously 'political' approach here is merited, an approach all the more compelling when the conduct of other branches of the federal government is considered.

GOVERNING INSTITUTIONS

The Court's predicament is made still more acute by the practical politics of gay rights. As we saw previously, the Court frequently takes account of public opinion and the actions of other branches of government when it adjudicates on controversial social and political issues. In this case, the attitudes of most Americans and their elected officials are fairly clear: any move to advance gay equality substantially is not a step that they would welcome.

PRESIDENTIAL POLITICS

No openly gay candidate has won election to the White House (although it is sometimes claimed that there have nevertheless been a few gay presidents). The first time that homosexuality was mentioned explicitly in a presidential campaign was in 1968, when Ronald

Reagan made an unsuccessful bid for the Republican presidential nomination. Referring to homosexuality as a 'tragic disease', Reagan argued that sexual relations among gays and lesbians should remain illegal. In his successful campaign during 1980, Reagan again reiterated that, 'in the eyes of the Lord, homosexuality is an abomination'. Yet many gay Republicans supported his campaign (some even advanced the circuitous argument that, as a former Hollywood actor, Reagan had to have gay friends who would battle from the inside of his administration to advance gay rights). Until the later 1980s, however, little coverage was accorded gay issues by either candidates or the mainstream media in presidential elections.

In office, no president has publicly sought to move America decisively in the direction of supporting equal rights for gays. The Carter administration made some minor regulatory changes that had a marginal impact on gay concerns: the Internal Revenue Service began to allow tax deductions for contributions to gay charities and the Immigration and Naturalization Service ceased asking visitors to America if they were homosexual. But despite being the most outspoken proponent of fundamental human rights to occupy the White House since FDR, Carter showed little interest in gay issues. Harassment and purges of gays from the military increased under Carter. As an avowed born-again Christian, Carter had to confront both the growing activism of gays in his party and the anti-gay sentiment of many traditionalists (as a result of his lack of support, many gays voted for Ted Kennedy in the 1980 Democratic primaries and the independent campaign of Republican John Anderson in the general election, the latter having announced a sweeping endorsement of gay rights as part of his socially liberal but fiscally conservative appeal).

Despite having made effective appeals for their support in Democratic Party primaries, the Clinton administrations proved to be something of a disappointment to the most vocal gay rights groups. Although he appointed gays and lesbians to his administration and consistently voiced opposition to discrimination, Clinton's policy impact was mixed. In 1993 Clinton set up the first official liaison office for the gay community in the White House. In August 1995, Clinton issued Executive Order 12968 that prohibited the denial of security clearances 'solely on the basis of the sexual orientation of the employee' (an Eisenhower-era directive had classified homosexuality as a 'sexual perversion' that was automatic grounds for denying a clearance). The order encouraged many gay and lesbian CIA intelligence officers to 'come out'. Three years later Clinton issued an executive order barring discrimination based on sexual orientation in the federal workforce. Clinton also issued an executive order on June 23, 2000 that barred discrimination on the basis of sexual orientation in federally conducted education and training programmes.

Not only did Clinton quickly abandon his pledge to end discrimination against gays in the armed forces and refuse to resign as honorary president of the discriminatory Boy Scouts of America after the 2000 Court ruling, however, but he also signed federal legislation passed by the Republican 104th Congress that protected states from recognizing gay marriages and denied those in same-sex marriages eligibility for federal benefits typically accorded to (heterosexual) married couples.

Not a great deal altered at presidential level during the 2000 election race. During the second presidential debate, both Al Gore and George W. Bush stated that they opposed the concept of gay marriage. Gore, however, argued that some type of recognition of 'civil unions' for gay couples should be reached – a reaction that Bush derided as inconsistent with the Vice President's stated opposition to same-sex marriage. In common with his recent predecessors, Gore secured the overwhelming majority of gay and lesbian votes, but Bush's attempt to reject the more homophobic elements of the GOP's more recent

TABLE 7.4   The gay and lesbian presidential vote, 1992–2000 (per cent)

1992		1996		2000	
Bill Clinton	72	Bill Clinton	66	Al Gore	70
George H.W. Bush	14	Bob Dole	23	George W. Bush	25
Ross Perot	14	Ross Perot	17	Ralph Nader	4

Source: Voter News Service exit polls.

election appeals helped him to win one-quarter of the vote (see Table 7.4).

The general absence of presidential enthusiasm to advance gay policy preferences is explicable by three factors:

- *Partisanship.* Opposition to gay rights is a required and relatively cost-free stance by which Republicans appeal to their party's base. The importance of the Christian Right, and the centrality of traditionalist positions on marriage and the family to the party's broader appeal, makes active support for gay equality anathema to most Republicans. Gay rights groups are hence unlikely to achieve executive support for their goals without a Democrat in the White House. But too strong an association with gay and lesbian causes is perceived by many Democrats as damaging to their prospects for winning 'mainstream' voters. The local electoral strength of gay voters, especially in cities like New York and San Francisco, is insufficient to induce a strongly pro-gay presidential stance by either party. Neither Carter nor Clinton fulfilled the initial hopes of gay rights advocates.

- *Strategy.* Because gay rights remains a controversial issue, with a decisive public majority opposed to measures advancing homosexual equality, few presidents will champion the cause with vigour. As Clinton discovered to his cost with the 'gays in the military' débâcle, any attempt to do so is likely to squander precious political capital, undermine other legislative measures of broader public salience, and even cause long-term damage to the

president and his party's popular image among marginal or floating voters (see Exhibit 7.7).

- *Personal.* Reagan and George W. Bush were both professed born-again Christians. Democratic presidents Carter and Clinton were southern Baptists. The best presidential hope for gay rights groups – a secular president for whom biblical condemnations of homosexuality are irrelevant considerations – is also the least likely to win nomination or election. Some presidents (for example, Nixon) have also opposed gay rights out of sincere personal conviction. That some recent presidents opposed gay equality measures but simultaneously enjoyed the friendship of gays and lesbians (especially from the world of entertainment, in the cases of Reagan and Clinton) is another oddity.

Nevertheless, pressures for embracing a more positive approach to gay rights have secured some modest successes. President George W. Bush, for example, became the first Republican president to appoint an openly gay person to head a federal office when he appointed Scott Evertz as the director of the Office of National AIDS Policy (though the office was one he had initially moved to abolish). Bush did not reverse Clinton's anti-discrimination executive orders regarding federal employees. Moreover, he refused to cave in to socially conservative groups who opposed his nominations of Paul Cellucci as ambassador to Canada (as the Republican governor of Massachusetts, Cellucci had been accused of allowing schools in the state to 'promote homosexuality' as part of their sex education curriculum) and of Michael Guest, an openly gay Foreign Service officer, to be ambassador to Romania. Bush also signed legislation that would allow the District of Columbia government to provide domestic-partner benefits to city employees. Such actions prompted the socially conservative Culture and Family Institute to issue a condemnatory report entitled 'The Bush Administration's Republican Homosexual Agenda'.

Exhibit 7.7   Gays in the military: 'don't ask, don't tell'

As Randy Shilts writes, 'The history of homosexuality in the United States armed forces has been a struggle between two intransigent facts – the persistent presence of gays within the military and the equally persistent hostility toward them' (Shilts, 1993: 3). Prior to 1993, servicemen and women could be dismissed from the forces through expedited hearings for homosexual acts or even declaring themselves to be gay. During the 1980s, investigations and courts martial were vigorously pursued with the aim of encouraging gay and lesbian soldiers either to resign, accept an administrative discharge or (for officers) leave quietly under the vague rubric 'conduct unbecoming'.

From 1983 to 1993, some 14,000 personnel had been so dismissed, over half of them Navy personnel. The incalculable human cost of careers destroyed and lives ruined was supplemented by the millions of dollars spent on the cost of investigations and replacing personnel. Issues not only of homophobia but also sex-based discrimination arose in that anti-gay regulations encouraged [hetero]sexual harassment: to refute accusations of lesbianism, women in an overwhelmingly male institution were pressurized into having 'consensual' sex with male colleagues.

President Clinton proposed to end discrimination by lifting the military ban. But Clinton's problems rapidly became apparent on entering the White House. Military leaders and congressional conservatives reacted furiously. Both Senator Sam Nunn (Democrat, Georgia), chairman of the Senate Armed Services Committee, and General Colin Powell, then Chairman of the Joint Chiefs of Staff, vehemently opposed the policy change. They argued that allowing open and practising gays in the forces would inevitably lead to a decline in morale, breakdowns in discipline, 'gay seduction' and, ultimately, a decline in America's defence capacity.

Clinton rapidly retreated and reached a compromise. The armed services would cease asking personnel if they were gay, an affirmative answer to which meant automatic dismissal. In turn, gay personnel would keep their sexual orientation secret and thus avoid triggering dismissal procedures. The policy became known as 'don't ask, don't tell'. Arising soon after Clinton's inauguration, the policy not only called his 'New Democrat' credentials into question but also signalled a political pragmatism that many saw as a chronic tendency to fudge on matters of principle.

The Gallup organization found public opinion split evenly on the issue. A January 1994 poll found 50 per cent supported the new policy, 47 per cent opposed, and 3 per cent had no opinion. But simultaneously, less than a third of those surveyed (32 per cent) endorsed Clinton's general handling of gay issues, 57 per cent disapproving and 11 per cent expressing no opinion. The compromise policy was struck down in March 1995 by the Federal District Court in Brooklyn, New York. Rejecting the government's argument that military morale and performance would suffer if openly homosexual men and women were permitted to serve, Judge Eugene H. Nickerson wrote: 'Congress may not enact discriminatory legislation because it desires to insulate heterosexual members from statements that might excite their prejudices'. But the ruling applied only to the six personnel who brought the lawsuit.

Congress

Between 1964 and 2001, Congress voted on almost 300 bills and amendments encompassing issues of sexual orientation. But with the exception of a handful of districts and states where gay communities are influential voting blocs (such as California, Illinois and New York), few incentives exist for most lawmakers to champion gay rights with vigour or clarity. That does not necessarily mean that support is politically disastrous. In Congress, for example, several lawmakers have 'come out' with no (or relatively few) adverse political consequences. Barney Frank (Democrat, Massachusetts) was a prominent and effective gay lawmaker during the 1980s and 1990s. In 1998, Tammy Baldwin (Democrat, Wisconsin) became the first openly lesbian (and the first non-incumbent openly gay) candidate to win election to the House (she was re-elected in 2000). While this strategy would be less likely to be rewarded in, say, rural Mississippi or Idaho, it indicates a basic level of tolerance – again, not approval – that reflects the values of liberty and equality at the core of the American Creed.

Moreover, although the number of such openly gay legislators is minuscule, this does not necessarily mean that Congress – even under Republican control – will consistently oppose measures beneficial to gays and lesbians. In 1990 Congress passed the Hate Crime Statistics Act (which required the FBI to collect statistics on crimes motivated by bias based on sexual orientation) and the Americans with Disabilities Act (which protects persons with HIV/AIDS from discrimination). In April 1996, the Republican 104th Congress also repealed legislation forcing the dismissal of military personnel with HIV, the virus that causes AIDS. Moreover, in June 2000, the Senate (under Republican control) voted to expand the definition of federal 'hate crimes' to include those committed because of the victim's sexual orientation (by 2002, 27 states had at least one type of law recording or punishing hate crimes motivated by bias towards perceived sexual orientation).

Where these individual instances face greater difficulties, however, occurs in relation to questions of 'family values'. For many Americans, it is one thing simply to disapprove of homosexuality but to recognize that discrimination based on sexual orientation violates a basic tenet of Americanism; it is another question entirely, however, to view homosexuality and heterosexuality as equal before the law where questions of marriage, children and taxation are concerned. Again, it is important to note that responses here reveal a mix of prejudice and beliefs that have nothing to do with sexuality as such. For example, the same Congress that acted in a progressive fashion on HIV military personnel also passed the Defense of Marriage Act in 1996.

Intermediary organizations

The main political parties have become increasingly polarized over gay issues since 1968. By the time of the Democratic National Convention in San Francisco in 1984, broad support among Democratic opinion leaders and traditional allies (such as the AFL-CIO) made the adoption of a gay rights plank in the party platform almost routine.

By contrast, Republicans have generally sought to make clear their distance from the aspirations of gay rights campaigners. Although President Reagan reiterated his opposition to discrimination of any kind in 1984, for example, he also reassured social conservatives of his disapproval of homosexuality. He released a statement celebrating 'the Judaeo-Christian tradition' of marriage and family and lamenting 'the erosion of these values has given way to a celebration of forms of expression most reject. We will resist the efforts of some to obtain government endorsement of homosexuality' (Shilts, 1993: 454). Although Reagan did not directly attack gays, GOP strategists dismissed their opponents as 'the San Francisco Democrats', a way of constantly linking the Democrats to gays, given the city's reputation.

The mounting campaigns and publicity accorded gay rights in turn moved the issue to even greater prominence for both parties. By 1992, Pat Buchanan's cultural *jihad* against liberalism specifically singled out gays in his prime-time speech at the Republican National Convention, claiming that the Clinton ticket represented

> the most pro-lesbian and pro-gay ticket in history. . . . Hillary believes that twelve-year-olds should have the right to sue their parents, and she has compared marriage as an institution to slavery and life on an Indian reservation. . . . Friends, this is radical feminism . . . abortion on demand . . . homosexual rights. . . .

By 2000, the GOP sought under George W. Bush to present a more inclusive front to the public. Seeking to advance the Bush agenda of 'compassionate conservatism', the national convention in Philadelphia in July 2000 even featured a speaking spot for an openly gay Republican congressman, Jim Kolbe from Arizona. Not only did Kolbe speak on trade rather than gay rights, however, but a number of delegates on the convention floor turned their backs on him in a symbolic show of opposition to gay rights. Clearly, the presence of avowedly conservative religious organizations within the Republican Party coalition remains a problem for those in the GOP seeking to reach out to gay Americans, notwithstanding the fact that some notable Republicans have gay relatives (Newt Gingrich's sister, for example) and siblings (the lesbian daughter of Vice President Dick Cheney).

While the partisan divide is fairly clear, two factors make the interest group universe on gay rights unusually complex. First, because sexual preference cuts across a range of beliefs and experiences, the gay 'constituency' is heterogeneous, taking in a variety of socio-economic, ethnic, racial, regional and religious categories (some surveys, for example, suggest that self-identified gays and lesbians are moderately more wealthy than heterosexuals across these categories). As

Urvashi Vaid notes, it 'is possible for gay people today to live in a supportive gay community, shop at gay businesses, vacation at gay resorts, participate in gay community and cultural events, but still deny the truth of their lives to families, employers, friends and government' (Vaid, 1995). At the same time, the growth of such communities threatens to isolate gays in a 'lifestyle closet', where gays and lesbians withdraw from political involvement, leaving important policy goals such as domestic-partners legislation, support for AIDS funding and anti-discrimination laws either partially or substantially unmet.

Secondly, as a result of their heterogeneity, gays and lesbians are divided over the optimum political strategies to advance equal rights. Homosexuals have a unique status as neither a visible nor an insular minority. Unlike blacks, women and even first-generation immigrants, homosexuals have had the choice of remaining invisible to the heterosexual population. A high psychic cost frequently accompanies doing so, but it has been a feasible option for many gays. Moreover, unlike the other groups, homosexuals have not been unified by obvious political or economic goals in the ways that abolitionism and the franchise were bonds for blacks and women during the nineteenth century. Even the battle against AIDS, which has provided a political focus, is unlike these other struggles as it is widely recognized as a major social problem by gays and straights alike, and government is funding research and health benefits (albeit not to the degree that activists would prefer).

The result is that pro-gay interest groups possess distinct goals, strategies and tactics. Beyond insisting that the federal government outlaw job discrimination based on sexual orientation, these groups are frequently pitted against each other and divided between progressive radicals, pragmatists and gay conservatives. For example, some groups on the left, such as the National Gay and Lesbian Task Force (NGLTF), champion issues (such as rights for bisexuals and people changing gender) that groups on the

Exhibit 7.8 Donations by gay and lesbian PACs to federal candidates

		Democrats (%)	Republicans (%)
Human Rights Campaign			
1997–98	$803,125	89	11
1999–2000	$971,236	86	14
2001–02	$316,193	84	16
Gay & Lesbian Victory Fund			
1997–98	$34,678	99	1
1999–2000	$31,664	69	31
2001–02	$6,500	100	0
Log Cabin Republicans			
1997–98	$11,550	0	100
1999–2000	$6,267	0	100
2001–02	$1,750	0	100
National Stonewall Democratic Federation			
1997–98	$8,339	100	0
1999–2000	$17,500	100	0
2001–02	$0	0	0

Note: 2001–02 figures through to October 2001.
Source: Center for Responsive Politics.

right avoid and they refuse to cooperate with Republicans. But the largest gay lobbying group, the Human Rights Campaign (HRC), is willing to work with and fund Republicans (see Exhibit 7.8). Some on the right, such as the Log Cabin Republicans, take no position on measures such as the proposed Employment Non-discrimination Act, while issues such as abortion and 'globalization' pit liberals and conservatives against each other. Some groups, such as NGLTF, also favour local and state-based grass-roots activism, while others, such as the HRC, prefer to focus on federal action as the best way to secure anti-discrimination measures for gays nationwide.

In terms of partisanship, some activists favour linking gay rights with progressive causes and finding a clear home in the Democratic Party. Others, such as the Log Cabin Republicans, seek assimilation in the wider society as economic and political conservatives. Still others, such as Queer Nation, espouse an almost separatist agenda that

rejects liberal tolerance as sufficient to achieve meaningful equality for gays. Thus far, no single leader or organization has managed to unify these groups. Some activists have tried to network with the National Organization for Women, and in 1994 persuaded the black civil rights group, the National Association for the Advancement of Colored People, to endorse a gay march for the first time. Gay organizations have also worked closely with groups dedicated to protecting individual rights more generally, such as the American Civil Liberties Union and Amnesty International, to safeguard egalitarian protections for homosexuals.

Although there is no lobby on the other side that bases its operation on an expressly and exclusively anti-gay rights purpose, many organizations exist that have opposition to equality as a key part of their broader platforms. Some of these are centred on the protection of the traditional two-parent, heterosexual family (such as the Family

Exhibit 7.9   A free market road to gay rights?

In June 2000, the largest three American car producers announced that they would offer full health benefits to the same-sex domestic partners of their nearly 500,000 employees. Ford Motor Company, General Motors Corporation and Daimler-Chrysler Corporation jointly announced that they would offer the benefits to the domestic partners of all employees who had shared a 'committed relationship for no less than six months'. (The benefits were not offered to unmarried heterosexual couples.) The auto-makers stated that 'offering health care benefits to same-sex domestic partners is consistent with each organization's commitment to diversity in the workplace and is responsive to competitive trends among the *Fortune* 500 companies'. In short, the need to recruit and maintain skilled labour in an increasingly tight labour market had encouraged the car firms to follow the lead of airlines (such as United and American) and corporations (such as Microsoft and Disney) in extending health care benefits to gay workers and their partners. On this approach, achieving gay equality is merely a matter of time: the economic costs of neglecting an important part of the skilled workforce are simply too prohibitive to tolerate inequality. (By 2002, court orders and legislation in eight states and over 80 localities had also mandated some type of domestic-partner benefit – such as health insurance – for public employees.)

Source: Adapted from Frank Swoboda, 'Big 3 Extend Benefits to Domestic Partners', *Washington Post*, June 9, 2000, p. A01.

Research Center). Others, such as the American Center for Law and Justice, monitor judicial developments on gay issues. Still others form part of the broad range of religious organizations active in political affairs, such as the Christian Coalition. In the 1970s and 1980s, the National Conservative Political Action Committee (NCPAC) spent several million dollars on television campaign advertisements linking Democrats to support for gay rights (despite the irony that Terry Dolan, NCPAC's founder and director, frequented gay bars in DC and gay resorts in California). As gay activists mobilize over issues of same-sex marriages and child adoption, the importance of gay issues to organizations dedicated to defending the traditional family is likely only to increase.

Moreover, many of these organizations have enjoyed success in using mechanisms of direct democracy, such as initiatives and referendums, to attack gay rights. From 1972 to 2001, opponents of gay rights placed 92 anti-gay measures on state and local ballots, covering topics such as prohibiting same-sex marriages and 'promotion' of homosexuality

in public schools to repeals of gay civil rights laws and domestic-partner benefits. Most of these measures succeeded in gaining electoral majorities. Although gay rights groups also sought to use this route, most pro-gay measures have been defeated at the ballot box. This suggests strongly that gay and lesbian equality is unlikely to be achieved – or maintained – through majoritarian mechanisms, particularly at state or local levels.

CONCLUSION

As the political struggles about homosexual equality intensified during the 1990s, some critics noted how odd it was for a group to be prioritizing concerns such as getting married and joining the military at the beginning of the twenty-first century. But for many gay and lesbian Americans (and heterosexuals, too), sexual orientation is a key part of their individual identity and an important expression of that individuality. Sexual identity is not somehow akin to smoking or hunting, a choice of 'lifestyle' activities that can as easily be relinquished as taken up in the first instance. Being gay is as much a defining characteristic and a 'given' as being a mother, Latino, man or woman. 'Leaving' homosexuality, as born-again Christians advocate, is no more possible than leaving being black. The stakes for many members of this substantial part of the American population are, therefore, as profound as they could possibly be in terms of achieving equal treatment.

As with other cultural value issues, however, much of the political conflict about gay rights turns on the supposed implications for others in society: children, the institutions of heterosexual marriage and the traditional family, and the legitimation that society confers on particular practices – in this case, 'sexual morality'. Like abortion, gun control and pornography, the views of the most animated participants in the political struggle are close to irreconcilable and the controversy assumes a passionate and polarized character generating much heat and only modest light. On gay rights, it is not simply the case that reasonable people can disagree about constitutional interpretation, the law and public policies; they can and, at times, do go to extreme lengths in order to voice their disagreement.

For gay rights activists, allowing the state to sanction homosexual marriage as equal before the law to heterosexual marriage, and allowing gay and lesbian couples to rear or adopt (and, in the case of the latter, bear) children, is a matter of fundamental human equality. As an aspect of citizenship and equality before the law, these questions say nothing about wider issues of the family or the 'moral tone' of society. For their opponents, however, to enact such changes is to encourage and abet the spread of an immoral state – homosexuality – and thereby to discourage and discredit traditional institutions that have been the foundation of American society.

In this respect, prohibitions on gay marriage do not resemble those state laws that existed on inter-racial marriage until 1967. While both types of statute were informed by brute prejudice against a class of Americans,

no one ever doubted the expressly heterosexual nature of the racial couplings that antimiscegenation laws were directed against. (It is mildly ironic that some of the most vigorous opponents of gay rights continue to be African Americans, a group whose experience of state-sponsored discrimination and malign sexual stereotyping might lead them to side with homosexual rights campaigners.) Black–white intermarriage remains rare in America for many reasons, but those Americans who do cross the racial divide are unlikely today to be seen as acting immorally – in public, at least.

It may therefore be that, in future years, this period will be looked on as another undistinguished – but, ultimately, transient – episode in American history. Historically, popular opposition to equal rights – based partly on biblical injunctions – was part of the rationale for opposing racial desegregation, gender equality and various categories of ethnic and religious immigration. Those battles were, at least partially, won, and the struggle for homosexual equality may be seen similarly as analogous to that of blacks during the 1950s and 1960s. Supreme Court decisions such as *Romer* may come, in retrospect, to be viewed by gays as important steppingstones on the road to equal citizenship in the way that many blacks look back on *Brown*.

Equally, however, those decisions may be seen as simply symbolic and hollow gestures running against a visceral majoritarian reaction against gay equality. The fact that mainstream films such as *Philadelphia* or television shows like *Ellen* depict gay issues and present a strongly positive image of gay men and women does not necessarily suggest that gays and lesbians have moved into the mainstream. An illiberal passion for conformism has historically been latent in American society, an intolerant tendency that has sometimes been made manifest by intense political struggles in which social groups seek to enforce particular moral or religious codes against competing claims of individual liberty or privacy. Perhaps no other contemporary social issue remains more likely to animate the competing tolerant and illiberal tendencies of the American public than gay rights.

FURTHER READING

Dennis Altman, *AIDS and the New Puritanism* (1986) is a detailed account of the effect of AIDS on political life in America, especially as it affected gay and lesbian Americans.

James W. Button, Barbara A. Rienzo and Kenneth D. Wald, *Private Lives, Public Conflicts: Battles over Gay Rights in American Communities* (1997) is a pioneering, empirically based textbook on the local politics of gay rights and public policy.

Martin Durham, *The Christian Right, the Far Right and the Boundaries of American Conservatism* (2000, Chapter 3) provides a comprehensive discussion of the changing role of opposition to gay equality in the strategy, tactics and rhetoric of the diverse American right.

Didi Herman, *The Antigay Agenda: Orthodox Vision and the Christian Right* (1997) is an excellent analysis of the Christian Right's strategies to resist the advance of gay rights.

Ken Kersch, 'Full Faith and Credit for Same-Sex Marriages?', *Political Science Quarterly* 112 (1) (1997), pp. 117–36 is a detailed discussion of the constitutional politics of same-sex unions.

Richard Posner, *Sex and Reason* (1992) is a balanced and thorough account of the key issues concerning homosexual rights in America.

Craig A. Rimmerman, Kenneth D. Wald and Clyde Wilcox (eds), *The Politics of Gay Rights* (2000) analyses gay politics, public opinion and policymaking at federal, state and local levels.

Randy Shilts, *Conduct Unbecoming: Gays and Lesbians in the US Military* (1993) is a detailed and comprehensive examination of the history of gay and lesbian experiences in the American armed forces.

Raymond A. Smith and Donal P. Haider-Markel, *Gay and Lesbian American and Political Participation* (2002) is a reference book assessing gay political participation from voting and interest groups to representation in government.

Andrew Sullivan, *Virtually Normal: An Argument about Homosexuality* (1996) is a balanced and thoughtful approach to the theoretical and practical issues concerning gay rights in America.

WEB LINKS

National organizations: traditionalist

American Family Association
http://www.afa.net

Christian Coalition
http://www.cc.org

Eagle Forum
http://www.eagleforum.org

Family Research Council
http://www.frc.org

Focus on the Family
http://fotf.org

National organizations: pro-gay rights

ACLU briefing papers in Supreme Court cases
http://www.aclu.org/issues/gay/argl.html

Gay and Lesbian Advocates and Defenders
http://www.glad.org/

Gay and Lesbian Victory Fund
http://www.victoryfund.org

Human Rights Campaign
http://www.hrc.org/

International Gay and Lesbian Human Rights Commission
http://www.iglhrc.org/

Lambda Legal Defense and Education Fund
http://www.lambdalegal.org/cgi-bin/pages/

Log Cabin Republicans
http://www.lcr.org/index.asp

National Gay and Lesbian Task Force
http://www.ngltf.org/

National Stonewall Democrats
http://www.stonewalldemocrats.org/main.html

Parents, Families and Friends of Lesbians and Gays
http://www.pflag.org

Traditional Values Coalition
http://64.55.184.74/tvc1/

Local and state organizations

California Alliance for Pride and Equality
http://www.calcape.org/

Georgia Equality Project
http://www.georgiaequality.org

Equality Illinois
http://www.ifhr.org

Indiana: Justice, Inc.
http://www.justiceinc.org/

Kentucky Fairness Alliance
http://www.kentuckyfairness.org/

Lesbian Avengers Organizers' Project
http://www.octobertech.com/october/handbook.nsf

New York: Empire State Pride Agenda
http://www.prideagenda.org

Equality North Carolina
http://www.equalitync.org

Lesbian Gay Rights Lobby of Texas
http://www.lgrl.org

Media and general resources

The Advocate
http://www.advocate.com

The Source
http://www.gaysource.com/index.html

Queer Resources Directory
http://www.qrd.org/qrd/

The Washington Blade
http://www.washblade.com/

QUESTIONS

- To what extent and why are gay and lesbian Americans still the victims of 'majority tyranny' in the United States?

- Evaluate the arguments for and against the constitutionality of same-sex marriage.

- What factors determine the relative political influence of homosexuals in American government and politics?

- Is a refusal of the federal judiciary to strike down laws against same-sex marriage justifiable on either constitutional or pragmatic grounds?

- Compare and contrast the opportunities for, and limits on, the political influence of gay Americans and either women or African Americans in the United States.

8 Religion in Public Life

Neither a state nor the Federal Government can set up a church. Neither can pass laws which aid one religion, aid all religions, or prefer one religion over another. . . . In the words of Jefferson, the clause against establishment of religion by law was intended to erect 'a wall of separation between Church and State'.

> Hugo L. Black, for the Court, *Everson v. Board of Education*, 330 U.S. 1 (1947), at 15–16

We are a religious people whose institutions presuppose a Supreme Being.

> William O. Douglas, for the Court, *Zorach v. Clauson*, 343 U.S. 306 (1952), at 313

- **The Historical Context**
- **Public Opinion**
- **Explaining the Politics of Religion**
- **School Prayer and Public Education**
- **Governing Institutions**
- **The Christian Right**
- **Conclusion**

Chapter Summary

As Al Gore's selection of the Orthodox Jewish Senator Joseph Lieberman (Democrat, Connecticut) as his vice presidential candidate vividly confirmed in 2000, one of the most distinctive features of the United States is the pronounced level of religiosity – the extent and intensity of religious belief and practice – that exists among Americans. Although they adhere to many different faiths, most Americans are religious believers and many regularly attend churches, synagogues, mosques and other places of worship. The secularizing trends of post-Second World War western Europe have not been present in America. Partly as a result, the relationship between religion and public life has been and remains politically controversial. Historically, the 'separation of church and state' has been a key part of the explanation for America's standing as an inviting refuge to thousands of individuals fleeing religious (and political) persecution. Freedom to practise religion without state interference has been a crucial element underpinning individual liberty more broadly. However, religion has not only informed conflicts such as abortion and gay rights, but has also become a distinct and controversial issue itself since the 1960s. Because of the political activism of religious groups such as the Christian Right, some Americans fear that their nation is in danger of becoming a theological republic, while other Americans of faith fear that the barriers between religion and public life have already turned the nation into a secular one where religion and traditional morality have been eroded, marginalized and even eliminated from the public sphere. In particular, the latter hold that judicial interpretations of the First Amendment's prohibition against an establishment of religion have left American public institutions, not least schools, as 'religion-free zones'. But the messy political and legal compromises that have been reached by governing institutions about the appropriate relationship between government and religion in recent decades reflect a typically American compromise. As President George W. Bush's strong emphasis on tolerance towards Muslim and Arab Americans suggested after September 11, 2001 the marked diversity of Americans today – religious, ethnic, racial and regional – suggests that religious pluralism is less a challenge to the nation's system of constitutional government than a powerful reinforcement of the core pluralist values of American democracy.

Prior chapters have emphasized the important and wide-ranging roles that religion plays in the various political battles of the contemporary American culture war. Continuing political controversies over the issues of abortion, the death penalty, pornography and gay rights have featured a strong religious component, with moral traditionalists frequently deriving their views on these issues from deeply held faiths. Many progressives, too, espouse their views partly from a religious foundation (such as Sister Helen Prejean's opposition to capital punishment). Not only does religious faith and observance provide a key context for these battles, however, but religion itself has also emerged as a distinct and controversial issue in the culture war since the 1960s. The role that religion should play in American public life has become the subject of heated political disagreement.

Such conflict is neither new nor surprising. Religion has been one of the most powerful forces in American life since the first Pilgrims landed on the continent – as influential, in its way, as the rule of law or regular elections. But religion has also been a highly problematic political question for many decades. In 1960, for example, Senator John F. Kennedy had to reassure American voters, most of whom were Protestants, that electing the first (and, thus far, only) Roman Catholic to the presidency would not endanger the republic. (In the event, a narrow majority was sufficiently confident that the Pope would not dictate American foreign or domestic policy to vote for JFK.) Subsequently, presidential candidates such as Jimmy Carter in 1976 and George W. Bush in 2000 made much of their 'born-again' Christianity. Al Gore's selection of an Orthodox Jewish running-mate, Senator Joseph Lieberman of Connecticut, in 2000 once again placed religion at the centre of public attention.

Social movements have also drawn powerfully on religious doctrines. For example, although the civil rights movement of the 1950s and 1960s was partly based on Christian teachings, epitomized by the non-violent approach of Martin Luther King Jr., many blacks rejected pacifist philosophies and turned instead to the unorthodox, quasi-Islamic teachings of black separatist groups like the Nation of Islam (including Malcolm X and the boxer Cassius Clay, who changed his name to Muhammad Ali). Mass movements against abortion rights, dating from 1973 and encompassing both Protestants and Catholics, were also heavily influenced by religious beliefs.

Even the composition of the Supreme Court is affected by religious considerations, with many Americans eager for the highest Court to 'look like' America in terms of religious affiliation as well as race, region and gender. Judicial nominations regularly feature discussion of the religious backgrounds of the justices and the presence of, in particular, Jewish and Catholic members of the Court. President Clinton appointed two Jewish justices, Ruth Bader Ginsburg and Stephen Breyer. Notoriously, populist conservative politicians such as Pat Buchanan and extreme right-wing groups such as the Ku Klux Klan also make use of images of America as a Christian or Protestant nation in order to justify their purist positions on issues from immigration to abortion rights.

The contemporary controversy over religion stems from two basic features of modern America. First, the diverse nature of America's social base encompasses a remarkable range of religious beliefs, with a myriad of different faiths now existing in the nation. However much Protestants founded and still dominate the nation, Americans now profess a remarkably wide range of faiths. Not only Protestants, Catholics and Jews, but also Mormons, Buddhists, Hindus, Muslims, Sikhs, Shintoists, Scientologists and other faiths are well represented among Americans today. This remarkable heterogeneity reinforces the diversity and pluralism of the

United States but also serves as a source of substantial social and political conflict, both between indigenous religious groups and among traditionalists who fear 'alien' faiths coming to dominate or subvert traditional American values and practices.

Secondly, a series of controversial decisions by the federal courts – and the Supreme Court, especially – have proven crucial in strongly politicizing the role of religion in public life since 1962. While the separation of church and state has been a foundation-stone of American life from the beginning of the republic, such that no official state church (like Britain's Church of England) could be established, many Americans now believe that the court-driven displacement of religion from public life has contributed powerfully to social breakdown, an erosion of morality and a growth of cynicism among the citizenry. The balance between government being impartial between religions and acting against religion as such has tilted, on this view, too far in favour of the latter position. Partly as a result, Americans of different religious beliefs have felt themselves to be an embattled minority and have increasingly engaged in expressly political action to achieve their aims of reaffirming the centrality of religion and spiritual faith to private and public life.

THE HISTORICAL CONTEXT

Religion has been a part of American life from before the United States was founded and remains a crucial and pervasive social force today. America was founded by Puritan settlers and has long cherished its historical reputation for offering a welcoming home to those fleeing religious (and political) intolerance, coercion or persecution in other parts of the world. Some of the most obvious manifestations of religion's continued importance can be gleaned from long-established features of public life. For example, presidents are sworn into office at their inauguration – in

Exhibit 8.1   Religion: some definitions

- The belief in a superhuman controlling power, especially in a personal God or gods entitled to obedience and worship.
- The expression of this belief in worship.
- A particular system of faith and worship.
- A life under monastic vows (the way of religion).
- A thing to which one is devoted ('football is their religion').

the January succeeding the presidential election of the previous November – with their hand on the Bible, ending their declaration to defend the Constitution with a plea for divine assistance: 'so help me, God'. (In the 2000 election, Joe Lieberman even sought to reassure non-Jewish voters about his faith by noting that, if elected, he could not violate the Constitution since to do so would also, in virtue of this phrase at the end of the oath, be a sin against God; the same approach had been used previously by JFK in 1960.) America is also fabled for being, according to the Pledge of Allegiance, 'one nation under God' and even for vowing on its dollar bills that 'In God We Trust'.

A key concept underlies America's boast as a beacon of religious freedom: 'the separation of church and state'. Although the term can be found in neither the Declaration of Independence nor the Constitution, during the eighteenth, nineteenth and (to a lesser, but still significant, extent) twentieth centuries, thousands of migrants from across the globe sought refuge from religious persecution in their host nations by emigrating to America. The concepts of individual freedom and the equal protection of the laws have powerfully reinforced the pull of the 'American Dream' of individual betterment. 'Freedom of religion' – the right to follow whatever religion one chooses without interference from the state – is a constitutionally protected right contained in the First Amendment to the federal Constitution. Together, these features of America's political culture suggested a capacious liberty for individual citizens to practise their religious beliefs, free from government interference, that has frequently been denied elsewhere. (Throughout the postwar era, for example, the American doctrine of containment of communism was partly premised on the atheistic content of communist belief and practice suppressing religious freedom behind the 'Iron Curtain'.)

Partly as a result of this distinctively tolerant approach, American society has continued to display powerful and remarkably widespread levels of 'religiosity': the condition of being religious. As long ago as the 1830s, de Tocqueville was amazed at how religious Americans were in comparison to Europeans, and that contrast has only deepened further as the decades have progressed and many European nations (both Protestant and Catholic) have experienced secularization since 1945 – the process whereby individuals shed beliefs in the spiritual or sacred. By contrast, America has remained among the most religious countries in the world. For example, the average American is significantly more likely than the average European to believe in God, pray on a daily basis, and acknowledge clear standards of right and wrong. Surveys in 45 countries conducted from 1990 to 1993 revealed that America was the only industrialized nation in which over 80 per cent of citizens identified themselves as religious. Similarly, only 1 per cent of Americans claimed that they were atheists, a strikingly low proportion in a country of over 270 million people (Lipset, 1996). To many non-Americans, Americans can even appear guilty of religionism: excessive religious zeal that can manifest itself in such exotic phenomena as 'speaking in tongues' and snake-handling in churches.

Beyond the comfort and guidance that they offer the faithful, however, religious beliefs have also played a significant and wide-ranging role in politics. From the outset, they contributed powerfully to the impulse of the Framers of the 1787 Constitution to disperse and check the powers of government. To the original colonists, mankind suffered from original sin, symbolized by Adam and Eve eating the forbidden fruit in the Garden of Eden. Since no one was born innocent and human nature is fundamentally depraved, no single human being could therefore be trusted with power. The religious revivalist movement of the late 1730s and early 1740s (known as the 'First Great Awakening') transformed the political life of the colonies. Religious ideas fuelled the break with England for violating, according to the Declaration of Independence, 'the laws of nature and nature's God'. Religious belief therefore reinforced the colonies' negative experiences with British rule to help shape the Constitution so as to curb the darker sides of human nature by fragmenting power among competing tiers and branches of government.

Subsequently, religious leaders were central to the moralistic struggles over the abolition of slavery in the nineteenth century and the temperance movement that achieved Prohibition of alcohol in 1919. During the second half of the twentieth century, religious faith remained a powerful resource for political activism. Both progressives and conservatives shrewdly used the pulpit either to promote or halt social and political change. The civil rights movement of the 1950s and 1960s was led mainly by black religious leaders. Relying heavily on non-violence and Christian teachings, the movement's humanistic and egalitarian appeals drew together a range of faiths – Protestants, Catholics and Jews – and ultimately proved irresistible to most Americans. With new and controversial federal court decisions on issues such as prayer in school, obscenity, contraception,

birth control and abortion during the 1960s and 1970s, many previously depoliticized Protestants and Catholics entered political life energized by opposition to such liberalizing measures. The Reverend Billy Graham drew hundreds of thousands of Americans to his evangelizing rallies while, during the 1980s, a conservative religious group known as the 'Moral Majority' advocated constitutional amendments that would allow prayer in public schools and ban abortion. Individual preachers such as Jerry Falwell, Pat Robertson and Jim Bakker came to national attention as the moralistic vanguard of the conservative right. In the 1990s, another strongly conservative religious group, the Christian Coalition, attracted an enormous amount of media attention and became an influential force in many national, state and local election campaigns and state political parties (such as the Republican Party in Texas).

The absence of an established or official religion for the nation as a whole, reinforced by a constitutional prohibition of such an establishment and by migration, meant that religious differences were both inevitable and politically significant. Since there could be no official religion, it became difficult for a corresponding political orthodoxy to emerge. Moreover, the differences between the Puritan tradition, with its emphasis on faith and good works, and the Catholic Church, with its devotion to the sacraments and priestly authority, provided a recurrent source of conflict in public life with the mass immigration of Catholics (most notably from Ireland and Italy) in the later nineteenth century. Differences in values between these groups showed up not only in religious practices, but also in areas involving the regulation of morals and the choice of political party.

Even though there was no established church, there was certainly a dominant religious tradition from the republic's founding: Protestantism, and especially Puritanism. Protestant churches provided many citizens with a set of religious beliefs and organizational experience that had profound effects.

Exhibit 8.2   Religion and immigration

The religious foundations of American life directly reflect the successive waves of immigration that have occurred since America's founding. Dominated by Anglo-Saxon Protestants for most of its first century as a republic, substantial numbers of Roman Catholics entered the nation with the growth of Irish and southern European immigration – principally from Italy, Spain and Austria – during the late nineteenth century. One hundred years later, during the 1980s and 1990s, Latino and Asian immigration added substantially to the religious diversity in America: not only Catholics but also Buddhists, Hindus, Muslims, Sikhs and Shintoists. Currently, American religious affiliations are markedly heterogeneous by comparative standards. Approximately 60 per cent of Americans call themselves Protestant and 25 per cent Roman Catholic, with about 8 per cent undesignated, 1 per cent adhering to the Orthodox Church and another 1–2 per cent to each of the Mormon, Jewish, Muslim and 'other' religions. Among Protestant denominations, the Southern Baptists and Baptists each constitute about 10 per cent, Methodists 10 per cent, Presbyterians 5 per cent, Episcopalians 2 per cent, Lutherans 7 per cent, Pentecostals 3 per cent, members of the Church of Christ 2 per cent, members of other denominations approximately 11 per cent, and members of non-denominational churches 5 per cent. Such religious pluralism not only underscores the extent to which Americans are people of faith and that hence religion in general has a role to play in public life, but also reinforces the long-standing American belief that government should not discriminate either in favour of or against a particular religion.

Those beliefs encouraged – even required – a life of personal achievement as well as religious conviction: a believer had to work hard, save money, obey the secular law and do good works. Religion thereby reinforced core American values. Churches also offered opportunities for developing civic and political skills. Since most Protestant churches were organized along congregational lines, with the church controlled by its members, who erected the building, hired the preacher and supervised the finances, they were, in effect, miniature political systems, with leaders and committees, conflict and consensus. Developing a participatory political culture was therefore made easier by the existence of a religious culture that strongly encouraged individualism and faith.

The absence of a British-style church–state link also meant that American religions were strongly influenced by sects – bodies of people subscribing to religious doctrines that are usually different from those of an established church from which they have separated (sometimes referred to as 'non-

conformists'). This has once again reinforced the diversity of religious faiths. A bewildering variety of religious groups exist which practise their own distinctive versions of orthodox doctrines. One result, however, is that the place that religion should occupy in American public life and politics is the subject of notable disagreement.

PUBLIC OPINION

Public opinion surveys consistently demonstrate that religion remains a powerful force in American social life and politics. For over 60 years, Gallup surveys have shown sizeable majorities of Americans identifying religion as either 'very important' or 'fairly important' in their personal lives. Admittedly, 'only' 35 per cent of Americans can be classified as 'religious', using a definition that requires them not only to consider religion important but also to attend religious services almost every week or more frequently. Not only is this figure impressive in itself in comparison

Exhibit 8.3   God v. monkeys: the Scopes trial and 'Creation Science'

The most notorious example of conflict between traditional religious belief and a changing America occurred in 1925 with the infamous Scopes trial. The case pitted those progressive forces that believed in the Darwinian theory of evolution against American traditionalists who found it repugnant and wrong to see humans as descended from apes and who instead believed in the literal truth of the Bible and the doctrine of 'Creationism'. Such was the political importance of the case at the time that the former presidential candidate, William Jennings Bryan, agreed to act as the prosecution's lawyer.

The background to the case was simple enough. In 1925, the Tennessee state legislature passed a bill that prohibited the teaching of Darwinian evolution theory in public schools. Immediately after the new law took effect, the officers of the American Civil Liberties Union offered to challenge the law in court. John Scopes, a 24-year-old science teacher in Dayton, Tennessee, was persuaded to provoke a test case by declaring publicly that he taught biology from an evolutionary standpoint. Scopes was arrested and brought to trial in the summer.

The trial featured intense battles between Bryan, for the prosecution, and the legendary counsel Clarence Darrow, Scopes's lawyer. Scopes was eventually fined $100 for breaking the law (Tennessee's Supreme Court later upheld the case but rescinded the fine on a technicality). The trial was in essence a battle between the rigid, orthodox, accepting, unyielding narrow, conventional mind and the broad liberal, cynical, sceptical and tolerant mind.

Near the end of the trial, Bryan was asked by the defence to take the stand. Darrow went on sarcastically to question Bryan, revealing his opponent's sincere faith in the literal truth of the Bible. While Darrow delighted in belittling his testimony as 'fool ideas that no intelligent Christian on earth believes', Bryan proclaimed in response that 'it is better to trust in the Rock of Ages than to know the ages of rocks'. Ultimately, both sides saw the Scopes trial as a victory but the episode merely illustrated how little tolerance secular and fundamentalist groups had for each other. The reverberations of the trial have continued and its echoes can still be heard currently in heated debates in several states – especially in the South and Midwest – over the place of so-called 'Creation Science' in public schools.

to European nations, but the percentage of Americans who report attending a religious service within the past seven days has remained remarkably steady since 1939, averaging just over 40 per cent. Moreover, as Table 8.1 shows, compared to Europeans, Americans profess a stronger religious faith, even when certain basic indicators about the existence of God, the importance of prayer, and questions of good and evil are considered. Prayer assumes an important part of almost four out of five American lives, compared to just fewer than two in five British lives, for example.

On specific questions of faith, the marked religiosity of most Americans emerges even more clearly. In a February 1995 poll, for example, nearly all Americans (96 per cent) stated that they believed in the existence of God, and 88 per cent affirmed the importance of religion. Since 1939, Gallup found that approximately 40 per cent of Americans attended a church or synagogue once a week or almost every week, while another 12–15 per cent attended once every month. Evidently, Americans may not turn out to the polling booths in remarkably large numbers, but they do turn out to churches in an impressive and regular fashion now unknown in much of Europe – in both numbers and frequency.

Many Americans believe in a hereafter of

TABLE 8.1   Religious belief in the US and Europe, 1991

Statement	Percentage agreeing				
	USA	UK	Germany	Italy	France
'I never doubt the existence of God.'	60	31	20	56	29
'Prayer is an important part of my daily life.'	77	37	44	69	32
'There are clear guidelines about what is good and evil.'	79	65	54	56	64

Source: *The Public Perspective*, November/December 1991, pp. 5, 8.

heaven and hell and in a world populated by angels, devils and miracles. For example, a 1994 poll revealed that 96 per cent of Americans celebrate Christmas, only 8 per cent do not believe in heaven, and only 12 per cent do not believe in miracles. By any measure, Americans remain strongly attached to important spiritual beliefs. Gallup data from December 1994 showed, for example, that 90 per cent of Americans believed in heaven, 73 per cent in hell, 70 per cent in miracles, 72 per cent in angels, and 65 per cent in the devil.

But Americans are not alone in the west in professing an active spiritual existence. A recent survey in the United Kingdom, for example, suggested that conventional assessments of the British as a secular people may not be entirely accurate. The survey (commissioned for the BBC) between April 25 and May 7, 2000, revealed that 32 per cent of Britons believed in the devil and 28 per cent in hell – figures far less high than those of Americans but nevertheless a substantial proportion. Despite a high divorce rate, 80 per cent of British respondents disagreed that marriage was an outdated institution and 76 per cent said they expected it to last a lifetime.

TABLE 8.2   Spiritual belief in the United Kingdom, 2000

Belief in:	Yes (%)	No (%)	Don't know (%)
God	62	30	8
Jesus	62	29	8
Life after death	51	37	13
A soul	69	25	6
The devil	32	63	6
Hell	28	66	6
Heaven	52	41	8
Sin	71	26	4
Resurrection	32	61	8
Reincarnation	25	65	10

Note: the question posed was 'What, if any, do you believe in?'
Source: *The Sunday Telegraph*, May 28, 2000, p. 3.

While most Americans view religion favourably, religious differences can also lead to important political divisions. Much as Americans adhere to the American Creed yet differ in their applications of it to the real world, so their near-universal commitment to religious faith feeds differing views about practical political and religious/moral issues.

As Table 8.3 reveals, religious differences inform or reinforce political differences. Secular views, for example, tend to be associated with politically progressive stances on questions such as abortion rights and gender equality. Fundamentalist views tend, conversely, to be strongly associated with more conservative and traditionalist positions. While these divisions do not exactly parallel those between Democrats and Republicans, the basic differences share much in common. For example, secular Americans were almost three times as likely to support (Southern Baptist) Clinton's presidential candidacy in 1992 as were fundamentalists, while a mere 7 per cent of fundamentalists considered themselves to be ideological liberals, compared to almost half of all secular respondents.

Such differences have generated a great deal of popular and academic attention in America. In particular, the distinctive world-views of fundamentalist Christians has generated a great deal of academic and popular attention since the late 1970s. A March 1994 poll found a remarkably high percentage of respondents (45 per cent) identifying themselves as 'born-again' or evangelical Christians, but only 11 per cent of respondents labelled themselves members of the 'religious right' and 20 per cent as 'conservative Christians'. Only 9 per cent said public issues and political candidates were discussed often in church, 43 per cent said occasionally, and 36 per cent said never. Nonetheless, when asked in a September 1994 poll whether government should promote traditional values or not favour any particular set of values, by a 61 per cent to 34 per cent margin respondents said government should promote traditional values.

In the early 1990s, a broad-based political

TABLE 8.3 Religious orientation and political opinion

Political opinion	Religious orientation		
	Secular (%)	In between (%)	Fundamentalist (%)
Increase domestic spending	48	41	32
Institute national health insurance	63	56	38
Guarantee good living standard	38	23	21
Permit all abortions	70	50	14
Prohibit mandatory school prayers	67	60	51
Allows gays in the military	68	59	32
Encourage equal role for women	99	93	71
Fund more AIDS research	63	52	46
Cut defence spending	77	70	42
Oppose Gulf War	17	11	10
Increase aid to Russia	35	33	24
% Democratic (of party identifiers)	41	40	30
% liberal (of ideological identifiers)	48	38	7
% for Clinton (1992)	57	49	23

Source: Erikson and Tedin (1995).

movement arose to represent these views: the Christian Coalition, an activist organization founded by the televangelist Pat Robertson and led by a shrewd conservative political strategist, Ralph Reed. Unlike the older 'Moral Majority', the Christian Coalition took seriously the task of entering conventional politics at the grassroots and recognized the need to build working alliances with mainstream politicians, especially within the Republican Party. Within a short time, people allied with the Christian Coalition won power in many local Republican Party organizations and its national conferences became important venues for Republican presidential candidates to address. Although strongest in the South, Midwest and West, the Coalition became a significant national force. During the 1994 election, for example, it distributed over 30 million voter guides nationwide and affiliated local organizations distributed several million more. Since 1960, evangelical Christians have become increasingly attached to Republican presidential candidates (with the exception of 1976, when 'born-again' Democrat Jimmy Carter ran), while Jews and those without a religious orientation have become consistently supportive of the Democratic Party at the national level.

But the effects of increasing participation by religious activists such as the Christian Coalition have become unclear. Some Americans see such activism as divisive and counterproductive for the place of religion in public life. In the 2000 presidential election, for example, Americans were evenly divided on whether the leading candidates should publicly discuss their religious beliefs (see Table 8.4). Majorities among Republicans, low-earners (those under $25,000 per year) and those over 65 years of age – groups that tend to be more religious – favoured public discussions of faith. Majorities of Democrats, high-earners and younger voters preferred candidates to keep their faiths to themselves. (The results were ironic, given that it was the Democratic nominee, Gore, rather than the Republican, Bush, who selected a running-mate who regularly spoke of his faith in public.)

Such dissensus among the public over the place of religion in political campaigning also applies to specific public policy issues. For example, one of the most consistently controversial questions about religion in public life concerns allowing public schools (state schools, in British parlance) to either allow or require their pupils to recite prayers (private or 'parochial' schools are free to act as they wish). The Supreme Court declared in 1962

TABLE 8.4 Should presidential candidates publicly declare their religious faith?

	Publicly discuss religious beliefs (%)	Keep religious beliefs to themselves (%)
All Americans	45	47
Republicans	58	35
Democrats	39	57
Independents	43	48
Under $25 million	51	42
Over $75 million	38	54
Age 18–34	42	52
Age 65+	53	40

N = 1,0004 adults, 3-point margin of error.
Source: ABCNEWS.com survey, January 19–23, 2000.

that states could not allow public school prayer since this would breach the long-established church–state separation doctrine. But that ruling aroused passionate resentment among traditionalists that has endured to the present.

Overwhelming majorities profess support for enacting a constitutional amendment (the only way, short of a judicial U-turn, that the Court's decision can be overturned) that would allow states to mandate moments of prayer in the public schools. Only a decided minority of Americans approved the Court ruling that outlawed prayer in public schools. A Gallup poll conducted in May and June of 1995 found that, by a margin of 71 per cent to 25 per cent, Americans favoured a formal amendment to the Constitution that would permit prayer in public schools. Despite the overwhelmingly Christian faith of most Americans, however, only 13 per cent of respondents said that spoken prayer in school should be exclusively Christian, while 81 per cent preferred an ecumenical approach. In the absence of school prayer, by a margin of 70 per cent to 24 per cent, Americans preferred that public schools provide a moment of silent contemplation.

So certain are most Americans of the value of religion to raising children that 74 per cent speculated that only a 'small percentage' of students' parents would object to spoken prayers in schools. By contrast, a decided minority (21 per cent) believed that verbal prayers would offend a large percentage of parents. Insistence on spoken prayer was most intense among strong supporters of a constitutional amendment, who believed in the spoken-prayer requirement by a two-to-one margin. But respondents to a June 2000 poll by *Newsweek* found that 68 per cent disagreed with a Supreme Court decision that public school districts cannot promote prayer before high school football games (Taylor, 2000: 2207). By no stretch of the imagination, then, can the majority of Americans be seen as endorsing the breadth and depth of separation of the church and state that has developed in America since 1962.

EXPLAINING THE POLITICS OF RELIGION

At a basic level, since religion is important to so many Americans, successful politicians must devote significant resources to cultivating the support (or minimizing the opposition) of influential religious groups. This can take symbolic forms (for example, professing the importance of religion to the individual's political beliefs or publicly endorsing measures such as a constitutional prayer amendment) or can assume more substantive contacts (such as appearing at particular churches to make direct appeals to specific groups or co-opting religious leaders on to campaign teams or staffs). Whichever approach is adopted, the goal is to gain the support of religious groups in terms of formal endorsements, financial contributions, sympathetic mass mailings and votes.

For individual politicians, demographics assume a crucial importance, depending on the region, state or city. In New York, for example, candidates for statewide office must typically be sensitive to the concerns of Jewish voters, who make up a significant proportion of the electorate – especially in New York City – and participate in politics at very high rates (hence Hillary Clinton's happiness as a prospective US Senator from New York when Lieberman was selected to be Gore's vice presidential candidate in 2000). In Deep South states such as Mississippi and Alabama, where evangelical Protestantism is a powerful force, candidates who take up positions that offend elements of that faith, such as being pro-choice on abortion or in favour of legalizing gay marriage, are unlikely to succeed. In a state such as Utah, with a strong Mormon population, sensitivity both to religious diversity and particularity is a prerequisite of successful electioneering.

But, as Exhibit 8.4 notes, the basic fact of religious faith or the presence of particularly influential groups in a state does not always yield straightforward decisions for politicians facing conflicting pressures. Moreover,

Exhibit 8.4   Taking a gamble with God: casinos and churches as tests of faith

A high-stakes political conflict developed in several states during the 1980s and 1990s that posed acute difficulties both for many Americans of faith and their elected representatives: the promotion or prohibition of legalized gambling. In many states, powerful economic arguments in favour of legalizing distinct forms of gambling drew significant public support. Many states operated (or introduced) state lotteries, whose proceeds would then be directed towards public-minded projects, such as funding state schools. In several, the establishment of gaming casinos offered lucrative rewards to the areas – typically economically depressed or relatively impoverished states such as Mississippi and Alabama – where they were set up, attracting tourists and visitors not only from neighbouring states but also from around the nation. But these economic arguments faced a powerful counter-argument: that gambling is inherently sinful. To endorse and encourage such activity was therefore immoral (and could also drain resources from the state lottery) and those politicians who did so effectively rejected the word of God and threatened to bring the decadent values and practices of Las Vegas to God-fearing local communities. That several states comprised simultaneously some of the most economically disadvantaged and religiously zealous citizens made the political conflict all the more acute. In many cases, public officials attempted to escape the problem by sponsoring specific ballot propositions that allowed the voters to decide the issue directly. More often than not, the gambling initiatives tended to meet with sufficient voter approval to succeed – a triumph for Mammon over God. In Mississippi, the political compromise reached between the economic and religious impulses was that no gambling would be allowed to occur physically on the soil of the state (other than on Native American land). Hence riverboat gambling was the approved method, making the state the third largest centre for gambling in America after Las Vegas and New Jersey.

Americans are not wedded to their particular faiths when it comes to political matters. In 2000, for example, 11 American states were represented by Jewish senators (both of California's senators were Jewish women), despite only 3 per cent of the total American population being Jewish.

The politics of religion are also complicated further by the fundamental conflict between respecting religion in general without either privileging or prejudicing particular religious faiths. In this regard, many Americans believe strongly that the First Amendment to the Constitution not only guarantees freedom of expression, but also requires government not to be party to religious activity. But, for many others, the First Amendment does not require this separation – at least, it does not do so in the strict manner that many of their compatriots hold to be the case.

Two aspects to this important dispute are crucial. The first, which is normally referred to as 'the free-exercise clause', states that Congress shall make no law prohibiting the 'free exercise' of religion. The second, the 'establishment clause', states that Congress shall make no law 'respecting an establishment of religion'. The competing claims of these constitutional clauses – both of which are contained in the language of the First Amendment, makes for a highly complex and contentious constitutional regime.

The best way to assess what these clauses mean in practice is to start with the simplest cases. In this regard, certain basic facts about the church and state relationship are not in dispute. The 'free exercise' clause obviously means that Congress cannot, for example, pass a law prohibiting Catholics from celebrating Mass or requiring Baptists to become Episcopalians, or preventing Jews from holding bar mitzvahs. Even the most zealous opponent of the Court's decisions since 1962 does not contest this. Moreover, since the First Amendment was applied via the due process clause of the Fourteenth Amendment by the courts during the twentieth century to encompass the states as well as the federal government, it means that state governments cannot pass such discriminatory laws either on religious matters.

Beyond such stark examples, however, matters become more difficult to judge clearly and dispassionately. For example, even some laws that do not appear on their face to apply to churches may be unconstitutional if their enforcement imposes particular burdens or places greater burdens on some churches than others. A state cannot, for instance, apply a licence fee on door-to-door salespersons when the salesperson is a Jehovah's Witness selling religious tracts. Similarly, the federal courts have ruled that the city of Hialeah, Florida, cannot ban animal sacrifices by members of an Afro-Caribbean religion called Santería. Since killing animals in America in general is not illegal (pro-gun advocates tend to see hunting as an important part of American heritage), the ban in this case was clearly directed against a specific religion and hence was unconstitutional.

The courts have made other notable but controversial protections for the exercise of religious freedom. For example, American draft laws exempted a conscientious objector from military duty and the Supreme Court has upheld such exemptions. But the Court went further, to rule that people cannot be drafted even if they do not belong to any religious tradition or believe in a Supreme Being, providing their 'consciences, spurred by deeply held moral, ethical, or religious beliefs, would give them no rest or peace if they allowed themselves to become part of an instrument of war'. The Court has also ruled that Seventh-Day Adventists must be paid unemployment compensation even if they refuse to work on a Saturday when an available job exists and that the state cannot require parents to send their children to public schools beyond the eighth grade (which members of the Amish sect, for example, refuse to do).

But having the right to exercise religion freely does not mean that Americans are exempt from laws binding other citizens, even when the law runs directly against their religious beliefs. A man cannot have more than one wife even if (as once was the case with Mormons) polygamy is thought to be desirable, or divinely required, on religious grounds. For religious reasons, an American may object to being vaccinated or having blood transfusions but if the state passes a compulsory vaccination law or orders that a blood transfusion be given to a sick child, the courts will not block them on grounds of religious liberty. Similarly, if a person belongs to a Native American tribe that uses a drug – peyote – in religious ceremonies, he or she cannot claim that his or her freedom was abridged if the state decides to ban the use of peyote, provided that the law applies equally to all. In yet another case, since American airports have legitimate needs for tight security measures, begging can be outlawed in them even if those doing the begging are part of a religious group (in this particular case, the Hare Krishnas).

The lines between ensuring the free exercise of religion and not privileging religion are, therefore, finely calibrated. The Supreme Court has interpreted the vague phrase prohibiting an establishment of religion to mean that the Constitution erects a 'wall of separation' between church and state. But that often-quoted phrase does not appear in the Bill of Rights. It was instead penned by one of the Founding Fathers and America's third president, Thomas Jefferson. (The phrase owes its genesis to Jefferson's passionate opposition to having the Church of England as the established church of his native state of Virginia.)

The Court has interpreted the phrase not simply to mean that 'no national religion' or church can be established in America, but also that no governmental involvement can occur with religion, even on a nonpreferential basis. Its first statement to this effect occurred in 1947. The case involved a New Jersey town that reimbursed parents for the costs of transporting their children to school, including parochial (in this case, Catholic) schools. The Court ruled that this reimbursement was constitutional but made clear that the establishment clause of the First Amendment also applied (via the Fourteenth Amendment) to the states and meant that the government cannot require a person to profess a belief or disbelief in any religion, cannot aid one religion, some religions, or all religions, and cannot spend any tax money in support of religious institutions or activities. By contrast, however, bussing black and white children to achieve racially balanced school systems was deemed to be a religiously neutral activity, akin to providing fire and police protection to Catholic schools, and hence did not breach the wall of separation. Such a ruling was controversial enough, but it was the activism of the Warren Court from 1953 to 1969 that nationalized and politicized the role of religion in public life in an unprecedented fashion.

SCHOOL PRAYER AND PUBLIC EDUCATION

The most consistently controversial issue in the post-Second World War era concerning religion has been its place in public education. Since 1947, the Supreme Court has applied the 'wall of separation' theory to strike down as unconstitutional every effort to have any form of prayer in public schools, even if it is non-sectarian, voluntary or limited to reading a passage of the Bible. In 1963 the Court considered the legality of a Pennsylvania school district's push to have students read at least ten verses from the Bible every day. The Schempp family argued that the requirement clearly violated their children's constitutional rights, with the state self-consciously engaging in religious instruction. In defence, the state argued that the aim of

Bible-reading was to teach morality without imposing either religion or theology on students. By an 8–1 majority, the Court found for the Schempps, declaring that Pennsylvania's policies encroached on the First Amendment because reading from the Bible was essentially a religious act.

The extension of judicial prohibitions on religious expression in public school since then has been steady and, to many Americans, farcical. Since 1992, for example, it has been unconstitutional for a public school to ask a rabbi or minister to offer a prayer – an invocation or benediction – at the school's graduation ceremony. The Supreme Court barred clergy-led prayers at public school graduation ceremonies in what was viewed as a strong affirmation of its 1962 decision banning organized, officially sponsored prayers from public schools. In a ruling hailed by supporters as an expression of religious pluralism but decried by its opponents as taking the wall of separation to an absurd length, the Court's 1992 decision stated, 'The Constitution forbids the state to exact religious conformity from a student as the price of attending her own high school graduation.'

In 1993, however, the Court refused to review a federal appeals court ruling that allowed student-led prayers at graduation ceremonies in Texas (a decision conflicting with another federal appeals court ruling that barred student-led graduation prayers in nine western states). In the 1999–2000 term, the Court accepted the first review of a school prayer case in almost a decade, deciding whether a school district in Galveston County, Texas, can allow student-led prayer at football games and other school activities. Lower courts had struck down the Galveston school board policy on grounds of violating the separation of church and state. The Court agreed.

But school prayer has not been the only area of controversy for the courts to resolve. For example, the Court has held that state laws prohibiting the teaching of the theory of evolution or requiring schools to provide equal time to 'Creationism' are religiously inspired and therefore unconstitutional. On another matter, again reflecting the highly complex case law emerging on religion, a public school may not allow its pupils to take time out from their regular classes for religious instruction if this occurs within the schools, but 'released-time' instruction is reasonable if it is done outside the public school building – such is the controversy attached to government involvement with religion.

Almost as controversial have been Court-imposed restrictions on public aid to parochial schools. It is permissible for the federal government to provide aid for constructing buildings on denominational (and non-denominational) college campuses and for state governments to loan free textbooks to parochial school pupils, grant tax-exempt status to parochial schools, allow parents of parochial school children to deduct their tuition payments on a state's income tax returns and pay for a deaf child's sign-language interpreter at a Catholic school, but the government cannot pay a salary supplement to teachers who teach secular subjects in parochial schools, reimburse parents for the cost of parochial school tuition, supply parochial schools with services such as counselling, give money with which to purchase instructional materials, or create a special school district for Hasidic Jews.

With the five Reagan–Bush appointments to the Supreme Court from 1981 to 1993, the wall of separation began to experience some cracks, though not as many as conservatives had anticipated. The result has been a perplexing and untidy regime whose nuances and subtleties can confuse even constitutional lawyers. In theory, according to the Supreme Court, government involvement in religious activities (whether federal or state) is properly constitutional if three conditions are met together:

- The government intervention has a secular purpose.
- The primary effect of government

intervention neither advances nor inhibits religion.
- The intervention does not foster an excessive government entanglement with religion.

But having developed this three-pronged test, the Court then decided that it was reasonable for the government of Pawtucket, Rhode Island, to erect a nativity scene as part of a Christmas display in a local park. Yet five years later it ruled that Pittsburgh could not put a nativity scene in front of the courthouse but could display a *menorah* – a Jewish symbol of Chanukah – next to a Christmas tree and a sign extolling liberty. And this despite the fact that the Court itself established a Christmas tree in its own building in Washington, DC, and celebrated the season with carols (the protests of some law clerks about this were ignored).

At least as curiously, although the Court has struck down prayer in public schools, it has upheld prayers in Congress (since 1789, the House of Representatives and Senate have opened each congressional session with a prayer). Similarly, while a public school cannot have a chaplain, America's armed forces can, according to the courts. In yet another confusing example, the Supreme Court has ruled that the government cannot 'advance' religion but has not objected to printing the phrase 'In God We Trust' on the back of every dollar bill issued in America. As with other areas of cultural value conflict, then, the judicial clarity and consistency on church–state relations are, at best, not entirely satisfactory and, at worst, contradictory, confused and incoherent. Nor, as we discuss next, have such confusions been resolved by the expressly political branches of government.

GOVERNING INSTITUTIONS

American public officials face competing political pressures over the place of religion in public life. On the one hand, elected

Exhibit 8.5   Key Supreme Court rulings on church and state

West Virginia State Board of Education v. Barnette (1943). 6–3. The Court ruled that Jehovah's Witnesses in public schools had the right to refuse to participate in required flag-saluting ceremonies (overturning *Minersville School District v. Gobitis* [1940] that had upheld a Pennsylvania law requiring this, despite its offence to their religion).

Everson v. Board of Education of Ewing Township (1947). 5–4. The Court upheld a New Jersey law mandating public funds to pay for bussing parochial school students to and from school. Its significance was more in stating for the first time that the First Amendment's establishment clause applied to the states as well as the federal government.

Abington School District v. Schempp (1962). 8–1. The Court ruled that a Pennsylvania law requiring daily bible reading in public schools advanced religion in breach of the First Amendment's establishment clause.

Engel v. Vitale (1962). 7–1. In interpreting the separation of church and state doctrine, the Supreme Court held that organized prayer in the public schools was unconstitutional.

Lemon v. Kurtzman (1971). 7–0. Established the three-pronged 'Lemon Test'. At issue was whether Rhode Island and Pennsylvania laws allowing the states directly to support the salaries of teachers of secular subjects in parochial and other non-public schools were constitutional. The Court found these unconstitutional, adding a new 'excessive entanglement' prong to existing requirements that such laws be for a secular purpose and their primary effect should neither advance nor inhibit religion.

Wallace v. Jaffree (1985). 6–3. The Court ruled that an Alabama law authorizing a moment of silence for 'meditation or voluntary prayer' violated the establishment clause.

Aguilar v. Felton (1985). 5–4. The Court held that New York City could not use government funds to send public school teachers into private religious schools to provide remedial education for disadvantaged children. Although a federal statute, Title I of the Elementary and Secondary Education Act of 1965, had authorized the programme, the Court ruled that the New York programme led to excessive entanglement of church and state in violation of the Constitution.

Employment Division, Department of Human Resources v. Smith (1990). 5–3. The Court ruled against state employees who were denied unemployment benefits after being dismissed from their jobs for religion-related reasons. The employees, who were Native Americans, practised a religion with rituals involving the smoking of peyote, an illegal substance under state law. Because they were dismissed for violating a state law, the Court upheld the denial of unemployment compensation. Scalia wrote for the Court that 'the right of free exercise does not relieve an individual of the obligation to comply with a valid and neutral law of general applicability'.

Zobrest v. Catalina School District (1993). 5–4. The Court ruled that a deaf student in a private religious school could be helped by a sign-language interpreter supported by government funds. This type of public aid was held directly to assist the student – and not the private religious school or church that sponsored it – and hence did not violate the establishment clause.

Capitol Square Review and Advisory Board v. Pinette (1995). 7–2. A private group may place religious symbols on government property if there is no appearance of government support for religion.

Exhibit 8.5   Key Supreme Court rulings on church and state *continued*

Rosenberger v. Rector and Visitors of the University of Virginia (1995). 5–4. A state university cannot discriminate against a student religious publication by denying it financial support on equal terms with other student publications.

City of Boerne v. Flores (1997). 6–3. The Court supported a Texas federal district court's ruling that the Religious Freedom Restoration Act of 1993 is unconstitutional as a violation of the separation of powers.

Agostini v. Felton (1997). 5–4. The Court ordered a federal district court in New York to lift an injunction established in 1985 that forbade public school teachers from entering on parochial school grounds to provide remedial education, thereby overturning *Aguilar v. Felton*. Public funds could be provided to support programmes that directly aid students of private religious schools and clearly promote secular purposes that contribute to the public good. The establishment clause is not violated as long as the religious mission of the private schools is neither advanced nor obstructed by a government programme.

Santa Fe Independent School District v. Doe (2000). 6–3. The Court ruled that public school districts could not let students lead stadium crowds in prayer before high school football games. The majority stated that such prayers violate the constitutionally required separation of government and religion and that 'School sponsorship of a religious message is impermissible because it sends the ancillary message to members of the audience who are non-adherents that they are outsiders, not full members of the political community, and an accompanying message to adherents that they are insiders, favored members of the political community.'

Good News Club v. Milford Central School (2001). 6–3. The Court held that a New York state school could not prohibit an evangelical Christian children's club from meeting on its premises after school when it allowed non-religious groups access to its premises.

figures are strongly aware of the importance of religious belief to citizens (and, with few exceptions, share this conviction). On the other hand, members of governing institutions must deal with different religious groups and respect the authority of the federal courts. The result has seen American politicians imitating their judicial peers: steering a careful course between professing respect for religion and seeking to maintain limits on how far religious activities can influence public life.

Presidential politics

Given its unique position, the presidency assumes a particularly important place in the politics of religion. In terms of qualifications for office, religious belief is an informal prerequisite in America, one that effectively matches the Constitution's formal requirements (atheists, agnostics and heathens, for example, need not apply). Moreover, in terms of the office, the president is conventionally expected by citizens to provide a good example to the nation in his personal life, to profess a faith that Americans can recognize (even if they do not share his particular religion), and to help shape the moral climate and direction of the nation. (It was partly for this reason that the 'inappropriate behaviour' of President Clinton, a Southern Baptist who regularly invoked his faith as a guiding force in his life, aroused so much indignation among Americans.)

What presidents can achieve in practical terms is, however, less obvious. Consultations with religious figures can assuage

Exhibit 8.6   Religious affiliations of twentieth-century presidents

Not surprisingly, the vast majority of presidents have been Protestants, the one exception being John F. Kennedy. Episcopalians have been the most regular occupants of the White House – 11 in total since 1789.

President	Religious affiliation
William McKinley	Methodist
Theodore Roosevelt	Dutch Reformed
William Howard Taft	Unitarian
Woodrow Wilson	Presbyterian
Warren G. Harding	Baptist
Calvin Coolidge	Congregationalist
Herbert Hoover	Quaker
Franklin D. Roosevelt	Episcopalian
Harry S. Truman	Baptist
Dwight D. Eisenhower	Presbyterian
John F. Kennedy	Roman Catholic
Lyndon B. Johnson	Disciples of Christ
Richard M. Nixon	Quaker
Gerald R. Ford	Episcopalian
Jimmy Carter	Baptist
Ronald Reagan	Disciples of Christ
George H.W. Bush	Episcopalian
Bill Clinton	Baptist

religious groups that their priorities and preferences are being taken seriously by the White House. Presidents Nixon and Reagan, for example, made sure that they were publicly seen to consult the Protestant evangelist Billy Graham. Clinton regularly invited the Reverend Jesse Jackson to the White House and attended 'prayer breakfasts'. Appointments to the executive branch and judiciary can also assist forging ties with religious groups. Reagan, for example, staffed many positions in the White House with self-conscious 'born-again' Christian activists (George H.W. Bush, as his Vice President, once left a White House meeting of evangelical Christian officials quipping that he was the 'only one present who'd been born just once').

Four main resources inform the presidential approach to religious matters in terms of exercising political influence:

- *The bully pulpit.* By far the most common course for presidents to adopt is to use the Oval Office to bring attention to particular causes. For example, Ronald Reagan made repeated professions of his religious faith, most notably in a March 1983 speech to evangelical Christians, in which the president described the Soviet Union as an 'evil empire'.
- *Appointments.* Presidents can use the appointments process to signal affinity with particular groups and causes or to reward supporters. Presidents Eisenhower and Clinton appointed Jewish justices to the Supreme Court, for example. Reagan also appointed Antonin Scalia, the first Italian American and the first Catholic on the Court since Ike appointed

William Brennan in 1957. George W. Bush appointed John Ashcroft, an avowed fundamentalist Christian, to be his Attorney General in 2001.

- *Legislative recommendations.* As with other policy areas, the president can make suggestions to Congress on specific aspects of the question of religion. President Clinton was willing, for example, to sign the Religious Freedom Restoration Act of 1993 despite the reservations of some congressional Democrats about the measure.

- *The veto.* Presidents can veto, or threaten to veto, legislation that favoured groups oppose. In August 2000, for example, Bill Clinton (pocket) vetoed the 'Marriage Tax Relief Reconciliation Act' passed by the Republican 106th Congress, a measure to ease the tax burden on married couples strongly supported by Christian organizations. His successor, President George W. Bush, supported the measure strongly.

As he did in so many areas after his first two years in office, President Clinton consistently sought a middle ground in the religious and political debate from 1995 to 2001. In particular, the president sought to reassure important religious organizations and draw clear lines between what is constitutional and what is not with regard to prayer in public schools. Clinton declared in July 1995, for example, that the First Amendment does not 'convert our schools into religion-free zones'. He also urged Americans to encourage religious activities in public schools, including the use of Bibles in study halls and prayers at commencements. But the president declined to endorse a constitutional amendment that would allow prayer in public classrooms, on the grounds that freedom of religious expression is already protected under the First Amendment and that a prayer amendment might coerce students to compromise their own religious beliefs.

Partly as a result of Clinton's personal scandals, aspirant presidential candidates of both main political parties during the 2000 election made explicit appeals to religion.

Candidates frequently discussed their faith on the campaign trail and invoked the Bible in stump speeches. In a Republican Party debate in Iowa in December 1999, for example, no fewer than three prospective presidential candidates (George W. Bush, Senator Orrin Hatch of Utah, and Gary Bauer of the Family Research Council) named Jesus Christ as the philosopher or thinker who had exerted the most influence on their lives. Bush also raised the national profile of religious tolerance markedly, though not intentionally, by giving a speech at Bob Jones University in South Carolina in February 2000 (the university's fundamentalist Christian founder has described Catholicism as a 'satanic cult', conferred on the Reverend Ian Paisley of Northern Ireland an honorary doctorate, and banned inter-racial dating at the university – the ban was lifted after the furore surrounding Bush's appearance, so that students could date members of other races providing they had a letter of approval from their parents). Bush's subsequent efforts to court Catholic voters confirmed still further the critical role of religion in the election battle, mirrored in August 2000 by Lieberman's historic selection for the Democrats.

Congress

Religious issues have been important to federal legislators but have played out in Congress in several ways. Religious convictions about abortion, capital punishment, gay rights and school prayer have strongly influenced federal appointments (to the courts, in particular), national legislation, and even American foreign policy. But congressional responses to important religious questions have a long and complex history.

In the early 1970s, for example, Senator Henry Jackson (Democrat, Washington) introduced legislation that made trade exports to the USSR dependent on the Soviets liberalizing their restrictive policy on Jewish emigration. The Jackson–Vanik Amendment of 1974 represented a strong statement in favour of religious freedom. That Congress should

Exhibit 8.7   Faith in the millennium

In the 2000 presidential election, the main contenders for the presidency made explicit references to religion to assist their campaigns. George W. Bush regularly discussed his experience of having been 'born again'. Vice President Al Gore referred to the purpose of life being 'to advance God's will'. Leading contenders also proposed involving religious groups directly in efforts to revive decaying cities and combat drug abuse and crime. Rarely had a presidential election seen so many religious themes raised so directly and explicitly. But some commentators argued that the explanation was a simple one. After eight years of political scandal whereby President Clinton's personal behaviour had shocked and shamed many Americans and disappointed most, a restoration of moral probity in the White House appeared attractive to a weary, if prosperous, American electorate. The selection of Joe Lieberman, a senator who had headed efforts to insert the 'V-chip' in televisions, criticized Hollywood for sex and violence, and described Clinton's conduct as immoral, was expressly designed to reinforce Gore's appearance of moral probity and integrity as well as political boldness in choosing an Orthodox Jewish running-mate. Strictly observant Jews are not supposed to write, use electricity, operate machinery, watch television or talk on the telephone during the Sabbath (from sunset on Friday to sunset on Saturday), but Jewish law allows such rules to be broken if matters of 'human life' are at stake. Although Lieberman refused to campaign on the Sabbath in 2000, he declared that he was prepared to take important actions and decisions on public policy on the holy day.

approve such a law, when it strongly undermined the policy of détente that President Nixon and his National Security Adviser Henry Kissinger (himself Jewish) were pursuing, was an early indication of the potency of religious appeals. Subsequently, when the question of why Jackson–Vanik was not also applied to communist China, then-President George H.W. Bush (certainly not a racist or anti-Semite) reputedly murmured 'no Jews in China' (Mann, 2000: 107).

In 1993, Congress passed (and Clinton signed into law) the Religious Freedom Restoration Act (RFRA). The congressional majority was concerned about possible state government infringement of rights to religious liberty due to the Supreme Court's decision in *Employment Division Department of Human Resources of Oregon v. Smith* (1990). This ruling had overturned a constitutional standard set in *Sherbert v. Verner* (1963) which declared that to survive judicial scrutiny, a law restricting the free exercise of religion must advance a compelling public interest of government in the least restrictive manner

possible. The RFRA was intended by Congress to restore the 'compelling interest' and 'least restrictive means' standard of *Sherbert*. The law therefore limited the power of federal, state and local governments to enforce laws that 'substantially burden' the free exercise of religion. Such a law could only be carried out if the government could demonstrate a 'compelling' public justification for so doing and if it was the least restrictive means of furthering that interest.

Four years later, however, the Supreme Court ruled the RFRA unconstitutional in *City of Boerne, Texas v. Flores* (1997). By a 6–3 vote, the Court held that Congress had gone beyond its constitutionally sanctioned power by substantially attempting to interpret the Constitution through legislation. Congress not only usurped a power belonging exclusively to the federal courts (violating the constitutional principle of separation of powers), but also had unconstitutionally infringed on the autonomy of state governments to regulate the health, safety or general welfare of their citizens (violating the constitutional principle of federalism).

Such ongoing battles between the different branches of the federal government encouraged rather than defused the conflict over religion and public life. In the spring of 1995, for example, conservative Christians presented GOP lawmakers with a detailed legislative agenda, including a school prayer amendment, the curtailment of the campaign for gay and lesbian rights and the abolition of the Department of Education. Hostile critics saw the Christian Coalition's 1995 'Contract with the American Family' (modelled on the Republicans' 1994 'Contract with America') as a radical, religiously biased and deeply prejudiced political agenda, a gambit at religious domination by a presumed majority to use a revised US Constitution to repress minorities. Partly because of opposition based on these concerns, and despite the Republican majority in Congress, the Coalition was ultimately denied enactment of its favoured initiatives.

These congressional battles over religion reflect the mixture of motives animating lawmakers. As Table 8.5 demonstrates, most members of Congress are Protestants but the

TABLE 8.5   Religious denominations in the 106th Congress, 1999–2000

House of Representatives		Senate	
Catholic	127	Catholic	25
Baptist	58	Episcopalian	13
Presbyterian	42	Jewish	11
Methodist	40	Baptist	8
Protestant	31	Methodist	8
Episcopalian	30	Presbyterian	7
Jewish	23	Lutheran	5
Lutheran	17	Mormon	5
Christian	11	Protestant	4
Mormon	11	United Methodist	4
United Methodist	11	Congregationalist	3
Christian Scientist	5	Greek Orthodox	2
Seventh-Day Adventist	3	Assembly of God	1
African Methodist Episcopal	2	Eastern Orthodox	1
Assembly of God	2	Unitarian	1
Congregationalist	2	United Church of Christ	1
Disciples of Christ	2	No religious affiliation	1
Unitarian	2		
United Church of Christ	2		
Christ Church	1		
Christian Reformed	1		
Eastern Orthodox	1		
Greek Orthodox	1		
Reformed Church of America	1		
Reorganized Church of Christ of Latter Day Saints	1		
Southern Baptist	1		
No religious affiliation	7		

Source: *The Almanac of American Politics 2000; National Journal*, March 18, 2000, p. 865.

largest single group in the House and Senate is made up of Catholics. Only eight of the 535 voting members of the 106th Congress expressed no religious affiliation. Faith in God is one of the few forces that almost all federal legislators share, regardless of party, ideology, region, race or ethnicity. Many also belong to inter-faith groups that visit each other's districts and share regular prayer breakfasts on Capitol Hill. But these religious affiliations typically co-exist with, and encourage, a concern to ensure that the wall of separation between church and state remains a solid one.

Religious conservatives have countered a perceived relative lack of respect for faith by creating their own legal organizations to combat what they regard as an assault, especially by the federal courts, on important religious liberties. During the 1990s, more than half a dozen religious liberty law firms began to wage battles in courts, schools and city halls to establish a larger public space for religious activity and to respond to those institutions that they held to be attempting to curb religious expression. In an ironic but politically shrewd reversal of traditional roles, religious groups increasingly resorted to the 'secular' language of rights and victimization – only this time it was those groups professing religious faith who found themselves discriminated against by an increasingly secular state and progressive elites wedded to a dangerous doctrine of secular humanism. The extent to which this strategy has succeeded remains unclear. Most of the key priorities of organizations such as the Christian Coalition remain (as described below) unaddressed by the elected branches of government. Nonetheless, the partial retreat from a strict church–state separation by the federal judiciary, and the increasing political appeal of measures such as federally funded faith-based charity work (see Exhibit 8.8) suggests that the forces of secularism have not been entirely triumphant.

Intermediary organizations

The two main political parties have invariably had to take religious issues and organizations into account. This partly reflects the distinct and changing social bases to the parties' electoral coalitions. The Democrats have needed to demonstrate sensitivity to the concerns of Jews, Baptists (especially strong among African Americans) and Catholics (notable among white 'ethnic' voters, certain sections of the Latino community, and key Electoral College states such as Pennsylvania, Ohio and Michigan), as well as Protestant denominations. The Republican Party has had to pay particular attention to the strong evangelical Christian community across America, not only in the South but also in the Midwest and parts of the West.

As a consequence, both parties profess their religious credentials but typically with differing emphases. The Republican Party has tended since 1980 to wear its religiosity on its sleeve with varying degrees of enthusiasm and reluctance. In 2000, for example, John McCain's insurgent presidential nomination campaign made a deliberate attempt to seek the votes of those Republicans alarmed at the influence of religious conservatives in the GOP by casting George W. Bush as being a captive of the religious right. Outspokenly describing Falwell and Robertson as 'agents of intolerance', McCain even labelled Bush a 'Pat Robertson Republican' – in other words, someone too extreme to be acceptable to most Americans and hence unelectable. Bush had certainly developed well-established ties to the Christian Right even prior to becoming governor of Texas in 1995, having acted as a key liaison with evangelical organizations for his father during the senior Bush's administration between 1989 and 1993. But George W. Bush's ease with religious conservatives was far more a help than a hindrance during his primary campaign, as McCain discovered to his cost after his early upset wins in New Hampshire and Michigan were reversed in a succession of states, beginning with South Carolina, where

Exhibit 8.8 Knocking holes in the wall of separation? Faith-based healing v. civil rights

The far-reaching welfare overhaul legislation of 1996 (proposed by the Republican 104th Congress and signed into law by President Clinton) allowed faith-based groups to receive federal funds for welfare-to-work programmes. Congress added a similar provision to the Community Services Block Grant when it re-authorized the programme in 1998, opening the door to other faith-based anti-poverty efforts. By 2000, several bills in Congress sought to expand 'charitable choice' to include measures from school violence prevention to literacy for low-income fathers. But can and should churches, synagogues and mosques serve as deliverers of publicly subsidized services such as day care, care of the elderly or temporary housing? Is it legitimate to promote religiously based associations or institutions through public subsidy (tax exemptions for religious schools and other institutions already represent one way that this occurs)?

Both Governor Bush and Vice President Gore called, during the 2000 election, for new partnerships between government and faith-based organizations to attack social problems that government alone has been unable to solve. Some examples of these, such as Victory Fellowship, a Christian substance abuse programme in San Antonio, Texas, puts addicts through a three-month, total-immersion programme of chapel services and Bible studies to help clients kick their habits and establish a 'personal relationship with Jesus Christ'. Supporters of such groups argue that they take a more comprehensive approach to healing, dealing with the mental, physical and spiritual aspects of the sufferer.

But critics fear that giving taxpayers' money to the nation's churches, synagogues and mosques raises serious civil rights issues. They warn that religious organizations are already free to discriminate in their hiring practices because of an exemption in the Civil Rights Act of 1964 (that bans public and private discrimination on the basis of race, colour, religion, sex or national origin). Other concerns also animated critics: Should the government allow churches to hire and serve only those who agree with their religious views? Should the needy be required to attend prayer breakfasts or take communion to receive the help they need? How many strings can be attached to government aid before sectarian groups will lose interest? According to the Congressional Research Service, American courts have already protected a Christian college that refused to hire a Jewish professor; a Catholic university that refused to hire a professor because it did not agree with her views on abortion; a Baptist university that would not allow a professor to teach because his theological views conflicted with the dean's views; and a Christian retirement home that fired a Muslim receptionist who insisted on wearing a head covering.

The issue has proven highly divisive, splitting those who are drawn to encourage the positive activities of church-based groups (especially in cities and among African-American communities) and who do not see why they should deny their religious preferences in order to qualify for federal funds, and those who hold that government should not subsidize the spread of God's word.

the religious right exerted an important influence.

By contrast, although the Democratic Party has made strides to break down religious barriers (see Exhibit 8.9), the party generally has been less overt and ostentatious in its public displays of religious convictions. Admittedly,

Jimmy Carter made much of his born-again Christian faith during the 1976 election, but this was to rather mixed effect. In the aftermath of Vietnam and Watergate, Carter's obvious piety and concern for moral integrity assisted his appeal among many traditionalist Americans, but his admission to *Playboy*

Exhibit 8.9 Televangelism: ministering to the millions

Traditionalists have normally railed against changing technological developments which have threatened to undermine their vision of America. For example, as we saw in Chapter 6, the invention of the press, photography, film, television, the video and the Internet helped successively to disseminate pornography, create a formidable sex industry and expand the market for sexually explicit materials. But in the case of television and the Internet, the religious right has found an especially enticing and powerful ally in its battle against social change. New technologies enabled evangelical preachers to reach audiences of millions of Americans directly in their homes: to appeal to their faiths, influence their beliefs and ask for their donations, all free from any interference by secular authorities. As a result, multi-billion dollar TV-based ministries arose from the late 1970s, financed by millions of religious subscribers across the nation. Helped by a mass mailing base and television network, the Reverend Jerry Falwell warned millions in *Listen America!* in 1980 that 'liberal forces such as the abortionists, the homosexuals, the pornographers, secular humanists, and Marxists have made significant inroads' in Christian America. But by the late 1980s, the activities of leading figures threw a cloud over the entire Christian wing. Jimmy Swaggart, a fire-and-brimstone Louisiana preacher, was caught consorting with prostitutes in 1988 and 1991. Jim Bakker, creator of the PTL ('Praise the Lord') Ministry and Heritage USA (a Christian theme park that for a brief period was second only to Disneyland as a holiday destination for Americans), was accused of sexual misdemeanours in 1987, including adultery to his flamboyant wife Tammy Faye, bisexual encounters and rape of an assistant (and latterly *Playboy* centrefold) Jessica Hahn, and was eventually sent to prison for swindling supporters of his PTL Ministry out of $150 million. Pat Robertson, who had declared in 1986 that the key moment in his life had come when the Lord had told him, 'Pat, I want you to get an RCA transmitter' and observed later that the American feminist agenda 'is not about equal rights for women. It is about a socialist, anti-family political movement that encourages women to leave their husbands, kill their children, practice witchcraft, and become lesbians', authored books and preached around the nation about the dangers of a Zionist world government headed by the United Nations and Scottish homosexuals. Jerry Falwell, founder of the Moral Majority, was associated with disseminating accusations that Bill and Hillary Clinton were involved in murder plots. The 'electronic church' had gone X-rated and beyond. Creative artists from Frank Zappa (*Broadway the Hard Way*) to middle-of-the-road but aptly titled Genesis (*Jesus He Knows Me*) took their cue to ridicule some of the most influential figures in American public life for their alleged hypocrisy and un-Christian activities.

one month before the election that 'I've looked on many women with lust. I've committed adultery in my heart many times' struck many Americans as rather less impressive. Generally, Democrats have proven to be more cautious about expounding their religious convictions. In the 2000 election, for example, former Senator Bill Bradley was the only aspirant presidential candidate who refused to discuss his religious convictions in public. Lieberman's religious affiliations attracted notable comment in the media, mostly focused on its historical novelty – the first time that a Jew had been selected on a ticket for national office – and on how his Orthodoxy would affect his politics (such as in regard to the Middle East). The more acute observers speculated on whether a born-again Christian or Muslim would have received as positive a media commentary as Lieberman did for his regular and explicit public references to his particular faith.

Exhibit 8.10   Catholicism and the presidency: JFK in 1960

When John F. Kennedy accepted the Democratic Party's nomination in July 1960 in Los Angeles, he was the youngest man (at 43) and only the second Catholic (after New York Governor Al Smith, who lost to Republican Herbert Hoover in 1928) to be nominated for the presidency. In his acceptance speech, he declared that: 'I am fully aware of the fact that the Democratic Party, by nominating someone of my faith, has taken on what many regard as a new and hazardous risk – new, at least, since 1928. But I look at it this way: The Democratic Party has once again placed its confidence in the American people, and in their ability to render a free, fair judgment.'

Both refusing to engage religion and devoting excessive attention to religion are hazardous courses for most politicians. The range of active religious organizations is remarkable, and their concerns are equally far-reaching and heterogeneous in scope. The Christian Family Network (CFN), for example, devotes a substantial amount of its resources, along with more secular organizations such as Morality in Media, to monitoring the media for anti- and irreligious content. Programmes and films that have drawn the wrath of the CFN include the comedy show *Ellen* and, as Exhibit 8.11 records, the cult cartoon *South Park*.

THE CHRISTIAN RIGHT

No religious force in American politics has attracted more critical commentary than the Christian Right. The Christian Right is a broadbrush term for a heterogeneous collection of somewhat disparate groups. A reaction to the New Left and liberation movements of the 1960s (Black Power, student rights, women's and gay rights), the political activism of Christians who had previously rejected mainstream forms of politics reflected deep-rooted concerns that the public philosophy of liberalism had become too morally permissive, reliant on unelected

Exhibit 8.11   Cartoons v. Christianity? 'The Problems With: *South Park*'

The Christian Family Network (CFN) distributed a booklet in 1998 entitled 'The Problems With: *South Park*'. Its view of the cartoon show was unequivocal:

South Park's content is irreligious and blasphemous. . . . Our children need to be rooted in a strong moral foundation, one with a strong sense of faith and values. Parents who have trained their children in these precepts need to have their teaching reinforced to their children. *South Park* does nothing but undermine traditional, foundational values of our belief systems.

The CFN went on to criticize the depiction of Jesus as living in *South Park*, hosting a cable-access television show entitled 'Jesus and Pals', being portrayed as 'evasive and wimpy'. As well as blasphemy, CFN accused the show of encouraging drug and alcohol use, homosexuality, violence and for instilling disrespect for authority. Its content analysis of one episode, 'Cartman Gets an Anal Probe', calculated that an offensive use of language occurred every 18.5 seconds.

Source: Christian Family Network (1998).

courts and bureaucracies, and distant from traditional moral norms by the end of the 1960s.

As Steve Bruce (2000) argues, what unites the constituent parts of the Christian Right is not substantially greater than what divides them. In essence, the movement has attempted to reverse what it views as decades of liberalizing measures that assault traditional values with regard to abortion, marriage, heterosexuality and the nuclear family. In particular, the coalition has sought to influence the Republican Party, elect sympathetic candidates to public office, lobby Congress and state legislatures, and litigate in the courts to achieve its goals. Its objectives have included the overturn of *Roe v. Wade*, the prohibition of 'promoting' homosexual rights, the restriction and elimination of pornography, and the reassertion of traditional gender roles. The coalition won particularly widespread attention in 1980, when it claimed – and was accused by its opponents – of having played a key role in electing Ronald Reagan to the presidency and defeating several leading liberal Democrats in the Senate.

Despite popular assessments of the Christian Right as a powerful force, however, its impact has been relatively limited. For the most part the movement has largely failed to advance its agenda in public policy outcomes: abortion remains legal, gay rights have advanced and public school prayer remains unconstitutional. Even in electoral terms, despite plenty of media attention (take-overs of state Republican parties, a strong presence in GOP primary elections, elections to school boards and influence on the national Republican platform) most assessments suggest that its participation and influence in electoral politics has been relatively limited. In 1998 and 2000, for example, candidates supported by religiously conservative groups and evangelicals fared badly in states such as Alabama and Georgia, while Republican candidates, including Jeb Bush in Florida, distanced themselves from the Christian Right. This is not to deny either the movement's extensive activism or selective influence, but few serious analyses suggest that these are especially significant on a consistent or nationwide basis.

The reasons for this are not difficult to explain. The Christian Right's strengths – highly motivated and disciplined supporters strongly committed to particular beliefs and goals – also provide the movement's most debilitating weaknesses: an inability to compromise and engage in long-term cooperation and tolerance of differences that can build successful political coalitions. As Bruce notes:

> Most Americans are reasonably content with the present place of religion in public life. Most think religion a good thing and have some of it themselves. But they also appreciate its potential for conflict and are content with the general accommodation that modern America has reached in its interpretation of the constitutional requirements. Great liberty should be permitted to the individual and the family in the private sphere and the price of that liberty is something approaching neutrality in the public arena. Ordinary Americans may not often consciously articulate their happiness with the public–private divide but they regularly endorse it when they vote against referenda which they see as religious meddling and when they refuse to translate their general dislike for, say, abortion, into support for single-issue anti-abortion candidates. (Bruce, 2000: 278–9)

Although its concerns about 'public decency', parental authority and the importance of religious institutions in civil society therefore represent broader themes that resonate among Americans who do not adhere to its central preoccupations, the Christian Right has never influenced the views of the American public in the way of other social movements (such as the civil rights, women's and gay rights movements). As such, it remains an active but only modestly influential force.

CONCLUSION

Perhaps no more perplexing a contrast exists than that of the most technologically advanced, self-consciously capitalist and consumerist society in the world simultaneously professing the most religiously inclined citizenry of any western nation (although in comparative terms, of course, it is secular Europe that is exceptional when it comes to religious belief). Despite their basic tension, rationality and faith can co-exist in any society. But America remains alone among western industrialized democracies in the extent to which religious belief and practice pervade its diverse and comparatively affluent population. Americans' commitment to religion cuts across sex, age, region, community (urban/suburban/rural), race, education, politics and income. The idea of religion abides in the hearts and minds of most Americans, who cherish tradition in general and their specific faith in particular. What is most troubling to Americans is typically not that a citizen believes in another faith, but rather one who adheres to no faith at all.

Given the dramatic transformations in economics, society and government that occurred over the twentieth century, the religiosity of the United States remains a strikingly distinctive feature – arguably a phenomenon that contributes more to American exceptionalism than any other, and much more so today than the absence of a serious socialist movement (a phenomenon now characteristic of most industrialized liberal democracies). The public praise of God or the Bible has worked for both progressive and traditionalist political goals, but the efforts of the federal courts to limit the reach of religion in public life have been broadly successful. The tenacious hold of faith on millions of Americans ensures that questions of morality and ethics will continue to occupy American politics deeply and broadly – and, partly as a result, that the culture war is unlikely to diminish in the foreseeable future.

FURTHER READING

Steve Bruce, *The Rise and Fall of the New Christian Right: Conservative Protestant Politics in America 1978–1988* (1988) is a detailed and excellent analysis of the NCR by the leading British authority on the Christian Right.

Steve Bruce, 'Zealot Politics and Democracy: The Case of the Christian Right', *Political Studies*, 48 (2) (2000), pp. 263–82 is a concise and lucid summary of the relative success of the Christian Right and the dilemmas it confronts in America's pluralist democracy.

Frederick Clarkson, *Eternal Hostility: The Struggle between Theocracy and Democracy* (1997) is a lucid examination of the tensions between democratic principles and the role of religion in public life.

James W. Fraser, *Between Church and State: Religion and Public Education in a Multicultural America* (1999) is a comprehensive history of the key political battles in the church and state debate from the founding of the republic to today.

Jeffrey C. Isaac, Matthew F. Filner and Jason C. Bivins, 'American Democracy and the New Christian Right: A Critique of Apolitical Liberalism', chapter 13 in Ian Shapiro and Casiano Hacker-Cordon (eds), *Democracy's Edges* (1999) is a well-crafted examination of the 'threat' posed American liberalism by the Christian Right.

William Martin, *With God on Our Side: The Rise of the Religious Right in America* (1997) is a detailed account of the resurgence of the religious right from the 1970s on.

Justin Watson, *The Christian Coalition: Dreams of Restoration, Demands for Recognition* (1997) is a balanced critical discussion of the leading force on the Christian Right during the 1990s.

Clyde Wilcox, *Onward Christian Soldiers? The Religious Right in American Politics* (1996) is a comprehensive and impartial discussion of the role and influence of the religious right.

WEB LINKS

Resource Center on Religion
http://speakout.com/activism/religion/

'Divining America': The National Humanities Center – historical essays on religion, from the Scopes Trial to Islam in America
http://ipmwww.ncsu.edu:8080/tserve/divam.htm

Christian Coalition
www.cc.org

Reverend Jerry Falwell's site
www.falwell.com

A Christian Identity movement site
http://www.kingidentity.com/

A particularly extreme Christian site that interprets the Bible and its injunctions on matters such as adultery and homosexuality literally
www.tencommandments.org

The Christian Broadcasting Network
http://www.cbn.com/

Religious Right Resources
http://www.spiritone.com/~gdy52150/rrgs.htm

The Interfaith Alliance (opposed to the Christian Coalition)
http://www.interfaithalliance.org/

Association of Moderate Christian Voters
http://www.amcv.org/

Atheist site
www.atheists.org

Americans United for Separation of Church and State
http://www.au.org/

People for the American Way (a liberal group dedicated to opposing the Christian Right)
www.pfaw.org

United Synagogue of Conservative Judaism
http://www.uscj.org/

Jewish Reconstructionist Federation
http://www.jrf.org/

United States Conference of Catholic Bishops
http://www.nccbuscc.org/

Catholic Information Center
http://www.catholic.net/

Anglicans Online
http://anglicansonline.org/

The Episcopal Church, USA
http://ecusa.anglican.org/

United Methodist Church
http://www.umc.org/

Presbyterian Church USA
http://www.pcusa.org/

American Baptist Churches
http://www.abc-usa.org/

Southern Baptist Convention
http://www.sbc.net/sbcsplash/

Evangelical Lutheran Church
http://www.elca.org/

QUESTIONS

- How influential is religion in American politics, and why?

- 'The influence of the Christian Right in American politics been massively exaggerated'. Discuss.

- Should the 'wall of separation' between church and state in America be strengthened, relaxed or abandoned?

- Evaluate the constitutional arguments for and against allowing prayer in American public schools.

- Can democratic pluralism and religious pluralism co-exist in America?

9 Drugs

We're rejecting the helpless attitude that drug use is so rampant that we're defense-less to do anything about it. We're taking down the surrender flag that has flown over so many drug efforts. We're running up the battle flag. We can fight the drug problem, and we can win.

President Ronald Reagan, June 1982

It is a peculiar irony of American exceptionalist mythologizing that the right to bear arms, which harbor the potential for instant lethal violence, is regarded as sacro-sanct, while the right to bear drugs, whose potential is rarely so, is regarded as taboo.

David Downes (2001: 212)

- **The Historical Context**
- **Drugs Control: The Punitive Paradigm**
- **The Failure of Punitive Policies**
- **Public Opinion**
- **Explaining the Politics of Drugs**
- **Governing Institutions**
- **Conclusion**

Chapter Summary

Since the end of the 1960s successive administrations in America have declared and waged a 'war on drugs'. Following a 'punitive paradigm', the war's targets have included not just suppliers of illegal drugs but also drug users, regardless of the type of drug or quantity of consumption. For supporters of the drugs war, the growth of drug usage is a legacy of an indulgently permissive 1960s counterculture. Drug use is not only a moral hazard in itself, but has also contributed to serious public health and crime problems for millions of Americans. For critics, the war has been at least as disastrous and ineffective as that in Vietnam. Some progressives see the punitive paradigm that has dominated government approaches to drugs as misguided. Reflecting these concerns, the Clinton administration made some marginal efforts to place preventive and curative policies alongside the strongly punitive criminal justice policies of the Reagan/Bush years. But attempts to de-escalate the drugs war and its expansive bureaucracy have proven brief and unsuccessful since 1974. Instead, attempts to stem the drug trade have encompassed not only punishments for drug dealers and consumers in America but also efforts by presidents and Congresses to shape foreign policy towards Central and Latin America and Southeast Asia. Despite this, the figures on drug use have continued to grow and the war has failed to achieve its objectives. For some critics on the left and the libertarian right who look to the precedent of Prohibition of alcohol, only the decriminalization of drugs promises to ameliorate the problems associated with its current usage. For others, a public health approach is the key. The conflict over drugs stands as another paradigmatic example of cultural value conflict more broadly, featuring an ongoing controversy in a free society about how to balance the community's legitimate needs for order and safety against the individual's constitutional rights to liberty. As with firearms and capital punishment, traditionalists have dominated, if not determined, drugs policy.

The United States is a republic but on December 21, 1970 'the King' visited 'the Prez' – Elvis Presley met President Richard Nixon in the White House. Presley had written the president a six-page letter requesting the visit and suggesting that he be made a 'Federal-Agent-At-Large' in the Bureau of Narcotics and Dangerous Drugs. Nixon, not a president for whom rock and roll was an obvious or straightforward association, was reported to have commented to Presley, 'You dress pretty wild, don't you?' The singer responded with characteristic eloquence that, 'Mr. President, you got your show to run and I got mine.' The president then inducted Presley as a special agent. The official photographs of the summit that were released to the press suggested that Presley had already eagerly embraced his new role by 'going native' with narcotics – as he later was to do with burgers and fries – ultimately to fatal effect. (More requests for reproductions of the photo are made to the National Archives than for the Bill of Rights or the Constitution.)

That odd vignette seemed peculiarly appropriate for America's drugs politics, for the so-called 'drugs war' that was largely Nixon's creation, and for the prominent place that the issue of drugs has assumed in the culture war. At one level, that politics has been extremely heavy on symbolism and light on substance. Periodic declarations of all-out wars on drugs, the appointment of new 'drugs czars' to coordinate federal action, and the introduction and reform of federal, state and local laws on punishing drug suppliers, dealers and users have become constants in American public life since 1969. Yet the importation and consumption of drugs continues unabated, with attendant public health and crime problems, not to mention the psychological and emotional traumas of the families and friends of those drug users and addicts who are victims of health and crime problems.

Drugs might not be thought to form part of the cultural value battleground of contemporary politics, but the politics of drugs regulation underlines many of the central features of American politics, and the core themes of this book that have already been sketched. Traditionalists have tended to demonize drug users as well as dealers and to favour strongly punitive penalties against them. Many traditionalists make no distinctions between 'hard' drugs such as cocaine and heroin and 'soft' drugs such as marijuana; all drug use is, by definition, immoral and needs to be prohibited and punished. Progressives, while mostly reluctant to condone or legalize drug use, have tended instead to emphasize the need for empathy and programmes of prevention and treatment for drug addicts as being at least as important as sanctions and punishments on either them or drug suppliers.

Political conflict over drugs therefore involves many of the central questions of American politics more broadly: the rights and liberties of individual citizens versus the interest of communities in social order; the appropriate means of government ensuring adequate public health; the role of political parties in clarifying public debate and offering meaningful policy alternatives; the limits to judicial intervention to thwart elected bodies' will; the regulation of commercial interests supplying a tenaciously resilient domestic demand; and the power of particular 'special interest' lobbies to influence Congress and the executive bureaucracy in their favour.

In some respects, drugs symbolize more than any other cultural value issue the stark political divisions between traditionalists and progressives, with their public association with the 1960s counterculture and that decade's supposedly permissive or radical challenges to conventional American morality. But unlike abortion or gay rights, drugs are an issue where the harmful social consequences of drug usage are broadly agreed upon in America. A strong public consensus exists that drugs are harmful, by definition, to those who consume them and, through the by-product of social breakdown, violence and black markets in drugs trading, those who pay directly and indirectly for the costs of drug use. Relatively few Americans dissent from the conventional 'common sense' wisdom that the nation's drugs problem is the drugs themselves, not drug policies, and that the only way to tackle the nation's drugs problem is to adopt punitive sanctions against suppliers and consumers alike.

The identity of the protagonists on these issues is particularly ironic when compared to another controversial practice: smoking. While progressives have been among the forceful proponents of bans on tobacco advertising, restrictions on where smoking can occur, and pay-outs by tobacco companies, some have also been among the relatively few vocal supporters of decriminalizing drug use (selectively or completely). Many progressives experimented with casual drugs in their youth and in college and, at least in regard to drugs like marijuana and hashish, view them as harmless stimulants. Conversely, where traditionalists figure among the most implacable opponents of decriminalizing drugs, many also tend to be among the least enthusiastic prohibitionists when it comes to tobacco (and alcohol).

Yet both groups have enlisted appeals to American moralism behind their respective causes. Such is the social stigma surrounding drugs that politicians can demonize not only drug pushers but also drug users as easily as demonizing pornographers. To some extent, with generational change, attitudes to politicians and drugs have softened since the height of the 'moral panic' over drugs in the 1980s. For example, opinion surveys in 1999–2000 showed that most Americans professed not to care whether or not George W. Bush had taken cocaine as a young man.

More common, however, is the forceful and regular denunciation of drug use by prominent political figures. Not unrepresentative were the comments in a speech in August 1994, of Newt Gingrich, Speaker of the House of Representatives from 1995 to 1998, who urged Congress to enact a mandatory death penalty for the importation of large quantities of illegal drugs – and then carry out mass executions of those convicted of the crime:

> The first time we execute twenty-seven or thirty or thirty-five people at one time, and they go around Colombia and France and Thailand and Mexico, and they say, 'Hi, would you like to carry some drugs into the U.S.?', the price of carrying drugs will have gone up dramatically. (Bedau, 1997: 28)

In 1989, Bill Bennett, the 'drugs czar' of the Bush administration, had informed a national radio audience that there was nothing 'morally' wrong with beheading drug traffickers while Los Angeles Police Department Chief Daryl Gates testified before Congress that casual drug users 'ought to be taken out and shot'. In such a climate, it is unsurprising that, despite marginal setbacks, traditionalists have dominated public policymaking.

THE HISTORICAL CONTEXT

Much as imbibing alcohol has a history of thousands of years, so consuming addictive narcotics has long been a favoured American pastime. Such was American demand for cigarettes and cigars during the twentieth century, for example, that the production of tobacco became an important and highly profitable domestic industry, particularly in states such as North Carolina, South Carolina and Virginia. Companies such as RJR Nabisco and Philip Morris became multi-million dollar corporations with substantial economic – and hence political – influence, and tobacco-related symbols (such as 'Marlboro Man' and 'Joe Camel') became cultural icons.

But health and moralistic concerns also encouraged social movements regularly to press government to regulate and prohibit the distribution and consumption of such substances. Part of the motivation here was a traditional American Puritanism (what H.L. Mencken once dubbed 'the fear that somebody, somewhere is happy') that strongly informed the movement to ban alcohol consumption. Along with this, however, was a strong fear among many Americans that the weed, to a lesser but significant extent, encouraged deeply anti-social forms of behaviour, threatened traditional family and marital ties, and led to joblessness and poverty.

Following such notions, drug use is still frequently conceived of as a social and, in some cases, criminal problem that many attribute to moral failure. But, in markedly different forms, use of drugs has extensive historical roots in the American experience. Daniel Patrick Moynihan, for example, has noted that the second law passed by the first-ever Congress was a tariff on Jamaican rum, an act intended not to deter the drinking of alcohol but rather to promote the consumption of American-made whiskey. Moynihan pointed out further that, '[d]istilled spirits in early America appeared as a font of national unity, easy money, manly strength, and all-round good cheer. … It became routine to drink whiskey at breakfast and to go on drinking all day' (quoted in Lipset, 1996: 271). The historical record bears out the observation. Annual per capita consumption of distilled spirits was five gallons in 1830 – almost five times what the average American consumes today. This pattern, and the consequent social ills accompanying it, eventually encouraged the temperance movement of 1820–50, reducing the per capita annual consumption rate to 'merely' two gallons by 1840.

Perhaps more surprising than the notion of alcohol being as American as apple pie is the testimony of St John de Crèvecoeur, who, in his *Letters from an American Farmer* (1782) remarks on the adoption by the women of Nantucket of 'the Asiatic custom of taking a dose of opium every morning'. Between 1840 and 1870 opium imports to America increased seven times faster than the population growth. Reminiscent of the media's role currently in raising and reinforcing public concerns about drug use, the press during the 1870s and 1880s shocked the public with exposés on the widespread use of opiates and other narcotics for both medicinal and recreational purposes (Lipset, 1996: 271).

Most analysts have concluded that Americans' historic inclination to use drugs is culturally based. As technology has offered modern society more sophisticated, varied and powerful narcotics – from morphine during the Civil War to cocaine in the late nineteenth century to 'free-base' cocaine and crack in the 1980s – many Americans have been keen to use them. Consequently, while there is no doubt that the connection between crime and the violent drug trade since the 1960s presents serious social problems for the nation (especially in urban centres), whether these developments indicate a suddenly declining state of societal morality in America is more questionable. According to Seymour Martin Lipset, current patterns of drug use instead reflect new manifestations of cultural strains brought on by the development of new and sometimes pernicious technologies, not a change in values (1996: 271).

Such analyses are cold comfort to many Americans today. The moral state of young Americans, as evidenced by media reports of spreading drug abuse in the nation's schools, particularly in inner cities, has been of especially acute concern, and recent studies show that the proportion of today's youth who

report using illicit drugs appears to be increasing. For example, national survey data on drug use by eighth, tenth and twelfth graders from 1975 to 1994 gathered by the Institute for Social Research at the University of Michigan reveal that marijuana use increased during the 1990s after a period of decline beginning in the late 1970s. The percentage of twelfth graders who said that they had used any illicit drug, which had dropped steadily from a peak of 66 per cent in 1981 to 41 per cent in 1992, went back up to 50 per cent in 1994. Alcohol consumption by high school seniors, however, was on a downward slope, with daily use falling from 4.8 per cent in 1987 to 3.4 per cent in 1992 and 2.9 per cent in 1994.

As Table 9.1 reveals, easily the most popular drugs in America are alcohol and

TABLE 9.1   Drug use, by type of drug and age group, 1974–94 (per cent)

Age and type of drug	Ever used			Current user		
	1974	1985	1994	1974	1985	1994
12–17 years old						
Marijuana	23.0	23.2	16.0	12.0	11.9	7.3
Cocaine	3.6	4.8	1.3	1.0	1.4	0.4
Heroin	1.0	0.4	0.4	na	0.1	na
Alcohol	54.0	55.4	41.2	34.0	31.0	16.3
Cigarettes	52.0	45.3	33.5	25.0	15.3	9.8
18–25 years old						
Marijuana	52.7	59.4	43.4	25.2	21.9	12.2
Cocaine	12.7	24.4	9.6	3.1	7.5	1.0
Heroin	4.5	1.3	0.2	na	0.3	0.1
Alcohol	81.6	92.0	86.8	69.3	70.7	63.8
Cigarettes	68.8	75.2	68.6	48.8	36.6	26.5
26 years and older						
Marijuana	9.9	26.6	35.0	2.0	6.0	3.0
Cocaine	0.9	9.2	10.9	na	1.9	0.6
Heroin	0.5	1.1	1.3	na	na	na
Alcohol	73.2	89.2	91.0	54.5	59.8	55.6
Cigarettes	65.4	80.6	76.8	39.1	32.7	24.7

Note: Current users are those who used drugs at least once within the month prior to the study.

Source: *Statistical Abstract of the US* (1996: 144).

cigarettes. Although the figures for current users are lower than for those who have ever used these drugs, they remain easily more popular than other 'soft' and 'hard' drugs. Although these official government figures almost certainly understate the full extent of drug consumption, they suggest two points: (i) that alcohol and cigarettes remain the drugs of choice, and (ii) the consumption of almost all drugs has declined over the 20 years surveyed.

Although it may surprise many accustomed to the rhetoric of the 'war on drugs' of the last two decades, marijuana, cocaine and LSD were part of a widely accepted culture in America as late as the 1970s. In 1970, for example, Congress repealed tough statutory penalties on marijuana possession and established a maximum penalty of one-year probation for first-time possession. If probation were successfully completed, the proceedings would be dismissed. For those aged 21 and younger, successful completion of probation also expunged the arrest and indictment and no record would remain of the offence. This relatively relaxed culture was reflected in 1971, when NORML (the National Organization for the Reform of Marijuana Laws) was formed to press for the legalization of marijuana. In 1974, a new American journal, *High Times*, was even published to celebrate the flourishing drug culture.

President Nixon named conservative Pennsylvania Governor Raymond Shafer to chair a congressionally mandated Commission on Marijuana and Drug Abuse. In 1973, much to the president's displeasure, the Commission recommended that Congress decriminalize possession of marijuana for personal use. The relatively permissive attitude to drugs was such that, in 1977, President Carter (a 'born-again' Baptist) asked Congress to eliminate criminal penalties for possession of less than one ounce of marijuana and replace them with a $100 fine. The head of the Department of Health, Education and Welfare from 1977 to 1979, Joseph Califano Jr., later observed that 'we were more concerned with herbicides used to kill marijuana than marijuana

itself' during the Carter administration (Califano, 1999). The relative lack of a vehement punishment culture on drugs was not confined to federal officials. During the 1970s, 11 state legislatures, representing about one-third of the total American population, decriminalized consumption of marijuana. The Alaska Supreme Court also held that the privacy clause in its state constitution protected the possession of marijuana in the home for personal use.

But such a culture was sharply challenged by subsequent social and political developments. By the early 1980s, it was estimated that more than 60 million Americans had tried illegal drugs, including 50 million who had smoked pot. Approximately one in ten high school seniors was estimated to smoke marijuana on a daily basis; and nearly four in ten were current smokers (that is, they had smoked at least once within the last month). Cocaine was not as widely used as marijuana but the number of regular users (at least monthly) in the late 1970s and early 1980s was nonetheless counted in millions, not thousands. By 1982, some 22 million Americans had tried cocaine at least once. By the mid-1980s, the American people – approximately 5 per cent of the world's total population – were consuming 50 per cent of the world's total production of cocaine (a situation that has effectively remained the same since that time).

It has only been since the mid-1980s that broad public perceptions about drugs in general have altered in the face of new medical evidence that cocaine was addictive and could incite states of paranoia and violence; and that marijuana could undermine short-term memory and increase the risks of turning to harder drugs. 1983 was arguably the key year in which a serious social ill among some Americans became a national catastrophe. The transformation occurred when baking soda and water were cooked with cocaine to produce 'crack' cocaine. In the early 1980s, it had cost 'social snorters' of coke somewhere between $100 to $150 for a teaspoonful of powder, good for a 'high' for

Exhibit 9.1   The precedent of Prohibition of alcohol

Like drugs today, the issue of Prohibition of alcohol previously exposed deep fissures in American society as well as acute problems of law enforcement. After the Civil War, the temperance movement, fuelled by Protestant moral reform fervour, gathered substantial popular support by linking drink to every manner of vice and evil in the public mind. Drink ruined families, caused workers to agitate for higher wages (to pay for more booze) and made immigrants the willing dupes of political bosses. The Prohibition issue turned on the class, ethnic and religious make-up of individual communities, not merely on whether the community was rural or urban. Broad support ushered in the Eighteenth Amendment in 1919 as the apparent dawn of a new era. The Amendment prohibited the manufacture, sale, transportation, import and export of intoxicating liquors in America and authorized Congress and the states to enforce the ban by appropriate legislation.

At first, Prohibition's apparent success in combating drinking muted its many critics. During the 1920s, distilleries and breweries shut down, saloons locked their doors and alcohol-related deaths all but disappeared. Compliance, however, had less to do with piety and public support than laws of supply and demand: since illegal liquor remained in notably short supply, its price rapidly rose beyond the average worker's wage.

As could be expected, in quintessential American fashion, private enterprise filled the void. Enterprising smugglers supplied wealthy drinkers who could afford the best liquor and wine, but less affluent Americans had to rely on small-time operators who produced for local consumption. Due to high shipping and storage charges, it cost more to procure beer or wine, so the price of liquor, relative to other alcoholic beverages, dropped. Drinking habits shifted accordingly. The consumption of hard liquor (such as whiskey and bourbon) rose while beer and wine sales declined, while ordinary Americans sometimes turned their hand to producing 'moonshine' liquor of dubious quality.

Much of this booze ran the gamut from swill to poison. According to one widely circulated story, for example, a potential buyer who sent a liquor sample to a laboratory for analysis was shocked when the chemist replied: 'Your horse has diabetes.' For others, the problem of 'killer batches' was no laughing matter. Hundreds, perhaps thousands, of Americans died from drinking concoctions with names like 'Jackass Brandy'. Supposedly 'dry' counties – strictly enforcing prohibition – defended themselves by pointing to the number of alcoholics as proof of their rigid enforcement: 'We're the driest county in the state and we've got the alcoholics to prove it.'

Despite the constitutional amendment, neither federal nor state authorities had enough funds to enforce Prohibition in anything approximating effective terms. The Federal Prohibition Bureau began the 1920s with 1,520 agents, for example, and by 1930 the number had grown only to 2,836. Lax enforcement, coupled with huge profit margins, inevitably enticed large-scale operators to enter bootlegging. Organized crime, of course, had long been a fixture of urban life, with gambling and prostitution as its base, but it was predominantly small-time, local operators who managed these vices. Liquor demanded production plants, distribution networks and sales forces, attracting large-scale operators with the capital and business skills to tackle big-time bootlegging.

Bootlegging thereby turned into a veritable gold mine for organized crime. By the late 1920s, crime syndicates sold 150 million quarts of liquor each year, generating revenue in excess of $2 billion annually (more than 2 per cent of America's gross national product). Chicago's notorious mobster, Al Capone, had a gross income of $60 million in 1927 and employed an army of workers in his operation. A ruthless figure accused of ordering numerous gangland killings, Capone preferred to think of himself as a businessman. 'All I do is supply a public demand', he insisted. 'I do it in the best and least harmful way I can.' In one of the greatest ironies in American history, the traditionalist moralists who had lobbied for Prohibition had become unwitting supporters of organized crime.

Exhibit 9.1 The precedent of Prohibition of alcohol *continued*

> From the outset, cynics insisted that Prohibition could not be enforced. Ultimately, they were right. Where the public backed Prohibition, it had teeth; where it lacked support, particularly in large cities, people often flaunted it. Public authorities were not immune: on more than one occasion journalists even saw President Warren Harding's favoured boot-legger drive to the back door of the White House and unload cases of liquor in broad daylight.
>
> In 1923 (just four years after the Eighteenth Amendment was ratified) New York became the first state to repeal its enforcement law, and by 1930 six more states had followed suit. Others remained firmly committed to Prohibition, prompting Walter Lippmann to conclude: 'The high level of lawlessness is maintained by the fact that Americans desire to do so many things which they also desire to prohibit.' Not until the 1930s, when the Great Depression and mass unemployment gave the country something genuinely serious to worry over, did Prohibition lose political steam. After a presidential commission reported that Prohibition could not be enforced, Congress finally repealed it in 1933 with the ratification of the Twenty-First Amendment, making liquor control a state and local matter – precisely the jurisdiction where many Americans had always thought it belonged.

two people of several hours. The equivalent in crack cost just $5.

Unsurprisingly, the illicit trade in crack exploded, concentrated disproportionately among the poor rather than the affluent and ambitious, and with it an epidemic of violence shocking even to a country inured to leading the civilized world in the macabre leagues of murders and prison populations. Rapidly becoming a business generating tens of billions of dollars for its suppliers and pushers, dealers fighting for 'turf' steadily transformed areas of major cities such as Chicago, Los Angeles and Detroit into *de facto* war zones during the 1980s. The number of Americans sent to prison for drug crimes had, by 1990, exceeded the number sent for property crimes but the police were hard-pressed to contain the warfare. The Center on Addiction and Substance Abuse at Columbia University found alcohol and/or drug abuse implicated in some three-quarters of all murders, rapes, child molestations and deaths of babies and children from parental neglect.

Faced by such indicators of social breakdown (frequently framed as a crisis of American morality), public figures ratcheted up the rhetorical assault on 'drugs culture' and lawmakers responded by boosting the budgets of

agencies charged with drug busting and rounding up drug dealers and users. The nation rapidly turned against drug use, reviving and increasing criminal penalties (especially for drug dealers and those who sold to children) and mounting major public health campaigns to educate the young about the dangers of drug abuse (by 1990, casual drug use had dropped by half, partly as a result of these campaigns).

Partly as a result of the efforts of presidents Nixon, Reagan and George H.W. Bush to demonize all drug users as criminals, much of the public's concern about drugs became focused on their association with criminal behaviour – both within and outside the United States. Such a preoccupation is, to a degree, understandable. As Table 9.2 shows, in all but one of the major cities sampled (Houston), a majority of men arrested by law enforcement officers were found to have tested positive for drug use. In several, in excess of half of those arrested tested positive for cocaine (although heroin was much less commonly present among those arrested). While these figures do not for a moment support the notion that drug users in general commit crimes, they do demonstrate that those who are arrested on charges of criminal behaviour tend to be drug users.

But, as Table 9.3 reveals, significant differences exist between the arrest rates of drug dealers and consumers. In terms of those selling or manufacturing drugs, the most common arrest is for the most prevalent forms of 'hard drugs': heroin and cocaine. Compared to the arrest rate in 1980, this increased almost nine times by the early 1990s. But in terms of arrests for possession of drugs, the 'soft' drug marijuana is almost as common a cause of arrest as heroin and cocaine, reinforcing the point that the punitive paradigm so popular among politicians since the 1980s casts all drugs users as criminals. Again, though, the arrest rate for possession of heroin and cocaine has also increased

dramatically – by six times as many arrests in 1993 as 1980 – reflecting the growing concern among public authorities about heroin and cocaine abuse.

The history of drug usage is of a common practice steadily transformed by technological developments. Periodic outbreaks of public anxiety or 'moral panics' over drugs neither eliminated the consumption of existing drugs (even during Prohibition) nor prevented the distribution, sale and use of new drugs. But once drugs became increasingly linked in the public mind with criminal activities – and especially with the crack epidemic of the 1980s – few policymakers felt able to dissent from a self-consciously 'punitive paradigm' that increasingly dominated

TABLE 9.2   Drug use by male arrestees in major US cities, by type of drug, 1994 (percentage testing positive)

City	Any drug	Marijuana	Cocaine	Heroin
Atlanta, GA	69.4	24.7	57.3	2.5
Birmingham, AL	69.2	28.1	50.4	3.6
Chicago, IL	78.9	38.2	56.6	27.1
Cleveland, OH	65.9	27.5	47.9	2.7
Dallas, TX	57.4	32.7	34.9	3.0
Denver, CO	67.1	38.6	40.2	4.0
Detroit, MI	65.5	37.6	34.1	7.4
Fort Lauderdale, FL	58.1	29.4	40.8	1.1
Houston, TX	47.7	22.6	29.0	2.8
Indianapolis, IN	69.4	39.1	47.2	2.6
Los Angeles, CA	66.4	19.6	48.4	9.5
Manhattan, NY	82.0	24.2	67.9	18.9
Miami, FL	66.3	27.8	55.6	2.2
New Orleans, LA	63.3	28.5	46.7	4.7
Omaha, NB	59.2	44.2	25.8	2.4
Philadelphia, PA	76.1	32.3	54.2	14.4
Phoenix, AZ	64.8	28.8	28.4	6.4
Portland, OR	65.3	26.9	32.2	11.8
St Louis, MO	73.5	36.4	50.2	10.9
San Antonio, TX	51.8	29.5	30.9	12.4
San Diego, CA	79.2	36.2	30.0	12.4
San Jose, CA	55.0	29.7	19.1	5.9
Washington, DC	63.8	30.2	38.1	9.1

Source: *Statistical Abstract of the United States* (1996: 209).

TABLE 9.3 Drug arrest rates for drug abuse violations, 1980–94

Offence	1980	1990	1993
Drug arrest rate, total	256.0	435.3	437.2
Sale and/or manufacture	57.9	139.0	129.8
Heroin and cocaine	10.8	93.7	84.1
Marijuana	28.4	26.4	27.1
Synthetic drugs	2.8	2.7	2.5
Other dangerous non-narcotic drugs	15.9	16.2	16.1
Possession	198.1	296.3	307.4
Heroin or cocaine	22.2	144.4	136.1
Marijuana	146.2	104.9	120.6
Synthetic drugs	6.7	6.6	5.2
Other dangerous non-narcotic drugs	23.0	40.4	45.6

Note: Figures are rate per 100,000 inhabitants.

Source: *Statistical Abstract of the United States* (1996: 210).

political discourse about America's drugs problem and the regulatory 'solutions' to it.

DRUGS CONTROL: THE PUNITIVE PARADIGM

The prevailing model of drug control in America relies primarily on law enforcement to seize drugs and imprison those whom the law defines as drug offenders (whether dealers or users). This punitive paradigm has informed the federal government's approach to drug control since the 1920s and rests on three related premises:

- The use of any drug is defined as criminal and morally wrong without distinctions being made between different types of drug.
- The government's central task is identified as stopping all drug use in America as speedily as possible.
- Coercion and punishment are regarded as the appropriate means to the policy end of eliminating all drug use.

The federal- and state-level public policies inspired since 1969 by this three-pronged punitive paradigm have clearly succeeded in arresting and imprisoning large numbers of Americans. At the height of the drugs war (thus far) under President George H.W. Bush, some 1,089,500 people were arrested in 1990 for drug abuse violations; 1,126,300 Americans were arrested in 1993 under a supposedly less zealous anti-drug warrior, Bill Clinton. As of June 1996, 5.5 million Americans were under some form of control by the justice system (approximately one in every 35 adults in the United States) and over 1.7 million Americans were behind bars. According to the Department of Justice, 85 per cent of the overall increase in the federal prison population from 1985 to 1995 was due to drug convictions. From 1980 to 1995, the proportion of drug offenders in the American jail and prison population increased twelve-fold, and a similar rise in drug overdose deaths also occurred over the same period.

But while these punitive efforts have produced impressively large numbers of arrests, incarcerations and seizures (107 metric tonnes of cocaine and 815 kilograms of heroin were seized in 1990; 110.7 tonnes of cocaine and 1,600.9 kilos of heroin in 1994), drug overdose deaths in America increased 540 per cent from 1980 to 1997 (according to the Drug Enforcement Administration) and drug-related problems have worsened significantly across the nation: emergency room visits, adolescent drug use and the spread of fatal diseases (particularly AIDS and hepatitis) have risen substantially, and drug-related crime continues at high levels across the nation (concentrated particularly in central cities).

The result of this apparent disjuncture between increasingly punitive policies and their marginal effects on drug use and drug-related crime and disease is an ongoing (but rather one-sided) political conflict about the reasons for the relative ineffectiveness of existing punitive approaches. For many (and perhaps most) traditionalists, the lack of success in America's war on drugs is attributable essentially to the expenditure of insufficient political and financial effort: a lack of funding for key enforcement agencies and programmes, a political and/or military reluctance to engage in combating head-on the supply of drugs abroad, and a refusal to enact sufficiently harsh punishments within and outside America effectively to deter drug dealing and consumption. For some progressives, however, the main problem is that the punitive paradigm itself is ill-suited (at least in and of itself) to address the complex problems associated with drug use. As we will see, despite marginal changes since the late 1960s and the evidence against established approaches discussed in the next section, it has been the traditionalist endorsement of the punitive paradigm that has dominated American public policies on drugs.

THE FAILURE OF PUNITIVE POLICIES

As was the case with gun regulation, the fact that both traditionalists and progressives agree that a problem exists (gun violence, drug-related crime and disease) says little about what solutions should be adopted. But it is important initially to document that the existing policies have not worked before considering why they remain the preferred model.

Demand for drugs

How effective the punitive approach has been in combating drug use is hotly contested. Government policy has sought, for example, to prevent children from gaining access to illegal substances. Since 1975, the federal government has asked high school seniors how easy it is for them to obtain marijuana. In 1975, 87 per cent said it was 'very easy' or 'fairly easy'; in 1998, 89 per cent said it was easily obtained. Despite the efforts of public authorities, then, no change apparently occurred in marijuana availability over the 13-year period.

Moreover, several federal surveys showed a rise in the incidence of adolescent drug use after 1992. In particular, cocaine and heroin use have been increasing among America's youth. Since 1991, twice as many eighth grade students report using heroin and three times as many report using crack. Some American organizations that analyse drugs policies, such as Common Sense for Drug Policy, argue that since these developments have occurred at the same time as record government spending, arrests and incarceration rates, the escalating drug war has not reduced adolescent drug use. In addition, the prevailing model of drug control – relying essentially on the random chance of arrest, increasing use of locker searches, drug-sniffing dogs, and 'just say no' television ads – utilizes relatively unsophisticated methods of countering youth drug use in America.

Supply of drugs

An additional method of countering drug consumption, which is especially important to proponents of the punitive paradigm, is to tackle the supply of drugs. If successful, this could reduce the volume of drugs in the nation and/or make them more costly to obtain. Moreover, the indicators of policy success are relatively clear to identify: rising drug prices and decreasing drug purity levels. But, according to the federal drug czars' own staff, the Office of National Drug Control Policy, the price of heroin has dropped over time in America while its production has at the same time greatly risen. Similarly, the price of cocaine in the United States dropped from $275.12 per gram in 1981 to $94.52 in 1996. Despite massive federal government investments in border patrols, overseas crop eradication efforts, Department of Defense involvement and arrests of drug smugglers and dealers, the drug war has not reduced the supply of drugs into America nor made them more costly to obtain.

In terms of the economics of the drugs trade, the market prices for illegal drugs, like that of illegal alcohol during Prohibition, follow the same fundamental laws of supply and demand that apply to all commodities. The drug war created an artificially high commodity price and the resultant huge profit margins encouraged more drug producers to enter the market. Greater production then created economies of scale with lower production costs. Since then, lower production costs have allowed drug cartels to earn the same profit margin with lower retail prices. The cartels could also accommodate the interdiction efforts of federal agencies and the US military by over-producing their commodity to account for the likely losses. Since a kilogram of raw opium sold for approximately $90 in Pakistan in the late 1990s was worth $290,000 in America, law enforcement seizures at American borders had relatively little impact on cartel operations or profitability. (Indeed, the United Nations estimated in 1997 that the global drug business was equal to approximately 8 per cent of total world trade.)

An additional problem confronting American authorities charged with implementing punitive policies concerns the practical logistics of stopping the supply of drugs. For example, a mere 13 truck loads of cocaine is sufficient to satisfy the prevailing demand for drugs in America for a period of one year. The United States has 8,633 miles of shoreline, 300 ports of entry and more than 7,500 miles of border with Mexico and Canada. Stopping drugs at the borders is hence akin to trying to find the proverbial needle in a haystack. However much interdiction is necessary (as is shutting down the open-air 'drug bazaars' that frequently occur in American central cities), even some of the enforcing federal authorities concede that controlling supply cannot be more than a holding operation when in excess of five million Americans annually find themselves unable to apply Nancy Reagan's preferred solution of just saying 'no'.

Public health

Easy availability, increased purity and lowered prices have together resulted in high levels of overdose deaths and drug-related hospital emergency room visits in America. Also alarming has been the disparate demographic impact, especially the devastating expansion of the HIV and hepatitis C epidemics due to the prohibitions on needle possession in most American states. The sharing of needles is an important engine for the spread of HIV and hepatitis C. It was estimated in 1998, for example, that every day 33 more Americans are infected with HIV due to injection drug use. The epidemics have been particularly onerous on African American and Latino communities. By the end of 1997, for example, it was estimated that more than 110,000 African Americans and 55,000 Latinos were living with injection-related AIDS or had already died from it. (But it is important to note that by almost every measure – use of marijuana, cocaine, LSD, stimulants, barbiturates, crack, alcohol and cigarettes – blacks are consistently less prone to use illicit substances than either whites or Latinos.)

Taken together, the available data suggest strongly that the punitive model of drug control had not reduced the levels of adolescent drug use, nor reduced the demand for or supply of drugs into the United States, nor reduced the public health damage to many Americans (and the attendant financial and psychological effects on drug users and their friends and families) caused by drug addiction. As with gun control and capital punishment, however, the empirical realities about drug consumption are contested and, even where these are difficult to refute, they have not yielded a political consensus among Americans on an acceptable alternative to punitive policies. Elected officials, in particular, remain so tenaciously wedded to the punitive paradigm that 'most Americans today simply accept it as conventional wisdom' (Bertram et al., 1996: 101), as the next section illustrates.

PUBLIC OPINION

One of the main reasons for the attachment of American politicians to punitive drugs policies is that the public attitudes on drugs are predominantly negative – and in many cases, vociferously so. A political 'vicious cycle' therefore occurs in which an assumed public antipathy to drug users (both widespread in scope and strong in intensity) informs public officials' steadfast reluctance to criticize the punitive paradigm, while that official reluctance in turn fuels continued public support for further punitive policies as the only plausible 'solutions' to America's drugs problems.

The history of public opposition to drugs is extensive. In a June 1951 Gallup poll, for example, in response to an open-ended question about punishing drug dealers, over one in ten Americans (14 per cent) said that they favoured the death penalty for 'selling drugs to teenagers'. In January 1969 only 2 per cent of Americans mentioned the death penalty as a possible punishment for 'dope peddling'. In both years, the plurality of respondents favoured long prison sentences. Those are the only two national surveys before 1985 to ask about the death penalty for selling drugs. Since then 11 surveys have asked about it but their questions are so different that support ranges from 1 per cent (AP/Media General, November, 1986) in which only the 40 per cent who said they favoured the death penalty for crimes other than murder were asked about specific crimes, to 73 per cent (*Times Mirror*, May 1990) in which 42 per cent of the respondents 'strongly favoured' and 31 per cent 'favoured' the death penalty for 'drug traffickers'. The idea of death for drug dealing is a relatively new one, and question wordings suggest everything from the little kid who sells cocaine on his block to major drug 'kingpins', so it is difficult to say precisely how the public feels on the issue (Bedau, 1997: 106).

Like other issues, public responses can be strongly shaped by presidential addresses, comments by prominent public officials, and consequent media attention. In July 1989, for example, only 20 per cent of Americans in a *New York Times*/CBS survey considered drugs to be the most important problem facing the nation, but two months later, after President Bush's first national television address focused on drugs, 64 per cent of respondents declared drugs to be the country's greatest problem. A *Washington Post*/ABC News poll at the time also revealed that 62 per cent of those polled were even willing to give up 'a few of the freedoms we have in this country' for the war on drugs: 52 per cent said they would approve of homes being searched for drugs; 67 per cent were willing to have cars stopped and searched without court orders; and 82 per cent would permit the military to join the war on drugs (Bertram et al., 1996: 115–16).

But mass concern about drugs is not simply episodic in nature. For example, drug abuse and drug-related crime trailed only violent crime in a December 1995 ranking of America's social, economic and political

Exhibit 9.2   Invading the smokers' paradise: the anti-smoking campaign in America

Prohibition of alcohol was not the end of attempts to eliminate particular drugs from America. Reflecting the illiberal and prohibitive impulses latent in the American Creed, attempts to prohibit tobacco smoking are not at all new. During the nineteenth century, the anti-tobacco campaign in America remained an appendage of the temperance movement, and critics of the 'vile weed' denounced pipes, cigars, plugs and snuff with equal venom. After the introduction of machine-made cigarettes in the 1880s, however, opponents concentrated their fire on the 'little white slavers', insisting that cigarettes damaged the public's health more than previous forms of tobacco because smokers inhaled fumes filled with poison.

As early as the Civil War, a few cities in America had banned smoking in restaurants, theatres, public buildings, trolleys and railway cars. After anti-smokers organized the National Anti-Cigarette League in 1903, scores of prominent leaders joined the crusade. Between 1896 and 1923, 14 states (mainly in the Midwest) outlawed the sale of cigarettes, promoting calls for a constitutional amendment for national prohibition similar to that of alcohol.

But smokers had little to fear. By the end of the 1920s every state had repealed its law against cigarette sales. The crusade against tobacco was the last hurrah of the Prohibition movement. Prohibition of alcohol devolved into a legal fiasco and the public considered smoking the lesser vice of the two. Nor did the style of the anti-smokers help their cause. Many Americans dismissed them (not inaccurately) as moral zealots and opponents of individual liberty who wanted to expand the power of the state over private behaviour.

Largely because a national consensus had not formed against tobacco, smokers had no difficulty defending their right to smoke. The tobacco industry strongly supported them by opposing every legislative effort to restrict the sale of cigarettes and by spending millions of dollars on advertisements to reassure the public smoking was sophisticated, sexy and even healthy. Industry spokespeople hammered home the message that smoking should be left to individuals to decide, with no state interference.

Politically, smokers were traditionally protected by one of America's most successful 'iron triangles', the tobacco sub-government that focused on policies relating to promoting the consumption of tobacco products. The three main sets of actors in the sub-government were members of Congress from tobacco-growing states (especially North Carolina, South Carolina and Kentucky) who sat on the Agriculture and Appropriations committees and subcommittees, lobbyists representing tobacco growers and cigarette manufacturing companies, and federal bureaucrats from tobacco-related programmes at the Agriculture and Commerce Departments. Meeting regularly to work out policies favourable to tobacco products, these three actors created public programmes that helped tobacco farmers and the giant tobacco industry to fend off attacks from those who sought policies contrary to their interests.

Not until the 1950s, when scientists linked smoking to lung cancer, did reformers win public support for their war against 'slow motion suicide'. The phoenix of prohibition emerged from the ashes of a previous era with much greater political and social force. In 1964, the tightly knit sub-government community began to fragment. That year the surgeon general of the United States issued a report linking cigarette smoking to lung cancer, heart disease and emphysema. The report was followed by a Federal Trade Commission proposal that cigarette packets and advertising contain health warnings. The cosy triangle no longer had the low visibility that had made it so politically effective. Nevertheless, the tobacco sub-government remained intact, though its members faced increasingly stronger threats to their ability to set public policies related to tobacco. For years they fought a more or less constant battle to maintain what remained of their subsidy and international

Exhibit 9.2 Invading the smokers' paradise: the anti-smoking campaign in America *continued*

marketing programmes. More recently, members of Congress, in conjunction with federal agencies from the Public Health Service and the Environmental Protection Agency to the Food and Drug Administration have led a direct attack on the tobacco industry that indicates a future of greater regulation of cigarette production and consumption.

The battle has not been all one way. During the debate in Congress over a national health care programme in 1993–94, for example, the tobacco industry mobilized thousands of tobacco growers and workers to Washington to lobby against a proposed cigarette tax increase to fund the programme. That attempt at putting a human face on the industry and reminding members of Congress of the large number of people employed in the tobacco industry had the effect of significantly reducing the proposed size of the cigarette tax, even if it failed to prevent any tax being imposed.

But the Food and Drug Administration finally declared tobacco a drug in 1995. In 1998, a $368.5 billion settlement failed to gain the required approval of Congress. Subsequently, however, attorneys general from eight American states unveiled a $206 billion deal with tobacco companies to settle all state lawsuits against them. The largest legal settlement in history, it required the monies to be paid over 25 years and involved restrictions on cigarette advertising and marketing.

problems. An overwhelming 94 per cent of respondents in the poll said that drug abuse in America is a 'crisis' or 'serious problem'. In an unusual exception to the punitive approach, however, most of these respondents believed that education and prevention were the most effective of four strategies used in the 'war against drugs'. Forty-one per cent listed education as the best approach, compared with 32 per cent for reducing the supply of drugs, 23 per cent for tougher punishments for drug offenders, and only 4 per cent for improved treatment programmes for drug users. Previously, a September 1995 survey had found that more than half of the respondents (51 per cent) felt so passionately about the drugs issue that they favoured the death penalty for anyone convicted of smuggling 'a large quantity' of drugs into the United States (Golay and Rollyson, 1996: 6).

In some respects, the drugs battles most closely resemble those over firearms regulation. Drugs and guns both raise American passions to an intensity that appears bizarre to much of the rest of the world. Both drugs and guns harm people (albeit in very different ways). How best to warn of their dangers and regulate their use is an issue that occupies policymakers within and outside America. Fear of a total ban on guns animates many of the same Americans who most keenly press for a total ban on drugs. Yet many who doubt that a total ban on guns could be enforced simultaneously believe that such a prohibition is possible in relation to drugs. Moreover, no other developed country has chosen to turn smokers into social pariahs and drug users into criminals while making it easier and easier to carry guns, even concealed ones. But a society armed to the teeth but with clear lungs and an aversion to hallucinatory states evidently seems a worthy aim to many Americans. For example, a poll in April 2000 asked Americans which posed a 'greater threat' to young people today, guns or drugs. The respondents chose drugs over guns by the overwhelming margin of 74 per cent to 22 per cent (*National Journal*, August 22, 2000: 2360).

EXPLAINING THE POLITICS OF DRUGS

Drugs became a fully fledged national political issue in America in 1969, but their enduring persistence on the national agenda and the politicized character of the debate dates from the early 1980s. The nationalization and politicization of the issue stemmed from the greater drug usage by Americans that had commenced as far back as the 1960s. Partly, however, this politicization reflected the deadly potent threat to 'family values' that such usage was perceived by millions of Americans to pose with the spread of cocaine, crack and heroin. And partly, this new focus on drugs arose from the concern among lawmakers and the public alike – based on considerable empirical evidence – that drugs were strongly linked to anti-social behaviour, dangers at the workplace and crime against property and persons.

Enmeshed with these important concerns was the increasing personalization of American politics, such that few public officials who had consumed even 'soft' drugs could any longer be confident of a long political career. President Reagan's Supreme Court nominee, Douglas Ginsburg (his first-choice replacement for the failed nomination of conservative crusader Robert Bork), was obliged to withdraw his candidacy in 1987 when it was revealed that he had smoked cannabis as a law professor at Harvard University – a grievous embarrassment to conservative Republicans and to the president's recently announced 'Just Say No' initiative. In 1992, presidential candidate Bill Clinton invited widespread ridicule when he claimed prior to the New Hampshire Democratic Party presidential primary election that he had smoked cannabis but not inhaled it as a student. By 1999, prospective presidential nominees were asked by the *New York Post* whether they had tried cocaine amidst widespread rumours of Governor George W. Bush's 'partying' lifestyle as a young man (his refusal explicitly to state whether or not he had taken cocaine led some wags to suggest that, following

Clinton's precedent of non-inhalation, he'd 'sniffed but not snorted').

But however much post-Second World War generational change has meant that more Americans have had experience of drugs personally, the behaviour of public officials in governing institutions rarely focuses on such activities. As a result, America's public policies reflect a near-universal preoccupation with punishing drug suppliers and consumers even when the punishments seem out of step with comparable criminal offences (see Exhibit 9.3).

GOVERNING INSTITUTIONS

Compared to other issues of cultural value conflict, drug regulation has seen relatively little dissent from the prevailing punitive paradigm among members of America's governing institutions. Although some critical voices have been raised in Congress, the federal courts and the mass media, the key institutional players in drug politics – the executive bureaucracy, Congress and the federal judiciary – have mostly adhered strongly to the central punitive tenets of the 'war on drugs'.

Presidential politics

The question of which type of citizen is likely to make it to the White House first – a woman, an African American, a gay or lesbian, an atheist or a self-confessed drug user – consistently poses one of the more intriguing matters for speculation about American politics in the twenty-first century. In this particular case, the prospects of an active drug user entering the Oval Office are about as slim as those of a homosexual or atheist. (For both Al Gore and George W. Bush in the 2000 elections, the rumours of their youthful experimentation with marijuana and cocaine, respectively, were remnants of the past and managed to cancel each other out politically.)

From Lyndon Johnson's presidency (1963–69) onwards, successive occupants of

Exhibit 9.3   Drugs and guns in New York State

The penalties for the illegal sale or possession of drugs and guns, respectively, in the New York State Penal Code are listed below.

Class of felony (first-time offender)	Gun offence	Drug offence
Maximum prison sentence: Life	Not applicable	Selling two or more ounces of heroin or possessing four ounces of cocaine
Max: Life Min: 3–8.5 years	Not applicable	Selling 0.5 ounces of heroin or possessing two ounces of speed
Max: 25 years Min: 5 years	Illegally selling 20 or more firearms*	Selling one vial of crack or one bag of heroin
Max: 15 years Min: 3.5 years	Illegally selling ten or more fireams*	Selling 16 ounces of marijuana or possessing one milligram of LSD
Max: 7 years Min: 1–3 years	Illegally selling one firearm* or illegally possessing an explosive bomb or machine-gun	Possessing 0.5 grams of cocaine or 16 ounces of marijuana
Max: 4 years Min: Probation or 1–3 years	Not applicable	Possessing eight ounces of marijuana or selling 25 grams of marijuana

* Effective November 1, 1999.
Source: New Haven Police Department, cited in *The Nation*, September 20, 1999.

the Oval Office have publicly declared their deep and abiding concern over drug use in America. Richard Nixon placed drugs at the centre of the political stage in 1969 when he declared drugs a 'national threat'. Although Nixon established a commission on drugs, he also enlisted drugs as part of his more general attack on crime. It was not until the Nixon presidency that crime and drug use became automatically linked in the public mind. In June 1971 Nixon told Congress that drugs had 'assumed the dimensions of a national emergency' and informed media executives that 'Drug traffic is public enemy number one domestically in the United States today and we must wage a total offensive, worldwide, nationwide, government-wide and ... media-wide' (Bertram et al., 1996: 106). While Nixon consolidated the executive branch's Bureau of Drug Abuse Control, the Office of Drug Abuse Law Enforcement, the Office of National Narcotics Intelligence and the Customs Service Drug Investigation Unit into a new drug super-agency, the Drug Enforcement Administration (DEA), Congress passed the Comprehensive Drug Abuse Prevention and Control Act (1970) and increased spending on drug enforcement from $43 million in fiscal year 1970 to $321 million in fiscal year 1975.

In terms of their political agendas and electoral coalitions, exploiting the drugs war was not attractive to Gerald Ford or Jimmy Carter but neither possessed the political will or skills to reverse the established approach. Despite their de-escalation of Nixon's anti-drug rhetoric and the downgrading of the priority of combating drug use, the federal anti-drug apparatus continued to expand under their administrations. Like many of his other legislative initiatives, Carter's proposal to decriminalize marijuana and replace criminal penalties for possession of the drug with civil fines – seeking not to rewrite national drug strategy but alter the law on controlling a particular drug – died in Congress, while drug law enforcement budgets continued to grow, to $382 million in fiscal year 1977 under Ford to $855 million by fiscal year 1981 under Carter.

It was during the 1980s, however, that the most substantial escalation of the drug war occurred under successive Republican administrations. Anti-drugs law enforcement funding went from $855 million to more than $7.8 billion by 1993. Republican anti-drug campaigns were shaped by the party's increasingly conservative electoral coalition and the new pattern of crack/cocaine-centred drug consumption in America. President Reagan launched – with his wife Nancy – a high-profile national effort to tackle drugs, inaugurating in 1986 the 'Just Say No to Drugs' campaign that appealed not only to parents' groups recently organized to combat drugs in schools but also represented a powerful symbolic attack on the left, the 'counterculture' and permissive 'secular humanism'. When combined with an anti-crime platform and negative images of minority Americans (the new crack epidemic was especially visible among urban black and Hispanic neighbourhoods), the broad appeal of a punitive approach was especially marked among traditionalist whites.

Reagan's successor, George H.W. Bush, described the drugs trade in his first televised address to the nation on September 5, 1989, as America's 'gravest domestic threat' and called for 'an assault on every front'. He also adopted a particularly expansive view of the enemy in the drug war: 'Who's responsible? Let me tell you straight out. Everyone who uses drugs. Everyone who sells drugs. And everyone who looks the other way.'

Unlike his Republican predecessors, for whom attachment to the punitive paradigm was a near-exclusive preoccupation, President Clinton also emphasized the need to reduce the demand for illegal drugs rather than simply cutting down on the supply reaching America – a strategy that congressional Republicans held responsible in large part for the drug problem spiralling during the 1990s. Although Clinton stated at the Democratic National Convention in July 1992 that he would fight 'a real war on crime and drugs', he sought a shift in priorities to address the need for adequate treatment and health services, especially for hard-core drug users.

But such is the pressure on politicians to 'talk tough' on drugs that Clinton, perhaps unsurprisingly, succumbed. The defeat of health care in 1994 lost some nascent changes while Congress granted merely $57 million of a proposed $355 million increase in treatment-centred spending. (The drug budget for fiscal year 1996 had treatment and prevention at 31 per cent, the same figures as the final Bush budget.) When the Centers for Disease Control and Prevention issued a report in 1994 concluding that needle-exchange programmes diminish transmission of the AIDS virus without increasing drug use, the administration refused to release the report for fear of a political backlash. On the very morning that his Secretary of Health and Human Services, Donna Shalala, was to announce federal funding for needle-exchange programmes, the president took the advice of his National Drug Control Policy Director, Barry McCaffrey, and withdrew administration support. In the end, Clinton 'succeeded only in moving drug policy off the political agenda and out of the public spotlight' (Bertram et al., 1996: 125), thereby creating a false impression that the drugs war was a relic of the past.

The resources at the disposal of presidents to combat the drugs trade and drug consumption, though increasing, have remained fundamentally limited. Moreover, to the extent that they involve delicate questions of foreign policy (well before September 11), combating drugs is a highly problematic enterprise. Presidents have nevertheless tended to resort to a mixture of formal and informal powers in their battles against drugs:

- *The bully pulpit.* Nixon was the first president to seek to make drugs an issue at the top of Americans' agenda of public policy problems in his national addresses, a strategy repeated by Reagan and Bush in their rhetorical assaults on America's 'drugs culture'. In 1986, Reagan and several dozen presidential assistants even submitted to urine tests to set a moral example to the nation. While Clinton lowered the hostile rhetoric – attacking drugs publicly was to a certain extent politically problematic for this particular president – his administration continued to implement the types of punitive policy that his Republican predecessors sponsored.
- *Executive orders.* Both Reagan and Bush issued orders that drafted the federal intelligence apparatus (including the CIA) and the military into the drugs war and widened the authority of federal agencies to fight drugs. Bush, for example, issued a 1989 order that directed all agencies to check for drug violations before awarding hundreds of federal benefits.
- *Legislative recommendations.* Successive presidents have regularly pressed Congress to enact measures to combat the spread of drugs in America and expand the executive bureaucracy dealing with the drugs war.
- *Foreign policy measures.* Successive administrations have sought to use foreign policy instruments, such as foreign aid, training and military assistance, in efforts to induce drugs-trading nations to combat the spread of drugs. In particular, chief executives have asserted the right of the United States under the 1823 Monroe Doctrine to protect its hemispheric interests in the Americas, and have sought to link offers of increased economic assistance to Latin American nations to their efforts to curtail the trade in narcotics. By 2001, America's relations with Colombia, in particular, hinged on the drug trade and the civil war it fuelled.

- *Drugs czars.* In keeping with the 'war on drugs' metaphor, presidents have resorted to appointing individuals as drugs 'czars', charged with coordinating the administration approach. In 1999, the federal drug control budget amounted to $17.9 billion. Under the auspices of the Office of National Drug Control Policy (created by Congress in 1989), 66 per cent of these funds were apportioned to law enforcement activities, 22 per cent to treatment measures and 12 per cent to youth drug use.

Congress

Although the executive branch since Nixon has been central to initiating the drugs war, the president cannot act alone. The funds that support the war can only be appropriated by Congress and the national legislature faces the obligation to check and redirect misguided executive policies (either through its oversight authority or through the power of the purse). But Congress has not only acquiesced in punitive presidential approaches to drugs, it has also participated actively in expanding those approaches. Quite why is not difficult to understand. A representative example came in 1988 when the Senate was discussing efforts to increase the role of the US military in the drugs war. Senator John McCain (Republican, Arizona) simply noted that, 'This is such an emotional issue – I mean, we're at war here – that voting no would be too difficult to explain.'

In some respects, the issue of drugs resembles that of pornography, to the extent that millions of Americans consume the items in question – on a regular basis, in some cases as 'addicts', and frequently in breach of federal, state and local laws – but relatively few

Exhibit 9.4   The narco-enforcement complex

America's drug-enforcement bureaucracy began in 1914 as a small bureau in the Treasury Department (charged with ensuring that only doctors and pharmacists sold cocaine and heroin-based drugs). Even in the 1960s, it remained a small operation with only a few hundred agents. But under Nixon this underwent a transformation until the consolidated agencies in the Drug Enforcement Administration (DEA) had by 1981 amassed a formidable $219.4 million annual budget. By fiscal year 1996 this had spiralled to $857.4 million with 6,098 employees in 170 offices in America and in 48 foreign countries. Approximately 40 federal agencies or programmes – in seven of the 14 Cabinet departments – were involved in drug enforcement, whose total budget exceeded $8.2 billion in 1995.

In the Justice Department: the FBI conducts investigations into organized trafficking groups; the Immigration and Naturalization Service detects and apprehends drug smugglers and illegal aliens at or near the US border; the US Marshals Service detains and transports prisoners and manages seized assets. At the Treasury Department, the US Customs Service interdicts and disrupts the illegal flow of drugs by air, sea and land; the Internal Revenue Service (IRS) seeks to disrupt the money-laundering organizations' flow of funds. At the Pentagon, the military trains local forces in Latin America, searches cargo and tracks drug smugglers. Even the National Park Service and the Fish and Wildlife Service (in the Department of the Interior) were charged with fighting drug production and smuggling on the vast lands they control.

But the combination of such fragmentation and the logic of bureaucratic politics has both entrenched and expanded the drugs war:

- *Band-wagoning.* A 'hot' issue often entices bureaucrats seeking funds, not least when other programmes (poverty programmes in the 1970s, post-Cold War defence programmes in the 1990s) are being cut or eliminated.
- *Turf wars.* Competition between agencies over both jurisdictions and effectiveness tends to expand funding for all sides and reinforce the fragmentation of the war on supply and users into multiple missions.
- *Evaluation.* Rather than assessing the overall policy, drug agencies are concerned with their particular missions: seizing shipments, arresting smugglers, prosecuting dealers. Such statistics may mean little even on their own terms (increased seizures of cocaine in absolute terms, for example, may be entirely irrelevant if the overall supply is expanding or if figures for the latter are unknown) much less without data on the overall strategy's relative success.

The cumulative result is intense pressure by bureaucrats (and their political bosses) on Congress to set up new agencies and win more funds to achieve missions that are, in principle, difficult to achieve: halting drug production outside America, sealing America's borders, eliminating drugs from the nation's streets and preventing users from buying or possessing drugs.

organized lobbies exist either to defend or protect their actions. Since the 'pro-drugs' constituency in America is neither sizeable nor vocal (nor does it enjoy the countervailing constitutional arguments about free speech that libertarians conventionally point to on pornography), one might expect that risk-averse members of Congress would respond to mainstream, middle America by taking up harsh stances on drug production, consumption and trading. That has largely been the case. As Exhibit 9.5 records, the fragmentation of the executive bureaucracy is mirrored by that of Congress, with the sweeping reach of drugs policies cutting across over 70 congressional committees and subcommittees by the 1990s. This has meant that a substantial number of legislators possess influence over drugs policies and, crucially, can be held accountable at election time. (Most major legislation on drugs has been passed in election years.) This has meant not only that some lawmakers have sought to claim credit for out-toughing their opponents on drugs, but that even more moderate and pragmatic legislators among both main parties have tried to avoid the charge of being 'soft on drugs'. Since the 1980s, rival candidates for elective office have sought not only to outdo each other in their support for efforts to crush the illegal drugs trade, but have also challenged each other to take drug tests to prove their personal ethical purity on the drugs issue.

In 1988 a new federal death penalty statute was enacted for murder in the course of large-scale drug-trafficking, and from then until 1999 six persons were sentenced to death for violating the law (though none was executed). Congress also enacted legislation imposing mandatory prison sentences for drug dealing in 1994. Dealers in crack cocaine, however, are punished more severely than those who supply cocaine powder. Someone convicted of dealing more than 50 grams of crack must be sentenced to at least ten years imprisonment: a dealer in powder, however, must be found with over 5,000 grams before the same mandatory minimum sentence is imposed. The main justification offered for the distinction is that crack dealing typically involves greater and more serious violence than trade in powder cocaine.

That view is not universally accepted. Ostensibly, no racial dimension exists on this issue. But the US Sentencing Commission reported to Congress in 1995 that the law clearly has a disparate racial impact, disadvantaging African Americans. It produced figures that gave some support to the popular view that powder is a drug used by 'yuppie'

Exhibit 9.5   Creating an omnibus drugs law: 1988

The creation of the 1988 House omnibus drugs bill offers a good example of the fragmented congressional process. On June 9, the Banking, Finance and Urban Affairs Committee was the first to approve language for the omnibus bill, adopting new money-laundering controls designed to detect drug smugglers who collected cashier's cheques from several banks. In a separate committee hearing on the same day, the Ways and Means Committee voted to create 500 new positions for the Customs Service and to increase the penalty for failing to declare a controlled substance. Several days later the House Foreign Affairs Committee endorsed proposals that required the State Department to revoke the passports of convicted drug offenders and re-authorized the Agency for International Development to withhold economic and military aid from countries known to be involved in narcotics trafficking. On June 21, the Merchant Marine and Fisheries Committee approved provisions that would allow the United States to prosecute US citizens aboard drug-carrying vessels that were seized outside US territorial waters and authorized $346 million in additional funds for new helicopters, patrol boats and other drug enforcement needs of the Coast Guard. Also on that day, the Public Works and Transportation Committee voted to give the Federal Aviation Administration a role in stopping the flow of drugs entering through US airspace. Two days later the Education and Labor Committee approved funds for the Department of Health and Human Services to establish drug-abuse prevention and education programmes aimed at youth gangs. Additional proposals came from the Judiciary, Government Operations, Science, Energy and Commerce, and other committees. The draft was 400 pages long when it reached the floor on August 11.

(professional and upwardly mobile) whites, while crack is almost exclusively the drug of black ghetto youths, and it is the latter, as a result, who suffer disproportionately in the criminal justice system.

While there is undoubtedly a disparate racial impact here, it is far less clear that there is a discriminatory intent behind the policy. The same sentencing standards apply to people of all races convicted of dealing in crack. But whether Congress – an over-whelmingly white institution – would have passed such a law if its effect was to treat whites more severely than blacks has been questioned. Fifty-five per cent of all federal drug defendants are low-level offenders such as street-dealers, while only 11 per cent are classified as high-level dealers. Moreover, according to the United States Sentencing Commission, only 5.5 per cent of federal crack defendants are considered high-level crack users.

Considerations of race, whether conscious or unconscious, seemed operative here to some observers. According to The Sentencing Project, a Washington-based organization

Exhibit 9.6   Race and the drugs war

- Only 11 per cent of the nation's drug users are black, but blacks constitute almost 37 per cent of those arrested for drug violations, over 42 per cent of those in federal prisons for drug violations, and almost 60 per cent of those in state prisons for drug felonies.
- One in three black men between the ages of 20 and 29 years old is under correctional supervision or control.
- At current incarceration levels, newborn black males have more than a one in four chance of going to prison during their lifetimes, while Latino males have a one in six chance and white males have a one in 23 chance of serving time.
- In 1986, before mandatory minimums for crack offences became effective, the average federal drug offence sentence for blacks was 11 per cent higher than for whites. Four years later, following the implementation of harsher drug sentencing laws, the average drug offence sentence was 49 per cent higher for blacks.
- 54 per cent of blacks convicted of drug offences get sentenced to prison, against 34 per cent of whites convicted of the same offences; 44 per cent of blacks get prison sentences for possession versus 29 per cent of whites; 60 per cent of blacks are sentenced to prison for trafficking while 37 per cent of whites are sentenced to prison for the same crime.
- Regardless of similar or equal levels of illicit drug use during pregnancy, black women are ten times more likely than white women to be reported to child welfare agencies for prenatal drug use.
- The Latino community has been disproportionately affected by HIV/AIDS. Although Latinos represent 12 per cent of the US population, they represent 17.8 per cent of all AIDS cases.
- In 1995, the incarceration rate for white and Latino women combined was 68 per 100,000. For black women it was 456 per 100,000.
- All major western European nations' incarceration rates are about or below 100 per 100,000. In America, in 1995, the incarceration rate for black women was 456 per 100,000 and for black men 6,926 per 100,000.
- 1.46 million black men out of a total voting population of 10.4 million have lost their right to vote due to felony convictions.

Source: Wright and Lewin (1998: 41–2).

that researches issues of criminal justice, a total of 4.2 million Americans were not allowed to vote in the 2000 elections because they were in prison or had felony convictions. Of those, more than one-third (1.8 million) were black, amounting to 13 per cent of black men. In two states – Alabama and Florida – approximately 31 per cent of all black men were permanently disenfranchised because of convictions, many for non-violent offences. Many of these were guilty of drugs felonies. As Exhibit 9.6 indicates, the facts about race, drugs and incarceration make disturbing reading. Like capital punishment, they suggest that even if there is no clear or consistent intent deliberately at work, the results of existing punitive policies have a powerfully negative effect on American racial and ethnic minorities in particular.

Like the elected branches of government, judicial action on drugs has generally reflected the conservative, punitive approach. The Supreme Court, in *Edwards v. United States* (1997), unanimously upheld the constitutionality of the law concerning crack cocaine penalties. But lawyers for the black crack dealer involved in the case maintained that 'There is a perception among African Americans that there is no more unequal treatment by the criminal justice system than in the crack v. powder cocaine racially-biased federal sentencing provisions.' That perception can even lead to claims that the government is intentionally spreading drugs among black communities in America (see Exhibit 9.7).

Another issue that has provoked political disagreements is the question of drug tests.

Exhibit 9.7 The war on drugs: a war on the people?

On November 15, 1996, John Deutsch, the then head of the Central Intelligence Agency (CIA) stood before a neighbourhood group in Los Angeles and called the accusation made against his organization 'an appalling charge that goes to the heart of this country'. To say that 'an agency of the United States government, founded to protect Americans, helped introduce drugs and poison into our children and helped kill their future – no one who heads a government agency . . . can let such an allegation stand. I will get to the bottom of it, and I will let you know the results of what I've found.'

Deutsch had come to South-Central Los Angeles to respond to growing controversy spawned by a series of newspaper articles published in the *San Jose Mercury News*. For three days the paper carried a reporter's investigation into the crack cocaine epidemic, which had spread throughout the United States and had its most devastating impact on black neighbourhoods like South-Central. The story traced the drugs trail back to a San Francisco-based drug ring, which 'sold tons of cocaine to the Crips and Bloods street gangs of Los Angeles and funnelled millions in drug profits to a Latin American guerrilla army run by the US Central Intelligence Agency'.

For those in the black community trying to understand the roots of the suffering brought on by the crack cocaine epidemic, the stories confirmed what many had suspected all along – that once again they were the victims of a conspiracy in which government played a key role. It did not matter that the *Mercury News* reporter had found no explicit evidence of a government-based conspiracy. There were links and associations between the drug ring and a CIA-supported rebel group from Nicaragua, which seemed to benefit from the profits of crack sales, but there was nothing to indicate that the CIA either knew or was involved in this. Agency denials and internal investigations meant little or nothing to many in the black community. Local US representative, Juanita Millender-McDonald, stated that it was 'not up to us to prove the CIA was involved in drug trafficking in South-Central Los Angeles. Rather, it is up to them to prove that they were not.'

Such tests directly pit the interests of communities and organizations in public order against the civil liberties and rights of individual Americans. In the wake of growing public concern about the spread of drug abuse, President Reagan in 1986 signed an executive order requiring many federal government employees to be tested. Numerous private firms and major league sports organizations had already required such testing of job applicants and athletes. There is no obvious constitutional reason why a private

Exhibit 9.8   Liberty curtailed? Drug-testing student athletes

In Vernonia, Oregon, a small community of approximately 3,000 people faced a serious problem of drug use among its local public school students. The Vernonia School Board approved an anti-drug policy that required random drug testing of students wanting to participate in inter-school athletics.

The drug-testing programme required all middle school and high school student athletes to provide a urine sample at the start of their team's season. During the remainder of the season, on a weekly basis, 10 per cent of the team members would be selected randomly for a new test. Athletes refusing to take the test would be prevented from participating in inter-school sports activities for two years. Students with a positive result would be suspended from participating in the school's sports programme for an unspecified period while undergoing counselling to remedy their problems.

The drug-testing policy appeared to be acceptable to Vernonia parents and none objected when the School Board approved the programme in 1989. However, when James Acton wanted to join his school's seventh-grade football team, his parents challenged the policy. They refused to sign a urinalysis consent form to permit the son to take the test and filed suit in the federal district court in 1991 to stop the policy because they held it violated the Fourth Amendment's prohibition on 'unreasonable' searches.

The federal district court in Oregon dismissed the suit but on appeal the Court of Appeals for the Ninth District supported the Actons and voided the drug-testing programme. But the ruling conflicted with a 1988 ruling of the Fifth Circuit Court of Appeals that allowed random drug testing in public schools in Illinois, Indiana and Wisconsin.

On appeal to the Supreme Court, a 6–3 majority upheld the Vernonia policy. The Court held that the School Board's objective on behalf of the community to protect the public against drug abuse – a 'rampant problem' – outweighed the minimal limitations of an individual's Fourth Amendment rights associated with the drug-testing regulations. The Court noted that only members of sports teams were subjected to drug testing and that participation in inter-school athletics was voluntary. Scalia wrote for the Court that:

> The most significant element in this case is . . . that the Policy was undertaken in furtherance of the government's responsibilities, under a public school system, as guardian and tutor for children entrusted to its care . . . when the government acts as a guardian and tutor the relevant question is whether the search is one that a reasonable guardian and tutor might undertake.

In dissent, three justices (O'Connor, Souter and Stevens) argued that the policy allowed 'suspicionless searches' of students, violating their Fourth Amendment rights and potentially leaving innocent students 'open to intrusive bodily search'.

Federal government officials praised the Court's ruling as supportive of their war against illegal drug use. Lee Brown, President Clinton's then advisor on drugs policy, described the decision as 'a victory for kids'. In response, a spokesperson for the American Civil Liberties Union criticized the justices for failing to protect the rights of students in schools, rendering them 'second-class citizens'.

organization should not be able to test its members, but the Constitution restricts what the government may do. Hence drug testing by a government agency could be considered an improper 'search' of a person.

Initially, some federal district courts took the view that the mandatory drug testing of, for example, fire fighters was an unreasonable search unless the fire fighter who was tested had been suspected of some wrongdoing. However, in two cases in 1989 (*National Treasury Employees Union v. von Rabb* and *Skinner v. Railway Labor Executives' Association*) the Supreme Court held that certain categories of employees could be subjected to drug tests without a search warrant or even any individual suspicion. These were employees involved in law enforcement (in particular, Customs Service agents) and railroad employees involved in accidents. In short, a concern for public safety or national security can justify government-ordered drug tests. Using the same reasoning, the Court has upheld state laws that authorize the police to set up roadblocks and randomly check drivers to see if they are sober (*Michigan v. Sitz* (1990)). As Exhibit 9.8 records in detail, the Court has also upheld the random drug testing of high school athletes in *Vernonia School District v. Acton* (1995).

Employers have lobbied for random drug testing in order to protect themselves from lawsuits resulting from injuries caused by employees on drugs. Federal courts have ruled that, with the exceptions of screening airline pilots and train conductors to ensure public safety, random drug testing violates the Fourth Amendment's prohibition against unreasonable searches and seizures (see Exhibit 9.9).

Such is the fear of lawmakers that electoral punishment will result from anything other than a strong 'anti-drugs' stance, that most will refuse to back policies that move away from the punitive paradigm. Just as opposition to the death penalty is amenable to opponents depicting an elected official as 'soft on crime', so support for public health, treatment and liberalizing measures equate with being 'soft on drugs'. There are few electoral rewards, and many dangers, in taking up such positions, however rational they are as public policy.

The actual implementation of a war on drugs is also complicated by the fact that Congress – typically – refuses to give the task to a single bureaucratic agency. Stopping drug trafficking is the shared task of the Customs Service, the FBI, the Drug Enforcement Administration, the Border Patrol and the Defense Department (among others). Such fragmentation facilitates inter-agency wrangling, makes communication more complex

Exhibit 9.9   Key Supreme Court rulings on drugs

United States v. Ross (1982). Police officers may search an entire vehicle they have stopped without obtaining a warrant if they have probable cause to suspect that drugs or other contraband is in the vehicle.

Michigan v. Sitz (1990). The police may stop automobiles at roadside checkpoints and examine the drivers for signs of intoxication. Evidence obtained in this manner may be used to bring criminal charges against the driver.

Vernonia School District v. Acton (1995). Public school officials may carry out a policy of drug testing for students involved in inter-school athletic programmes.

Chandler v. Miller (1997). State laws cannot require candidates for public offices to be tested for drugs. This requirement constitutes an unreasonable search under the Fourth Amendment.

Exhibit 9.10   Annals of the drugs war: America and Latin America

American concern over the foreign supply of drugs had its origins in the international drug control efforts of American missionaries in the nineteenth century and remained a focus for nativist and anti-vice crusaders since then. The Nixon administration deployed agents on the Mexico border in September 1969 to search trucks and other vehicles crossing into America and applied strong diplomatic pressure on Turkey to stop drug exports. However, these efforts – and the major increase in foreign efforts to curb the drug supply under Reagan and Bush – have not eliminated the trade. Profit margins are high for drug producers and supply routes have frequently shifted. The end of the Cold War and the European Union's Schengen Agreement (lifting border restrictions among its signatory member states) offered new supply lines through former Soviet republics, eastern and western Europe during the 1990s that have proven especially problematic for American authorities to counter. By the end of 2000, Colombia alone was growing or processing approximately 90 per cent of America's cocaine and much of its heroin.

1986 Foreign Aid

In an atmosphere of increased concern over drug trafficking, Congress passes an omnibus measure (PL 99–570). A country where drugs are produced or shipped can receive US narcotics control aid only if the president certifies that it is fully cooperating in the drug war. Those not certified would receive a 50 per cent cut in US aid.

1988 Noriega Indictment

Panamanian dictator Manuel Noriega is indicted by a federal grand jury on charges of racketeering and drug trafficking. Congress passes a defence-spending bill (PL 100–463) that includes $300 million for drug interdiction. Congress also passes a $2.7 billion omnibus anti-drug law that authorizes $101 million in fiscal year 1989 for international narcotics-control programmes.

1989 Military Aid and 1990 Panama Invasion

President Bush proposes the Andean Initiative. Under this plan the US would give Colombia, Peru and Bolivia an additional $129 million in military aid for fiscal year 1990. Congress passes legislation (PL 101–231) authorizing $125 million in US military and law enforcement aid to the Andean nations. US forces invade Panama on December 20, and Noriega surrenders on January 3, and is flown to Florida to face charges.

1990 Latin America Accord

Bush and the presidents of Peru, Bolivia and Colombia meet in Cartagena, Colombia, and sign an accord for more cooperation in the fight against illegal drug trafficking.

1992 Latin America Accord

Bush and officials from six Latin American countries sign an accord in San Antonio, Texas, that calls for increased cooperation in fighting drug trafficking.

1995 Colombia Waiver

The US withholds full certification for Colombia in anti-drug cooperation but waives penalties in the national interest.

Exhibit 9.10 Annals of the drugs war: America and Latin America *continued*

1996 Colombia Decertified

Colombia is decertified and disqualified from most US economic aid. Mexico is certified despite the opposition of some lawmakers.

1997 Mexico Controversy

Colombia is again denied certification. However, President Clinton in August grants a waiver of penalties on the grounds of national security. Some members of Congress are upset that Mexico is certified, but Congress does not overturn Clinton's decision. Clinton and Mexican President Ernesto Zedillo sign an accord calling for broader cooperation in fighting drug trafficking. The US and Colombia sign an End Use Monitoring memorandum of understanding that stipulates that US counter-narcotics assistance to the Colombian military is conditional on human rights screening of proposed recipient units.

1998 Colombia Aid

Colombia is denied full certification but is given a waiver that would allow it to receive US aid. Mexico is certified, despite criticism from lawmakers. An agreement is signed between the US and Colombia providing the latter with more than $280 million in assistance to combat drugs trafficking.

2000 Plan Colombia

President Clinton visited Colombia in September 2000 and proposed $1.3 billion of aid, along with 60 American helicopter gunships and some 300 troops and military advisors.

and raises problems in attributing responsibility for both successes and failures in the drugs war.

Crucial to shaping the drugs war is also the international dimension of the booming trade. While the root cause of the popularity of drugs is domestic demand, the plentiful and cheap supply of drugs from outside the United States – in particular from Latin America, Pakistan and Southeast Asia – has made the issue of drugs as much a foreign policy question for the executive branch and Congress as a domestic one. But for many members of Congress, the issue is one essentially of criminal justice and defence, not foreign policy. As a result, and under pressure from concerned constituents, Congress has taken a stronger lead on drugs policy during the later 1990s than at any period previously.

Republican lawmakers, in particular, strongly opposed the Clinton administration's main focus on treatment and enforcement at home, preferring instead to try to halt supplies of drugs at the source. In November 1999, the discovery of mass graves near the Mexican city of Juarez (just over the American border, near the Texan town of El Paso) that held up to 100 victims of Mexico's powerful and ruthless drug cartels provided further impetus to their case. But such attempts not only bring accusations of congressional micro-management of foreign policy, but also provoked many Democrats to question the effectiveness of the strategy and to state concerns over the human rights records of the military and police forces in Central and Latin America charged with stemming the flow of drugs.

Intermediary organizations

One of the key reasons for the triumph of the punitive paradigm on drugs regulation has been the absence of a partisan polarization over drugs. Competition between the two parties might be expected to clarify differences, sharpen debate and provide policy alternatives to the failed drug strategy. Instead, party competition since the 1980s has expanded tough anti-drug policies still further. Unlike gun control and abortion, the issue of drugs has seen both the Democrats and the Republicans occupy broadly similar ground.

This has not always been the case. It was the Nixon administration, for example, that introduced America's first large-scale experiment with federally funded treatment efforts during the 1960s. But the Republican Party since Nixon's presidency has consistently located the source of America's drug problem in the moral degeneration of society and has backed a government response based on absolute intolerance of any and all drug use. The party's 1988 platform stated that:

> The Republican Party is committed to a drug-free America. Our policy is strict accountability, for users of illegal drugs as well as for those who profit by that usage. The drug epidemic didn't just happen. It was fueled by the liberal attitudes of the 1960s and 1970s that tolerated drug usage. Drug abuse directly threatens the fabric of our society. It is part of a worldwide narcotics empire whose $300 billion business makes it one of the largest industries on earth. The Reagan–Bush administration has set out to destroy it. (quoted in Bertram et al., 1996: 141)

In contrast to the GOP focus on enforcement and sanctions, the Democrats emphasized a balance between enforcement and assistance both at home and abroad. Preventive education, treatment and concern for civil liberties occupied prominent places in the

Exhibit 9.11   Selective list of organizations supporting access to marijuana

AIDS Action Council (1996)
AIDS Treatment News (1995)
Alaska Nurses' Association (1998)
American Academy of Family Physicians (1995)
American Medical Student Association (1994)
American Public Health Association (1994)
American Society of Addiction Medicine (1997)
Being Alive: People with HIV/AIDS Action Committee (1996)
California Academy of Family Physicians (1994)
California Legislative Council for Older Americans (1993)
California Pharmacists' Association (1997)
Colorado Nurses' Association (1995)
Florida Medical Association (1997)
Kaiser Permanente (1997)
Life Extension Foundation (1997)
Lymphoma Foundation of America (1997)
National Nurses' Society on Addictions (1995)
New England Journal of Medicine (1997)
New York State Nurses' Association (1995)
North Carolina Nurses' Association (1996)
Oakland City Council (1998)
San Francisco Mayor's Summit on AIDS and HIV (1998)
Virginia Nurses' Association (1994)

Democratic agenda of the 1980s, but by 1988 even the Reverend Jesse Jackson on the left of the party was arguing that children had to be convinced that 'drug pushers are terrorists'. The 1988 election saw the erosion of these party differences as Michael Dukakis, the Democratic presidential candidate, failed to out-toughen Bush on drugs and crime (the first question in the first presidential debate was on drugs). In seeking to inoculate (or 'de-Dukakisize') themselves against charges of softness, the Democrats simply encouraged congressional Republicans to seek out ever-tougher proposals, such as mandatory death sentences. Consequently, the parameters of the drugs debate on Capitol Hill and in the nation narrowed and hardened during the 1990s. As John Conyers (Democrat, Michigan), a supporter of treatment and prevention measures, observed:

Drug education and treatment have gained a name as a wimp activity. If you favour these things, you're a softy. When these proposals come up in Congress, most members want to know, before they vote, which one is the toughest? It's sort of, 'I don't know if this is going to work, but nobody is going to blame me for not being tough'. (Bertram et al., 1996: 163)

The interest group universe on drugs is also heterogeneous. Opposition to liberalizing drugs policy is a prominent part of the agendas of the Christian Coalition, religious and 'pro-family' groups such as the Family Research Council. Many of these traditionalist and moralistic conservative groups have proven to be important parts of the Republican Party's electoral coalition since the 1970s.

However, many organizations and prominent individuals from across the political spectrum have issued calls for either partial or complete decriminalization of drugs. Among those favouring the legalization of drugs are, for example, some notable conservative

Exhibit 9.12   De-emphasizing law enforcement?

Progressive groups such as Common Sense for Drug Policy (CSDP) advocate a decrease in the focus on law enforcement, favouring instead a public health approach involving:

- After-school programmes, mentor programmes and activities for youth
- Treatment on request for drug-dependent persons
- Rehabilitation programmes, including skills building, job training and education programmes
- Disease prevention programmes, emphasizing education, syringe exchange and other public health strategies
- Alternatives to incarceration
- Educational activities to keep children in schools.

By de-emphasizing law enforcement, CSDP argue policy can:

- Dramatically reduce the prison population
- End racial disparities in drug arrests and imprisonment
- Restore civil liberties eroded as a result of the drugs war
- End mandatory sentencing and restore judicial authority
- De-militarize law enforcement activities
- Restore due process to property forfeiture
- Reduce the burdens on the justice system caused by drug enforcement.

figures such as former Secretary of State George Shultz, William F. Buckley and Milton Friedman. As Exhibit 9.11 shows, many organized groups have been particularly opposed to the continuing laws against marijuana, especially those organizations most actively concerned with caring for the medically ill.

Relatively few groups that support more liberal and preventive approaches reject entirely the need for government to combat the supply of drugs into America and to punish the criminals associated with their manufacture and distribution. But as Exhibits 9.12 and 9.13 record, organizations that favour less punitive policies tend to emphasize the need for a more rounded approach to the drugs war.

Exhibit 9.13 Alternatives to the punitive paradigm? Legalization and public health approaches to drugs

Legalization

The movement for legalization of drugs has its roots in the marijuana reform movement of the 1960s and 1970s, a campaign that rallied student protestors and libertarian conservatives together under the banner of decriminalizing the consumption of the drug. Proponents of legalization differ on both the scope and justification, but most identify the central problem as the harm caused by drug policies, not drug-taking. Their concern is the damage caused by prohibition to individual lives and liberties, with drugs not seen as good or bad in and of themselves. That drugs can alter moods and have negative effects on health is accepted, but adults are deemed to be free to choose whether or not to take drugs. Addiction and dangerous behaviour are individual matters, but ones for which laws exist to punish illegal or harmful behaviour to others. The drugs war is not only ineffective but represents an invasion of privacy and a threat to constitutional rights.

Critics argue that:

- Legalization would inevitably increase drug usage and hence abuse and addiction.
- In the case of drugs the distinction between harm to self and to others is frequently blurred. A seemingly private act may have consequences, albeit not direct ones, for others.

Public Health Approaches

Public health approaches were used in the twentieth century on matters such as the environment, mental illness, smoking and drinking. Public health proponents tend to seek not prohibition through prevention and regulation but, instead, safe or responsible rather than heavy use of drink, cigarettes and, by extension, drugs. In contrast to legalization, public health advocates stress that:

- Drug use is a public, not an individual, health issue that demands an emphasis on the social causes and consequences of drug problems.
- The social environment (such as local subcultures, jobs and peer influences) need emphasis.
- Prevention as well as treatment is essential.

But for critics of such approaches, the public health paradigm is simply a plea for vast new federal programmes and funds that essentially admit defeat in the war on drugs.

CONCLUSION

Midway through *Bob Roberts*, the Tim Robbins movie savagely satirizing American politics in the 1990s, the right-wing folk singer turned senatorial candidate of the title duets with 'Miss Broken Dove' on a country number pithily entitled 'Drugs Stink'. The song's not-so-subtle message was that the cure for drugs and their associated problems was to deal harshly with drug users ('pot-smoking weirdos', 'sex deviants' and 'dirty hippie freaks') – to follow Newt Gingrich, Bill Bennett and their allies and 'hang 'em high for a free-living land'.

Like abortion and firearms, even if they wish that they would no longer be present, relatively few Americans believe that drugs will disappear from American life. Just as many Americans who hold that a gun-free United States is utopian still desire stronger regulation of firearms, so many who see a drugs-free America as an impossibility want federal, state and local governments to do all that they feasibly can to combat drug consumption. And like the controversy over pornography, the fact that many Americans want to criminalize activities that many others engage in on a routine recreational basis – and who view drug consumption as uncontroversial, benign and even beneficial – makes political conflict over drugs an abiding feature of the culture war. The impulse to prohibit drugs, as with alcohol in the first half of the twentieth century and smoking in the latter half, has become a proxy for wider conflicts over values, morality and identity.

Largely as a result, drugs and tobacco have become increasingly emotive issues. The likelihood of addiction and the costs – health, mental, psychological and even physical – that this poses both to the consumer and to others partly explains the intensity which many Americans bring to the controversies.

But these issues also provide outlets for the deeply ingrained tradition of moralism and the desire to enforce morality – to deter or prevent activities that many disapprove and some detest – to resurface. Traditionalists have been keenest to root out drugs in general as a social evil and a moral menace to American families. Unlike gay rights or abortion, however, it is progressives who are most zealously in the front-line of trying to ban selective drug-taking activities that they dislike (in the case of tobacco).

Sceptics have tended to view the 'war on drugs' in much the same way as Lyndon Johnson's mid-1960s 'war on poverty', namely that both drugs and poverty emerged victorious. But this type of approach tends merely to reinforce the emotive and intemperate language that generally characterizes the American debate. Progressives have tended to reject traditionalist arguments about drugs by focusing on structural socioeconomic problems of economic inequality and inner-city decay. Traditionalists, by contrast, have tended to present drugs exclusively as an issue of crime, law enforcement and public order and morality. The reality is that some drugs are both relatively harmless recreational and medicinal stimulants and others pose a severe public policy problem, partly by virtue of their addictive qualities but especially because of the criminal activity surrounding their distribution and use. Most informed American observers argue that a combination of law enforcement, treatment and prevention efforts is a requisite part of any effective drugs control policy. As with the other American dilemmas in this book, however, qualifications and nuances, compromises and concessions, and rational and cool contemplation can often get lost amid the vociferous populism and heated position-taking of both sides in the controversy.

FURTHER READING

Eva Bertram, Morris Blachman, Kenneth Sharpe and Peter Andreas, *Drug War Politics: The Price of Denial* (1996) is a comprehensive and detailed analysis of the politics and policies of the 'war on drugs'.

Craig Reinarman and Harry Levine (eds), *Crack in America: Demon Drugs and Social Justice* (1997) is a set of critical essays discussing the policies, politics and racial aspects of the crack epidemic in America.

Lynn Zimmer and John P. Morgan, *Marijuana Myths, Marijuana Facts: A Review of the Scientific Evidence* (1997) is a survey of the data on marijuana and the case for its decriminalization.

Joseph Dillon Davey, *The Politics of Prison Expansion: Winning Elections by Waging War on Crime* (1998) is an excellent analysis of how 'toughness' on crime by American politicians has led to America possessing the world's largest prison population.

WEB LINKS

Citizen Agenda: Drug Policy Reform
http://www.fpif.org/cgaa/drug.html

Citizen Agenda: Stop US Military Involvement in Colombia
http://www.fpif.org/cgaa/milcol.html

National Organization for the Reform of Marijuana Laws
http://www.norml.org

Information on Marijuana Laws and Usage
http://www.marijuanafacts.org

Views on US government and drugs policy
http://www.druggingamerica.com

Focus on the Family
http://www.fotf.org

Christian Coalition
http://www.cc.org

Eric Sterling, 'Drug Policy: Failure at Home', *Focus on Foreign Policy* 6 (16), May 2001
http://www.fpif.org/briefs/vol6/v6n16drugfail.html

Documentary records and photos of the 1970 Presley–Nixon meeting
http://www.gwu.edu/~nsarchiv/nsa/elvis/elnix.html

QUESTIONS

• Has the 'war on drugs' been a relative failure primarily because of insufficient funding or excessively punitive goals?

• What relevance do the arguments of gun rights groups that a ban on firearms in America would be unenforceable have to the regulatory regime on drugs?

• 'The primary obstacle to a more permissive regulatory regime on drugs is Congress'. Discuss.

• To what extent, and why, does the politics of drugs resemble that of other cultural value issues?

• What explains the high levels of drug imprisonment for black and Latino Americans compared to whites?

10 Conclusion

Unless the United States wants to go the way of Iran and Saudi Arabia, we shall not be able to return to the era of premarital chastity, low divorce, stay-at-home moms, pornography-free media, and the closeting of homosexuals and adulterers.

Richard Posner (2001: 300)

America will always stand firm for the non-negotiable demands of human dignity, the rule of law, limits on the power of the state, respect for women, private property, free speech, equal justice, and religious tolerance.

President George W. Bush, State of the Union address, January 2002

In the autumn of 1999, Senator Sam Brownback (Republican, Kansas) sponsored a resolution calling for the US Senate to commission an investigation into America's 'cultural breakdown', a troubling malaise featuring everything from divorce, 'deadbeat dads' and child gun killings to presidential perjury, teenage sex and trashy television. Senate Democrats, fearful that the proposed probe would focus mainly on Hollywood and the music industry and exclude the 'culture of guns', brokered a deal with Republican Party leaders that established a rather less prestigious task force. Such was the conflict that even the task force's name was changed from its bold original, the 'Special Committee on American Culture', to the more blandly flavoured 'Task Force on the State of American Society'. At least, some observers said, the fact that members of both parties could agree on the need for an investigation could be counted as progress of a sort in America's ongoing culture war.

If official federal government channels came to recognize the fact and importance of cultural divisions rather late, however, they at least acceded to the point that the pressing political dilemmas it has raised have become a defining and distinctive feature of American public and private life. That this should be the case is perhaps an oddity, given that the last decade of the twentieth century saw America enjoying remarkable levels of peace and prosperity, unseen for a generation. But amid such affluence and apparent security the BBC's American correspondent, Gavin Esler, was moved to examine a *United States of Anger* (1997), while historian Arthur Schlesinger, Jr., wrote of the nation's 'disuniting' and cultural critic Robert Hughes lamented a growing and divisive *Culture of Complaint* (1993). For these and other observers, much of the heated emotion animating many Americans prior to September 11 stemmed directly from intense domestic battles over culture, values and identity.

In describing such conflicts, these critics echoed the influential commentator, E.J. Dionne, who argued in *Why Americans Hate Politics* (1991) that a large part of the blame for that revulsion should be attributed to the culture war. America's political system had become loaded since the late 1960s with cultural value conflicts in which political opponents cast their foes as moral lepers. In a mixture of exasperation and hope, Dionne advised:

> If we are to end the cultural civil war that has so distorted our politics, we need to begin to practice a certain charity and understanding. We need politics to deal with the things it is good at dealing with – the practical matters like schools and roads, education and jobs. Paradoxically, by expecting politics to settle too many issues, we have diminished the possibilities of politics. After years of battling about culture and morality through the political system, voters are looking for a settlement that combines tolerance with a basic commitment to the values of family and work, compassion and the rule of law. Americans welcomed many of the liberating aspects of the sixties. They also welcomed the rediscovery during the eighties that certain 'traditional' rules and values were socially useful and even necessary. In the 1990s, we have a choice. We can join the old battles all over again and set the sixties against the eighties. Or we can try to move on. (Dionne, 1991: 343–4)

More than a decade has now passed since Dionne's advice, but Americans have not moved on. The passionate and bitter divisions manifested in the Clinton impeachment and the aftermath of the 2000 presidential election showed graphically how divided America remains between a (mostly white) traditionalist heartland and a (racially and ethnically mixed) bi-coastal progressive front. As many historians have observed, it is frequently periods of material prosperity and rising public expectations – not economic downturns – that generate political tumult, constitutional crises and even revolutions. Until September 11, 2001, and despite well-publicized warnings of an impending and intractable 'clash of civilizations' around the globe pitting an American-inspired 'McWorld' against an Islamic 'Jihad', it was the social and political divisions at home that

occupied most American energies during the Clinton years. But even since 9/11, the cultural battles have raged on with no immediate or straightforward resolution in sight. What, then, do they say about American politics and the prospects for an eventual cessation of hostilities?

STRUCTURAL FEATURES

The first point worth noting is that however much social changes drive political conflicts over culture, values and national identity, the American context is continually affected by certain core structural features of a unique system of government. The cultural battles are unresolved in large measure because Americans are divided themselves. Rival conceptions of what it is to be an American shape rival conceptions of what it is that Americans ought to believe and the ways in which they should behave. As the political theorist George Lakoff observes, on questions of identity, culture, morality and ethics, 'Contemporary American politics is about worldview. Conservatives simply see the world differently than do liberals, and both often have a difficult time understanding accurately what the other's worldview is' (Lakoff, 1996: 3).

But these vexing cultural battles are not only about basic differences in value systems. They are also prolonged by central features of the political system: the constant election campaign; the weakness of political parties and consequent phenomenon of risk-averse candidates for elective office 'running scared'; the slow-moving, reactive and often obstructionist character of Congress; and the changing composition and fluctuating interventions of federal courts. All of these – expressly institutional – factors play additional and important parts in sustaining the fundamental hostilities of the divergent world-views that many Americans harbour, for they provide ample opportunities for the articulation of divergent views while offering relatively little prospect of reconciling them decisively.

In some respects, there exists a marked irony that a system of government whose constitutional design has remained essentially intact over 200 years should give birth (or at least be the midwife) to a cultural conflict whose central driving force – a profound divergence in basic world-views – is a relatively recent phenomenon. Historically, however much the battles over values and identity preceded these years, the contemporary culture war is a product of the 1960s and 1970s. Those turbulent decades, alternately celebrated and censured, left an indelible – but sharply disputed – imprint on the nation:

The cultural divide in American politics was no longer between Catholic and Protestant, North and South, city and countryside. It was a divide along lines of values, in which those who believed in liberation from the traditional mores of 1940s America were on one side and those who believed in honoring those values were on the other. This transformation was apparent by the 1968 election and was exacerbated by the fact that the elites of America, especially in the political and communication capitals of Washington and New York, were moving rapidly toward the liberation side, while most voters, especially in the South and in the growing suburban rings around the shrinking central cities, were rallying to the national standard. (Barone, 1997: 40)

But if historical developments have played their role in precipitating and perpetuating the culture war, so too has a unique and revered document of more than 200 years' pedigree. For central to each of the conflicts surveyed in this book is the US Constitution. Compared to economic policy, international affairs or trade, the Constitution is not only more clearly present and pervasive on cultural matters, but also more ambiguous and powerfully contested in its application. Combatants in cultural battles invariably claim constitutional validity for their particular case. This is a familiar feature of American politics: as Foley (1991) observed, what is needed to achieve enduring change in public policy in America is not merely weight of numbers but the priceless sanction of constitutional support. The impressive weight of that argument is especially heavy on matters of cultural conflict where the Founding Fathers' intentions and current social interests frequently collide.

Constitutional interpretation has therefore revealed inconsistencies and challenges to all sides in the culture war as a result not so much of reasonable persons disagreeing over an 'objective' reading of the document, but more as a function of the different policy outcomes that the contending sides are seeking to achieve. There exist some profound ironies in this regard. During the Clinton impeachment proceedings, many of the progressives who normally adhere to the 'living Constitution' approach looked to an originalist reading of the Constitution to defend the president: the Framers never intended 'high crimes and misdemeanors' to cover such tawdry issues as illicit sexual liaisons by the Head of State, they noted. Yet on issues such as gun control and capital punishment, what the Framers intended assumes a much less important part – an irrelevance, even – for these same progressives when the merits of these policies are considered. Equally, for originalists who see a search for meaning in the founding document as an overarching condition of law, the notion that the Founding Fathers deliberately injected leeway into the Constitution is a frequent matter of selective interpretation.

The constitutional aspect to the culture war is partly about history and interpretation. In some cases, the meaning of particular provisions is disputed, such as the Eighth Amendment's prohibition of 'cruel and unusual punishment'. In others, where the document contains no explicit language, questions of interpretation are even more acrimonious, nowhere more so than in regard to the 'right to privacy'. In this regard, a shrewd advertisement appeared in magazines in late 1999 and early 2000, sponsored by the National Rifle Association. Amid new public clamour for stronger gun controls, it reproduced the Second Amendment but with various of its words crossed out and new qualifications written in. Underneath were the profiles of eight leading revolutionaries and Founding Fathers, with (selective) quotes from each on the virtues and necessity of gun ownership. The caption – and punchline – read: 'Before anyone edits the Bill of Rights, the authors would like a word with you.' In no other industrialized democracy would interest lobbies so effectively use the provisions of a constitution to build public support for their cause.

Disagreement over constitutional interpretation has therefore been fundamental to the genesis of many cultural value conflicts. Their resolution has also been sought – but rarely achieved – through resort to constitutional change, either by changing the composition of the federal judiciary to render new interpretations or to seek formal amendments to the founding document. However profound their disagreements, both traditionalists and progressives look to the Constitution as the source of authority and sanction against their opponents' views.

In most contemporary cultural battles, movements have arisen to amend the Constitution in order to guarantee certain rights and liberties or to advance egalitarian values. But these movements display the ironies associated with the politics of constitutional amendment. If a cause is so overwhelmingly popular that it secures passage in Congress and ratification by the states, it is rarely likely to be especially divisive. But if an issue provokes widespread social divisions, by definition, it cannot meet the rigid requirements for ratification that the Constitution prescribes. The Constitution allows as few as 13 states out of 50, representing as little as 4.5 per cent of the population, to block constitutional change, no matter how modest.

In this sense, the inherent conservatism of the Constitution helps to prolong the cultural conflicts or, at least, preclude their definitive and abiding resolution. The Constitution often offers hope to the cultural combatants for securing desired social change, but more frequently disappoints them by frustrating their aspirations. A means of potentially resolving the divisive societal battles that the Founding Fathers anticipated would occur, the document – or, more accurately, its invocation by diverse political coalitions and changing interpretation by state and federal courts – tends instead to perpetuate them.

Part of the constitutional contribution to the persistence of cultural conflict also stems from the character of the key institutional players that the Constitution determines should perform particular roles in policy-making at federal and state level. The main governing institutions that matter in the culture war are generally the federal courts, Congress and state and local institutions, not the presidency. Political conflict is an odd one in as much as the central player in American politics more broadly is notable either by his frequent absence from these disputes or his marginal effect. Hence, in one sense at least, this means that the picture of politics in this book is somewhat distorted. For all the many academic volumes on law and politics that are dedicated to the courts and Congress, the presidency has been the focus of recent American political science. But the president is a marginal figure on these issues, his influence confined to occasional interventions of varying consequence.

In another respect, however, we do see several important, if not necessarily timeless, truths about American politics revealed in the culture war. For all of the congressional resurgence that has occurred on foreign policy matters since 1966, the president's power in domestic affairs remains substantially more constrained than in international matters – even prior to 9/11. In domestic politics, presidents face a powerful and attentive Congress, an independent and assertive judiciary, an active and complex interest group universe, an aggressive media, engaged mass publics (albeit selectively so), and a powerful set of countervailing state and local governments. While they can articulate preferences, issue executive orders and use the 'bully pulpit' to build public attention and support for particular goals, achieving their implementation in domestic matters remains difficult. Setting out a destination for the ship of state is one thing; successfully steering the vessel along that route is another burden entirely.

These matters are not eased by the character of American intermediary organizations. In some respects, the picture of political parties here is unusual. On most issues in this book, clear partisan differences exist between the two main parties. Much of the reason for this reflects the divergent public philosophies that inform the two parties' current approaches. For the Democrats, with a new heartland in the northern tier of the country, from New England and New York, across the Upper Midwest and including the Northwest Coast, cultural liberalism is formidably strong. Instinctively dovish, multilateralist, supportive of liberation from traditional sexual mores and gender roles, Democrats are strongly backed by the 'care-giving' professions, ethnic and racial minorities, and public employee unions. For the Republicans, with strong support in the Rocky Mountains, Plains states and a solid southern base, and informed by a deep faith in America's manifest destiny, special mission in the world and unique goodness as a nation, the GOP is sustained by traditionalists for whom cultural conservatism remains dominant.

The result is that partisan divisions are now powerfully, though not exclusively, founded on strong cultural value differences. Even economic issues are now less an argument over the distribution of income than they are an argument between those who want more money to go to a public sector imbued with liberation-minded values and those who want the money to remain with a private sector where tradition-minded values are free to compete in the marketplace of ideas. As Barone notes, the parties offer 'a choice, if you will, between therapy and discipline, a choice that parties offer on issues from crime to foreign policy to public sector employee strikes – and even in their

candidates' personalities' (Barone, 1997: 42–3). The Republicans are the party that is most obviously pro-capital punishment, anti-gun control, 'pro-life' on abortion, and hostile to gay rights. The Democrats, by contrast, have emerged as the party for gun control, women's reproductive rights and (to a certain extent) gay equality and the party that is less certain in support of the death penalty.

Admittedly, students of American politics are frequently reminded that conservatives are not in favour of less government when it comes to issues such as the defence budget, military expenditures or the Drugs Enforcement Administration. But there exists an instinctive hostility to government regulation of economic life among Republicans that is less apparent in the case of social issues. On these, state intervention either to encourage or prohibit certain ways of life is a mainstay of Republican thinking. For many Republicans, the empirical evidence that reveals capital punishment as arbitrarily enforced, restrictive laws on early-term abortions as encouraging later ones, or drugs policy as an abject failure is flawed or, if correct, essentially irrelevant. A visceral desire to honour and enforce traditional moral codes – to instill responsibility and punish irresponsibility – powerfully informs many Republican views on politics and culture.

Beyond the parties, the cultural battles also reveal an interest group universe in remarkably robust health. Some organizations, such as the National Rifle Association, the National Association for the Repeal of Abortion Laws and the American Civil Liberties Union have proven adept and shrewd campaigners over several decades. Groups such as these have adapted their campaigning techniques, political strategies and tactics to the changing context of American politics. The more effective evangelical organizations, such as the Christian Coalition, abandoned fire-and-brimstone oratory in favour of pitching their appeals in terms of the rights of ordinary Christians and religious minorities. Organizations opposed to capital punishment, though woefully under-resourced, altered the focus of their tactics from the judiciary to the elected branches as the courts took up increasingly pro-death penalty positions during the 1980s and 1990s. Even on an issue such as pornography, groups have taken up the burden of opposing the forces of censorship, either directly or indirectly, from across the political spectrum.

Finally, the mass media remain central players on these battles. As much as most television journalists are liberal in their personal political convictions, the medium of television is especially suited to traditionalist messages. It is difficult to counter the arguments of those who demand retribution for certain crimes when the scenes of carnage that accompanied the bombing of the federal building in Oklahoma or the collapse of the World Trade Center occupy every prime-time news channel. Arguments about arbitrary sentencing, the absence of a deterrent effect, or the nuances of international relations often become muted in the face of such graphic footage. 'Abstract' claims about free speech assume less weight when faced by female and child victims of sex crimes whose assailants had fed upon a steady diet of pornography. Equally, protestations about the 'right to life' or being motivated by love rather than hate somehow ring rather hollow when juxtaposed by images of murdered physicians or crowds yelling homophobic chants at the funerals of young men murdered simply because of their sexual orientation.

Partly as a result of the intensity that accompanies the contending claims of graphic images and more or less subtle or abstract arguments, the tone of public discussion of these issues is more emotive, shrill and raw than typically occurs on other issues. It becomes easier to demonize opponents as enemies, portray enemies as 'un-American', and appeal to visceral emotions. Images of crime victims, drug addicts and foetuses take over from dry statistics and complex, competing arguments about public policies and regulation. In real wars, opposing sides see the utility of propaganda, dropping leaflets on enemy lines and broadcasting directly to the enemy's population. In the culture war, traditionalists and progressives know the value of shock tactics and strategies. The aim is to harness vivid images to dramatic dialogue, to reinforce those Americans already instinctively on one side and convert those who are uncertain or confused. The same tactic applies to trade and taxes and other socioeconomic issues, of course, but the emotive resonance is rarely equivalent.

IS AMERICA (STILL) DIFFERENT?

Given the highly charged nature of much cultural conflict in America, the question arises of whether the United States remains a distinctive (even unique) polity and society. Is America still different from other industrialized democracies or increasingly converging with them on a similar form of political economy, governmental structure and social regulatory regime?

The case for America's continued distinctiveness draws on many supportive examples, but three features stand out as especially important. On the one hand, they mark America as a distinctive (if not unique) social and political arrangement and together suggest that the existing political hostilities over cultural values may ebb and flow in intensity but are unlikely to disappear entirely in the immediate future. At the same time, however, they also demonstrate how finely calibrated the American system is to enable a pluralistic society divided by deep disagreements over fundamental values to reconcile extensive individual freedoms and tolerance with majority rule – the basic task of all liberal democratic forms of government.

First, compared to other democracies, religion and religiosity remain profoundly influential in America. From black church congregations joining with Jews and white Christians to march for civil rights to Catholics and Christian evangelicals blocking the entrances to abortion clinics, religious activism in politics has been a long-established tradition. As long as millions of Americans see cultural value issues in moral terms, hold strong views about the enforcement of morals, and practise their faiths to this end, conflict with the forces of modernity is inevitable. 'Post-materialism' exists as a reality of daily life for most Americans but many remain strongly wedded to a 'pre-material' set of spiritual and moral values that cast doubt on the current direction of social regulatory policy. That need not prove especially significant were these Americans reluctant to act on their values and beliefs. But many of religious faith have little in the way of doubt, either about their faith or the need – even duty – to realize it in today's America. A commitment to the rule of law is part of America's political culture yet many of the nation's citizens claim, ultimately, only to follow laws that are divine in origin.

It might be objected that since these issues did not provoke such enduring and intense battles prior to the 1960s, they could equally well recede from view as the years progress. Many traditionalists, such as Paul Weyrich and Bill Bennett, saw the refusal of the Senate to convict Clinton during his impeachment trial in 1999 as a disheartening sign that the culture war was already over and that traditionalists had lost. No longer could there be any case for the existence of a 'moral majority' when most Americans supported the president's acquittal in luridly full knowledge of his adulterous, perjurious and obstructive conduct. Faced by the brute reality, some traditionalists even argued that the time had arrived to disengage from politics entirely: to find alternative ways of reaffirming traditional values away from public life after three decades of frustration and rejection.

But the point here is that the reason why these cultural issues did not appear previously was that the ways of life cherished by millions of traditionalists were not threatened. Once the federal government (and the Supreme Court in particular) intervened to regulate or prohibit particular activities, a full-scale and long-lasting confrontation was

likely to arise. In this regard, given the pervasive and tenacious hold that religion still exerts on most Americans, it is improbable that conflicts over rival conceptions of good public policy will lessen in their intensity. It is remarkable – astonishing, even – that of modern, democratic industrialized nations, only America can still cast doubt on Darwinian evolution theory and seek to exclude it from schools or render it equivalent to 'Christian Science'. But it is a fact. And as long as Americans continue to believe that this is so, battles from Creationism and school prayer to abortion and gay rights will continue.

Secondly, the nature of American identity looms large over these cultural value questions. Historically, America has not known a pull between nationalism and ideology. Because national identity is defined in normative terms, conflicts about what it is to be an American and what an American should or would do in a particular circumstance are inevitable. Conflicts over identity have occurred previously and the 'threat' posed to America from supposedly alien immigrants was a mainstay of public life from the end of the nineteenth century to the 1950s. But the vividness of this conflict is clearer – and broader in scope – today thanks to technological developments, competitive rivalries in education and employment, and demographic trends. Mass immigration at the turn of the nineteenth century was never of a scale that threatened to make the Protestant white population a minority. The fear of some Americans is that Latino immigration, especially, is doing exactly that and that 'their' nation is unlikely to remain theirs much longer. Rightly or wrongly, for better or worse, the context is very different today.

But perhaps more crucial than changing racial, ethnic and demographic patterns is the intimate connection between American national identity and the concept of rights. More than the citizens of most comparable democracies, Americans are preoccupied – even obsessed – by the question of individual rights and liberties and the appropriate role of government in safeguarding these. Issues that were once confined to the private sphere, from pregnancy terminations to same-sex relations, have steadily emerged as matters for debate in American public life, confronting federal, state and local governing institutions with competing demands for government action. In this respect, traditionalists, for whom such issues are necessarily cast in terms of morality, have encountered an increasing array of Americans for whom 'the personal is political'. Compromise on these matters is difficult, and perhaps impossible, to achieve.

Thirdly, the framework of government remains ill-equipped to deal rapidly or decisively with these issues. Parliamentary systems are more likely to achieve quick and 'decisive' results in public policy, particularly those where plurality rather than proportional electoral systems exist. Elected majorities in such systems, whether of one party or more, typically enjoy the full fruits of legislative victories. American government balances the federal government against the states and pits individual and minority rights against legislative majorities. A multitude of venues for citizen participation in politics and citizen influence on governing institutions exist. Beyond these, veto points abound within and between distinct tiers and branches of government. In nations with less open, accessible and balanced governmental systems, from the UK to Australia, issues such as capital punishment or gun control are likely to be more easily and decisively resolved.

Cooperation and compromise are essential to overcome the conflicts inherent in the constitutional design. But cultural conflicts are not ones where the combatants feel easily disposed to compromise. Such conflicts may resist definitive resolution in any system, at least in the sense that battles occur at the margins of policy. The American one, however, guarantees their enduring presence. America is a genuine liberal democracy, tempering the power of government and the outcomes of elections by checks and balances that intrude upon unrestricted state authority.

But it is also a populist democracy in which politics is suffused by the imperative of attending to the people's demands, be they for executions or firearms. The fragmentation of American institutions ensures that a lobby that loses in one arena may invariably turn to several others in which to press the same issue. On each issue in this book, recent decades have therefore seen constant competition between traditionalist and progressive forces across the nation, at each level and within each branch of government.

Underlying all these questions, however, is a basic fact about American life since the 1960s, as disconcerting to many as it is fundamental to all: change. Like their predecessors during the Progressive Era, Americans during the final quarter of the twentieth century have been buffeted by economic, social and political changes of far-reaching – indeed, transformative – scope. Changing economic conditions and modes of work have created opportunities for some, ruin for others, and uncertainty for most. Family life has been transformed, not only in regard to increased rates of divorce, births outside marriage and single mothers, but also to the lack of time that parents report having with their children and each other. Dependent on people and agencies outside the home, children are often less closely supervised and young Americans can celebrate their autonomy with all manner of clothes, hairdo, tattoos and body piercings. While crime declines in large cities, suburban and rural areas appear less and less safe, with those who can afford to do so flocking to 'gated communities' served by private security forces. Despite declining official levels of violent crime during the 1990s, vicious crimes dominated news stories and 'Fortress America' existed behind security fences and private guards. As one set of academics commented:

> It is not hard to understand why so many Americans feel as though we have lost way, that something has gone profoundly awry. Prohibition is again before us, though this time around drink is not the target. In complex, overlapping, and even contradictory

ways, we are being urged to prohibit, among other sorts of presumed evils, abortion, drugs, and guns as paths to restored virtue and 'normalcy.' Like their precursors, these moral reform movements encourage participants to see the world in the stark oppositions of good and evil. (Dizard et al., 1999: 12)

That juxtaposition is characteristically American. Esler has rightly noted that no industrialized democracy debates 'guns, god, gays and gynecology' with such regularity and frequent hysteria as America. His view exaggerates but nonetheless captures the essence of the difficulties that Americans face on issues of cultural value conflict:

Complex social and moral issues guided by genuine religious faith are difficult to solve in any democratic society, but in the United States achieving reasonable consensus is impossible because each discussion is framed in the most polarizing terms. You either believe, in the end, that abortion is a kind of murder, or you do not. You either believe that homosexuals are born homosexual and as a group have 'rights', or that they 'have a choice' in the matter and pursue perversion because they are morally 'bad' and their lifestyle is 'an abomination'. And you either believe that the Constitution gives Americans the unrestricted right to bear arms – any gun, anywhere, any time – or alternatively it suggests something far more limited in the context of raising a local militia. (Esler, 1997: 162)

Even during the unprecedentedly good economic conditions that existed from 1995 to 2001, many Americans were angry about the direction in which their nation was headed.

In this respect, it is important to note that no one group possesses a monopoly on either tolerance or intolerance in America. The desire to 'enforce morality' is effectively shared by both coalitions in the culture war, albeit with varying degrees of intensity and scope. It is commonplace to observe that traditionalists seeking to prohibit abortions or same-sex marriages are asserting moral and religious precepts about the right way to live.

But progressives are ultimately acting in similar fashions, in two important respects.

In one respect, seeking to legislate pro-choice positions or to allow gays to marry does not materially affect those who do not wish or need to seek an abortion or who are not gay, but it does preclude one set of values underpinning public policy – traditionalism – being enacted. In the second course, progressives themselves seek to abolish or prohibit certain forms of action: owning handguns, implementing capital punishment and (for some) consuming pornography. No less than traditionalists, progressives on these issues have clear views about activities that should be heavily regulated, discouraged and even banned. The salient difference, such as it is, is that the progressives are generally more concerned than traditionalists with 'banning the bans': ending rather than enforcing prohibitions on activities.

Ironically, then, the illiberalism latent in America's political culture finds frequent expression on both sides of the culture war. The deep-seated impulse to prohibit and ban, denounce and demonize, condemn and censure, is not monopolized by any one grouping. America has seen several deeply illiberal policies enacted 'in the name of liberalism': sterilization, work-welfare programmes and immigration control. It is salutary to remember that illiberal policies such as these, as well as suppressions of free expression in the name of racial or gender equality, can be championed by erstwhile progressives as much as self-proclaimed conservatives.

Against all this, however, two important qualifications need to be taken into account. The first derives from the work of the sociologist Alan Wolfe (1998) which strongly suggests that, far from 'disuniting' or balkanizing in the manner that Schlesinger and others contend, America is 'One Nation After All.' On this view, it is clear that Americans do harbour strong views about public morality which distinguish clearly between activities and behaviour that they believe to be fundamentally right and others they hold fundamentally wrong. Approving and disapproving of particular activities is as American as apple pie (or, in 'multicultural' America, burritos and dim sum). But there is no logical necessity that disapproval need equate with a desire to prohibit or discriminate. In practice, millions of American citizens combine, perfectly consistently and rationally, the disapproval of particular modes of conduct with a recognition of the rights of individuals to engage in that conduct. Americans are more tolerant than even they often suspect. The majority possess non-judgemental attitudes about women's and civil rights, for example, even in the Bible Belt.

Indeed, even on the issue of gay rights, tolerance has grown substantially from a time during the 1950s and 1960s when homosexuality was widely regarded as a psychological disorder and suspected gays were denied security clearances by the CIA to a point where, in June 2000, the agency hosted a gay pride celebration for its gay and lesbian intelligence workers at its Langley, Viriginia, headquarters. Despite the general dominance of traditionalists on the issue and continuing rejection of homosexuality as morally equivalent to heterosexuality, a broad consensus against anti-gay discrimination has emerged since the 1980s. Moreover, in most respects, the bulk of ordinary Americans display a marked tolerance towards those on the 'extremes' of social and political life in the United States that is frequently absent in other (western and non-western) nations.

The second reason to cast a little doubt upon the intensity of the culture war is related to the first. That is, over time, established public policy on many, if not most, of these cultural value issues has come to reflect the broad swathe of relatively moderate mass opinion in the country at large. On abortion, the constitutional right of a woman to terminate her pregnancy remains in place despite the peculiar basis of the *Roe* ruling and the intense efforts of pro-lifers to get the decision overturned. But states may regulate the exercise of that abortion right in a variety of fashions, from parental consent laws to the conditions in which terminations are carried out. Similarly, the federal government achieved new regulations of firearms with passage of the Brady bill and the partial assault weapons ban. But the states have responded by a variety of measures, both tightening controls over gun purchases and registrations and decontrolling firearms laws regarding 'concealed carry' weapons. Although most states have affirmed their belief in capital punishment, the new millennium saw moratoriums on executions in several states, new laws over protecting innocent life and the use of DNA evidence, and changes to the methods by which capital punishment can be carried out.

These compromises reflected and expressed the broad sweep of opinions among Americans at large: in support of the basic abortion right but desirous of strong regulations conditioning its exercise; in support of the basic right to own guns but wanting federal laws to regulate access to them; in favour of capital punishment but sensitive to wrongful executions; in accepting the spread of sexually explicit materials but wanting their more egregrious public displays regulated. That these compromises have taken a long time to achieve, and at the cost of much expenditure and acrimony, is less significant than the fact that they have, eventually, been reached with broad-based support. Most Americans reflect, albeit not always consciously, what Richard Posner describes as the modern incarnation of John Stuart Mill: 'the anti-paternalism and affection for the free market that are components of the ideology of the Republican Party and the tolerance of "deviant" personal behavior that is characteristic of the Democratic Party' (2001: 356).

Readers of this book will have their own views on the substantive rights and wrongs of particular public policy questions and may disagree that particular public policies, for example decontrolling guns, disallowing same-sex marriages, liberalizing laws on drugs or obscenity, are the correct ones to ameliorate or resolve existing social problems. In that regard, those of us outside America are no different from the mass of Americans themselves. What is perhaps more important to recognize, however, as students of the United States, is that Americans not only differ from many non-Americans on these issues but are also strongly divided among themselves. Popular stereotypes of Americans as responding in the same ways – to government, terrorism, or war – all too often miss the mark.

It is also worth taking a check on our own particular prejudices and stereotypes. Students of politics are sometimes prone, whether consciously or unknowingly, to a marked cultural relativism with regard to customs, practices, values, beliefs and attitudes when it comes to Africa, Asia and other regions: to assert respect for alternative cultural traditions and religious faiths to the west being different but not deficient. Often, however, that reluctance to judge or hastily condemn is much less present in discussions of the different traditions, religions and faiths that are present in America. A double standard often prevails here, no doubt reflecting in large part the cultural dominance of America in western life and the singular influence of American foreign policy – economically and militarily – around the world.

To this extent, it is important to record that the American political system performs a remarkable job not merely of attempting to give expression to, but also to reconciling, markedly different value systems and conflicting demands. The frustration that many within America typically feel about government – that it is slow, cumbersome, reactive and frequently ends up producing public policies that invariably resemble a lowest common denominator set of outcomes designed to placate as many interests as possible – is understandable. But it also neglects the key features of the remarkable societal heterogeneity and diversity that characterize America and the many dangers to that

society and its political stability were untrammelled majoritarianism – of the traditional British type – allowed to triumph. Public policies that emerge from the fragmented American system do so after prolonged and sometimes intense conflict, but they tend ultimately to enjoy a broad public legitimacy as a result. That is no mean political achievement: it is a relatively unusual, enviable and significant one.

It would be a mistake to paint too rosy a picture. Complacency is misplaced when so many of the problems of the twentieth century remain with us – racism, gender inequality, poverty, drugs, crime, the threat of weapons of mass destruction, the disparity between rich and poor within and between nations, the decay of the natural environment and central cities, the dilution of educational standards, and the basic political dilemma of where personal freedom ends and public responsibility and collective duties begin. The cultural battles surveyed in this book are unlikely to disappear from political conflicts. As such, America's remarkable history of progress and innovation, and its capacity to absorb and transcend social, economic and political problems, continues to confront these substantial historical tests – at the same time as it faces new challenges from global terror networks and 'rogue states'.

But politics is a dynamic process, and liberal democratic government is necessarily a series of adaptations to new challenges, problems and changing national and international environments. America possesses a unique constitution, an unusually complex governing system and a remarkably heterogeneous social base. The three remain extremely well matched. Only an inveterate optimist could confidently predict America's successfully rising to meet and overcome each of the formidable challenges it faces at home and abroad. But only the most cynical could deny the capacious ability of the United States and its people to confront, absorb and transcend such challenges. In checking and balancing state power and in steadily extending the bounds of liberal tolerance, the idea of America epitomizes the advice of Judge Learned Hand that 'the spirit of liberty is the spirit that is not too sure it is right'. In that respect, the continued existence of cultural conflicts may be less a threat to American democracy than an expression of its remarkable, and continued, vitality.

Bibliography

Altman, D. (1986) *AIDS and the New Puritanism.* London: Pluto Press.

Attorney General's Commission on Pornography (1986) *Final Report.* Washington, DC: Government Printing Office.

Barone, M. (1997) 'Our Country: The Shaping of America from Roosevelt to Clinton', in Byron Shafer (ed.), *Present Discontents: American Politics in the Very Late Twentieth Century.* Chatham, NJ: Chatham House Publishers, pp. 31–45.

Barone, M. (2000) *The Almanac of American Politics 2000.* Washington, DC: National Journal Inc.

Bedau, H.A. (ed.) (1997) *The Death Penalty in America: Current Controversies.* Oxford: Oxford University Press.

Bellesiles, M.A. (2000) *Arming America: The Origins of a National Gun Culture.* New York: Alfred Knopf.

Bertram, E., M. Blachman, K. Sharpe and P. Andreas. (1996) *Drug War Politics: The Price of Denial.* Berkeley, CA: University of California Press.

Beschloss, M. (ed.) (1997) *Taking Charge: The Johnson White House Tapes, 1963–1964.* New York: Simon and Schuster.

Bork, R. (1990) *The Tempting of America: The Political Seduction of the Law.* New York: The Free Press.

Bork, R. (1996) *Slouching Towards Gomorrah: Modern Liberalism and American Decline.* New York: Harper Collins.

Bruce, S. (1988) *The Rise and Fall of the New Christian Right: Conservative Protestant Politics in America 1978–1988.* Oxford: Clarendon Press.

Bruce, S. (2000). 'Zealot Politics and Democracy: The Case of the Christian Right', *Political Studies*, 48 (2): 263–82.

Bruce, J.M. and C. Wilcox (eds) (1998) *The Changing Politics of Gun Control.* New York: Rowman and Littlefield Publishers.

Button, J.W., B.A. Rienzo and K.D. Wald (1997) *Private Lives, Public Conflicts: Battles over Gay Rights in American Communities.* Washington, DC: CQ Press.

Califano, J. (1999) 'White Line Fever: What an Older and Wiser George W. Should Do', *Washington Post*, August 24, p. A17.

Chafe, W. (1991) *The Unfinished Journey: America Since World War Two* (2nd edition). New York: Oxford University Press.

Christian Family Network (1998) *The Problems With South Park.* New York: CFN.

Clarkson, F. (1997) *Eternal Hostility: The Struggle between Theocracy and Democracy.* Monroe, ME: Common Courage Press.

Clinton, H. (1996) *It Takes a Village: And Other Lessons Children Teach Us.* New York: Simon and Schuster.

Clinton, B. and A. Gore (1992) *Putting People First: How we can change America.* New York: Times Books.

Craig, B.H. and D.M. O'Brien (1993) *Abortion and American Politics.* Chatham, NJ: Chatham House Publishers.

Davey, J.D. (1998) *The Politics of Prison Expansion: Winning Elections by Waging War on Crime.* London: Praeger.

De Grazia, E. (1993) *Girls Lean Back Everywhere: The Law of Obscenity and the Assault on Genius.* New York: Vintage Books.

Dees, M. (1996) *Gathering Storm: America's Militia Threat.* New York: Harper Collins.

Diaz, T. (1999) *Making a Killing: The Business of Guns in America.* New York: The New Press.

Dionne, E.J. (1991) *Why Americans Hate Politics.* New York: Simon and Schuster.

Dizard, J.E., R.M. Muth and S.P. Andrews, Jr. (eds) (1999) *Guns in America: A Reader.* New York: New York University Press.

Downes, D. (2001) 'The Macho Penal Economy: Mass Incarceration in the US – A European Perspective', in A. Giddens (ed.), *The Global Third Way Debate*. Cambridge: Polity Press, pp. 210–23.

Durham, M. (2000) *The Christian Right, the Far Right and the Boundaries of American Conservatism*. Manchester: Manchester University Press.

Dworkin, A. (1981) *Pornography: Men Possessing Women*. New York: Perigee.

Easton, S. (1994) *The Problem of Pornography: Regulation and the Right to Free Speech*. London: Routledge.

Epstein, L., J.A. Segal, H.J. Spaeth and T.G. Walker (1994) *The Supreme Court Compendium: Data, Decisions and Developments*. Washington, DC: CQ Press.

Erikson, R. and K. Tedin (1995) *American Public Opinion*. Needham Heights, MA: Allyn and Bacon.

Esler, G. (1997) *The United States of Anger*. London: Michael Joseph.

Fiorina, M. (1992) *Divided Government*. Boston: Allyn and Bacon.

Foley, M. (1991) *American Political Ideas*. Manchester: Manchester University Press.

Fraser, J.W. (1999) *Between Church and State: Religion and Public Education in a Multicultural America*. Basingstoke: Macmillan.

Freedland, J. (1998) *Bring Home the Revolution*. London: Fourth Estate.

Frymer, P. (1999) *Uneasy Alliances: Race and Party Competition in America*. Princeton, NJ: Princeton University Press.

Garrow, D. (1994) *Liberty and Sexuality: The Right to Privacy and the Making of Roe v. Wade*. New York: Macmillan.

Golay, M. and C. Rollyson (1996) *Where America Stands 1996*. New York: John Wiley and Sons.

Goodall, R. (1995) *The Comfort of Sin: Prostitutes and Prostitution in the 1990s*. Folkestone: Renaissance Books.

Griffin, A. (1997). 'Another Case, Another Clause – Same-Sex Marriage, Full Faith and Credit, and the US Supreme Court's Evolving Gay Rights Agenda', *Public Law*, 315–27.

Grossman, M. (1998) *Encyclopedia of Capital Punishment*. Santa Barbara, CA: ABC-CLIO.

Haines, H.H. (1996) *Against Capital Punishment: The Anti-Death Penalty Movement in America, 1972–1994*. New York: Oxford University Press.

Halbrook, S. (1984) *That Every Man Be Armed*. Albuquerque, NM: University of New Mexico Press.

Heins, M. (1993) *Sex, Sin and Blasphemy: A Guide to America's Censorship Wars*. New York: The New Press.

Hellinger, D. and D.R. Judd (1994) *The Democratic Façade* (2nd edition). Belmont, CA: Wadsworth.

Henigan, D.A., E.B. Nicholson and D. Hemenway (1998) *Guns and the Constitution: The Myth of Second Amendment Protection for Firearms in America*. Amherst, MA: Aletheia Press.

Herman, D. (1997) *The Antigay Agenda: Orthodox Vision and the Christian Right*. Chicago, IL: The University of Chicago Press.

Hershey, M. (1989) 'The Campaign and the Media', in G. Pomper (ed.), *The Election of 1988: Reports and Interpretations*. Chatham, NJ: Chatham House Publishers, pp. 73–102.

Hickok, E. (ed.) (1991) *The Bill of Rights in America: Original Meaning and Current Understanding*. Charlottesville, VA: University Press of Virginia.

Hoffman, J.L. (1993) 'The "Cruel and Unusual Punishment" Clause: A Limit on the Power to Punish or Constitutional Rhetoric?', in D.J. Bodenhamer and J.W. Ely, Jr. (eds), *The Bill of Rights in Modern America after 200 Years*. Bloomington, IN: Indiana University Press, pp. 139–54.

Hughes, R. (1993) *Culture of Complaint: The Fraying of America*. Oxford: Oxford University Press.

Isaac, J.C., M.F. Filner and J.C. Bivins (1999) 'American Democracy and the New Christian Right: A Critique of Apolitical Liberalism', in I. Shapiro and C. Hacker-Cordon (eds), *Democracy's Edges*. Cambridge: Cambridge University Press, chapter 13.

Jenkins, H. (2001) 'Pornography, Main Street to Wall Street', *Policy Review*, 105: 3–11.

Kennet, L. and J. Anderson (1975) *The Gun in America: The Origins of a National Dilemma*. Westport, CT: Greenwood Press.

Kersch, K. (1997) 'Full Faith and Credit for Same-Sex Marriages?', *Political Science Quarterly*, 112 (1): 117–36.

Kettle, M. (1998) 'You Do? The Hell You Do!', *The Guardian*, G2, August 4, pp. 2–3.

Ladd, E.C. (1997) 'The 1996 Vote: The "No Majority" Realignment Continues', *Political Science Quarterly*, 112 (1): 1–28.

Lakoff, G. (1996) *Moral Politics: What Conservatives Know That Liberals Don't*. Chicago, IL: The University of Chicago Press.

Langton, J. (1999) 'The Texas Terminator Keeps Death Row Busy', *Sunday Telegraph*, July 18, p. 29.

Leitzel, J. (1998) 'Evasion and Public Policy: British and US Firearms Regulation', *Policy Studies*, 19 (2): 141–57.

Lipset, S.M. (1996) *American Exceptionalism: A Double-edged Sword*. New York: W.W. Norton and Company.

Lipset, S.M. and G. Marks (2000) *It Didn't Happen Here: Why Socialism Failed in the United States*. New York: W.W. Norton.

Lockhart, W. (1990) *National Commission on Obscenity and Pornography*. Washington, DC: Government Printing Office.

Lott, J. (1998) *More Guns, Less Crime*. Chicago, IL: The University of Chicago Press.

MacKinnon, C.A. (1989) *Toward a Feminist Theory of the State*. Cambridge, MA: Harvard University Press.

MacKinnon, C.A. (1993) *Only Words*. Cambridge, MA: Harvard University Press.

Malcolm, J.L. (1998) *To Keep and Bear Arms: The Origins of an Anglo-American Right*. Cambridge, MA: Harvard University Press.

Mann, J. (2000) *About Face: A History of America's Curious Relationship with China, from Nixon to Clinton*. New York: Vintage Books.

Martin, W. (1997) *With God on Our Side: The Rise of the Religious Right in America*. New York: Broadway Books.

McFeeley, W.S. (2000) *Proximity to Death*. New York: W.W. Norton and Company.

McKeever, R. (1993) *Raw Judicial Power? The Supreme Court and American Society*. Manchester: Manchester University Press.

McKeever, R. (1995) *Raw Judicial Power? The Supreme Court and American Society* (2nd edition). Manchester: Manchester University Press.

Mulloy, D.J. (ed.) (1999) *Homegrown Revolutionaries: An American Militia Reader*. Norwich: EAS Publishing.

Myrdal, G. (1944) *An American Dilemma: The Negro Problem and Modern Democracy*. New York: Harper and Brothers.

Orwell, G. (1957) *Inside the Whale and Other Essays*. London: Penguin Books.

Peele, G. (1998) 'Political Parties', in G. Peele, C. Bailey, B. Cain and B.G. Peters (eds), *Developments in American Politics 3*. Basingstoke: Macmillan, pp. 137–61.

Pines, B. (1982) *Back to Basics: The Traditionalist Movement that is Sweeping Grass-roots America*. New York: Morrow.

Pomper, M. (2001) 'Bush Order Gives GOP an Edge in Annual Struggle Over Abortion', in *CQ Weekly*, January 27, pp. 235–6.

Posner, R. (1992) *Sex and Reason*. Cambridge, MA: Harvard University Press.

Posner, R. (1998) *Overcoming Law*. Cambridge, MA: Harvard University Press.

Posner, R. (2001) *Public Intellectuals: A Study of Decline*. Cambridge, MA: Harvard University Press.

Posner, R. and K. Silbaugh (1998) *A Guide to America's Sex Laws*. Chicago, IL: The University of Chicago Press.

Prejean, H. (1993) *Dead Man Walking*. New York: Random House.

Reinarman, C. and H. Levine (eds) (1997) *Crack in America: Demon Drugs and Social Justice*. Berkeley, CA: University of California Press.

Rimmerman, C.A., K.A. Wald and Clyde Wilcox (eds) (2000) *The Politics of Gay Rights*. Chicago, IL: The University of Chicago Press.

Rosenberg, G. (1991) *The Hollow Hope: Can Courts Bring About Social Change?* Chicago, IL: The University of Chicago Press.

Rubin, E. (1987) *Abortion, Politics and the Courts: Roe v. Wade and its Aftermath*. New York: Greenwood Press.

Sarat, A. (ed.) (1999) *The Killing State: Capital Punishment in Law, Politics and Culture*. New York: Oxford University Press.

Schlafly, P. (1984) *Child Abuse in the Classroom*. Alton, IL: Pere Marquette Press.

Schlesinger, A. (1992) *The Disuniting of America: Reflections on a Multicultural Society*. New York: W.W. Norton and Company.

Schlosser, E. (1997) 'Pornography in America', *US News and World Report*, 10 February, pp. 43–5.

Shafer, B. (ed.) (1998) *Partisan Approaches to Postwar American Politics*. New York: Seven Bridges Press.

Shafer, B. and W. Claggett (1995) *The Two Majorities: The Issue Context of Modern American Politics*. Baltimore, MD: The Johns Hopkins University Press.

Shapiro, M. (1990) 'The Supreme Court from Early Burger to Early Rehnquist', in A. King (ed.), *The New American Political System*. Washington, DC: American Enterprise Institute Press, pp. 47–85.

Shilts, R. (1993) *Conduct Unbecoming: Gays and Lesbians in the US Military*. New York: St Martin's Press.

Smith, R.A. and D.P. Haider-Markel (2002) *Gay and Lesbian American and Political Participation*. Denver, CO: ABC-CLIO.

Spitzer, R. (1995) *The Politics of Gun Control* (2nd edition). Chatham, NJ: Chatham House Publishers.

Staggenborg, S. (1991) *The Pro-Choice Movement: Organization and Activism in the Abortion Conflict*. New York: Oxford University Press.

Strossen, N. (1995) *Defending Pornography.* New York: Scribner.

Sullivan, A. (1996) *Virtually Normal: An Argument about Homosexuality.* New York: Vintage Books.

Sunstein, C. (1999) *One Case at a Time: Judicial Minimalism on the Supreme Court.* Cambridge, MA: Harvard University Press.

Tang, I. (1999) *Pornography: The Secret History of Civilisation.* London: Channel 4 Books.

Taylor, S. (2000) 'How the "Conservative" Supreme Court Leans to the Liberal Side', *National Journal,* July 8, pp. 2207–8.

Tribe, L. (1992) *Abortion: The Clash of Absolutes.* New York: W.W. Norton and Company.

United States Government (1996) *Statistical Abstract of the United States.* Washington, DC: Government Printing Office.

Vaid, U. (1995) *Virtual Equality: The Mainstreaming of Gay and Lesbian Liberation.* New York: Anchor Books.

Van Dyke, V. (1995) *Ideology and Political Choice: The Search for Freedom, Justice and Virtue.* Chatham, NJ: Chatham House Publishers.

Verhovek, S.H. (1995a) 'Why Not Unconcealed Guns?', *New York Times,* The Week in Review, September 3, p. 1.

Verhovek, S.H. (1995b) 'Across the US, Executions are Neither Swift Nor Cheap', *New York Times,* February 22, p. 1.

Ware, A. (1998) 'The American Political System in Transition to a New Century', in G. Peele, C.J. Bailey, B. Cain and B. Guy Peters (eds), *Developments in American Politics 3.* Basingstoke: Macmillan, pp. 357–82.

Watson, J. (1997) *The Christian Coalition: Dreams of Restoration, Demands for Recognition.* New York: St Martin's Press.

West, D. (1997) *Air Wars: Television Advertising in Election Campaigns, 1952–1996.* Washington, DC: CQ Press.

Wilcox, C. (1996) *Onward Christian Soldiers? The Religious Right in American Politics.* Boulder, CO: Westview Press.

Williams Committee (1979) *Report on Obscenity and Film Censorship.* London: HM Government.

Wolfe, A. (1998) *One Nation After All.* New York: Penguin Books.

Wolfe, T. (1993) *The Purple Decades.* London: Pan Books.

Woodward, B. and S. Armstrong (1979) *The Brethren: Inside the Supreme Court.* New York: Avon Books.

Wright, K. and P. Lewin (1998) *Drug War Facts.* Washington, DC: Government Printing Office.

Younge, G. (1999) 'Bad Vibes', *The Guardian,* section G2, March 9, pp. 6–7.

Zimmer, L. and J.P. Morgan (1997) *Marijuana Myths, Marijuana Facts: A Review of the Scientific Evidence.* New York: Lindesmith Center.

Index